July 2018

The
Sociological
Review
Monographs

Contents

The Sociology of Stigma

Edited by Imogen Tyler and Tom Slater

The
Sociological
Review
Monographs

The Sociological Review Monographs
2018, Vol. 66(4) 3–25
© The Author(s) 2018
Reprints and permissions:
sagepub.co.uk/journalsPermissions.nav
DOI: 10.1177/0038026118777425
journals.sagepub.com/home/sor

Rethinking the sociology of stigma

Imogen Tyler
Lancaster University, UK

Tom Slater
University of Edinburgh, UK

Abstract

Stigma is not a self-evident phenomenon but like all concepts has a history. The conceptual understanding of stigma which underpins most sociological research has its roots in the ground-breaking account penned by Erving Goffman in his best-selling book *Stigma: Notes on the Management of Spoiled Identity* (1963). In the 50 years since its publication, Goffman's account of stigma has proved a productive concept, in terms of furthering research on social stigma and its effects, on widening public understandings of stigma, and in the development of anti-stigma campaigns. However, this introductory article argues that the conceptual understanding of stigma inherited from Goffman, along with the use of micro-sociological and/or psychological research methods in stigma research, often side-lines questions about where stigma is produced, by whom and for what purposes. As Simon Parker and Robert Aggleton argue, what is frequently missing is social and political questions, such as 'how stigma is used by individuals, communities and the state to produce and reproduce social inequality'. This article expands on Parker and Aggleton's critique of the limitations of existing conceptual understandings of stigma, through an examination of the anti-stigma campaign Heads Together. This high-profile campaign launched in 2016 seeks to 'end the stigma around mental health' and is fronted by members of the British Royal Family. By thinking critically with and about this campaign, this article seeks to both delineate the limitations of existing conceptual understandings of stigma and to begin to develop a supplementary account of how stigma functions as a form of power. We argue that in order to grasp the role and function of stigma in society, scholarship must develop a richer and fuller understanding of stigma as a cultural and political economy. The final part of this introduction details the articles to follow, and the contribution they collectively make to the project of rethinking the sociology of stigma. This collection has been specifically motivated by: (1) how reconceptualising stigma might assist in developing better understandings of pressing contemporary problems of social decomposition, inequality and injustice; (2) a concern to decolonise the discipline of sociology by interrogating its

Corresponding author:
Imogen Tyler, Department of Sociology, Bowland North, Lancaster University, Lancaster, LA1 4YN, UK.
Email: i.tyler@lancaster.ac.uk

major theorists and concepts; and (3) a desire to put class struggle and racism at the centre of understandings of stigma as a classificatory form of power.

Keywords
capitalism, governmentality, mental health, neoliberalism, politics, power, racism, space, stigma

Heads Together (or why we need to rethink the sociology of stigma)

In May 2016 three members of the British Royal Family, Prince William and his wife Catherine (the Duke and Duchess of Cambridge) and Prince Harry launched Heads Together, 'a new campaign to end stigma around mental health' (Heads Together, 2017).
[1] Heads Together is an umbrella organisation for eight existing UK based mental health charities[2] that together have 'decades of experience in tackling stigma, raising awareness, and providing vital help for people with mental health challenges' (Heads Together, 2017). Bringing these charities together under one organisational 'brand', Heads Together seeks to harness the significant media power of the popular younger members of the Royal Family. The publicity for this campaign states that whilst there has been progress 'in recent decades', stigma remains a 'key issue' in preventing people with 'mental health challenges' in accessing the help and support they need (Heads Together, 2017). As Prince William stated 'people can't and won't seek help because they are ashamed about what people might think' (CALM, 2017). To this end, Heads Together is focused on eradicating stigma as a barrier to help-seeking, through initiatives that centre on promoting individual disclosures of mental distress. As they put it, 'shattering stigma on mental health starts with simple conversations. When you realise that mental health problems affect your friends, neighbours, children and spouses, the walls of judgement and prejudice around these issues begin to fall' (Heads Together, 2017). To facilitate these conversations, Heads Together has mobilised an array of communications technologies, developing a website, harnessing social media platforms (Facebook, Twitter and Instagram), and devising hashtags, such as #oktosay and #thereforme, under which people can share their experiences. To illustrate the 'stigma shattering' potential of disclosure the Heads Together website has also published a series of short films, featuring celebrities and public figures in conversation with family and colleagues: these include the American pop star Lady Gaga discussing her mental health with Prince William (over Skype), the ex-footballer Rio Ferdinand talking about bereavement with his agent, and the ex-New Labour Communications Director, Alastair Campbell, discussing his cyclical depressions with his partner, the journalist Fiona Miller (Heads Together, 2017). Alongside these well-known public figures, there are films featuring 'ordinary' members of the public, such as ambulance driver colleagues talking about experiences of mental distress in the aftermath of stressful events at work. Through this accumulation and dissemination of individual conversations, Heads Together aims 'to help change the national conversation on mental health', effecting a transformation in British public attitudes (Heads Together, 2017). Indeed, there is much to be admired about the values and

ambitions of Heads Together, including Prince Harry and William's candour about their own struggles with mental distress following the death of their mother, Diana. As William Davies writes:

> Harry's admission that he had ignored his own emotional distress for several years before eventually having counselling was a valuable contribution, from a figure more commonly associated with laddish machismo. William's focus on male suicide statistics was also a good use of his celebrity. (Davies, 2017)

All the existing evidence supports the claims of Heads Together that 'unresolved mental health problems lie at the heart of some of our greatest social challenges' (Heads Together, 2017). 'Shattering stigma' is certainly one step in meeting this challenge. Indeed, negative attitudes around mental health problems are not only damaging and discriminatory but often exacerbate mental distress. As clinical psychologist John Read and his colleagues argue:

> Negative attitudes … lead to discrimination in many domains, including the workplace and housing, and to rejection by family and friends. They can also lead, via anticipated and actual discrimination and internalized stigma, to decreased life satisfaction and self-esteem, and to increased alcohol use, depression and suicidality. (Read, Haslam, Sayce, & Davies, 2006, p. 304)

However, while Prince William states that '[it's time] to feel normal about mental health, it's the same as physical health', psychologists like Read have begun to question the effectiveness of the 'mental illness is an illness like any other' approach embraced by anti-stigma programmes (Heads Together, 2017). Indeed, research suggests that the embracing of biogenetic rather than social explanations of mental distress risks amplifying the very negative attitudes and discriminations which these campaigns ostensibly seek to eliminate (see Bonnington & Rose, 2014; Corrigan, 2007; Holley, Stromwall, & Bashor, 2012; McWade, 2016; Read et al., 2006). So while, as Davies argues, the 'idea that one is simply "unwell" ' might provide comfort 'to people wrestling with their own depression or anxiety', it simultaneously veils over '*a whole host of more fundamental cultural, political and economic questions regarding the distribution of distress in our society* – the sorts of questions that the Duke of Cambridge would be less likely to grapple with' (Davies, 2017, our emphasis; see also Davies, 2016).

'Hands Off Our Stories'

There is also concern amongst mental health survivors and activists about the impact that anti-stigma campaigns that solicit, share and publicise personal stories of mental distress might have on individuals given the facts of discrimination against people with diagnosed mental conditions. For example, in terms of potential consequences, there are substantive differences between a Prince or a pop star disclosing their struggles with mental health to the public, a precarious worker disclosing to an employer, or a mother disclosing to a social worker (on the latter, see Morriss, this issue). In 2012, a group of

Canadian scholar-activists affiliated with 'Mad Studies'[3] published an account of a community event, 'Recovering our Stories: A Small Act of Resistance', which sought to trouble the 'appropriation' of personal experiences of psychiatric distress by mental health organisations and charities (Costa et al., 2012, p. 85). As they detail, while the sharing of testimonies has long been a central strategy of grassroots mental health activism, particularly in struggles against 'psychiatric authority', what concerns them is the ways in which these strategies have been increasingly adopted (co-opted) by charitable and governmental bodies (Costa et al., 2012). In particular, they are apprehensive about the commodification of personal stories of psychiatric distress and recovery in mental health and wellbeing 'marketplaces' that are increasingly dominated by powerful corporate actors (Costa et al., 2012, p. 89). As they argue, this market is often aligned with the interests of those organisations (state, commercial or third sector), rather than those of 'mad people themselves' (Costa et al., 2012, p. 89). In this context, personal stories of mental health, they write, 'function to garner support from authority figures such as politicians and philanthropists, to build the organizational "brand" regardless of program quality, and to raise operating funds during times of economic constraint' (Costa et al., 2012, p. 86). Further, they argue, there is a marked shift away 'from the history of psychiatric survivor storytelling' as a means to critically question social norms and provisions, towards forms of storying which 'solidify hegemonic accounts of mental illness' (Costa et al., 2012, p. 87). This critique of mainstream anti-stigma campaigns draws attention to how 'mad stories' risk being 'sanitised' in ways which 'do little to change the way that agencies function or to address broader issues such as poverty, unemployment and discrimination' (Costa et al., 2012, p. 90; see also McWade, 2016). In short, in focusing on individualised stories of disclosure and recovery, sociological questions about the causes of mental distress are frequently airbrushed out of the picture.

In order to alert 'the community to the dangers of storytelling', the Canadian scholars and activists devised a project entitled 'Hands Off Our Stories', which included the production of a humorous button badge 'displaying the words *patient porn* stroked out by a red diagonal line' and information cards (Costa et al., 2012, pp. 91, 96). Designed to caution people to the risks of freely giving their personal stories to mental health organisations, these information cards had the following 'tips' printed on them:

- Participation is voluntary. You can always say no.

- Ask yourself, who profits from you telling your story?

- What purpose does personal story sharing serve?

- How do large organizations use stories to make material change?

- Story telling as an exercise of labour/work. Do you get paid?

- The internet lasts forever. Because of the technology available today, your interview or story will likely be accessible to the public for a very long time. That includes future employers and landlords. (Costa et al., 2012, p. 93)

The 'Hands Off Our Stories' project is a salient reminder that stigmatisation arises in contexts that are shaped by unequal relations of power, and that stigma *and* anti-stigma initiatives are the site of intensive social struggles. As the articles in this collection variously elucidate, attempts to ameliorate social stigma (of any kind) are limited from the outset, if they fail to take account of 'the political economy of stigmatization and its links to social exclusion' (Parker & Aggleton, 2003, p. 17)

The political economy of stigma

In January 2017, the Heads Together campaign was lent political support of the highest order when the British Prime Minister Theresa May stated in a speech to the Charity Commission, that: '[f]or too long mental illness has been something of a hidden injustice in our country, shrouded in *a completely unacceptable stigma* and dangerously disregarded as a secondary issue to physical health' (May, 2017, our emphasis). Alongside tackling stigma, May made a specific commitment to addressing 'shortfalls in mental health services', which she described as 'plans to tackle the burning injustice of mental illness' (May, 2017). However, the promise that mental health funding would be a key priority of her premiership, her assurances of additional resources for mental health services, and her promise to create parity between state funding for mental and physical health conditions were met with incredulity by many British health professionals. Mental health services in the UK are so 'notoriously underfunded' that they are 'often referred to as a "Cinderella service" ' (O'Hara, 2017, p. 37; see also McWade, 2016). Further, at the time of this announcement May's government was in the midst of 'austerity driven' welfare reforms which include draconian cuts to the National Health Service (NHS), as part of a broader ideological commitment to gradual privatisation. As Mary O'Hara details, '[m]ental health provision was hit hard and early by austerity measures and this pattern has continued' (O'Hara, 2017, pp. 37–38). To take one example, in 2017, an investigation by *Pulse*, a news forum for UK General Practitioners, found that:

> … increasing numbers of vulnerable children are being refused vital mental health treatment that is recommended by their GP. Figures obtained from 15 mental health trusts revealed that 60% of GP referrals to child and adolescent mental health services (CAMHS) lead to no treatment and a third are not even assessed. (Wickware, 2017)

These cuts to services are taking place in a context of increasing need. For example, in 2017 several regional NHS trusts reported a 60% increase in the previous 12-month period in referrals to mental health crisis teams (a crisis referral is made in urgent cases when, for example, an individual is in extreme distress and felt to be at risk of self-harm which may endanger their life or those of others). This surge in crisis referrals is likely, in part, due to people being unable to access essential services such as counselling at earlier stages of need.

One consequence of this marked increase in need is that the police are becoming Britain's de facto front line mental health service. As Vikram Dodd notes, '[t]he number of calls handled by the Metropolitan police [London's regional police force] in which someone was concerned about a person's mental health hit a record 115,000 in the last year: on average 315 a day, or about 13 an hour. Volumes have grown by nearly a third since 2011–12' (Dodd, 2017). Dodd, a journalist, reports cases in which 'ill people struggling to find help commit crimes to obtain treatment', noting how one woman 'on crutches walked a mile to smash a shop window in Hereford, then called the police herself, believing that was the best way to get access to mental health services' (Dodd, 2017).

If one of the aims of Heads Together is to eradicate stigma in order that people are willing and able to access services, the timing of this campaign inevitably begs the question, what kinds and what quality of services actually exist for those in need, both now, and if current programmes of cuts continue, in the future? Further, it is important to note that whilst the charities supported by Heads Together lead important programmes of mental health support, the form this takes is largely the provision of information, helplines and online forums and not the kinds of intensive counselling and/or acute psychiatric health services that many people in Britain are currently having problems accessing. This is not to say that talking about mental distress with friends and families cannot lessen social stigma, but rather that anti-stigma initiatives which want to remove barriers to help-seeking, but that do not simultaneously address *either* the erosion of public service provision *or* the deeper social causes of increased levels of mental distress, will be limited in their impact.

Let us unpack this a little further. In the UK, it is not only that mental health services have been historically underfunded, but that cuts to services are taking place in a period in which there has been a significant and sustained increase in anxiety, depression and suicides (see Cooper & Whyte, 2017; O'Hara, 2017; Stuckler & Basu, 2013). In *How Politics Make Us Sick: Neoliberal Epidemics*, Ted Schrecker and Clare Bambra detail the ways in which state adoption of neoliberal economic policies characterised by 'reductions in workplace rights, job security, pay levels and welfare rights', has 'led to large increase in chronic stress across large parts of the population of many countries' (2015, p. 42). This governmental production of chronic stress, is (unequally) distributed across the population, and 'gets under the skin', through multiple and 'well understood' psychosocial mechanisms (2015, p. 43). Research such as Schrecker and Bambra's reveals in the starkest terms the limitations of anti-stigma campaigns around mental health which do not consider the role of social and economic policies which are, by design, actively promulgating mental distress.

The 'neoliberal epidemic of insecurity' has been exacerbated in Britain (and elsewhere) by political responses to the 2008 global financial crisis (Schrecker & Bambra, 2015, p. 42). For example, the British Coalition government (2010–2015) and the subsequent Conservative government (2015 – current) responded to this crisis in the banking sector by implementing 'the deepest and most precipitate cuts ever made in social provision' (Taylor-Goodby, 2013, p. viii; see also Shildrick; Scambler; Slater in this issue). Vickie Cooper and David Whyte have described this governmental response as 'an attempt to permanently dissemble the protection state' (2017, p. 1). A decade of austerity measures have seen those most affected by cuts, such as disabled people, 'not only struggling under the financial strain' but 'becoming ill, physically and emotionally' (2017, p. 2). To paraphrase Davies, efforts to end the stigma around mental health conditions in the context of a political economy which actively produces depression, anxiety and other psychosomatic illnesses, are at best a forlorn attempt to ameliorate symptoms 'without confronting any serious political-economic questions' (Davies, 2016, pp. 9–10).

Further, it is not only that austerity-driven reforms have intensified an existing neoliberal epidemic of chronic stress, but that this programme of cuts to social provision *has been enacted and legitimated through strategies of (state-sanctioned) stigma production.* As Tracey Jensen and Imogen Tyler (2015) have detailed, since 2010 the British elites (including politicians, journalists and television producers) have engaged in an intensive programme of *welfare stigma production*, reanimating longer histories and figures of the undeserving poor, to justify austerity. In particular, the promotion of the idea that a large 'underclass' of people are 'trapped' in conditions of stupefying dependency on state hand-outs has been a central mechanism through which public consent for draconian cuts to services has been produced. In short, 'stigmatisation is intimately linked with neoliberal governance', that is with attempts to manage and/or change the behaviour of populations through deliberate *stigma strategies* which inculcate humiliation and shame (see Paton, this issue). Indeed, as Graham Scambler argues in this monograph, the governmental 'weaponisation of stigma', both in terms of intensification of stigma production from above, and in terms of the specific targets of stigmatisation (such as disabled welfare recipients), cannot be disentangled from the political and economic imperatives of financial capitalism (Scambler, this issue). The point we are making here is that we require *more thoroughly sociological* understandings of stigma. This necessitates supplementing approaches focused primarily on the effects of stigma towards a consideration of the social causes and indeed the political function of particular modalities of stigma production.

Stigma as a practice of 'capital accumulation'

In her contribution to this collection, Paton urges us to examine the 'processes of power and profit', which might motivate stigma production, by 'gazing up' to ascertain where and by whom stigma is crafted, and to what ends. Following Paton's call 'to gaze up', it is interesting to note that alongside the eight charitable partners who are the major beneficiaries of funds raised by Heads Together, that this campaign has four corporate partners. These include the retail bank Virgin Money, Dixons Carphone 'Europe's leading specialist electrical and telecommunications retailer and services company', the global corporate giant Unilever, and BlackRock, 'a global leader in investment management, risk management and advisory services for institutional and retail client' (Heads Together, 2017). In short, Heads Together is bankrolled by some of the very corporate and financial organisations who are the beneficiaries of neoliberal economic policies (and the austerity reforms) which are eroding state welfare and social care, and in so doing are exacerbating mental distress amongst the poorest and most vulnerable members of society.

To take just one example from amongst the list of Heads Together's corporate partners: Virgin Money (UK) began life as a personal finance company which primarily sold debt, though credit card services. In 2008, the British bank Northern Rock collapsed in the wake of the US sub-prime mortgage crisis, and the British government took the bank into national ownership. It then split the bank into two parts, Northern Rock plc., and Northern Rock Asset Management, with the bad debt (approx. £21bn) parcelled in the latter. It later sold Northern Rock plc. to Virgin Money at an estimated loss to the tax-payer of an estimated £400m to £650m. The figures continue to disputed, but what we can say with certainty is that British citizens not only effectively subsided Virgin Money in their acquisition of the salvageable part of this bank, but also absorbed a massive amount of private financial sector debt – monies which could, of course, have been used to fund health and social services. Virgin Money is one part of Virgin Group Ltd., a mul-tinational venture capital conglomerate. In 2010, Virgin set up a new arm, called Virgin Care, with which it sought to expand its interests into the private UK health services market, thus capitalising on the government's programme to privatise state health ser-vices, a process accelerated under the guise of austerity-driven reforms. At the time of writing, Virgin Care had acquired NHS (state) contracts amounting to over £1bn. Services run by Virgin Care include primary care (GP services and hospitals), adult social care (including social workers), community health, prison healthcare and child mental health services.[4] Several whistle-blowers, among them the current Labour MP for Dewsbury, Paula Sherriff, have spoken out about 'unethical practices' and 'misconduct' within some of the health services Virgin now runs in place of the state (Stewart & Booth, 2016). In short, Virgin Group has been a key beneficiary of government programmes of austerity-driven welfare reforms since 2010, profiting from the privatisation of social provision. Given this, we might want at least to question the claim of this predatory for-profit pri-vate healthcare provider that it shares the mission of Heads Together 'of ending stigma, changing the conversation on mental health and giving people the tools they need to help themselves and each other with their mental health' (Heads Together, 2017).

We began this introduction with the high-profile British anti-stigma campaign Heads Together in order to illustrate some of the restraints of current understandings of what stigma is, and to challenge some of the common-sense approaches to how stigma should be combated. We have taken as inspiration in this endeavour Parker and Aggleton's claim that 'in order to move beyond the limitations of current thinking about stigma ... we need to reframe our understandings of stigmatization and discrimination to conceptualize them as social processes that can only be understood in relation to broader notions of power and domination' (2003, p. 16). One of the primary motivations of this collection is precisely to expand sociological understandings of stigma as a form of power, and in the next section we will argue that this requires sociologists to move beyond Goffman's decidedly ahistorical and apolitical formulation of stigma.

Rethinking stigma after Goffman

Stigma is not a self-evident phenomenon but like all concepts has a history (see Tyler, forthcoming, on the long history of stigma). The conceptual understanding of stigma which underpins anti-stigma campaigns such as Heads Together has its roots in 20th-century North American sociology and social psychology, which in turn largely has its roots in the formative understanding of stigma penned by Goffman in his best-selling book *Stigma: Notes on the Management of Spoiled Identity* (1963). It is difficult to over-state the influence of Goffman's stigma-concept, both on scholarly research and on wider public understandings of what stigma is (see Tyler, this issue). As Stephen Hinshaw argues, '[t]here has been an explosive growth of research and theorising about stigma in the decades since Goffman's conceptualisation' (2009, p. 25). Proceeding from a definition of stigma as 'the situation of the individual who is disqualified from full social acceptance' (1963/1986, preface) Goffman in effect transformed stigma into 'a remarkable organizing concept' (Hacking, 2004, p. 18), a way of seeing, classifying and understanding a vast array of discriminatory social attitudes and practices.

Goffman made four important claims: first, that stigma is *a perspective* which is 'generated in social contexts' (1986, p. 138); second, that people learn to manage the potentially devastating effects of being socially stigmatised, by employing strategies of identity management, such as passing and concealment; third, and this remains more implicit in his account, that stigmatisation is historically specific in the forms it takes; and finally, that stigma functions 'as a means of formal social control' (p. 139). It is primarily the first two of these claims that have come to dominate and underpin research, policy-making and anti-stigma initiatives, while the third and fourth claims, neglected by Goffman himself (see Tyler, this issue), have been taken up within contemporary stigma research, but still remain somewhat marginalised. Indeed, in the wake of *Stigma*, since the mid-20th century, social scientists have become accustomed to thinking about stigma within a liberal framework as a problem of social norms that can be challenged and alleviated through what Goffman terms 'benevolent social action' (1986, p. 5). It is our contention that this understanding of stigma as something that can be ameliorated, either through forms of social action which focus on 'educating people' about particular stigmatised conditions, or by 'schooling the stigmatised' to better manage their stigmatised difference, frequently neglects to address structural questions about the social and political function of stigma as a form of power. Therefore, one of the aims of this monograph is to rebalance research on stigma by precisely focusing on the function of stigma as a form of governmentality. In short, we seek to retain what is potentially most radical about Goffman's account, in particular his understanding of stigma *as a relation* which emerges in social settings, but to further amplify the critical implications of this claim. In this regard, we also seek to employ Goffman's relational understanding of stigma to trouble the more conservative and reactionary aspects of his own account. For example, in her contribution to this monograph, 'Resituating Erving Goffman: From Stigma Power to Black Power', Imogen Tyler undertakes a critical rereading of Goffman's theory of stigma by resituating it within the context of the Civil Rights Movement; rereading *Stigma* in dialogue with a rich but largely marginalised lineage of stigma thinking within in the black sociological tradition.

To date, in terms of the discipline of sociology, Goffman's stigma-concept has been taken up most enthusiastically within the sociological subfield of symbolic interactionism. Developing the work of the early 20th-century sociologist and philosopher George Herbert Mead, his student Herbert Blumer, and the later contributions of Howard Becker, Goffman and others, sociologists working within a social interactionist tradition are concerned with researching how the relationship between the self and society is mediated via systems of communication. In brief, social interactionism is a form of 'sociology from below' which is focused on producing micro-level studies of social interactions, and examining how meanings are produced (modified, challenged and transformed) in everyday contexts. Employing mainly observational, ethnographic and participative methods, this body of scholarship focuses on: (1) how stigma arises in social settings; and (2) how stigma clusters around specific 'conditions'. Symbolic interactionism has been criticised for being 'conservative' because of its lack of concern with 'explanations of people suffering' and its tendency to over-state individual agency in terms of people's ability to influence or determine their own fates (see for example McNall & Johnson, 1975, p. 49). From the point of view of the concerns of this monograph, the best examples of social interactionist work on stigma reveal not only how stigma is (re)produced within everyday interactions, but how what and who is stigmatised transforms across time and place. Indeed, Stacey Hannem's and Chris Bruckert's edited book *Stigma Revisited: Implications of the Mark* (2012), while working within a social interactionist tradition, shares many of the concerns of this monograph in precisely attempting to bring questions of how stigma is lived and resisted into dialogue with broader questions of power and structure.

An excellent example of how micro-sociological approaches have been used to extend and trouble Goffman's original conceptualisation of stigma is Abdi Kusow's research with Somali immigrants in Canada. Focusing on racial stigmatisation, Kusow challenges one of Goffman's primary assumptions, namely 'the existence of a normatively shared understanding of the criteria for and the distribution of stigma' (Kusow, 2004, p. 194). He does this by demonstrating how the presence of 'mutually incomprehensible' or conflicting social and cultural beliefs within one geographical space transforms not only who and what is stigmatised, but how stigma is resisted and indeed in some cases reversed (Kusow, 2004, p. 180; see also Tyler, this issue). Kusow arrives at the conclusion that stigma is always already unstable, volatile and shifting, through a study of the social interactions of Somali migrants in Canada. He details how this group of migrants refuse the stigmas associated with being black, being African, being a migrant and being Muslim in Canadian society, by enacting an alternative Somali value system. Indeed, the Somalis in his study reveal they had never heard of the word 'race', or experienced racism, before they interacted with (racist) white Canadians. More specifically they had no prior knowledge of racist North American epistemologies of race, where racism frequently (but not exclusively) pivots around visible perceptions of skin colour. In Somali it is tribal affiliations within an ethnic clan system which is the primary driver of social stratification. Thus for Somali migrants, 'the use of skin color as a stratification device' is 'incomprehensible' (2004, p. 182). Kusow explores the strategies through which Somali migrants reject the racist identity assessments of Canadian citizens. This includes the avoidance of interactions with white Canadians, a rejection of 'Canadianness as a possible identity', a persistent restating of 'separate systems of honor' and the 'reverse stigmatisation' of white Canadian racism (2004, p. 188). As he notes:

> What I mean by 'stigma reversal' is illustrated in the following comment by a respondent: 'I kind of reverse it upon them [white Canadians]. I always reverse what they are thinking of another human being like that.' According to some of the respondents, stigmatizing someone else on the basis of skin color is itself stigmatizing. (2004, p. 193)

Kusow concludes that 'while Goffman's concept of stigma has provided a powerful analytic category for understanding how stigmatized individuals manage the everyday problems attached to their spoiled identities, his treatment does not go far beyond the issues of identity management' (2004, p. 195). In fact, Kusow's work is also a more radical application of Goffman's conclusion that stigma is a relational and contingent practice of social classification. However, whilst Goffman argues that the work of the micro-analyst necessitates a 'bracketing off' of the economic and political imperatives that structure behavioural settings, Kusow argues that interactional forms of stigma research need to proceed by identifying 'the social and social structural conditions' that shape the relationship between self and society (2004, p. 195; see Tyler, this issue). In short, in trying to make sense of his empirical findings, what Kusow reveals are the limits of micro-sociological approaches to stigma. As Hannem similarly concludes:

> Goffman's qualitative descriptions of individual struggles of identity management and shame need to be augmented not only with the experiences of 'normals' who come into interaction with the stigmatized, but also with a genealogy of the social structures of normalcy and difference that create generalized stigma and attitudes of prejudice. (Hannem, 2012, p. 27)

While some of the articles in this monograph draw on the kinds of methods and approaches familiar to the sociology of social interaction, this collection also highlights the limits of approaches which fail to take into account structural and structuring factors, such as history (time), geography (place), politics and economic conditions. In so doing, this monograph seeks to supplement the existing sociology of stigma by encouraging sociologists to 'look up' to the forces which shape the emergence of stigma in everyday contexts (Hannem, 2012; Paton, this issue; Tyler, forthcoming).

Interestingly, most of the social scientific work on redefining stigma post-Goffman has not taken place in sociology but in cognate and neighbouring disciplines: primarily social psychology but also in medical and health research, and to lesser extent law and criminology. Unlike social interactionist approaches, whose methods are primarily qualitative and which tend to favour small-scale studies, social psychology research on stigma has been driven by quantitative methods which seek to measure, classify and quantify stigma. One of the limits of quantitative approaches is that they have a tendency to produce an understanding of stigma as static attitudes, 'rather than a constantly changing (and often resisted) social process' (Parker & Aggleton, 2003, p. 14). Alongside and/or in conjunction with quantitative methods, social psychologists have developed social cognitive understandings of stigma, which focus on the mental processes involved in stigmatisation, and the interpersonal consequences of stereotyped perceptions. This research is motivated by a concern with changing attitudes and behaviours, through, for example, increasing people's 'tolerance' for stigmatised conditions (Parker & Aggleton, 2003, p. 15).

It is this social cognitive understanding of stigma that underpins many anti-stigma campaigns. For example, Heads Together offers a weak definition of stigma as the 'negative associations, experience and language' attached to mental health conditions, and imagines that the way to combat these negative connotations is by initiating face-to-face conversations which will (magically) change individual attitudes, and which in turn might cumulatively, when 'scaled up' to the level of a 'national conversation', transform wider social beliefs. In this understanding, stigma is conceived from the 'bottom up', as primarily a problem of individual beliefs and actions – 'as what some individuals do to other individuals' (Parker & Aggleton, 2003, p. 16). This individualistic starting point rarely considers the 'political economy of stigmatization' (p. 17), including macro-level structures and forces, from economic crisis, wars and international conflicts, which shape stigmatising attitudes and beliefs. So while social psychology might focus on understanding stigmatising beliefs or behaviours in order, ostensibly, to change people's behaviours, it often ignores the ways in which, for example, governments or corporations might deliberately *activate stigma* to 'nudge' people into desired patterns of behaviour. As a consequence, the social psychology of stigma suffers from 'serious conceptual limitations' (Parker & Aggleton, 2003, p. 15; see also Hatzenbuehler & Link, 2014; Link & Phelan, 2001). Indeed, there is now a general agreement within social psychology that the previous failures of many anti-stigma campaigns to effect much in the way of meaningful or sustained social change are 'linked to the relatively limited theoretical and methodological tools available' (Parker & Aggleton, 2003, p. 14; Pescosolido & Martin, 2015).

The recognition within social psychology of the constraints of the 'excessively individualistic focus' of stigma research has led to a new focus on 'macro-level factors that drive stigma processes' (Link & Phelan, 2014, p. 30). Most significant in this regard has been Bruce Link and Jo Phelan's development of the concept of 'stigma power', which turns to sociology, and specifically draws on Pierre Bourdieu's account of 'symbolic violence', to better understand how stigma is exercised 'to keep people down, in and/ away' (Link & Phelan, 2014, p. 30). There is an important recognition in this turn that 'stigma arises and stigmatisation takes shape in specific contexts of culture and power' (Parker & Aggleton, 2003, p. 17). This has led to attempts to 'expand and reorient stigma's theoretical lens to focus on meso and macro socio-cultural structures and power' (Bonnington & Rose, 2014, p. 7). This new emphasis on traditional sociological concerns with structures, institutions, classification and power, and with the ways in which 'stigma feeds upon, strengthens and reproduces existing inequalities of class, race, gender and sexuality' has largely emerged out of grassroots initiatives to combat specific kinds of social stigma (Parker & Aggleton, 2003, p. 13). Most notable examples include activism that has sought to reduce the social stigma of specific health conditions such as HIV and AIDS, body-positive feminism, disability activism, and more expansive social and political movements, such as queer pride. However, while research on stigma has started to critically engage with questions of power, it is still often hampered by a limited understanding of 'power': where power is still imagined primarily as a force exercised by individuals – 'the aims of stigmatizers' (Link & Phelan, 2014, p. 24) – rather than conceptualised vis-a-vis the motives of *institutions* and *states* within a broader political economy of neoliberal capitalist accumulation. In order to address these limitations, several of the articles in this issue further develop Link and Phelan's concept of 'stigma power' (2014) through a focus on stigma as a political apparatus: that is, stigma power as a productive and constitutive force which enables 'the structures, mechanisms, and justifications of power to function' (Foucault, 2008, p. 85).

The 're-turn' to classic sociological concerns with 'structure' in stigma research is evident in all the recent 'state of the field' reviews around stigma literature. For example, in 'The Stigma Complex' (2015) published in the *Annual Review of Sociology*, Bernice Pescosolido and Jack Martin surveyed the existing literature on stigma (primarily social psychology and health research literature) in an attempt to produce 'a more synergistic view' of 'the complicated nature and effects of stigma' (2015, p. 101). For Pescosolido and Martin what they term 'the stigma complex', attempts to advance an understanding of stigma as a 'heterogeneous system' which involves 'the individual to the society, and processes, from the molecular to the geographic and historical' and 'that constructs, labels, and translates difference into marks' (2015, p. 101). At the heart of their account is Goffman's understanding of stigma as a 'fundamentally a social phenomenon rooted in social relationships and shaped by the culture and structure of society' (2015, p. 101). The problem, as they identify it, is that research concerned with 'understanding and changing' stigma has focused on changing behaviours and beliefs rather than 'changing the structures that shape social relationships' (2015, p. 101). While in general agreement with Pescosolido and Martin's approach to stigma as a psychosocial complex, we disagree with their claim that research focused on 'changing structures' 'remains at an early stage' or is 'primitive in nature' (2015, p. 101). Indeed, we hope to illustrate that rich genealogies of stigma theorising – which are precisely focused on challenging structures – already exist but have been marginalised by mainstream social science: for example, research and writing within the long black sociological tradition, social history research on class struggle, postcolonial history and theory, feminist and queer theory, and more recently the theories of spatial stigma developed by critical human geographers (see Slater, this issue). We would also point to the ways in which 'stigma struggles' have been explored within literature and the visual arts, and conceived in activist writing and political manifestos. What we seek to illustrate through this collection is some of the ways in which sociologists, geographers, political economists, media scholars and historians might fruitfully extend and supplement the ongoing reconceptualisation of stigma as power, by bringing the expertise and theoretical resources of these alternative genealogies of stigma to bear on this field.

Neoliberal stigma power

The historical, geopolitical and theoretical context out of which our interest in stigma emerges is a very different one than that of the postwar society which confronted Goffman in the 1950s. In returning to stigma we were motivated by how reconceptualising stigma might assist in researching pressing contemporary problems of social decomposition, inequality and injustice which have emerged in the wake of neoliberalism. In *The Shock Doctrine: The Rise of Disaster Capitalism*, Naomi Klein details the ways in which 'the policy trinity' of neoliberalism, 'the elimination of the public sphere, total liberation for corporations and skeletal social spending' has been enabled through the invention and/or exploitation of crises, be they natural disasters or terrorist attacks (Klein, 2007, p. 17). As Tyler has previously argued, 'in such a climate public anxieties and hostilities are channeled towards those groups within the population, such as the unemployed, homeless people, welfare recipients, irregular migrants, disabled people, ill and elderly populations who are imagined to be a parasitical drain upon scarce resources' (Tyler, 2013, p. 211). Indeed, what we want to add precisely to Klein's diagnosis is that neoliberal modes of government operate not only by capitalising upon 'shocks' but through 'the daily, pervasive production and mediation of stigma' (Tyler, 2013, p. 210). This understanding was inspired by Loïc Wacquant's argument that one of the major characteristics of neoliberalism is conditions of heightened stigmatisation for minority subjects 'in daily life as well as in public discourse' (2008, pp. 24–25). Drawing on Bourdieu's concept of symbolic power, Wacquant develops an account of stigma as a form of 'violence from above' (2008, p. 24), stressing 'the distinctive weight and effects of territorial stigmatization as well as the insuperable political dilemmas posed by the material dispersion and symbolic splintering of the new urban poor' (2008, p. 7). Of particular concern to Wacquant is the 'intensity of the stigma' and the 'virulence of its negative effects in the context of the mass unemployment and political marginalization' (Wacquant, 2008, p. 174). Wacquant suggests that the patterns of stigmatisation evident today are not novel phenomena, but are 'more or less coextensive with the existence of the cities': we might think here of the revitalisation of 19th-century distinctions between deserving and undeserving poor (see Crossley, 2017). However, Wacquant suggests that the potency and weight of 'symbolic dispossession' have intensified under neoliberal conditions (Wacquant, Slater, & Pereira, 2014). In *Revolting Subjects: Social Abjection and Resistance in Neoliberal Britain*, Tyler (2013) extended Wacquant's analysis, arguing that stigmatisation is increasingly employed as a device to procure consent for punitive policies directed at those living at the bottom of the class structure. Through a series of case studies, *Revolting Subjects* tracks how the production and mediation of stigma is 'not simply an effect of neoliberal ideologies and policies' but is 'a core organ' of 'neoliberal governmentality' (Tyler, 2013, p. 212). As she concludes: 'stigmatization operates as a form of governance which legitimizes the reproduction and entrenchment of inequalities and injustices' (Tyler, 2013, p. 212).

This claim, that there is a relationship between 'stigma intensification' and neoliberal forms of government, is supported by social policy research on changing social attitudes towards poverty and welfare (Hills, 2014; Taylor-Gooby, 2013). Meanwhile, a recent multi-sited project, 'Shame, Social Exclusion and the Effectiveness of Anti-Poverty Programmes: A Study of Seven Countries' (2010–2012) led by Robert Walker, has identified a broader global shift from liberal welfare policies concerned with alleviating the shame of seeking relief, to forms of (neoliberal) policy-making designed to activate stigma. Walker concludes that shame (although we would argue this is stigma not shame) is 'a key mechanism in perpetuating the structures of self-interest that support the unequal distribution of resources in society' (Walker, 2015, p. 184). As Tracy Shildrick's contribution to this issue reveals, the amplification of poverty stigma has particularly potent effects in the context of consumer capitalism. Wacquant describes this as 'the curse of being poor in the midst of a rich society in which participation in the sphere of consumption has become a *sine qua non* of social dignity – a passport to personhood' (2008, p. 30).

This collection

In order to extend these initial attempts to rethink stigma sociologically in the context of neoliberalism, this collection brings together 'classic' sociological research on poverty, racism, disability, stigma and shame, with geopolitical perspectives on the activation of stigma at different scales (governmental, policy, media industries), scholarship on the stigma of place (territorial stigma) and historically orientated analysis of anti-stigma campaigns and activism. In so doing, it draws together contributions from scholars across Europe and North America, variously concerned with rethinking stigma as a contemporary mechanism of disenfranchisement in numerous forms and locations, and on multiple scales.

Through a range of methodological approaches and drawing on different kinds of data (interviews, ethnography, media analysis, policy documents, archival research), the articles in this monograph together produce new insights into how stigma functions as a form of power, contributing to a much fuller understanding of stigma as a 'cultural and political economy' (Jessop, 2010). This approach to stigma is one which seeks to guard against a tendency in both Marxist and Weberian approaches to sociology to underemphasise the importance of symbolic systems and especially media culture. This is achieved via the fusion of critical semiotic analysis with critical political economy, by emphasising the role of institutions in shaping the movement from social construal to social construction and their implications for the production of hegemony (and its contestation in the remaking of social relations), and its commitment to the de-naturalisation of economic and political imaginaries. Considered as a whole, the monograph demonstrates the importance of the role of symbolic structures and social mediating agencies in the production of inequality and marginality. Its overarching aim is to demonstrate how a sociology of stigma might work to 'untie the threads of stigmatization and discrimination that bind those who are subjected to it' (Parker & Aggleton, 2003, p. 18). Indeed, the approach to stigma we want to encourage is one which begins by calling 'into question the very structures of equality and inequality' which characterise contemporary societies (Parker & Aggleton, 2003, p. 18).

We have organised the articles in this special issue into two themed sections, *Living with Stigma* and *The Stigma of Place*. This reflects a clustering of interests in the contributions in first part of this collection with how stigma is negotiated and resisted in everyday lives, often in interactions with the state, and a focus in the second half of this collection with the concept of 'territorial stigma', namely how spatial taint is enacted and resisted.

Living with stigma

The collection opens with Imogen Tyler's article, 'Resituating Goffman: From Stigma Power to Black Power', which offers a critical rereading of Goffman, to expose how many of the limits of contemporary understandings of stigma are embedded in Goffman's original account. In order to extrapolate a sociologically informed understanding of stigma as power, Tyler resituates Goffman's conceptualisation of stigma within the historical context of Jim Crow and the black freedom struggles that were shaking 'the social interaction order' to its foundations at the very moment Goffman crafted his book. It is the contention of her article that these explosive political movements against the 'humiliations of racial discrimination' invite revision of Goffman's decidedly apolitical account of stigma (Robinson, 2000, p. 318). This historical revision of Goffman's stigma-concept builds on an existing body of critical work on 'the relationship between race, segregation and the epistemology of sociology within the United States' (Bhambra, 2014, p. 472). Throughout, it reads Goffman's *Stigma* through the lens of 'Black Sociology', a field of knowledge that here designates not only formal sociological scholarship, but political manifestos, journalism, creative writing, oral histories and memoirs. It is the argument of Tyler's article that placing Goffman's concept of stigma into critical dialogue with black epistemologies of stigma allows for a timely reconceptualisation of stigma as a governmental technology of 'racialized capitalism' (Robinson, 2000; see also Loyd & Bonds, this issue).

As Tyler argues, one of the major limitations of existing understandings of stigma is the ways in which they have 'bracketed off' key questions, such as where stigmatising attitudes come from, how and by whom is stigma crafted, mediated, produced and why, what social, political and economic functions stigmatisation might play in particular historical and geopolitical contexts, and how has stigma been resisted. As we see it, the challenge for future sociologies of stigma is to begin with these questions in order to better understand the role of stigma in the reproduction of social inequalities and injustices. To develop the conceptual tools adequate for this task means moving beyond the influential understanding of stigma developed by Goffman and the understandings of stigma which have followed in his wake.

The political economy of stigma is the major concern of the next article in this section, 'Heaping Blame Upon Shame: Weaponising Stigma for Neoliberal Times', where Graham Scambler focuses on the 'weaponising' of stigma in the neoliberal era. After a critical exposition of major sociological works on stigma, where he observes (a) the distinctions between enacted and felt stigma (involving norms of shame) and enacted and felt deviance (involving norms of blame), and (b) the novel neoliberal dialectic between these two sets of norms, Scambler finds significant limitations to these literatures as they are inattentive to the dynamics of financial capitalism. With reference to changing social policies vis-a-vis disability, he argues that research on stigma too often neglects the social relations of class, oppression and power that make financial capitalism possible. Not only does this have implications for knowledge of how stigma is used as weapon by the powerful, it also has implications for modes of resistance to the neoliberal elites who exercise stigma as a weapon. He argues that an effective struggle against pernicious forms of social abjection requires combinations of alliances across multiple fields that challenge not only policy but the systemic conditions under which policies are made, or in his words, 'the "real" social structures' that are critical for the maintenance and deepening of stigma power.

In 'Lessons from Grenfell: Poverty Propaganda, Stigma and Class Power', Tracy Shildrick extends her remarkable body of work on the lived experiences and representations of poverty in the UK to dissect the production, diffusion and implications of what she terms 'poverty propaganda'. This is achieved by way of an analysis of the aftermath of the Grenfell Tower disaster in London in June 2017 (when a devastating fire tore through a high-rise social housing block that had been 'regenerated' with cheap, combustible cladding solely to make it look visually more attractive to wealthy residents of the upscale district). Grenfell exposed the absolute political contempt for the rights and housing situations of working-class Londoners, and also exposed the protracted disinvestment in social housing and the disregard for the repeated warnings by tenants of an impending disaster. This led to widespread disquiet and anger about the extent of inequality in London and beyond, but poverty propaganda, according to

Shildrick, 'works to orchestrate confusion and muddies the waters, so clarity on issues of poverty and related disadvantages is never revealed'. As she demonstrates, poverty propaganda provides a critical resource for those with power in times of crises like Grenfell, as (1) its stigmatising messages are simple and far more likely to stick than arguments about causal complexity, and (2) it is malleable as it serves to divide the working class, fuelling mistrust of fellow citizens and neighbours, particularly in deprived neighbourhoods.

In 'Stigma, Housing and Identity after Prison', Danya Keene, Amy Smoyer and Kim Blankenship examine the power of stigma in their account of the ways in which 'the enduring and discrediting mark' of being as an ex-offender shapes and limits the ability of individuals to access decent and affordable housing on their release from prison. Drawing on interview data, the authors reveal the arduous processes ex-offenders go through in their quest to secure a decent home. As they reveal, the stigma enacted not only by individuals (such as landlords) but also by the state, both restricts access to housing and functions as a justification for the discrimination they face. They also show that the interconnected stigmas of prison and poverty are reinforced when former prisoners are denied the marks of decency and valorised self-sufficiency that access to a stable home can provide. Former prisoners' relegation to the streets, half-way houses, homeless shelters and other stigmatised places serves to strengthen the stigmas that are barriers to home in the first place. Their study is a welcome contribution to our understanding of how the stigmatisation of poverty, race and place are not experienced in isolation from each other, but rather work together to compound and harden inequalities and marginalisation.

Lisa Morriss also examines the impact of state produced and/or sanctioned forms of stigmatisation in 'Haunted Futures: The Stigma of Being a Mother Living Apart from her Child(ren) Following State-Ordered Court Removal'. Morriss's article draws on her experience as a researcher working in court archives, a role which 'involved reading documents concerned with parents and children involved in care proceedings in the Family Court: namely, the legal bundles and the social work electronic case files'. These archival data contained 'numerous types of material: social work case notes; legal orders and Judgments; psychiatric and psychological reports; care plans; police interviews; and minutes of various statutory meetings'. By critically rereading this archive, she details how the stigma of having a child removed from their care leaves mothers in states of silent mourning. Silenced both through the shame of court-ordered removal and by court-ordered reporting restrictions, this is a stigma which often remains unspoken, and is largely invisible in the public domain. As she notes, stigma operates here 'as a governmental form of classification and badging with the power to silence and constrain the (m) other'. There is though some resistance to stigma here, as the mothers continue to carry photographs of their children with them, and frequently have the names of their missing children tattooed on their bodies. Morriss also relates collective forms of resistance to this stigma, through the work of groups such as Mothers Living Apart from their Children, After Adoption's 'Breaking the Cycle', and the organisation Match Mothers (Mothers Apart from Their Children), all of whom provide spaces where mothers can talk to others, and learn to express their experiences through creative practices such as writing poems and letters and making art.

In 'Repelling Neoliberal World-Making? How the Ageing–Dementia Relation is Reassembling the Social', Joanne Latimer tackles the pressing issue of the biomedicalisation of ageing vis-a-vis dementia, or what she calls the 'ageing–dementia relation'. In particular, she is concerned with the proliferating framing of dementia as something that can be prevented, transformed and managed – a framing that serves to stigmatise ageing. As she demonstrates, widely circulating media representations of older people with dementia are creating 'spectacles of "othering" that reaffirm the values and modes of ordering that underpin dominant forms of world-making'. Fusing Zymunt Bauman's theories of how communities cope with the 'otherness' of 'others' with a body of work theorising the discursive creation of monsters, Latimer explains that the stigma of dementia relation is hardening because of neoliberal ideologies of 'aging well'. In short, dementia is increasingly portrayed as a moral condition (something that can be prevented through managing self and risk), rather than a neurodegenerative condition. In relation to the political economy of stigma that is a major concern of this publication, Latimer argues that the so-called crisis of dementia is 'partly constructed around an idea that "we cannot afford dementia" ' which in turn is intensifying the fear and stigma of this condition. From this perspective, the stigma associated with the dementia–ageing relation is not just the outcome of a political regime, but is helping 'to legitimate the biomedicalization of ageing, in general, and of dementia, in particular'. Through an exploration of alternative representations and accounts of dementia, Latimer explores how the neoliberal stigma power of dementia and ageing might be resisted.

The stigma of place

The introductory essay to a stimulating recent special issue of *American Behavioural Scientist* entitled 'Understanding Social and Community Stigma' sets out to provide 'an update of the state of stigma research' (Bresnahan & Zhuang, 2016, p. 1283), so it is rather remarkable that it missed entirely a rich strand of research among urban scholars on *territorial stigmatisation* going back more than a decade now (see Wacquant et al., 2014 for a bibliography). Whilst the stigmatisation of certain parts of cities is not a new development, the concept of territorial stigmatisation comes from Wacquant, who argues that spatial taint is a distinctive feature of advanced marginality in the 21st century due its autonomisation from other bases of stigmatisation, to the point where it is 'arguably the single most protrusive feature of the lived experience of those trapped in these sulphurous zones' (Wacquant, 2008, p. 169). He highlights how certain areas of disrepute in advanced societies become renowned across class levels, racialised, and portrayed as emblems and vectors of disintegration, unlike, for example, the disreputable wards of the metropolis in the industrial era which were perceived as an organised counter-society. This conceptualisation has spawned a large body of work, and this vibrant literature is both extended and critiqued in this section of the monograph.

In '*Voices* in the Revolution: Resisting Territorial Stigma and Social Relegation in Porto's Historic Centre (1974–1976)', João Queirós and Virgílio Borges Pereira offer a study of that city through a period of political revolution and social instability. Based on the close scrutiny of institutional archives, ethnographic work in several neighbourhoods, and semi-structured interviews with social actors involved in these processes, they reconstitute the main urban and housing properties of inner city Porto's working-class boroughs in the first three quarters of the 20th century and discuss the forms of political and social resistance developed by residents from the most degraded neighbourhoods following the revolutionary process of April 1974. The sociological analysis of the actions that gave origin to the *voice* of the residents in the historic centre of the city in this period is revealing of a significant mode of interaction with the processes of territorial stigmatisation, that of organised collective resistance. This is a major step forward in the literature on territorial stigma, which has tended to focus on individual responses and coping strategies in the face of such stigma, rather than pay close attention to collective action at the neighbourhood level.

In 'The Invention of the 'Sink Estate': Consequential Categorisation and the UK Housing Crisis', Tom Slater explores the history and traces the realisation of a category that was invented by journalists, amplified by free market think tanks and converted into policy *doxa* (common sense) by politicians in the United Kingdom: the sink estate. This derogatory phrase, signifying social housing estates that supposedly create poverty, family breakdown, worklessness, welfare dependency, antisocial behaviour and personal irresponsibility, has become the symbolic frame justifying current policies towards social housing that have resulted in considerable social suffering and dislocation. Slater advances a conceptual articulation of agnotology (the intentional production of ignorance) with Bourdieu's symbolic power (the capacity for consequential categorisation) to understand the institutional arrangements and symbolic systems structuring deeply unequal social relations. Specifically, the highly influential publications on housing by a free market think tank, Policy Exchange, are dissected in order to demonstrate how the activation of territorial stigma has fed into housing policy agendas that are geared towards profit interests. The 'sink estate', Slater argues, is a semantic battering ram in the ideological assault on social housing, deflecting attention away from social housing not only as urgent necessity during a serious crisis of affordability, but as incubator of community, solidarity, shelter and home.

Imogen Tyler's understanding of racism as 'a preeminent form of stigma' is developed in Jenna Loyd and Anne Bonds' paper 'Where Do Black Lives Matter? Race, Stigma, and Place in Milwaukee, Wisconsin'. Here Loyd and Bonds analyse how the spatial metaphor of *53206*, a zipcode within the city of Milwaukee, connects with crises in the legitimacy of policing and politicians' claims to care about black lives. In unpicking how 'liberal and conservative rhetoric about *53206* largely obscures the roles that decades of deindustrialization and labor assaults, metropolitan racial and wealth segregation, and public school and welfare restructuring play in producing racial and class inequality', Loyd and Bonds produce new understandings of the political function of stigma, and in so doing they challenge existing conceptual formulations of *territorial stigmatisation* to take account of 'historical and contemporary processes of racialized capitalism'. This is a striking challenge to Wacquant's argument that territorial stigma has become autonomised from other forms of stigmatisation, for Loyd and Bonds insist that a politically relevant analysis of this movement must be alert to how different forms of stigmatisation work together.

While many of the articles in this issue emphasise the intensification of stigma under neoliberal conditions, Loyd and Bonds underline the historical persistence, and indeed the *consistency*, of racial-spatial stigma in the US. As they argue, the very idea of distinct historical shifts and breaks are often 'recounted in ideological ways that serve to isolate structures of white racial rule to the past, thereby disavowing the role that accumulated white wealth and power play in the persistence of racialized poverty and racial and class conflict'. In short, they caution against claims that the intensification of stigma is a *general characteristic* of neoliberal forms of government. Pausing here, we want to note that there remains much to be learnt from histories of struggle against stigma. Four of the articles in this collection take a *longer view* on stigma, power and resistance (Tyler; Queirós & Pereira; Slater; Loyd & Bonds). Together they suggest a need for further fine-grained research on changing patterns of stigmatisation over time as well as in place.

The collection ends with Kirsteen Paton's article, 'Beyond Legacy: Backstage Stigmatisation and 'Trickle-Up' Politics of Urban Regeneration', which is principally concerned with systems of local profiteering from the urban regeneration projects which accompanied the Commonwealth Games in Glasgow. As she argues, 'the political economy of the Games reveals a support for private finance and a simultaneous withdrawal of social welfare support, which transfers the burden of debt from the state to the individual and wealth from public funds to private funds'. In particular, her article demonstrates how territorial stigmatisation and gentrification (resulting in displacement) are completely intertwined. The processes of value and devaluation which accompanied and facilitated the Games are a moral and economic class project which is realised in a distinctly spatial way. Extending her earlier work on working-class lives under gentrification, she argues that the management of working-class places and people is of material importance to neoliberal practices of elite capital accumulation and, crucially, stigmatisation helps realise this value. What is perhaps most important about Paton's impressive contribution to this collection, is how directly she evidences stigma power to be a 'vital' and 'key form of exploitation integral to capital accumulation'. Paton's study also underscores the need for sociologies of stigma to 'gaze up' to the site of stigma production and be alert to the role and motivations of stigmatisers. Indeed, a theme which cuts across the articles in this collection is a concern with rethinking stigma as 'a bureaucratised form of violence' that is frequently activated from above (Cooper & Whyte, 2017, p. 3).

Stigmatisation is never a static nor a natural phenomenon, but rather a consequential and injurious form of action through collective representation fastened on people and on places. The contributors to this monograph advance our empirical, theoretical and conceptual grasp of the role of stigma in the production of inequality and marginality in the societies they analyse. They furnish us with rich materials for drawing more complex and nuanced pictures of the production and mediation of stigma; of the relationship between stigma and social classification; of the relationship between stigma and neoliberal forms of capitalism; of the deployment of stigma as a weapon of domination over populations; and of the ways in which stigma is negotiated and resisted. In doing so, they directly counter the portrayals of people and places as perpetrators of moral dissipation and national debility, and point to the possibilities for social justice in deeply unjust times.

Funding

Professor Imogen Tyler acknowledges the support of the Leverhulme Trust. A Philip Leverhulme Prize (2015–2018) funded a project on the Sociology of Stigma, which is developing new historically informed understandings of stigma (as) power. This collection is one outcome from this project.

Notes

1. The decision to focus on stigma and mental health in this introduction came about because two of our original 'line-up' for this special issue where unable to submit articles due to circumstances outside their control. Both of these contributions would have had a mental health and disability focus. We felt that mental distress was so central to understanding both the history of the concept of stigma, the effects of stigma, the neoliberal political economy of stigma and stigma as a form of power, that we decided to address this theme in the introduction. In doing, Imogen wants to note her debt to Brigit McWade, who had many hours of conversations with her about stigma, mental health and politics. Brigit worked as a researcher on Imogen's stigma research project, pointed us to much of the academic literature drawn on here, and has pioneered the development of 'Mad Studies' in the UK.

2. Charity partners include organisations such as The Campaign Against Living Miserably (CALM), a national charity dedicated to preventing male suicide, and YoungMinds, 'the UK's leading charity championing the wellbeing and mental health of children and young people'.

3. For an account of the emerging scholar-activist discipline of 'Mad Studies', see Costa (2014) and McWade (2016).

4. Gill Plimmer notes that 'the provision of community services and mental healthcare is one of the biggest growth areas for healthcare companies and accounts for about half of all NHS outsourcing deals put out to tender'. As she writes, 'according to LaingBuisson, the industry analysts, the market for out-of-hospital services could be worth £10bn–£20bn a year' (Plimmer, 2017).

References

Bhambra, G. (2014). A sociological dilemma: Race, segregation and US sociology. *Current Sociology, 62*, 472–492.

Bonnington, O., & Rose, D. (2014). Exploring stigmatisation among people diagnosed with either bipolar disorder or borderline personality disorder: A critical realist analysis. *Social Science and Medicine, 123*, 7–17.

Bresnahan, M., & Zhuang, J. (2016). Detrimental effect of community-based stigma. *American Behavioural Scientist, 60*, 1283–1292.

CALM. (2017, April 18). William and Harry in their own words. *CALMzine, 25*, pp. 10–13.

Cooper, V., & Whyte, D. (2017). Introduction: The violence of austerity. In V. Cooper & D. Whyte (Eds.), *The violence of austerity* (pp. 1 – 31). London, UK: Pluto.

Corrigan, P. (2007). How clinical diagnosis might exacerbate the stigma of mental illness. *Social Work, 52*, 31–39.

Costa, L., Voronka, J., Landry, D., Reid, J., Mcfarlane, B., Reville, D., & Church, K. (2012). 'Recovering our stories': A small act of resistance. *Studies in Social Justice, 6*, 85–101.

Costa, L. (2014). Mad studies – what it is and why you should care. Retrieved from https://madstudies2014.wordpress.com/2014/10/15/mad-studies-what-it-is-and-why-you-should-care-2/ (last accessed 1 May 2018).

Crossley, S. (2017). *In their place: The imagined geographies of poverty*. London, UK: Pluto.

Davies, W. (2016). *The happiness industry: How the government and big business sold us wellbeing*. London, UK: Verso.

Davies, W. (2017, April 20). On mental health, the royal family is doing more than our government. *The Guardian*. Retrieved from https://www.theguardian.com/commentisfree/2017/apr/20/mental-health-royal-family-government-children-illness (last accessed 1 May 2018).

Dodd, V. (2017, August 28). Police dealing with record level of phone calls on mental health. *The Guardian*. Retrieved from https://www.theguardian.com/society/2017/aug/28/police-phone-calls-mental-health-nhs (last accessed 1 May 2018).

Foucault, M. (2008). *The birth of biopolitics: Lectures at the Collège de France, 1978–1979* (M. Sennelart, Ed., G. Burchell, Trans.). Basingstoke, UK: Palgrave Macmillan.

Goffman, E. (1986). *Stigma: Notes on the management of spoiled identity*. New York, NY: Simon & Schuster (Original work published 1963).

Hacking, I. (2004). *Historical ontology*. Cambridge, MA: Harvard University Press.

Hannem, S. (2012). Theorizing stigma and the politics of resistance: Symbolic and structural stigma in everyday life. In S. Hannem & C. Bruckert (Eds.), *Stigma revisited: Implications of the mark* (pp. 10–28). Ottawa, Canada: University of Ottawa Press.

Hannem, S., & Bruckert, C. (Eds.). (2012). *Stigma revisited: Implications of the mark*. Ottawa, Canada: University of Ottawa Press.

Hatzenbuehler, M., & Link, B. (2014). Introduction to the special issue on structural stigma and health. *Social Science & Medicine, 103*, 1–6.

Heads Together. (2017). *Heads Together [Website]*. Retrieved from https://www.headstogether.org.uk/ (last accessed 1 May 2018).

Hinshaw, S. (2009). *The mark of shame: Stigma of mental illness and an agenda for change*. Oxford, UK: Oxford University Press.

Hills, J. (2014). *Good times, bad times: The welfare myth of them and us*. Bristol, UK: Policy Press.

Holley, L., Stromwall, L., & Bashor, K. (2012). Reconceptualizing stigma: Toward a critical anti-oppression paradigm. *Stigma Research and Action, 2*(2). http://stigmaj.org/article/view/46

Jensen, T., & Tyler, I. (2015).'Benefits broods': The cultural and political crafting of anti-welfare commonsense. *Critical Policy Studies, 35*, 470–491.

Jessop, B. (2010). Cultural political economy and critical policy studies. *Critical Policy Studies, 3*, 336–356.

Klein, N. (2007). *The shock doctrine: The rise of disaster capitalism*. London, UK: Penguin.

Kusow, A. (2004). Contesting stigma: On Goffman's assumptions of normative order. *Symbolic Interaction, 27*, 179–197.

Link, B., & Phelan, J. (2001). Conceptualizing stigma. *Annual Review of Sociology, 27*, 363–385.

Link, B., & Phelan, J. (2014). Stigma power. *Social Science & Medicine, 103*, 24–32.

May, T. (2017). Prime Minister unveils plans to transform mental health support. Retrieved from https://www.gov.uk/government/news/prime-minister-unveils-plans-to-transform-mental-health-support (last accessed 1 May 2018).

McNall, S., & Johnson, J. (1975). The new conservatives: Ethnomethodologists, phenomenologists, and symbolic interactionists. *Insurgent Sociologist, 5*, 49–65.

McWade, B. (2016). Recovery-as-policy as a form of neoliberal state making. *Intersectionalities: A Global Journal of Social Work Analysis, Research, Polity, and Practice, 5*, 62–81.

O'Hara, M. (2017). Mental health and suicide. In V. Cooper & D. Whyte (Eds.), *The violence of austerity* (pp. 35–43). London, UK: Pluto.

Parker, R., & Aggleton, P. (2003). HIV and AIDS-related stigma and discrimination: A conceptual framework and implications for action. *Social Science & Medicine, 57*, 13–24.

Pescosolido, B., & Martin, J. (2015). The stigma complex. *Annual Review of Sociology, 41*, 87–116.

Plimmer, G. (2017). Virgin Care sues NHS after losing Surrey child services deal. *Financial Times*. Retrieved from https://www.ft.com/content/297e7714–089f-11e7–97d1–5e720a26771b?mhq5j=e5 (last accessed 1 May 2018).

Read, J., Haslam, N., Sayce, L., & Davies, E. (2006). Prejudice and schizophrenia: A review of the 'mental illness is an illness like any other' approach. *Acta Psychiatrica Scandinavica, 114*, 303–318.

Robinson, C. (2000). *Black Marxism: The making of a black radical tradition*. Chapel Hill: University of North Carolina Press.

Schrecker, T., & Bambra, C. (2015). *How politics makes us sick: Neoliberal epidemics*. Basingstoke, UK: Palgrave Macmillan.

Stewart, H., & Booth, R. (2016, October 12). Patients forced to make appointments to boost profits, says Labour MP. *The Guardian*. Retrieved from https://www.theguardian.com/society/2016/oct/12/virgin-care-patients-being-forced-to-make-appointments-to-boost-profits-says-labour-mp-paula-sherriff (last accessed 1 May 2018).

Stuckler, D., & Basu, S. (2013). *The body economic: Why austerity kills*. London, UK: Basic Books.

Taylor-Gooby, P. (2013). *The double crisis of the welfare state and what we can do about it*. Basingstoke, UK: Palgrave.

Tyler, I. (2013). *Revolting subjects: Social abjection and resistance in neoliberal Britain*. London, UK: Zed Books.

Tyler, I. (forthcoming). *Stigma machines*. London, UK: Zed Books.

Wacquant, L. (2008). *Urban outcasts: A comparative sociology of advanced marginality*. Cambridge, UK: Polity.

Wacquant, L., Slater, T., & Pereira, V. (2014). Tersritorial stigmatisation in action. *Environment and Planning A, 46*, 1270–1280.

Walker, R. (2015). *The shame of poverty*. Oxford, UK: Oxford University Press.

Wickware, C. (2017, April 25). CCGs cutting spending on mental health despite NHS pledges. *Pulse*. Retrieved from http://www.pulsetoday.co.uk/clinical/mental-health/ccgs-cutting-spending-on-mental-health-despite-nhs-pledges/20034293.article (last accessed 1 May 2018).

Author biographies

Imogen Tyler is a Professor of Sociology at Lancaster University. Her research is concerned with social inequalities (of multiple kinds), power, injustice and resistance and she has published widely on topics such as borders, migration, citizenship, class, racism and gender. Imogen's book *Revolting Subjects: Social Abjection and Resistance in Neoliberal Britain* (2013) was shortlisted for the Bread and Roses Prize for Radical Publishing. A Philip Leverhulme Prize (2015–2018) is supporting her current research project on stigma, of which this collection is an outcome. She is currently completing a solo-authored monograph, titled *Stigma Machines*, which employs historical methods to trace the long penal genealogy of stigma power.

Tom Slater is Reader in Urban Geography at the University of Edinburgh. He has research interests in the institutional arrangements producing and reinforcing urban inequalities, and in the ways in which marginalised urban dwellers organise against injustices visited upon them. He has written extensively on gentrification (notably the co-authored books, *Gentrification*, 2008 and *The Gentrification Reader*, 2010), displacement from urban space, territorial stigmatisation, welfare reform, and social movements. Since 2010 he has delivered lectures in 19 different countries on these issues, and his work has been translated into 10 different languages and circulates widely to inform struggles for urban social justice.

The
Sociological
Review
Monographs

The Sociological Review Monographs
2018, Vol. 66(4) 26–47
© The Author(s) 2018
Reprints and permissions:
sagepub.co.uk/journalsPermissions.nav
DOI: 10.1177/0038026118777450
journals.sagepub.com/home/sor

Resituating Erving Goffman: From Stigma Power to Black Power

Imogen Tyler
Lancaster University, UK

Abstract

This article offers a critical re-reading of the understanding of stigma forged by the North American sociologist Erving Goffman in his influential *Stigma: Notes on the Management of Spoiled Identity* (1963). One of the most widely read and cited sociologists in history, Goffman was already famous when *Stigma* was published in 1963. His previous books were best-sellers and *Stigma* alone has sold an astonishing 800,000 copies in the 50 years since its publication. Given its considerable influence, it is surprising how little sustained engagement there has been with the historicity of Goffman's account. This article resituates Goffman's conceptualisation of stigma within the historical context of Jim Crow and the Black freedom struggles that were shaking 'the social interaction order' to its foundations at the very moment he crafted his account. It is the contention of this article that these explosive political movements against the 'humiliations of racial discrimination' invite revision of Goffman's decidedly apolitical account of stigma. This historical revision of Goffman's stigma concept builds on an existing body of critical work on the relationship between race, segregation and the epistemology of sociology within the USA. Throughout, it reads Goffman's *Stigma* through the lens of 'Black Sociology', a field of knowledge that here designates not only formal sociological scholarship, but political manifestos, journalism, creative writing, oral histories and memoirs. It is the argument of this article that placing Goffman's concept of stigma into critical dialogue with Black epistemologies of stigma allows for a timely reconceptualisation of stigma as governmental technologies of dehumanisation that have long been collectively resisted from below.

Keywords
Black Power, civil rights, Goffman, Jim Crow, racism, stigma

Corresponding author:
Imogen Tyler, Department of Sociology, Bowland North, Lancaster University, Lancaster, LA1 4YN, UK.
Email: i.tyler@lancaster.ac.uk

Long we've borne the nation's

Shame. (J. Thompson 'Exhortation' 1933, in Kelley, 1996, p. 103)

I ask to be considered. I am not merely here and now, sealed into thingness. I am for somewhere else and for something else. (Fanon, 1952/2008, p. 170)

Stigma: A history lesson

In January 1960, a Black teenager called Joseph McNeil travelled back from a Christmas visit with his family in New York, to North Carolina Agricultural and Technical State University[1] in Greensboro. When McNeil got back to campus he described the bus journey to his friends: In Philadelphia, I could eat anywhere in the bus station. By Maryland, that had changed; by the time I arrived in Richmond, Virginia I was refused a hotdog at a food counter reserved for whites. 'It was a degrading experience; three hours ago I was a human being … three hours later … some kind of pariah' (Cerese & Channing, 2003). Travelling from the Northern to the Southern states in 1960 meant crossing, in Erving's Goffman's terms, from one 'social interaction order' into another. Arriving in the South in 1960 meant immersion in the spatial politics of white supremacy, manifest in the Jim Crow signs that segregated social spaces and in unspoken 'customs', rules, rituals and codes 'designed to degrade and divide' (Davis, 1970/2004, p. 496). McNeil and three teenage friends, Franklin McCain, David Richmond and Jibreel Khazan,[2] had spent the evenings of their first term at university discussing Ghandi, Langston Hughes, Martin Luther King, and Jim Crow – a period 'of institutionalized violence against African Americans' that had lasted by then for close to a century (Bhambra, 2014b, p. 480). They had talked long into the night about the failures of the Civil Rights Movement to effect meaningful change and the quotidian humiliations of living under white supremacy. Furious after his degrading bus journey, McNeil persuaded his friends to take direct action. On 1 February, the four went into the Woolworths store on South Elm Street in Greensboro and sat down at the 'Whites only' lunch counter.[3] They asked for coffee. The waitress refused to serve them: 'we don't serve Negroes here' (Langer, 2014). The police were called, an officer arrived, 'He took his knife stick out. He took his billy club and began to hit it on his hand' (Cerese & Channing, 2003). Taking their place in a long history of Southern Black freedom fighters, the four refused to move from their seats. The Greensboro Four returned to Woolworths lunch counter every day that week accompanied by growing numbers of students from A&T, Bennett College (a Black liberal arts college for women), and Dudley High School (then a segregated Black school). By 6 February, 1000 students were sitting-in at Greensboro Woolworths lunch counter. These initially minor 'dramaturgical' challenges to segregation escalated into the largest Black resistance movement in the history of the United States (Goffman, 1956).

The sit-in protests garnered extensive national television news coverage. By 1958 over 80% of American homes had television sets, and by 1960 the use of 16mm film and the development of wireless audio recorders transformed the ability of television journalists 'to capture volatile demonstrations as they unfolded' (Fleming & Morris, 2015, p. 113).[4] As a consequence of this rapidly growing television audience, and technical advances in shooting news footage, 'the sit-ins provided the nation with a unique experiment in moral theatre, where Black protestors (at times with white allies) nonviolently withstood verbal and physical abuse' (Joseph, 2014, p. 19).[5] Anne Moody, then a sociology student at Tougaloo College, described the scene at a sit-in at a Woolworths lunch counter in Jackson, Mississippi:

> … the white students started chanting all kinds of anti-Negro slogans. We were called a little bit of everything. The rest of the seats except the three we were occupying had been roped off to prevent others from sitting down. A couple of the boys took one end of the rope and made it into a hangman's noose. Several attempts were made to put it around our necks. The mob started smearing us with ketchup, mustard, sugar, pies, and everything on the counter. … a Negro high school boy sat down next to me. … the word 'nigger' was written on his back with red spray paint. (Moody, 1968, p. 238)

Being Black in the United States in 1960 was to be 'smeared with the stigma of "racial inferiority" ' (Haywood, 1948, p. 138). By putting their bodies in white-only spaces, these young people sought to dramatise 'the studied humiliations' of Jim Crow (Du Bois, 1903/2015, p. 160). Protesting the political and economic terrorism of white supremacy came at a price: people were heckled, intimidated, beaten, arrested and expelled from schools, colleges and jobs. As then student activist (and later sociology Professor) Joyce Ladner notes: 'It was very, very difficult to continue because the local police and all the towns had almost crushed us. They were closing in like … They murdered people, they beat people' (Ladner, Ladner, & Mosnier, 2011). What motivated young people to participate in the face of these 'terrible beatings, brutalities' was often a deeply personal need to express the anguish of living with anti-Black racism (Kelley, 1996, p. 79). These 'subversive demands for a dignified life free from harassment' (Gilroy, 2002, p. xiii) were acts of resistance against what Malcolm X described as the 'psychological and physical mutilation that is an everyday occurrence in our lives' (Malcolm X, 1964, p. 2). As Franklin McCain reflects, 'it really started out as a personal thing … we didn't like the idea of not having dignity and respect … and decided it was really up to us to find a solution to this thing we were suffering with' (Boyd, 2004: 78). McCain described the Woolworths protest as a reparative act: 'almost instantaneously after sitting down on a simple dumb stool, I felt so relieved, I felt so clean', 'a feeling of total freedom' (Cerese & Channing, 2003). Similarly, when Jibreel Khazan was asked what moved him to act he replied 'something had to be done *to remove the stigma*' (Khazan, n.d., my emphasis).

Introduction

Through the examination of the history of a particularly influential sociological concept, stigma, this article responds to calls for a reconstruction of 'the historical narratives that inform sociological conceptions of the contemporary world' (Bhambra, 2014a, p. 1). It emerges out of an ongoing Leverhulme funded research project on the Sociology of Stigma (2015–2018) which seeks to develop new historical understandings of stigma (as) power. One of the major aims of this project is to supplement the often individualistic, ahistorical and politically anaesthetised conceptualisation of stigma which dominates within the social sciences, with richer historical understandings of the social and political function of stigma as an instrument of social policy and 'component of the state's coercive apparatus' (Davis, 1970/2004, p. 494). In order to better understand the 'political economy of stigma', I am researching the long penal history of stigma as a practice of social control, stretching from the penal tattooing of slaves in the Greek and Roman Empires, through to the badging of the poor in Industrial Britain and the stigmatisation of migrants in contemporary political rhetoric (Tyler, 2017; Tyler, forthcoming). This article is guided by this research but the specific focus here is on the emergence of stigma as a sociological concept in the mid-twentieth century. To this end, the article reappraises the understanding of stigma forged by the North American sociologist Erving Goffman in his influential *Stigma: Notes on the Management of Spoiled Identity* (1963). The reason for returning to Goffman is that despite many subsequent refinements of his account, this short book established the conceptual understanding of stigma that continues to buttress contemporary sociological thinking.

This critical reading of Goffman's *Stigma* is an urgent one in the context of the wider movement to 'decolonise' the sociological canon. Decolonising sociology necessitates the development of a 'deep historical consciousness' and a commitment to 'unlearning' the epistemological foundations of the discipline, in order to confront 'more candidly the myriad of effects and consequences' of the concepts, vocabularies and methods which have shaped the discourses and practices of sociology since its invention as a science in the mid-nineteenth century (West, 1987/2016). The historical revision of Goffman's stigma concept that follows builds on a growing body of critical work on 'the relationship between race, segregation and the epistemology of sociology within the United States' (Bhambra, 2014b, p. 472). It is not only, as Gurminder Bhambra notes, that 'dominant historiographies have been silent' on the segregation of sociologists of colour and the sociology of racialisation and racisms from mainstream canons, but that this has had a profound epistemological and political impact on sociological knowledge (Bhambra, 2014a, pp. 1–2). This article draws particular inspiration from Roderick Ferguson's *Aberrations in Black: Towards a Queer of Color Critique* (2004). Concerned with 'the strategies of power that are immanent in canonical sociology's will to knowledge', Ferguson focuses on mid-twentieth century North American Sociology, and the ways in which 'techniques of racial domination' 'are obscured through the language of liberal progress' (Ferguson, 2004, pp. 55, 63). Reading sociological classics alongside Black American fiction from the same period, Ferguson examines how sociologists produced pathological knowledge about Black culture which functioned as 'an epistemological counter-part' to official forms of state racism. Sociology, he argues, was 'the supplicant of the American state' (p. 81) employed to regulate and legislate (against) non-white populations. This article brings Ferguson's insight to bear on both the concept of stigma and practices of stigmatisation, by rethinking stigma as a technology of racism.

One of the most widely read and cited sociologists in history, Goffman was already famous when *Stigma* was published in 1963. His previous books *Presentation of Self in Everyday Life* (1956) and *Asylums: Essays on the Social Situation of Mental Patients and Other Inmates* (1961) were best-selling titles, an unusual achievement for academic sociological texts. *Stigma* alone has sold an astonishing 800,000 copies in the 50 years since its publication. Given the considerable influence of *Stigma*, it is surprising how little sustained engagement there has been with the historicity of Goffman's conceptualisation of stigma; Heather Love's work on Goffman's 'stigma archive' being a notable exception (see Love, 2010, 2013). Reading Goffman historically is not an easy task for as Fredric

Jameson notes, his work is 'punctuated by frequent disclaimers that his material is drawn only from our own society and that his findings are therefore not necessarily binding on other social forms'; an admission which is 'not so much an invitation to comparative research and to a more genuinely historical approach … as it is a dismissal of those perspectives' (Jameson, 1976, p. 124). Despite the difficulty of reading Goffman against the grain, this article resituates his conceptualisation of stigma within the historical context of the Black freedom struggles which were shaking 'the social interaction order' to its foundations at the moment he crafted his account. It is one of the central contentions of this article that the explosive political movements against what Cedric Robinson termed the 'humiliations of racial discrimination' (Robinson, 2000, p. 318) in the 1960s invites revision of Goffman's decidedly apolitical account of stigma. Throughout it reads Goffman's stigma concept through the lens of Black Sociology, a field of knowledge which here designates not only formal sociological scholarship, but political manifestos, journalism, creative writing, oral histories and memoirs. It draws on the resources of this 'Black stigma archive' to challenge Goffman's account. In doing so, this article troubles 'the conceptual matrix' that has isolated 'the study of race and racism' from sociological (and social psychological) accounts of stigma (Magubane, 2016, p. 371). It also reveals how bringing racism to the front and centre of sociological understandings of stigma transforms existing understandings of stigma. In particular, it is the argument of this article that placing Goffman's concept of stigma into dialogue with Black epistemologies of stigma allows for a reconceptualisation of the social and political function of stigma as a governmental technology of 'racialised capitalism' (see Loyd & Bonds, this issue).

Struggles in the interaction order

What distinguishes Goffman's work is his career-long focus on social interaction defined as 'social situations … in which two or more individuals are physically in one another's response presence' (Goffman, 1982, p. 2). As he notes in 'The Interaction Order' (1982), his posthumously published Presidential Address to the American Sociology Association: 'my concern over the years has been to promote acceptance of this face-to-face domain as an analytically viable one – a domain whose preferred method of study is microanalysis' (p. 2). The interactional spaces which Goffman was interested in studying extended to all conceivable public settings: 'a local bar, a small shop floor, a domestic kitchen … factories, airports, hospitals, and public thoroughfares' (p. 4). Goffman was interested in observing these 'behavioural settings' (p. 4) for what they reveal about the rules, norms, conventions and procedures that allow for orderly social interactions to take place. Those familiar with Goffman's oeuvre will be reminded of his dramaturgical understanding of the interaction order as 'a natural theater', with a front and back stage, in which people perform anticipated and prescribed social roles (p. 4). He was particularly interested (and I will argue, politically invested) in how social order is maintained, including why individuals 'go along with current interaction arrangements' even in contexts where they might 'resent' or 'resist' the costs of social arrangements (p. 5). Goffman's concern with 'shared cognitive presuppositions' and 'self-sustained restraints' that underpin human interactions inevitably raises questions about what kinds of structures and values shape the interactions that comprise social worlds (p. 4). As Goffman states, 'questions do arise when we consider the fact that there are categories of persons – in our own society very broad ones – whose members constantly pay a very considerable price for their interactional existence' (p. 6). However, while Goffman acknowledges these questions, he refuses to dwell on them. Rather, he argues that the work of the micro-analyst necessitates a 'bracketing off' of the economic and political imperatives that structure behavioural settings. One of the 'warrants' he offers for this elision is that his approach is not 'informed by a concern over the plight of disadvantaged groups' (p. 2). What is striking about this statement is that Goffman's career as a sociologist spanned some of the most tumultuous decades of resistance by 'disadvantaged groups' – including Black people, women, disabled people, 'mad' people and queers – to the dominant social order in US history. More than this, the grassroots resistance movements which characterised this period were taking place within the very 'behavioral settings', and involved conflicts in exactly the kinds of 'service transactions', which were, ostensibly, at the very centre of Goffman's sociological interest (pp. 2, 7). As Stokely Carmichael put it in 1966, 'I am black. I know that. I also know that while I am black I am a human being, and therefore *I have the right to go into any public place*' (Carmichael, 1966, my emphasis).[6]

Two months after Greensboro electrified the Civil Rights Movement from below, the formation of the Student Nonviolent Coordinating Committee (SNCC) saw young people's actions against racial segregation extended to 'Freedom Rides' which challenged segregation on interstate travel, kneel-ins at segregated churches, sleep-ins at segregated motels, swim-ins at segregated pools, wade-ins at segregated beaches, read-ins at segregated libraries, play-ins at segregated parks, watch-ins at segregated cinemas and theatres, wait-ins at housing developments, chain-ins at city halls and participation in rent-strikes (Boggs, 2011). By the spring of 1960 it was estimated that 50,000 people had participated in 'interactional' forms of political resistance against the violent regimes of racial stigma which characterised Jim Crow. By 1963 'the southern struggle had grown from a modest group of Black students demonstrating at one lunch-counter to the largest mass movement for racial reform and civil rights in the 20th century' (Younge, 2013). It was in the midst of these political struggles in 'the interaction order' that Goffman crafted his concept of stigma.

Between 1960 and 1963, Goffman was teaching a course called 'Deviance and Social Control' at the University of California at Berkeley, and *Stigma* emerged out of his lectures for his course. While teaching at Berkeley Goffman would have been acutely aware of the Black freedom struggles which were exploding all around in 'sit-ins, marches, protest rallies and urban upheavals' (Collins, 2007, p. 585).[7] As indicated above, newspaper images and television footage of 'chanting demonstrators being sprayed by fire hoses and attacked by dogs, freedom riders being abused, sit-in participants being taunted or beaten, and small Black children requiring military escorts to enter public schools' made for powerful viewing in this period (Macdonald, in Robinson, 1997, p. 145). Moreover, as a consequence of the sit-in movement, the 'pernicious de facto segregation of the Urban North' was increasingly seen through the lens of the 'codified racial discrimination' of Jim Crow (Taylor, 2016, p. 37). From the spring of 1960, Berkeley students were picketing hotels and shops which were known to practise racial discrimination in their employment practices in solidarity with Southern sit-in movements (Freeman, 2004). We know that this anti-racist politics leaked into Goffman's classroom, as the sociologist Gary Marx, then a student in Goffman's 1961 'Deviance and Social Control' class, recalls:

At the end of the last class session a black student said 'this is all very interesting Professor Goffman, but what's the use of it for changing the conditions you describe?' Goffman was visibly shaken. He stood up, slammed shut the book he had open on the desk and said 'I'm not in that business' and stormed out of the room. (Marx, 1984: 657)

In what follows, I examine what happens to Goffman's account of stigma when we take seriously the question of this unnamed Black student:[8] 'what's the use of it for changing the conditions you describe?'

Social relations without power relations

In the opening pages of *Stigma*, Goffman offers a working definition of stigma as 'an attribute that is deeply discrediting' (1986, p. 2) and 'the situation of the individual who is disqualified from full social acceptance' (Preface). However, what is most novel and influential about the definition of stigma he proposes are the ways in which Goffman roots stigma in his existing understanding of social identities as 'perspectives' produced in interactional settings (p. 138). While stigma might be experienced as emanating from the body of the stigmatised, in fact *stigma describes a relation* between normal and stigmatised persons. What he means by this is that people acquire stigma in their exchanges with other people – be this a look, a glance, a comment or a more overt form of discrimination such as name-calling. Goffman's understanding of stigma, as something produced in social settings, pivots on the existence of a social consensus about 'what is normal'. For Goffman, society 'works' and 'coheres' to the extent that members of society implicitly understand and share, or at least accept, the norms in operation in a given social context. So, in social interactions, Goffman argues, 'there is some expectation on all sides that those in a given category should not only support a particular norm but also realize it' (p. 6). Stigma describes a particular kind of negative social relation then, as it arises when an individual fails to realise 'a particular norm' (p. 6). Further, stigma not only describes a relation between people, but also a relation of self to self. Goffman argues that it is through processes of socialisation that an individual 'learns and incorporates the stand-point of the normal' and in so doing understands how they are likely to be placed in a stratified order of normal–stigma positionalities (p. 32). Through this psychosocial process, people judge themselves against incorporated norms and anticipate 'the standards against which they fall short' (p. 32). In short, rather like Pierre Bourdieu's relational theory of social class, for Goffman social identities are not properties of a person, but emerge in encounters between social actors and in doing so become incorporated as part of oneself. However, unlike Bourdieu, his account of stigma as a relational classification excludes questions of how social relations are structured through power.

Where do these norms come from? Again, Goffman anticipates but does not this answer this question, stating on the first page of his book: 'Society establishes the means of categorizing persons and the complement of attributes felt to be ordinary and natural for members of these categories' (p. 2). Towards the end of *Stigma*, he admits that stigmatisation is historically specific in the forms it takes (p. 138), notes that 'shifts have occurred in the kinds of disgrace that arouse concern', and implicitly acknowledges that stigma functions 'as a means of formal social control' (p. 139). However, he expresses little curiosity about where norms come from, what they prescribe, what the effects of these prescriptions might be, or how they might be challenged or transformed. Rather, he is concerned with detailing the more abstract operations of the system within which face-to-face interactions take place, in *smooth* or *disordered* ways. That is, his interest is in *how* social rules work rather than in *what* they proscribe. So while a relational under-standing of stigma is at the core of Goffman's account, his understanding of normal–stigma relations is divorced from power relations – both the macro-level structural power relations of, for example, capitalism or patriarchy, or the power inflected micro-aggres-sions of everyday interactions. Fredric Jameson suggests that this suspension of ques-tions of power is deliberate, for Goffman's ambition is 'to evolve abstractions which hold for all social situations', rather than to develop an understanding which is 'concrete and historically determinate' (Jameson, 1976, p. 129). It is possible to read power back into Goffman, and indeed this is what many sociologists who draw on his stigma concept have subsequently done, by thinking about stigma as a form of oppression or discrimina-tion. However, it is the contention of this article that thinking with this absence of power in Goffman remains important for understanding some of the remaining limitations of stigma as a conceptual tool for sociology. Employing Greensboro and the challenging question of Goffman's student as a guide, I want to consider what 'this ambition to evolve' an abstract understanding of stigma which might 'hold for all social situations' implies in terms of Goffman's methodology (Jameson, 1976, p. 129). I ask what it means to argue that society informs stigma categorisations in advance of interactional encoun-ters without reference to, for example, colonial histories of power. And I want to reflect on how the structural absence of questions of power has shaped subsequent understand-ings of what stigma is, what stigma does and what stigma is for.

Atrocity tales: Goffman's methods

Despite his career-long concern with social interaction, *Stigma* is not grounded, as are some of Goffman's earlier studies such as *Asylums* (1961), or his PhD research in a Shetland Islands community which formed the basis of *The Presentation of Self in Everyday Life* (1956), in original ethnographic research. Indeed, despite being recog-nised as 'one of the founding figures of microsociology', and despite his self-presenta-tion as pioneer of observational methods, his 'links to both ethnography and empiricism are rather tenuous, since he rarely engaged in traditional fieldwork and drew on both fictional literary texts and fabricated anecdotes for his evidence' (Love, 2013, p. 419). Goffman states that his objective in *Stigma* is to explore what a burgeoning psychologi-cal literature on stigma – but 'especially popular work' – might 'yield for sociology' (Preface). As Love details, it transpires from his footnotes that what Goffman means by 'popular work' is memoirs and biographies, letters and newspaper articles, 'lightly fic-tionalized [medical] case histories, human interest stories, and counterfactuals' (Love, 2013, p. 420). Indeed, *Stigma* opens with an epigraph, a fictional letter written by a 16-year-old girl who was 'born without a nose' to a newspaper 'agony aunt', which Goffman has taken from Nathaniel West's bleak comic depression-era novel *Miss Lonelyhearts* (1933). Goffman's use of this fictional epigraph has been interpreted as signalling compassion (Taylor, Bogdan, & DeVault, 2016, p. 176). However, given

West's 'ironic' and 'dispassionate' treatment of 'emotionally and politically charged material' in this novel, it seems more likely that Goffman is making a playful statement about his own cool and detached approach to stigma (Love, 2013, p. 423). Indeed, I would argue that his use of this epigraph is best understood as a dry joke: the punchline being, as Goffman will argue at the end of *Stigma*, that 'we normals' might, just like the antihero in West's novel, find ourselves switched into the role of the stigmatised (Goffman, 1986, p. 5).

Stigma draws together a heterogeneous and eclectic archive of writing about blindness, facial deformities, cripples, amputees, alcoholics, gentleman criminals, ex-cons, prostitutes, homosexuals, the 'mentally deficient', 'the mad', anti-Semitism and anti-Black racism. Goffman describes his reading method as 'an exercise' in 'marking off the material on stigma from neighboring facts' and 'showing how this material can be economically described within a singular conceptual schema' (Preface). Love argues that this 'marking off' of 'facts' necessitates what she describes (approvingly) as 'thin description' (Love, 2013).[9] What this method amounts to in practice is that there is often no discernible difference in how Goffman deploys, for example, an extract from a clinical account of a facial disfigurement, or a personal memoir or fictional account on the same topic. Certainly, he rarely introduces the authors of the materials he quotes from in his text, but rather substitutes particular accounts of stigma in his text with abstract 'stigma figures', such as 'a blind writer', 'a multipole sclerotic', 'a cripple', 'a prostitute', 'a homosexual', 'a Negro', 'a Jew' (Goffman, 1986). This abstraction produces the 'stylistic effect, of impartial "realism" ' (Schweik, 2014). It is telling in this regard that *Stigma* is sometimes misread as based on Goffman's own first-hand observational research. What I want to draw attention to here is the politics of a method which deliberately eschews contextual information in this way.

What is veiled through this method of abstraction are the particular genres and aesthetics of the writing he draws upon, and the multiple perspectives encoded within these texts. Most significantly, in suppressing 'neighboring facts' Goffman erases the original intentions which might have motivated what is often confessional writing about stigma (Goffman, 1986, Preface). As noted, this suppression of authorial intention is deliberate on Goffman's part, for as he explains, his account of stigma is not written for 'them', and it is not 'informed by a concern over the plight of disadvantaged groups' (1986, p. 2). This point is underlined by his acerbic characterisation of some of the literature he draws upon as 'atrocity tales' written by 'stigma professionals' and 'heroes of adjustment' who seek to 'present the case for the stigmatized' (p. 25). In short, *Stigma* draws on the writing of people who understood themselves in various ways as stigmatised (or are concerned about the fates of stigmatised people) but it fails to engage with the authors of this stigma data as 'knowers' or understand these confessional literatures as knowledge. On the contrary, Goffman's method of abstraction proceeds from what Kristie Dotson has described as 'an active practice of unknowing' (2011, p. 243).

It is important to note at this juncture that *Stigma* was written during a resurgence in confessional writing in US and wider European culture. Indeed, this 'confessional turn' was central to social and political struggles of the period, beginning with the Civil Rights Movement and extending to feminist, queer, disability and anti-psychiatry movements (Goffman's *Asylums* played a central role in the latter). Goffman acknowledges the 'current literary fashion' for confessional writing, self-help literature and 'advice to the stigmatized' in which 'deeply hidden sores are touched upon and examined' (1986, p. 112). He dismissively cites James Baldwin in a footnote as an example of 'material of this kind in regard to Negroes' (fn. 18, p. 112). At the same time, he veils over any of the reformist, consciousness-raising and/or political intentions of these 'atrocity tales' (p. 25). More than this, by transforming the authors of these stigma experiences into abstract figures – such as 'negroes' in the aforementioned footnote about Baldwin – Goffman enacts a 'testimonial quieting' (Dotson, 2011, p. 242) which mimics the dehumanising effects that the concept of stigmatisation describes. Goffman's reproduction of stigma in his writing illustrates how stigma is a relation characterised by the relative power of 'the normal' to silence, constrain and misrepresent 'the other'. The argument I am signalling here is that reconceptualising stigma as a political economy of (de)valuation requires critical methods which are rooted not in the imagined 'neutral' observational methods of the sociologist, but in people's struggles against the social structures that produce them as 'markedly inferior' (Du Bois, 1916, p. 86).

The stigma of disability

While this article focuses on racial stigma, or more precisely stigma as another name for racism, I want to note at this juncture the understanding of stigma developed by disabled people in the early 1960s. In particular, I want to draw attention to the groundbreaking collection *Stigma: The Experience of Disability* (1966): a series of autobiographical essays written by physically disabled people and edited by activist and writer Paul Hunt. What Hunt develops, through the curation and editing of this extraordinary collection of essays, is a multi-perspectival account of stigma from below. Indeed, in his contribution to this collection, 'A Critical Condition', Hunt argues, in a thinly veiled critique of Goffman, that stigma should not be theorised from the perspective of 'normals' but from 'the uncomfortable, subversive position from which we act as a living reproach to any scale of values that puts attributes or possessions before the person' (Hunt, 1966, p. 159). In this essay, Hunt develops an understanding of stigma as a technology of disablement which stratifies people along a differential axis of in/humanity. Hunt's concept of stigma emerged from his concern with the ways in which stigma legitimated *the segregation* of disabled people from mainstream society. It is stigma, he argues, which allows disabled people to be perceived as 'unfortunate', 'useless', 'tragic' and 'abnormal' and thus undeserving of the rights or considerations of 'normal' able-bodied citizens (Hunt, 1966). Indeed, Hunt composed *Stigma* (1966) in a residential home in England where he was incarcerated against his will.

> All my adult life has been spent in institutions amongst people who, like myself, have severe and often progressive physical disabilities. We are paralysed and deformed, most of us in wheelchairs, either as the result of accident or of diseases like rheumatoid arthritis, multiple sclerosis, muscular dystrophy, cerebral palsy and polio. (Hunt, 1966, p. 145)

Hunt's understanding of stigma as a political economy emerges from the longer penal history of stigma (Tyler, 2017: Tyler, forthcoming), as a cruel system of classification which marks out categories of people in order to impede their freedom and mobility. Further, his understanding of the relationship between stigma and segregation – for his was an anti-segregationist disability politics – was directly inspired by the US Civil Rights Movement. While, as Hunt notes, the 'injustice and brutality suffered by so many because of racial tension makes our troubles as disabled people look very small', the dehumanisation of disabled people 'stirs in me a little of the same anger' which 'James Baldwin reveals in *The Fire Next Time*': a rather different reading of Baldwin and his centrality to freedom struggles against stigma than that suggested by Goffman (Hunt, 1966, p. 153). As Hunt concludes, stigma is a vital terrain of political struggle and 'we who are disabled are deeply affected by the assumptions of our uselessness that surround us. But it is vital that we should not accept this devaluation of ourselves' (Hunt, 1966, p. 149). While I cannot do justice to Hunt's pivotal contribution to disability activism and scholarship here, it is important to note the foundational role his conceptualisation of stigma as a pivotal force in the social segregation of disabled people played in the development of the social model of disability, and the policy and attitudinal changes which followed. Sadly, it is Goffman's, and not Hunt's, *Stigma* which is the most cited text in disability studies today.[10]

Professor Normal

The problems I have identified with Goffman's methods, his suppression of questions of power, and his silencing of the perspectives of the 'stigma knowers' he draws upon, are embedded within the very structure of his stigma concept. To further illustrate this, I want to briefly return to the status of norms in *Stigma*. As feminist, queer and critical race theorists have elaborated,[11] it is often by unpacking norms that we get to the crux of the problem, the problem here being how Goffman's 'neutral' sociological account of stigma in 1963 reproduces what Du Bois described as the 'National Stigma' of racism (Du Bois, 1916, p. 86).

Goffman uses the terms 'norms', 'normal' and those he designates as 'we normals' in multiple ways (1986, p. 5). At some points in *Stigma* norms seem to designate ideals 'and standards'; at others norms refer to foundational social rules which precede all social interactions; and at others norms are imagined as more akin to perceptual frames – the social optics – through which we perceive others (p. 128). In all these cases, norms describe accepted rules, conventions and ways of seeing. Indeed, Goffman is emphatic that 'a necessary condition for social life is *the sharing of a single set of normative expectations by all participants*' (pp. 127–128, my emphasis). The normal human being is also used to mark the authorial position of Goffman, the 'neutral' sociological observer, in the text, while the address 'we normals' is employed several times in *Stigma* as a proxy for the imagined readers of his book. What 'we' – his readers – are invited to imagine we have in common with the authorial 'I', is a shared normality. In short, while Goffman argues that stigma is relational, his stigma concept is crafted from the authorial position of 'the normal human being', the powerful positionality of one who attributes stigma to those imagined as failing pre-agreed social norms of appearance or behaviour. So while, as noted above, his account of stigma draws on the experiential knowledge of stigmatised people, Goffman mediates this stigma knowledge through the perspective of 'we normals' (p. 5). As he writes, 'norms regarding social identity pertain to the kinds of role repertoires or profiles *we feel* it permissible for any given individual to sustain' (p. 81, my emphasis). Goffman justifies grounding his definition of stigma in 'the notion of the "normal human being" ' by arguing, first, that this is 'the basic imaginary' through which 'laymen currently conceive of themselves' (fn. 10, p. 7), and second, that we live in rational societies characterised by 'the tendency of large-scale bureaucratic organizations, such as the nation state, to treat all members in some respects as equal' (fn. 10, p. 7). Yet as he wrote this justification, millions of American citizens were explicitly contesting 'the facts' of this equality, and 'the forms' which 'a normal human being' could take (fn. 10, p. 7). As we have established, Goffman was aware of ongoing social and political challenges to white normativity and racial stigma but refused to dwell on the political economy of stigma, noting that his 'is a statement about the social function of these processes and not about their cause or desirability' (pp. 129–130).

Unsurprisingly, and perhaps accurately in the context of the United States in the early 1960s, Goffman reveals that the singular norm he is writing about (and from the perspective of) is 'that of the young, married, white, urban, northern' male (p. 128). 'There is only one complete unblushing male in America', he argues, and '[e]very American male tends to look out upon the world' from the perspective of heterosexual able-bodied white masculinity (p. 128). Goffman describes this white male norm as the 'general identity-values' of American society adding that this ideal identity casts a 'shadow on the encounters encountered everywhere in daily living' (p. 129). Goffman does not reveal the figure of 'heterosexual able-bodied white masculinity' as the measure of 'general identity-values' until the reader is reaching the final chapters of *Stigma*. However, once the abstract normal collapses into the particularity of this figure, he grants us a key with which to unravel 'the normal perspective' through and from which he produced his account of stigma. Given the strictures of this ideal human, people's potential to fail this norm, and be stigmatised as a consequence, is extensive. Goffman's cast of 'stigma figures' includes the physically disabled, people with 'blemishes of individual character' such as 'weak will, domineering or unnatural passions, treacherous, mental disorder, imprisonment, addiction, alcoholism, homosexuality, unemployment, suicidal attempts' extending to 'radical political behavior' and those tainted by what he terms 'tribal stigma of race, nation, and religion' (1986, p. 4). Perhaps Goffman was reflecting on his own Jewish ethnicity, but it seems more likely he was reflecting on the stigma of *being Black* in the United States, when he added that 'tribal stigma' 'can be transmitted through lineages and equally contaminate all members of a family' (1986, p. 4).

Goffman's figures for racial stigma include the 'educated northern Negro' (p. 44) who finds themselves mistaken for a Southern Negro, 'urban lower class Negroes' (p. 44), 'an apprehended Negro' (fn. 1, p. 46), 'black-skinned Negroes who have never passed publicly' (p. 74), and 'a passing Negro and the white girl he wants to marry' (fn. 101, p. 95). Goffman also comments on how skin-lightening products are fraudulently sold as a remedy for the stigma of dark skin (p. 9), and reflects on the ambivalent social position of 'the light-skinned Negro' who 'can never be sure what the attitude of a new acquaintance will be' (p. 14). While Goffman suggests that many stigmas can be successfully concealed or managed, he reflects on the fact that visibly racialised minorities and members of the lower class 'who quite noticeably bear the mark of their status in their speech, appearance, and manner, and who, relative to the public institutions of our society find they are second class citizens' are 'all likely on occasion to find themselves functioning as stigmatized individuals' (p. 146). For sure, the version of white normativity which Goffman depicts in *Stigma* tallies with accounts such as W. E. B. Du Bois', who had argued two decades earlier in *Dusk of Dawn: An Essay Toward an Autobiography of a Race Concept* that being Black in America is to be 'badged' by colour, to be marked out 'for discrimination and insult' (Du Bois, 1940/2007, pp. 59, 126). However, what Black Sociology also tells us is that living as a person racialised as Black in the early 1960s did not mean being stigmatised 'on occasion', it meant daily confrontation 'with the realities of racism, not simply as individual acts dictated by attitudinal bias' but with an entire society organised through 'racial terrorism' (Davis, 1970/2004, p. 496). Further, unlike his Black sociological elders and contemporaries, Goffman offers no account of why 'to be unconditionally "American" is to be white, and to be black is a misfortune', or how historical norms of white supremacy were being challenged as he wrote his book (Killian & Grigg, 1964, in Carmichael & Hamilton, 1967/1992, p. 31). Moreover, we reach a major contradiction in Goffman's account of racial stigma when he suggests that there is a natural difference between what he terms the 'congenital' sign of skin colour and imposed social signs such as 'a brand mark or maiming' (1986, p. 46). Goffman is here not only illustrating existing racism in US society but also normalising racial difference as a 'fact' which is consequent of deeper genetic human difference. Indeed, his argument that the 'congenital' 'fact of blackness' is 'a permanent part of the person' (p. 46), seems to trouble Goffman's own conclusion in *Stigma* that 'the normal' and 'the stigmatized' are social roles – and that anybody might find themselves in either role in a given (interactional) context (p. 46). For Goffman, *blackness is a stigma which is it impossible to erase*. A 'stigma of inferiority that resides not merely in the label or designation of race', but is imagined as 'embodied in black presence' (Williams, 1990, pp. 542–543). In this sense, the figure of the normal human in *Stigma* does not only describe existing social norms but reproduces what Lewis Gordon describes as 'the in-advance claim of the white world to human status' (Gordon, 2006, p. 255). Indeed if, as Goffman argues, 'we believe the person with a stigma is not quite human' (p. 5), then Black readers of *Stigma* find both that they are 'not structurally regarded as human beings' and that this dehumanised positionality is their permanent fate (Gordon, 2015, p. 22).

For many sociologists, what is appealing about Goffman's conceptualisation of stigma is precisely that it is relational, contextual, contingent and historically malleable. However, by taking Goffman 'at his word', I have demonstrated that one of the limitations of his account is that he uses norms to obfuscate and naturalise existing arrangements of power. Goffman argues that 'we believe the person with a stigma is not quite human' and 'on this assumption we exercise varieties of discrimination, through which we effectively, if often unthinkingly, reduce his life chances' (Goffman, 1986, p. 5). He also stresses that the 'psychological price' of stigmatisation is 'living a life that can be collapsed at any moment' (p. 108). However, he offers neither compassion nor space for imagining alternatives to the system of confining and discriminating norms he describes. Rather, he argues that normal and stigmatised people should 'accept' social norms: 'Not doing so, one could hardly get on with the business at hand; one could hardly have any business at hand' (p. 5). That this is a *political* recommendation is most evident in one of the final sections of *Stigma*, when Goffman makes a series of proposals about how individuals might manage living with stigma. This is one of the few places in the book that Goffman addresses the stigmatised rather than 'we normals'. His proposals to those suffering with stigma are conservative, pragmatic and – given the relational character of his theory of stigma – oddly individualistic.

'Normals', Goffman reassures the stigmatised, 'really mean no harm', and 'should therefore be tactfully helped to act nicely' (p. 116). He argues that the stigmatised should not contest the norms that produce stigma, but instead develop strategies of stigma management in social settings where stigma might arise. Goffman's proposals for the stigmatised include 'information management' (p. 135) 'the arts of impression management' (p. 130), employing strategies of 'passing and covering' (p. 130), adopting a position of 'tolerance' (p. 121) and refraining 'from pushing claims for acceptance much past the point normals find comfortable' (p. 130). As he writes, 'When the stigmatized person finds that normals have difficulty in ignoring his failing, he should try to help them and the social situation by conscious efforts to reduce tension' (p. 116). In the context of Goffman's larger oeuvre, we might understand these proposals on the management of stigma as dramaturgical – in the sense that they offer suggestions to the stigmatised about how to play an assigned social role which minimises the discomfort of 'normals', and in so doing support, rather than challenge, the existing relations of power inscribed in social norms. Further, while Goffman cautions that the stigmatised should not 'ingratiatingly act out before normals the full dance of bad qualities imputed to his kind' (p. 110), he also advises they should *play the parts* society has assigned to them. To this end he quotes the Norwegian writer Finn Carling, who, reflecting on his own experience of living with cerebral palsy, notes:

> … the cripple has to play the part of the cripple, just as many women have to be what the men expect them to be, just women; and the Negroes often have to act like clowns in front of the 'superior' white race, so that the white man shall not be frightened by his black brother. (in Goffman, 1986, p. 110).

What we learn from Goffman is that for people racialised as Black, 'managing a spoiled identity' means interacting in public in ways which protect white people from 'the ferocious mythology of blackness … as the embodiment of inferiority' (Williams, 1990, p. 543). In order to decolonise Goffman's stigma concept, it is imperative that we question why he is so seemingly invested in maintaining an arrangement of normal–stigma relations in which only people who are socially marked as white can be normal. We also have to question why Goffman remained so empathically silent about the struggles against anti-Black racism – struggles which precisely sought to challenge white normativity by disrupting racist norms of social interaction – while they were unfolding all around him – including in his own classroom.

'A black boy hacked into a murderous lesson'

Reading *Stigma* through the lens of Black freedom struggles it is possible to discern 'the strategies of power that are immanent' within Goffman's stigma theory (Ferguson, 2004, p. 55). In effect, by arguing for the management of stigma, that is for its pacification, Goffman normalises stigma and conceals 'its violent underpinning and periodic atrocities' (Steinberg, 2007, p. 42). From this perspective, Goffman's stigma concept 'is not innocent of politics, but on the contrary, provides epistemic authority' for the suppression of Black humanity (Steinberg, 2007, p. 42).

To take just one example, the Greensboro Four, and many others amongst the Black students who would follow them in staging sit-in protests across the segregated Southern states, were haunted by the lynching of 14-year-old Emmett Till in Mississippi in 1955 – indeed Joyce Ladner coined this generation of civil rights activists 'the Emmett Till genera-tion' (Ladner et al., 2011). Born and raised in Chicago, Till was visiting relatives in the small town of Money, when he allegedly wolf whistled at a white woman[12] in a grocery store. Seemingly unaware of 'the subtleties of the Jim Crow Mississippi code of racial etiquette' (Rubin, 1995, p. 45), for this crime of alleged flirtation he was abducted, tortured, maimed and shot. His mutilated body was later recovered from the Tallahatchie River. Till's mother insisted her son's corpse be displayed in an open coffin in order, in her words, to 'rip the sheets off the state of Mississippi' (Mobley & Benson, 2004, p. 151). However, the terrible violent truth exposed by the circulation of photographs of Till's disfigured body, and the later acquittal of his killers by an all-white jury, left many Black teenagers fearful, angry and despairing. For this generation of young Black citizens, images of Till's body functioned as both an image of injustice and, as Audre Lorde put it, as a 'veiled warn-ing' – a 'black boy hacked into a murderous lesson' (Lorde, 2002, p. 340).

The death of Till, the publicity surrounding his death and the acquittal of his killers, reveals how whiteness as a 'general identity-value' cast its long shadow over Black lives in the 1960s (Goffman, 1986 p. 129). Franklin McCain described Till's death as a revelation which left his 15-year-old self in a suicidal depression: 'there seemed no prospect for dignity or respect as a young black man' (Younge, 1999, p. 108). This was a context where Black people daily negotiated interactional settings where not playing your socially assigned role as a racially stigmatised person, failing to appropriately manage your racial stigma by reduc-ing tensions in your interactions with white people, could led to your death. As Khazan recalled, this murder revealed 'what happened if we broke the code. If we spoke out of turn, we too could die like Emmett Till' (Cerese & Channing, 2003). The haunting of this genera-tion by the lynching of Emmett Till illustrates how stigma power works to confine and segregate, to keep people 'down and away' (Link & Phelan, 2014, p. 26). However, it also reveals how the violence of being stigmatised can become politicised and act as a catalyst for social change. Joyce Ladner describes, as a teenager, keeping a scrapbook of cuttings about Emmett Till which she would regularly weep over in her bedroom. As she states, 'That was the image for our generation that galvanised our generation, we all saw that image on the front cover of Jet magazine. … Every black southerner for sure had seen that photo-graph and it was like the clarion call for action … when we got older we were going to avenge his death' (Ladner et al., 2011). Ladner would later bring this activism to bear on the discipline of sociology itself, laying bare, in her edited volume *The Death of White Sociology* (1973), the white norms and racial bias at the heart of the discipline.

Stigma as struggle

Resituating Goffman's stigma concept within the context of Black freedom struggles against 'the legal stigma of second class citizenship' has revealed how his understanding of stigma proceeds from what was then, as now, a deeply contested understanding of white prototypicality and Black inhumanity (Marable, 2000, p. 106). While Goffman's stigma concept uncouples the perception of Black skin as a stigma from the history of racism – and specifically in the US the history of slavery – Black freedom struggles remind us that racial stigmatisation is a historical practice 'centuries in the making' (Spillers, 2003, p. 21). A regime of seeing, a 'stigma-optics', which was crafted in order to deny Black people personhood (Tyler, forthcoming). As Carmichael put it in his 'Black Power' speech to students at Berkeley in October 1966, 'we are now engaged in a psychological struggle in this country. … The question is, How can white society begin to move to see black people as human beings?' (Carmichael, 1966).

What is of interest – both sociologically and politically – is not only how stigma is lived and managed but how it is refused, reworked and resisted by those whom it abjects (Tyler, 2013). While Black (and disabled) readers of Goffman's *Stigma* find themselves not structurally regarded as human beings in this text, we also know that in 1963 many millions of Black American citizens sought 'to win recognition as human outside of the restrictive terms set by the racial order' (Gilroy, 2014, p. 7). By targeting the interaction order, their struggles made visible the concrete ways in which white supremacy invaded 'the lives of Black people on an infinite variety of levels' (Davis, 2004, p. 496). As James Boggs noted, this was unlike the preceding Civil Rights Movement of the 1950s in that 'it aimed at creating the issue, provoking it' (Boggs, 2011, p. 135). What Black activists realised is that in order to challenge 'the stigmata of degradation' they needed to remediate racial stigma (Du Bois, 1933, p. 199). Breaking the social rules around segregation, these Black activists provoked violent forms of stigmatisation. In doing so, they crafted new perceptual frames for understanding the operations of racial discrimination. Reflecting on what motivated him to join the sit-in movement as a teenager in 1960, Stokely Carmichael recalls how: 'when I saw those kids on TV, getting back up on the lunch counter stools after being knocked off them, sugar in their eyes, catsup in their hair – well, something happened to me. Suddenly I was burning' (Park, 1967, p. 80). As Abdelmalek Sayad notes:

> Black American sociology and colonial sociology teach that, as a general rule, one form of revolt, and undoubtedly the primary form of revolt against stigmatization … consists in reclaiming the stigma, which then becomes an emblem of [resistance]. (Sayad, 2006, p. 173, my translation).

Through acts of stigma dramaturgy, the Civil Rights Movement publicised, revolted against and reversed the power of stigma.

Conclusion: Stigma after Goffman

In 1963, the year *Stigma* was published, the pioneering Black sociologist and activist W. E. B Du Bois died in exile in Accra, Ghana – the US government had confiscated his passport. After Du Bois' death, 'Maya Angelou led a group of Americans and Ghanaians to the U.S. embassy in Accra, carrying torches and placards reading "Down with American Apartheid" and "America, a White Man's Heaven and a Black Man's Hell" ' (Euchner, 2010). A day later, at the March on Washington, Roy Wilkins, leader of the

National Association for the Advancement of Colored People (NAACP) led a minute's silence in remembrance of Du Bois. As he stated to the hundreds of thousands of marchers, 'his was the voice that was calling to you to gather here today in this cause. If you want to read something that applies to 1963 go back and get a volume of *The Souls of Black Folk* by Du Bois, published in 1903' (Euchner, 2010). While Goffman did not reference him, Du Bois was the first theorist of stigma power, identifying not only 'the problem of the Twentieth Century as the problem of the colour-line', but detailing how this line was enforced, reproduced and legitimated by the 'systematic humiliation' of Black lives (Du Bois, 1903/2015, pp. 1, 8).

There is a growing recognition that 'racism and intellectual segregation' have not only limited and divided the sociological tradition, but continue to diminish the capacity of the discipline 'to comprehend the key problems of the twenty-first century' (Back & Tate, 2015). When Goffman was teaching at Berkeley this segregation was challenged by Black students, as it is today in the transnational 'Why is My Curriculum White?' movement. In the spring of 1961 a group of Berkeley students formed a reading group, the Afro-American Association, which crafted an alternative 'Black Curriculum' featuring the work of scholars such as Du Bois, Frantz Fanon, James Baldwin, E. Franklin Frazier and Kwame Nkrumah (Kelley, 2016). This group soon extended their activities into the wider community, running a weekly radio programme that attracted other Bay Area college and university students, including Huey Newton and Bobby Seale who went on to form the Black Panthers. At the same time, in segregated Black universities in the Southern states, such as Tougaloo College in Mississippi, Black sociology students like Anne Moody, Joyce Ladner and their professors became active participants in the sit-in movements. Indeed, Jibreel Khazan of the Greensboro Four was also a sociology major. Together these students, activists and scholars were busy producing sociological knowledge about stigma, and developing anti-stigma strategies, which included the psychologically reparative work of protest itself (Taylor, 2016).

Of central importance to these Black freedom struggles was Carmichael and Hamilton's anti-stigma concept of 'Black Power' which reconfigured racial stigma into 'a revolutionary emotion': 'We aim to define and encourage a new consciousness among black people', they wrote, and facilitate 'a sense of peoplehood: pride, rather than shame, in blackness' (Carmichael & Hamilton, 1967/1992, pp. ix, viii).[13] In arguing that racial stigma functions as a form of psychosocial governmental power, Carmichael and Hamilton stressed the historic relationship between stigma and capitalism (racial capitalism), one which persists and continues to be resisted today. Indeed, as Jenna Loyd and Annie Bonds argue in this issue, *Black Lives Matter* marks another conjunctural moment in the history of racial capitalism in the United States – a period Michelle Alexander has coined 'The New Jim Crow' (Alexander, 2010).

Despite the sophisticated understanding of racial stigma developed over a hundred years of Black sociological thought, the conceptualisation of stigma in sociology has largely been 'structured by the absence of an address' to this tradition (Bhambra, 2014a, p. 12). Recent scholarship suggests a renewed sociological interest in the relationship between racism, stigma and power (see Howarth, 2006; Lamont et. al., 2016; Loury, 2003; Matory, 2015). In seeking to historically resituate Goffman's original account, this article has drawn on a longer and wider range of interlocutors working in a Black sociological tradition, including Mario Biondi, James Boggs, Stokely Carmichael, Patricia Hill Collins, Angela Davis, Kimberley Dotson, W. E. B. Du Bois, Roderick Ferguson, Frantz Fanon, the Greensboro Four, Paul Gilroy, Lewis Gordon, Charles Hamilton, Harry Haywood, Robin Kelley, Joyce Lamont, Manning Marable, Zine Magubane, Anne Moody, Cedric Robinson, Hortense Spillers, Cornell West, Patricia Williams and Gary Younge. The account of stigma which emerges through this Black genealogy of stigma-thinking challenges the individualism of psychological approaches to social problems, exposes the limits of Goffman's white normative perspective, and troubles 'race neutral' forms of interactional analysis. What this scholarship offers in place of a Goffman-esque approach, are rich historical, political and economic conceptualisations of stigma as technologies of dehumanisation, and stigma as a form of power which has been collectively resisted from below. It is the argument of this article that bringing racism and anti-racist scholarship to the front and centre of sociological understandings of stigma not only enriches its utility as an analytic for understanding racism but also other forms of 'dehumanisation' – such as classist, disablist and misogynist practices – which are also grounded in eugenicist and/or essentialist ideologies of human difference.

Funding

This research was supported by a Philip Leverhulme Prize (2015–2018). I gratefully acknowledge the support of the Leverhulme Trust.

Notes

1. North Carolina A&T State University was then a segregated Black university; it was established on 9 March 1891 as 'The Agricultural and Mechanical College for the Colored Race'. In 1969 a confrontation between the National Guard and student activists on this campus culminated in what Martha Biondi described as 'the most massive armed assault ever made against and American university', when the Army was drafted in to raid a male dormitory, which resulted in hundreds of students taken into police custody (Biondi, 2014, p. 158).
2. I am using Jibreel Khazan's chosen name here, but in 1960 he was known by his birth name Ezell Blair.
3. Sit-ins against anti-Black racism and segregation can be traced back to 1943 when Congress of Racial Equality (CORE) activists occupied a Chicago restaurant that refused service to Black customers (see Andrews & Biggs, 2006; Meier & Rudwick, 1973).
4. US television news footage of the sit-in movement from 1963, including some clips from Greensboro, can be viewed on the NBC online news archive here: http://www.nbcnews.com/video/today-in-history/22886961#22886961
5. There are interesting parallels between this moment in US television history, and the importance of mobile media, such as smart phones, in documenting and distributing footage of police violence against Black citizens and #Blacklivesmatter protests in the US today.
6. I have chosen to use Stokely Carmichael's birth name, rather than Kwame Ture, to reflect the name he used during the period of activism and in the writings referenced in this article.
7. The Free Speech Movement burst onto UC Berkeley campus in 1964, inspired first by the Civil Rights Movement, and later student-led opposition to the Vietnam War (see Freeman, 2004).
8. This student would have been in an extremely small minority at Berkeley in 1961. It is estimated that there were only 100 Black students enrolled at the University in 1960, out of a

student population of 20,000. Historical accounts of the University from this period describe the deep alienation experienced by Black students, both in terms of their minority status on campus, and in terms of the whiteness and the conservatism of academic curriculums (see Murch, 2010).

9. As Heather Love notes, his 'primary method of abstract synthesis is supplemented, perhaps even challenged, by the trace of the embodied, affective experience of social others, both fictional and real, archived in his footnotes' (Love, 2010, p. 118).
10. See 'Forum Introduction: Reflections on the Fiftieth Anniversary of Erving Goffman's Stigma' (2012) in *Disability Studies Quarterly* for reflections on Goffman and Hunt's different contributions to thinking disability stigma.
11. See for example Judith Butler's (1993) inspired work on the power of gender norms.
12. In 2017 Carolyn Bryant admitted that the testimony she gave in court, namely that Till had sexually harassed her, was untrue (see Caroll, 2017).
13. The transnational genealogical threads of Black epistemologies of stigma power are fascinating and important to note here. For example, it is in Frantz Fanon's work that we find the most developed understanding of racial stigma as a penal technology – an explanation of how and why the modern history of anti-Black racism came to be written on the skin. Fanon was born in the French colony of Martinique, but later renounced his French citizenship. Fanon in turn inspired Stokely Carmichael's development of the concept of Black Power – while Fanon was himself indebted to the writing of Du Bois, Richard Wright and James Baldwin.

References

Alexander, M. (2010). *The New Jim Crow: Mass incarceration in the age of colorblindness*. New York, NY: The New Press.

Andrews, K., & Biggs, M. (2006). The dynamics of protest diffusion: Movement organizations, social networks, and news media in the 1960 sit-ins. *American Sociological Review, 71*, 752–777.

Back, L., & Tate, M. (2015). For a sociological reconstruction: W.E.B. Du Bois, Stuart Hall and segregated sociology. *Sociological Research Online, 20*(3). Retrieved from http://www.socresonline.org.uk/20/3/15.html

Bhambra, G. (2014a). *Connected sociologies*. London, UK: Bloomsbury.

Bhambra, G. (2014b). A sociological dilemma: Race, segregation and US sociology. *Current Sociology, 62*, 472–492.

Biondi, M. (2014). *The Black revolution on campus*. Berkeley: University of California Press.

Boggs, J. (2011). *Pages from a Black radical's notebook: A James Boggs reader* (S. Ward, Ed.). Detroit, MI: Wayne University Press.

Boyd, H. (2004). *We shall overcome, volume 3 with 2 audio CDs: The history of the Civil Rights Movement as it happened*. Naperville, IL: Sourcebooks MediaFusion.

Butler, J. (1993). *Bodies that matter: On the discursive limits of sex*. London, UK: Routledge.

Carmichael, S. (1966). Black Power speech. *University of Berkeley*. Retrieved from https://www.youtube.com/watch?v=dFFWTsUqEaY (last accessed 2 May 2018).

Carmichael, S., & Hamilton, C. (1992). *Black Power: The politics of liberation in America*. New York, NY: Vintage (Original work published 1967).

Caroll, R. (2017, January 27). Woman at center of Emmett Till case tells author she fabricated testimony. *The Guardian*. Retrieved from https://www.theguardian.com/us-news/2017/jan/27/emmett-till-book-carolyn-bryant-confession (last accessed 2 May 2018).

Cerese, R., & Channing, S. [Directors] (2003). *February One: The story of the Greensboro Four* [documentary film]. Independent Lens. Retrieved from http://www.pbs.org/independentlens/februaryone/ (last accessed 2 May 2018).

Collins, P. (2007). Pushing the boundaries or business as usual? Race, class, and gender studies and sociological inquiry. In C. Calhoun (Ed.), *Sociology in America: A history* (pp. 572–604). Chicago, IL: University of Chicago Press.

Davis, A. (2004). Political prisoners, prisons, and Black revolution. In H. Zinn & A. Arnvoce (Eds.), *Voices of a people's history of the United States* (pp. 494–498). New York, NY: Seven Stories Press (Original work published 1970).

Dotson, K. (2011). Tracking epistemic violence, tracking practices of silencing. *Hypatia, 26*, 236–257.

Du Bois, W. E. B. (1916). The looking glass. *The Crisis: A Record of the Darker Races, 13*, 81–87.

Du Bois, W. E. B. (1933). On being ashamed of oneself: An essay on race pride. *The Crisis: A Record of the Darker Races, 40*, 199–200.

Du Bois, W. E. B. (2007). *Dusk of dawn: An essay toward an autobiography of a race concept.* Oxford, UK: Oxford University Press (Original work published 1940).

Du Bois, W. E. B. (2015). *The souls of Black folk.* New Haven, CT: Yale University Press (Original work published 1903).

Euchner, C. (2010). Excerpt: Roy Wilkins's reluctant tribute to W.E.B. *Du Bois*. Retrieved from http://www.beaconbroadside.com/broadside/2010/08/excerpt-roy-wilkinss-reluctant-tribute-to-web-du-bois.html (last accessed 2 May 2018).

Fanon, F. (2008). *Black skin, white masks* (C. Markmann, Trans.). London, UK: Pluto (Original work published 1952).

Ferguson, R. (2004). *Aberrations in Black: Towards a queer of color critique.* Minneapolis: University of Minnesota Press.

Fleming, C., & Morris, A. (2015). Theorizing ethnic and racial movements in the global age: Lessons from the Civil Rights Movement. *Sociology of Race & Ethnicity, 1*, 105–126.

Freeman, J. (2004). *At Berkeley in the sixties: The education of an activist, 1961–1965.* Bloomington: Indiana University Press.

Gilroy, P. (2002). *There ain't no black in the Union Jack: The cultural politics of race and nation.* London, UK: Routledge.

Gilroy, P. (2014). *Race and racism in 'the age of Obama': The Tenth Annual Eccles Centre for American Studies Plenary Lecture given at the British Association for American Studies Annual Conference, 2013.* London, UK: The British Library.

Goffman, E. (1956). *The presentation of self in everyday life.* Edinburgh, UK: University of Edinburgh.

Goffman, E. (1961). *Asylums: Essays on the social situation of mental patients and other inmates.* New York, NY: Anchor.

Goffman, E. (1982). The interaction order: American Sociological Association, 1982 Presidential Address. *American Sociological Review, 48*, 1–17.

Goffman, E. (1986). *Stigma: Notes on the management of a spoiled identity.* New York, NY: Simon & Schuster (Original work published 1963).

Gordon, L. (2006). Is the human a teleological suspension of man? Phenomenological exploration of Sylvia Wynter's Fanonian and biodicean reflections. In A. Bogues (Ed.), *After man, towards the human: Critical essays on the thought of Sylvia Wynter* (pp. 237–257). Kingston, Jamaica: Ian Randle.

Gordon, L. (2015). *What Fanon said: A philosophical introduction to his life and thought.* London, UK: Hurst & Company.

Haywood, H. (1948). *Negro liberation.* New York, NY: International Publishers.

Howarth, C. (2006). Race as stigma: Positioning the stigmatized as agents, not objects. *Journal of Community and Applied Social Psychology, 16*, 442–445.

Hunt, P. (1966). A critical condition. In P. Hunt (Ed.), *Stigma: The experience of disability* (pp. 145–159). London, UK: Geoffrey Chapman.

Jameson, F. (1976). On Goffman's frame analysis. *Theory & Society, 3*, 119–133.

Joseph, P. (2014). *Stokely: A life*. New York, NY: Basic Civitas.

Kelley, R. (1996). *Race rebels: Culture, politics, and the black working class*. New York, NY: Free Press.

Kelley, R. (2016, June 17). Cedric J. Robinson: The making of a Black radical intellectual. *Counterpunch*. Retrieved from https://www.counterpunch.org/2016/06/17/cedric-j-robinson-the-making-of-a-black-radical-intellectual/ (last accessed 2 May 2018).

Khazan, J. (n.d.). Interview. International Civil Rights Center & Museum Greensboro. Retrieved from http://www.sitinmovement.org/ (last accessed 2 May 2018).

Ladner, J. (1973). *The death of white sociology*. New York, NY: Random House.

Ladner, D., Ladner, J., & Mosnier, J. (2011, September 20). Dorie Ann Ladner and Joyce Ladner oral history interview conducted by Joseph Mosnier in Washington, D.C.. Retrieved from https://www.loc.gov/item/afc2010039_crhp0054/ (last accessed 2 May 2018).

Lamont, M., Silva, G., Welburn, J., Guetzkow, J., Mizrachi, N., Herzog, H., & Reis, E. (2016). *Getting respect: Responding to stigma and discrimination in the United States, Brazil, and Israel*. Princeton, NJ: Princeton University Press.

Langer, E. (2014, January 13). Franklin McCain, who helped inspire sit-ins for civil rights as part of Greensboro Four, dies. *Washington Post*. Retrieved from https://www.washingtonpost.com/national/franklin-mccain-who-helped-inspire-sit-ins-for-civil-rights-as-part-of-greensboro-four-dies/2014/01/13/8c39840e-7c6e-11e3-9556-4a4bf7bcbd84_story.html?utm_term=.f06a3b64c22e (last accessed 2 May 2018).

Link, B., & Phelan, J. (2014). Stigma power. *Social Science & Medicine, 103*, 24–32.

Lorde, A. (2002). *The collected poems of Audre Lorde*. New York, NY: W.W. Norton.

Loury, G. (2003). *The anatomy of racial inequality*. Cambridge, MA: Harvard University Press.

Love, H. (2010). Feeling bad in 1963. In J. Staiger, A. Cvetkovick & A. Reynolds (Eds.), *Political emotions* (pp. 112–133). Abingdon, UK: Routledge.

Love, H. (2013). Close reading and thin description. *Public Culture, 25*, 401–434.

Magubane, Z. (2016). American sociology's racial ontology: Remembering slavery, deconstructing modernity, and charting the future of global historical sociology. *Cultural Sociology, 10*, 369–384.

Malcolm, X (1964). Malcom X in Cairo urges African aid to U.S. Negroes. *The Militant*. Retrieved from http://hierographics.org/malcolmX.htm (last accessed 2 May 2018).

Marable, M. (2000). *How capitalism underdeveloped Black America: Problems in race, political economy, and society*. London, UK: Pluto.

Marx. G. (1984). Role models and role distance: A remembrance of Erving Goffman. *Theory & Society, 13*, 649–662.

Matory, J. (2015). *Stigma and culture: Last-place anxiety in Black America*. Chicago, IL: University of Chicago Press.

Meier, A., & Rudwick, E. (1973). *CORE: A study in the Civil Rights Movement, 1942–1968*. New York, NY: Oxford University Press.

Mobley, M., & Benson, C. (2004). *Death of innocence: The story of the hate crime that changed America*. New York, NY: Ballantine.

Moody, A. (1968). *Coming of age in Mississippi*. New York, NY: Dial.

Murch, D. (2010). *Living for the city: Migration, education, and the rise of the Black Panther Party in Oakland, California*. Chapel Hill: University of North Carolina Press.

Park, G. (1967, May 19). Whip of Black Power. *Life Magazine*, pp. 76–82.

Robinson, C. (1997). *Black movements in America*. New York, NY: Routledge.

Robinson, C. (2000). *Black Marxism: The making of a Black radical tradition*. Chapel Hill: University of North Carolina Press.

Rubin, A. (1995). Reflections on the death of Emmett Till. *Southern Cultures*, *2*, 45–66.

Sayad, A. (2006). *L'Immigration ou les paradoxes de l'altérité. L'illusion du provisoire* [Immigration or the paradoxes of otherness. The illusion of the provisional]. Paris, France: Raisons d'agir.

Schweik, S. (2014). Stigma management. *Disability Studies Quarterly*, *34* (1). Retrieved from http://dsq-sds.org/article/view/4014/3539 (last accessed 2 May 2018).

Spillers, H. (2003). *Black, white, and in color: Essays on American literature and culture*. Chicago, IL: University of Chicago Press.

Steinberg, S. (2007). *Race relations: A critique*. Stanford, CA: Stanford University Press.

Taylor, K. (2016). *From #BlackLivesMatter to Black liberation*. Chicago, IL: Haymarket Books.

Taylor, S., Bogdan, R., & DeVault, M. (2016). *Introduction to qualitative research methods: A guidebook and resource*. Hoboken, NJ: John Wiley.

Tyler, I. (2013). *Revolting subjects: Social abjection and resistance in neoliberal Britain*. London, UK: Zed Books.

Tyler, I. (2017). The hieroglyphics of the border: Racial stigma in neoliberal Europe. *Ethnic and Racial Studies*. Advance online publication. https://doi.org/10.1080/01419870.2017.1361542

Tyler, I. (forthcoming). *Stigma machines*. London, UK: Zed Books.

West, C. (2016). Race and social theory: Towards a genealogical materialist analysis [extract]. (Original work published 1987). Retrieved from http://www.versobooks.com/blogs/2568-race-and-social-theory-towards-a-genealogical-materialist-analysis (last accessed 2 May 2018).

West, N. (1933). *Miss Lonelyhearts*. New York, NY: Avon.

Williams, P. (1990). Metro Broadcasting, Inc. v. FCC: Regrouping in Singular Times. *Harvard Law Review*, *104*, 525–546.

Younge, G. (1999). *No place like home: A Black Briton's journey through the American South*. London, UK: Picador.

Younge, G. (2013, May 7). 1963: The defining year of the Civil Rights Movement. *The Guardian*. Retrieved from https://www.theguardian.com/world/2013/may/07/1963-defining-year-civil-rights (last accessed 2 May 2018).

Author biography

Imogen Tyler is a Professor of Sociology at Lancaster University. Her research is concerned with social inequalities (of multiple kinds), power, injustice and resistance and she has published widely on topics such as borders, migration, citizenship, class, racism and gender. Imogen's book, *Revolting Subjects: Social Abjection and Resistance in Neoliberal Britain* (2013) was shortlisted for the Bread and Roses Prize for Radical Publishing. A Philip Leverhulme Prize (2015–2018) is supporting her current research project on stigma, of which this collection is an outcome. She is currently completing a solo-authored monograph, titled *Stigma Machines*, which employs historical methods to trace the long penal genealogy of stigma power.

Article

Heaping blame on shame: 'Weaponising stigma' for neoliberal times

The Sociological Review Monographs
2018, Vol. 66(4) 48–64
© The Author(s) 2018
Reprints and permissions:
sagepub.co.uk/journalsPermissions.nav
DOI: 10.1177/0038026118778177
journals.sagepub.com/home/sor

Graham Scambler
University College London, UK; Surrey University, UK

Abstract

The focus of this article is the 'weaponising' of stigma in the neoliberal era. The article starts with a brief characterisation of the sociological literature on stigma before moving to characterise post-1970s financial capitalism, focusing on relations of class and command. It then examines (a) the distinctions between enacted and felt stigma (involving norms of shame) and enacted and felt deviance (involving norms of blame), and (b) the novel neoliberal dialectic between these two sets of norms. This critical exposition provides a platform for a sociological rethink. A case is made that the significance of stigma and deviance as defined here can only be grasped sociologically in terms of the prime macro-mechanism of financial capitalism, the *class/command dynamic*, and the interaction of relations of stigma and deviance with other social relations, most notably those of (class-based) exploitation, deriving from the possession of capital, and (command or state-based) oppression, deriving from the possession of power. This case is constructed via a consideration of changing policies in relation to disability, drawing on UK data but with a wider reference. The final part of the article addresses modes of resistance to the roles of capital and power in dictating the neoliberal dialectic of shame and blame. It is argued that effective resistance depends on the formation of alliances across and between diverse 'movement activities'. Expanding on the author's work with David Kelleher, it is suggested that there exists a plethora of 'resistance activities', ranging from specific and/or local campaigns to transnational, class, feminist and ethnic insurrections. What this adds up to is a strategy of 'permanent reform'. It is argued that the effective execution of this strategy *presupposes* a structural shift away from neoliberal ideology, the narrative of austerity and post-1970s financial capitalism. The potential effectiveness of the strategy of permanent reform is appraised, again, with reference to disability policy and practice.

Keywords

class, command, deviance, financial capitalism, neoliberalism, permanent reform, resistance, stigma

Corresponding author:
Graham Scambler, Research Department of Infection and Population Health, University College London, Gower Street, London WC1E 6BT, UK.
Email: g.scambler@ucl.ac.uk

Beyond Goffman

Stigma has of course always exacted a price from its 'victims'. Shaming is a social process that can catch in its net isolated individuals or groups or even sub-populations. Cultural norms proscribing attributes, traits or conditions defined as shameful have been omnipresent through history:

> ... according to Wittgenstein (1958), honourable upright behaviour, a staple of enduring sociability, is only possible if the breach of such norms is a realistic and publicly marked possibility. One of the core premises of Durkheim's proto-functionalism is that all social formations have discriminated between normal and abnormal, insiders and outsiders. There can be no 'normal/acceptable' in the absence of tangible exemplars of the 'abnormal/unacceptable'. As Goffman (1968) puts it, there is a 'self-other, normal-stigmatized unity'; stigmatized and non-stigmatized alike are products of the same norms. (Scambler, 2009, p. 442)

There is a considerable literature on shame and insider/outsider dynamics in ancient, traditional or premodern societies. It was Goffman, however, who provided the springboard for sociologies of stigma. I have argued that while his 'sensitisation' of the concept remains perspicacious and relevant, he neglected to ask a number of questions (Scambler, 2009). Some of these questions have been posed by disability theorists/activists and, latterly, by sociologists approaching stigma from a social structure or political economy orientation.

Goffman rightly stressed that stigma is a relational concept. Attributes are neither creditable nor discreditable *in themselves*. His principal interest was in the structure of interaction. The structure of face-to-face interaction in the lifeworld for him steadies and sustains the social order. His dramaturgical analysis is pertinent here. It is as if, he suggested, we are actors playing scripted parts in a theatrical production. Social life proceeds smoothly as long as individuals who find themselves together arrive at a working definition of the situation. While they perform to maintain face through lines in 'front regions' (e.g. hospital clinics), when no audience is present they can stop performing and act in a manner that contradicts their performance, in 'back regions' (e.g. at home).

Goffman (1961) recognised that definitions of situations can and often do reflect imbalances of power, as is the case in total institutions like long-stay hospitals. The self, he concluded, 'is not a property of the person to whom it is attributed, but dwells rather in the pattern of social control that is exerted in connection with the person by himself and those around him' (Goffman, 1961, p. 168). The self is a product of an institutional nexus of performances. Particularly important for order in day-to-day life is not only rule-following but rule-breaking, or 'remedial interchanges' (Goffman, 1971). In fact, rule-breaking is pervasive because social interaction is structured principally to afford individuals opportunities to 'adjust' with minimal fuss or stress while in pursuit of their own private goals. Rule-breaking in face-to-face interaction, generally articulated by means of 'accounts', 'apologies' or 'requests', gets the traffic moving again (Goffman, 1971, p. 108). In short, it can be more felicitous to overlook someone's rule infraction than to insist on rule-following behaviour. 'Deviant behaviour' of this kind is rarely sanctioned (Scambler, 2009).

So what is the case for going 'beyond Goffman'? What is missing, I have argued, is the causal role of social structures like class, command, gender, ethnicity and so on. These tend to be theorised outside of the symbolic interactionist/dramaturgical fold (Scambler, 2006). Social structures possess something of the external and constraining force of Durkheimian 'social facts'. It is to such structures that I now turn.

Class, command, stigma and deviance

Class and command

For all the unresolved and ongoing disputes about the nature of contemporary western capitalism, a loose consensus has emerged that a new phase commenced in or around the 1970s. The quadrupling of oil prices at this time provided a symbolic marker of this transition, if not an explanation for it. Repeated references to post-1970s processes of 'financialisation' make it natural and reasonable to label this new phase *financial capitalism*. I prefer to reserve the term 'neoliberalism' to signify the ideology that most comprehensively underpins and sustains financial capitalism. In prior publications I have, together with Sasha Scambler, spelled out the principal attributes of financial capitalism as we interpret them (most recently, see Scambler & Scambler, 2013, 2015). Taking our cue from French regulation theory we have maintained that throughout the capitalist era (a) regimes of capital accumulation (involving relations of class) and (b) their concomitant modes of regulation (involving relations of command) have tended towards inequalities of wealth and income, even when flows of material assets are strengthening across the population as a whole. Unchecked class relations lead to exploitation, while unchecked command relations lead to oppression. A much-misunderstood Adam Smith would not have baulked at this.

The regime of capital accumulation/mode of regulation specific to the latest phase of financial capitalism has been incontrovertibly associated with a steep rise in wealth and income inequality. It is in fact appropriate to refer to a 'new asymmetry' between exploitative class and oppressive command relations. This new asymmetry is encapsulated in what I have defined as the principal macro-social *mechanism* of financial capitalism, namely, its revised *class/command dynamic*. Put succinctly, 'objective' and (in a critical realist sense) 'real' class relations have become more dominant over objective and real command relations. Specifically, a small hard core or cabal within what I call the capitalist executive (see Clement & Myles, 1997) now exerts considerably more control than was the case during postwar or welfare capitalism over the decisions and activities of the power elite at the apex of the state apparatus. What this means in effect is that core owners of capital can and do buy policies that advantage them more cheaply from the state. Sayer (2015) has documented this and allied processes in his outstanding *Why We Can't Afford the Rich*.

Conventional empirical classifications of class, or rather occupational class or socio-economic group – like NS-SEC for example – have an important role in sociological enquiry (e.g. in studies of social mobility), but they skate over the presence of this cabal of capitalists who comprise a mere fraction of the 'top' 1%. Box 1 identifies these 'capital monopolists' and presents what I suggest is a neoclassical and deeper

Box 1. A new classification of class relations.

CATEGORY (A): *Capitalist executive* (significant, largely transnational and 'detached' *owners of capital*)
SOCIAL CLASS I
CAPITAL MONOPOLISTS (hard core of heavy capital-owners who are 'players')
SOCIAL CLASS II
CAPITAL AUXILIARIES (soft auxiliary core of heavy capital-owners who are non-players)
SOCIAL CLASS III
CAPITAL 'SLEEPERS' (insider higher management, light capital-owners who support players)

CATEGORY (B): *New middle class* (managers in the service of capital)
SOCIAL CLASS IV
INSIDER HIGHER MANAGERS ('Co-opted' higher/middle managers who support players)
SOCIAL CLASS V
OUTSIDER HIGHER MANAGERS (higher managers, independent of players)
SOCIAL CLASS VI
MIDDLE MANAGERS (middle managers, independent of players) (*P*)
SOCIAL CLASS VII
CAPITAL ASPIRERS ('aspirational', petit-bourgeoisie, independent of players) (*P*)

CATEGORY (C): *Old middle class* (established professionals)
SOCIAL CLASS VIII
INSIDER PROFRESSIONALS ('co-opted', high-status professionals who support players) (*P*)
SOCIAL CLASS IX
OUTSIDER PROFESSIONALS (high-status professionals, independent of players) (*P*)
SOCIAL CLASS X
SEMI-PROFESSIONALS (semi-professionals, independent of players) (*P*)

CATEGORY (D): *Working class* (waged workers)
SOCIAL CLASS XI
INSIDER WORKERS ('co-opted', supervisory, waged workers, support players) (*P*)
SOCIAL CLASS XII
OUTSIDER WHITE-COLLAR WORKERS (non-manual waged workers, independent of players) (*P*)
SOCIAL CLASS XIII
OUTSIDER BLUE-COLLAR WORKERS (waged manual workers, independent of players) (*P*)
SOCIAL CLASS XIV
OUTSIDER SEMI/UNSKILLED WORKERS (waged semi- and unskilled manual workers, independent of players) (*P*)

Box 1. (Continued)

CATEGORY (E): *Working class* (outside paid work)

DISPLACED WORKERS (never worked and long-term unemployed) (*P*)

Within the capital executive there exists a hard core of heavily 'globalised' capital owners personally committed to the accumulation of capital (or material) assets. I define these as 'detached'. This fraction of the 1% constitutes the class driver for order/change, exercising its will through the offices of those in the political elite, whose members have mostly been recruited or are allied to the capital executive. The governing oligarchy's personnel are – and this is the key sociological point – surfers of a revised class structuring of British society in financial capitalism (which is, as intersectionalists remind us, also structured by gender, ethnicity and so on).

I have made a distinction between supporters and non-supporters of players. This is important because the less than 1% critically 'rely on' the co-option of others in the capital executive, new and old middle classes and even the working class. This is not a matter of electoral or infrastructural support but of a compact of interest. These are people – from managers and accountants to lawyers and physicians to supervisors and union officials – whose cooperation with the governing oligarchy has been directly or indirectly hired or bought: they profit from the liaison.

The term 'precariat' (P) appears in parentheses. I do not accept that Standing's (2011) precariat is a class in – let alone or for – itself. But I certainly accept that there is a structural and cultural precariousness associated with financial capitalism. I here regard this as a cross-class matter, placing an emboldened question mark after the security and well-being of most members of the new, old and working classes (90%+ of the population as a whole). My employment of 'precariat' acknowledges this insecurity without making the 'error' of discovering a new class. Sociologists should in my view be focusing far more attention on: (1) the approx. 0.1% who comprise a cabal of globally heavy-hitting owners of capital who buy sufficient national state power to secure governance sufficient to further their agendas and interests; (2) the approx. 2% who comprise a governing oligarchy; and (3) the approx. 7–8% of 'supporters' and 'co-optees' (represented in each of the class categories (A) to (D)) who are critical for the viability of this governing oligarchy.

classification of class relations (see also Carroll, 2004). Time and empirical examination will be the judge.

There are two important riders to add. I have deliberately referred to *objective* and real relations of class. It is apparent that there is a different story to tell of *subjective* relations of class. I think this has confused some sociologists. While objective class relations have acquired renewed vigour and effect, subjective class relations have not: financial capitalism has been accompanied by a cultural shift such that people no longer identify by class or adopt class scripts as they did in welfare capitalism. Class is less salient for identity-formation now. A second error, I would suggest, is to conflate the structural 'materiality' of class with class-affiliated culture. This was written into the conception, design and methodology of the Great British Class Survey (GBCS) and has influenced subsequent debate. The GBCS does an even better job of hiding the capital monopolists than does NS-SEC; and it is more worrying in that it lets them off the class hook by resorting to elite theory (e.g. 'wealth elite'). This is not of course to say that *nothing* can be learned from the GBCS (Savage, 2015).

Box 2. Notions of stigma and deviance.

STIGMA (offences against norms of shame)	**DEVIANCE** (offences against norms of blame)
Enacted stigma Actual discrimination (shaming)	**Enacted deviance** Actual discrimination (blaming)
Felt stigma Fear of discrimination and sense of shame	**Felt deviance** Fear of discrimination and sense of blame
Project stigma Active resistance to enacted and felt stigma	**Project deviance** Active resistance to enacted and felt deviance

Box 3. Stigma and/or deviance, shame and/or blame.

Stigma + Deviance + *Abjects*	Stigma + deviance – *Rejects*
Stigma – deviance – *Normals*	Stigma – Deviance + *Losers*

Stigma and deviance

Having summarised my approach to class and command relations it is time to turn to stigma and deviance. It is implicit in Goffman's (1968) study that stigma has more to do with conformance than compliance. Stigma, I have suggested, might usefully be regarded as an offence against norms of *shame*, while deviance might be seen as an offence against norms of *blame*. It undoubtedly matters not a jot to 'victims' of either which category they fall into, but it is a distinction of sociological import, as I hope to show. Box 2 affords a breakdown of suggested concepts of enacted, felt and project stigma and deviance (Scambler, 2009). Enacted stigma and deviance denote actual discrimination due to unacceptable conformance and compliance respectively. Felt stigma and deviance point to internalisations of shame and blame and the fear, inhibiting in its own right, of encountering enacted stigma and deviance. Project stigma and deviance allow for the empirically recognised but neglected potential for people to resist enacted and felt stigma and deviance.

I recently experimented by devising a quartet of ideal types reflecting extant sociocultural norms of shame and blame (Scambler, 2015b). As I shall put it to use below I am reproducing it here (see Box 3). The logic is simple. There are four classes: stigma + deviance +; stigma + deviance –; stigma – deviance –; and stigma – deviance +. I shall for convenience and bite label these graphically as: *abjects, rejects, normals* and *losers*.

Three of these labels, each constructing, announcing and 'performing' abnormality, are as grim as it is to be assigned to any of them: they help focus the sociological imagination. Who aspires to be socially judged, dismissed and 'policed' as an abject, reject or loser?

A dozen theses

Enough has been said by way of preliminaries and positioning to articulate a dozen theses. They afford an example of what I have called sociological 'meta-reflection' (Scambler,

2015a). Meta-reflection acknowledges both that sociology is replete with under-utilised theories and research data and that its practitioners increasingly suffer from 'threatening', neoliberal and institutional pressures to satisfy an insatiable demand for funding *for its own sake* and outputs in internationally recognised high-impact journals *regardless of their content*. The realisation of the sociological project, in short, calls for a degree and strategy of resistance.

The theses, a sequential mix of philosophical, theoretical and substantive, are as follows:

1. Objects of sociological interest, in this article the structures or relations of class and command and cultural norms of stigma and deviance, are *real*, in a 'critical realist' sense (Bhaskar, 1979, 2016); that is, they are not just social constructions, but relatively enduring mechanisms the existence of which can be retroduced from our experience of actual events and event patterns.

2. Following on, despite sociology's 'transitivity', as a set or network of social processes, its objects are 'intransitive': they exist whether or not detected or studied. The mechanisms alluded to here – the structures/relations of class and command and the norms of stigma and deviance – can be said to issue in 'tendencies' in 'open systems'. Put differently, for any given social phenomenon in any given figuration or context the causal salience of a particular mechanism (e.g. class) can be annulled, undone or mitigated by other mechanisms (e.g. gender, ethnicity, age and so on). Potent mechanisms are not always detectable in the patterning of actual events.

3. Sociology typically only tells part of any story and rarely wraps things up explanatorily. Its objects are 'emergent from' but not 'reducible' to those of interest to the likes of geneticists or biologists (e.g. tennis is a social phenomenon and no genes or molecules have yet won Wimbledon).

4. If sociology has an overriding purpose, this might be to explore and come to terms with what Comte once highlighted as 'social dynamics' (or social change) and 'social statics' (or social order). Adapting Bhaskar, Archer (1995) has developed her morphogenetic/ morphostatic model that delineates three successive cycles, namely of *structural conditioning, sociocultural interaction* and *structural elaboration*, in any round or cycle of structural transformation or reproduction.

5. The prime structures/relations of relevance to sociologists interested in morphogenesis and morphostasis in general, and in justice and inequity in particular, with maximal explanatory purchase across the figuration of the British nation state in the era of financial capitalism, are those of class (via the capitalist executive) and command (via the power elite) that combine to comprise the class/command dynamic.

6. The class/command dynamic helps structure, without structurally determining, cultural norms like those of stigma and deviance that inform, reinforce and, if class push comes to command shove, *police* prescriptions of shame and blame.

7. In countries like Britain, financial capitalism has witnessed a class-motivated, command-delivered realignment of these norms to the advantage of Occupy's (less than) 1%, plus their class allies and co-optees, and to the disadvantage of the bulk of their populations (most conspicuously women, those disadvantaged due to their ethnicity, the un- and under-employed, the sick and the (dis)abled).

8. Less abstrusely, capital has bought the requisite power to secure policies that favour its accumulation over issues of justice, equity and the well-being of citizenries.
9. Habermas's (1975) perspicuous notion of a 'legitimation crisis', namely, a ubiquitous loss of faith in appropriate governance, remains the most likely trigger for structural/relational and cultural change.
10. The global financial crisis of 2008–2009 did not in the event trigger structural/relational and cultural change. It is important however to interpret the post-2010 protest campaigns and events – including in the UK, for example, those of the Occupy movement's sit-in outside St Paul's, student marches against the hiking up of fees, rearguard action against a Health and Social Care Bill designed to encourage the privatisation of NHS services, and culminating in the London riots of 2011, which were precipitated by the police shooting of Mark Duggan – as: (a) more or less inchoate shouts of anger and dissent against a status quo seen as exploitative, oppressive and more, and (b) a harbinger of, and apprenticeships for, subsequent structural transformation. Brexit in 2016 is a more recent reminder of the energy and power with which widespread disaffection, disconnectedness and hopelessness can release its potential for structural transformation.
11. There exists a broad range of possible triggers of a legitimation crisis against the background of the 'disaffection, disconnectedness and hopelessness' that I have epitomised in the notion of *disconnected fatalism* (Scambler, 2013). These include: political or social movements, identity politics, pressure groups, campaigns, pivotal incidents, and so on.
12. It is difficult to nominate social class as a likely trigger for the following reason. While class, understood as an *objective structure or relation*, remains a crucial mechanism in financial capitalism, it has lost *subjective* salience. In other words, it is no longer a key determinant of identity-formation. This subtracts from its immediacy as a force for oppositional or working-class consciousness and solidarity. If class does not suggest itself as a trigger for a legitimation crisis, however, it almost certainly remains a precondition for an effective one. For a trigger to be pulled and the bullet to hit its target, a class-based mobilisation will be required.

Phases in the weaponising of stigma

Stigma and deviance have always been deployed – 'weaponised' – for social and political ends. The mark literally scarred into the flesh of Attican and Athenian slaves 'othered', it is estimated, 115,000 of a total population of 315,000 (only 43,000 of whom were full citizens). Slaves were valuable assets and their branding – the mark was called a 'stigma' – minimised the risk of escape. In an Eliasian sense we have moved on, sanitising or 'civilising' our othering. I want to suggest that in the UK the era of financial capitalism has witnessed two distinctive phases with regard to stigmatisation. Periodisation is always tricky, but the first of these peaked in Thatcher's regime from 1979 to 1991 (which was in the event only a little ameliorated by New Labour), and the second crystallised within and beyond the Cameron-led Coalition government post-2010.

Thatcher's aspirations exceeded the politics of delivery. Moreover, she tilled ground illicitly acquired. But her policies also engendered new forms of opposition. This can be illustrated by reference to discourses on 'able-/disable-ment'. The ideology of 'free-market' neoliberalism that Thatcher espoused, alongside Reagan, called for a culling of welfare 'handouts', said to encourage dependency, extending to those whose cases for community-shared or pooled support had under postwar or welfare capitalism been unquestioned. Box 4 presents some core statistics on disability in the UK. Many Thatcherite policies had a negative impact, directly or indirectly, on people with disabilities; but the writing was certainly on the wall. During this period, and non-coincidently, the medical sociological orthodoxy on long-term illness and disability came under attack. The 'personal tragedy' bias was exposed. Above all, Bury's (1982) notion of 'biographical disruption' and its companion studies – including my own (Scambler & Hopkins, 1986) – were contextualised and opened up to critical interrogation.

Engaging explicitly with Bury and associates, disability theorists rejected medical sociology's use, from the 1950s through to the 1980s, of the 'social deviance' paradigm: structural functionalists, interactionists, conflict theorists and even postmodernists commenced from the notion of the sick and disabled as 'socially deviant individuals' (Turner, 1987, p. 2). The normal/deviant dualism was judged prejudicial and inappropriate for the study of disability or disabled people. This paradigm was consciously displaced by the 'oppression' paradigm. In Thomas's (2012) terms, disability studies, or the sociology of disability, edged towards a new branch of equality and diversity studies. In an earlier work Thomas (2007, p. 4) summarised the social deviance and oppression paradigms as follows:

> … sociologists in disability studies use a 'social oppression' paradigm: to be disabled, or to be discursively constructed as 'disabled', is to be subject to social oppression. 'Disablism' functions alongside sexism, racism, ageism and homophobia in society. Medical sociologists, I argue, theorize chronic illness and disability through the 'social deviance' lens, and have done so in different theoretical guises for many years. Ideas about social deviance have infused medical sociologists' analyses of two main themes: societal responses to people designated chronically ill or disabled, and the social experience of living with stigmatised body states. Theoretical diversity is evident in both the oppression and social deviance paradigms.

The Thatcher years saw a closing down of avenues and options for people with disabilities, a weakening of their asset flows; but it also heralded a new and oppositional consciousness and an embryonic movement.

The political ship was steadied somewhat through the New Labour years, 1997–2010, but gave way subsequently to governments with explicit Thatcherite agendas. The device of 'austerity' was utilised to undermine welfare statism at a faster pace in an ever more propitious political environment. The obstacles to, and any reticence about, cutting support for people with disabilities rapidly diminished. The outcome for them was stark.

It had been Blair who launched the work capability assessment (WCA) in 2008 in an attempt to cut the benefits bill. This cut was to be achieved through a redefinition of the

Box 4. Disability in the UK: Some statistics.

- Disability affects 1 in 5 people (19%) in the UK.
- Only 17% of disabled people are born with their disabilities.
- The prevalence of disability rises with age: in 2011–2012, 6% of children were disabled, 16% of adults of working age, and 45% of adults over state pension age.
- Disabled people are less likely to be in employment: in 2013, the UK employment rate for working-age disabled people was 49%, compared to 82% of non-disabled people.
- The two most commonly stated enablers of employment for adults with impairments are flexible hours/days and tax credits.
- The two most common barriers to work among adults with impairments are a lack of job opportunities (43%) and difficulty with transport (29%).
- Aged 18, disabled young people are more likely than their non-disabled peers to not be in any form of education, employment or training (NEET): 22% compared to 15%.
- The internet has become a key tool for those looking for work; but in 2013 one-third (33%) of disabled people had never used the internet: disabled people are four times more likely to have never used the internet than non-disabled people.
- Nineteen per cent of households that include a disabled person live in relative income poverty, compared to 15% of those without a disabled person.
- Disabled people's living costs are 25% higher than those of non-disabled people.
- The majority of impairments are not visible: fewer than 8% of disabled people use wheelchairs.
- Around 15% of households that contained one or more disabled person felt their current home was not suitable for their needs and required adaptations.
- Transport is the largest concern for disabled people in their local area: pavement/road maintenance, access and frequency of public transport are the biggest issues.
- More than 20% of disabled people have experienced harassment in public because of their impairment.
- Nine out of 10 people with a learning disability have been victims of hate crime and bullying.
- The annual cost of bringing up a disabled child is three times greater than that of bringing up a non-disabled child.
- About 60% of children and young people with both learning difficulties and mental ill health live in poverty.
- One in 4 people will experience mental ill health in any given year.
- Over 1 in 4 disabled people say that they frequently do not have choice and control over their daily lives.
- Disabled people are likely to be under-represented in public life: in 2012–2013, 1 in 5 people were disabled, but only around 5% of public appointments and reappointments were filled by disabled people.
- The WHO has predicted that depression will be the leading cause of disability by 2020.

Adapted from Papworth Trust (2013).

nature of disability. When people who had been receiving the old incapacity benefit were 'retested' to see if they were eligible for the new Employment and Support Allowance (ESA), the model predicted that 23% of them would be found fit for work. The initial tests were clearly flawed – people with terminal cancer were deemed fit for work – but the assessment was rolled out anyway in 2010 (starting the process of retesting around 1.5 million incapacity benefit claimants). Interpretations became polarised: British tabloids like the *Daily Mail* celebrated an overdue assault on the 'workshy', while critics condemned the initiative as a cruel, cuts-driven attack on the country's most vulnerable.

The Cameron Coalition government, 2010–2015, contracted out the retesting programme to ATOS and by 2012 hundreds of thousands were heading for tribunals to appeal their fit-to-work assessments (on average 40% of those refused the benefit go to tribunal, of whom 40% are subsequently granted the benefit). It was revealed in 2013 that 1300 people had died after being told they should start preparing to return to work. ATOS, previously a low-profile French IT firm, came under attack and eventually left the contract, which had been worth £80m a year. This was no great hardship, since it was in receipt of £700m in public sector and UK central government revenue in 2012–2013; staggeringly it was also awarded a separate contract to perform a different disability benefit assessment, Personal Independence Payments (PIP), designed to cut 20% from the bill. This was launched in 2013. Maximus took over from ATOS. Maximus already had a questionable reputation as a result of its contracts in the USA. In 2000 an audit revealed it had billed Wisconsin nearly $500,000 since 1997 in improper or questionable expenses. In 2007 Maximus settled a Medicaid lawsuit – mainly over whether or not it had falsified Medicaid claims – with a payment of $30.5m. It seems that Maximus was willing to step into ATOS's challenging footsteps as a way of expanding its operations into Europe. There was to be no amelioration of British policy when May took over from Cameron in 2015, following the referendum majority for Brexit.

Disability theorists and activists grew in sophistication even as their causes became more desperate. Oliver's (1990) ground-breaking 'social model of disability', epitomising early work within the oppression paradigm, was superseded by more nuanced studies (see Scambler & Scambler, 2010). There was a galvanising, too, of movement resistance to successive governments' calculated squeeze on poor and vulnerable citizens to replenish the bank accounts of the wealthy whose vested interests it rationalised. Groups like 'Disabled People Against Cuts' and 'Disability News Service' were particularly active on social media, a mode of dissemination and mobilisation used to some effect in a challenge to mainstream politics.

It is time now to explicate the notion of the weaponising of stigma. I have so far argued that the era of financial capitalism is notable primarily through the mechanism of the class/command dynamic. Expanding on American historian David Landes's claim that 'men of wealth buy men of power' [*sic*], I have long maintained that members of the capitalist executive, most especially the capital monopolists, together with their co-optees and allies in the new and old middle classes, use their (class) capital to buy sufficient (state or command) power to prioritise polices that serve their interests in capital accumulation. This class/command governing oligarchy rarely needs to 'conspire' since what C. Wright Mills (1956) in his discourse on the American power elite in the 1950s called a 'tacit understanding' typically does the trick. The power that capital attains in financial capitalism is more than it could attain in postwar welfare-statist capitalism, as has already been illustrated. That this has yet to provoke a legitimation crisis has its genesis in a family of factors.

First, the new class/command dynamic has fashioned a ubiquitous ideology of neoliberalism that feeds off and feeds a cultural intensification of individualism that has reduced empathy with and compassion for others. Surveys have documented a growing detachment and anti-Samaritan or American-style *habitus* mitigating against social solidarity and engagement. It has become harder to enlist people to fight for others than it has to 'other' the vulnerable, including those with disabilities. Second, to reiterate a point made earlier, ideology and individualism alike, part and parcel of a postmodern or cultural relativism, have also lessened the prospect of class-based resistance to exploitation and oppression, subjective class relations (and therefore 'working-class' consciousness) having lost salience relative to objective class relations). Third, as is also emphasised in Box 1, there is an accentuated 'precarity' in work status and relations that now extends well 'up' into professions and occupations seen a generation ago as secure and beyond threat. And fourth, in line with Standing's notion of precarity and a middle-range theory or model (namely, that of 'relative risk aversion') adduced by Goldthorpe and colleagues to help account for the long-standing lack of social mobility in Britain, people, even more conspicuously in the current cultural context, tend to opt to 'play safe' (in fact, to submit to exploitation/oppression) in the face of socio-political threats (Goldthorpe, 2016, pp. 118–121).

I contend that in the UK and elsewhere financial capitalism's (structural) class/command dynamic and its (cultural) sequelae have led to a political 'skewing' of social norms of shame and blame. This is what I term the *weaponising of stigma*. We have witnessed an historically rapid shift, alluded to by Jones (2012), according to which *stigma (norms marking an ontological deficit, non-conformance or shame) has been redefined as deviance (norms marking a moral deficit, non-compliance or blame)*. Hence the thesis that stigma has been 'weaponised'. If deviance can be effectively appended to stigma, then the austerity of neoliberalism that seeks to blame and punish vulnerable people like the dis-abled might obtain sufficient purchase to open the door to enhanced capital accumulation.

Drawing on the earlier discussion, and in particular on Box 3, and once again with acknowledgement of Tyler, if the stigmatised can be portrayed as deviants, then 'rejects' can be recast as 'abjects'. And abjects are both beyond the pale and deserving of their lot and their misery. Neoliberalism allows for the state's abandonment of people with disabilities.

The problematics of resistance

The scenario presented thus far is bleak. If the argument has substance, not only has stigma been weaponised in financial capitalism, but it has acquired structural and cultural underpinnings that threaten to neutralise critiques and oppositional collective action. How then to accomplish social change at the macro-level affecting the likes of the class/command dynamic? Harvey (2007) sets the scene: (1) organised labour and its capacity to defend wages has been sabotaged; (2) capitalism has become even more competitive, facilitating a territorial shift of power towards East Asia; (3) financial corporations have been *empowered*; (4) *accumulation by possession* has been used to augment class dominance; (5) the debt economy – governmental, corporate and house-hold – has become the default option; and (6) asset market bubbles have been used before *and after* the crisis of 2007–2008 to compensate for poor returns in production. He goes on to ask if global capitalism can survive it present traumas:

> Yes. But at what cost? This question masks another. Can the capitalist class reproduce its power in the face of the raft of economic, social, political and geopolitical and environmental difficulties? Again, the answer is a resounding 'yes'. But the mass of the people will have to surrender the fruits of their labour to those in power, to surrender many of their rights and their hard-won asset values (in everything from housing to pension rights), and to suffer environmental degradations galore to say nothing of serial reductions in their living standards which means starvation for many of those already struggling to survive at rock bottom. Class inequalities will increase (as we have already seen happening). All of that may require more than a little political repression, police violence and militarized state control to stifle unrest. (p. 79)

Given what has been said throughout this article, there seems little prospect of a legitimation crisis or occasion for optimism. What possible avenues and triggers for change are there? In the final paragraphs I briefly identify and appraise these and posit and defend a notion of 'permanent reform'.

Class action

While up to and including postwar welfare capitalism it was evident that collective action on the part of a solidary working class was the most likely threat to a then larger, more disparate and less compacted capitalist ruling class, this seems no longer to be the case. Workers' organisations have been disestablished; narratives undone, colonised and distorted; and solidarity compromised. I still judge this the most probable source and resource for change. It is within the working class, and most notably in what Paul Higgs and I nearly 20 years ago defined as its 'displaced segment' (incorporating the low paid and under- as well as un-employed), that true, deep suffering coupled with fatalist hopelessness coalesces (Scambler & Higgs, 1999). Misery, hate and reaction are natural byproducts of callous and anonymous exploitation and oppression. Class mobilisation in the absence of a ready class consciousness, however, is hard to accomplish, even more so in an era characterised by an atomised individualism. There will need to be apposite contexts and triggers.

Precariat (and precarity)

What about Standing's concept of the *precariat*, since (kind of) absorbed into the polemical Great British Class Survey? It is unquestionably the case that many conventionally designated middle- as well as working-class jobs are now less secure than was the case from 1945 to 1975. The post-baby-boomer generation has suffered from a deepening of the age- as well as gender-, ethnic- and – I would contend, fundamentally – *class-related* divisions of financial capitalism. The salariat has been overtaken by an enduring labour market unpredictability. But the putative precariat is not a class-in-itself, let alone a class-for-itself. In fact, it is not a class at all. Rather it is *a reservoir or pool of distal recruits for social change.*

New social movements

The postulation that new social movements, fuelled by identity-formation and senses of belonging and recognition, might precipitate change is a European one largely unac-knowledged in North American sociology; and probably with reason. New social move-ments are in my view: (1) significant precursors of cultural shifts (e.g. re-feminism, disability, ethnic and gay relations and rights), but (2) just potential triggers for a more revolutionary transformation of society. It should be noted, however, that many new social movements cannot fully realise their agendas in the absence of just such a transformation.

Hazan and Kamo (2013, p. 26) write of a 'wave' or 'surge' in this context: 'one suc-cess will bring others in its wake; the boldness of some will increase tenfold the prepar-edness of their neighbours to act'. A further observation or two are warranted. What the Occupy movement exposed was a vigorous philosophical consensus around critiques of capitalism ('in the spirit of Marx'), but the lack of any consensual alternative. Indeed, the anarchist arm of the movement comfortably prevailed over what might be précised as the neo-Marxist arm. It is in fact far from easy to construct and disseminate *any* compelling narrative for the future given the (postmodern or) relativistic character of the culture issued in by financial capitalism (Winlow, Hall, Treadwell, & Briggs, 2015). I have used the term 'foresight sociology' to capture a need on sociologists' part to explore 'alterna-tive futures', whether of workplaces, modes of transport, energy provision, housing, or large-scale institutions like the National Health Service; Giddens (1990) has referred to 'utopian realism' (although his own advocacy of a 'third way' suited the political status quo). Oppositional forces currently lack a *narrative* (that is, a navigational guide, not a blueprint) for transformatory change.

Thatcher's celebrated mantra of TINA ('There Is No Alternative'), once the sharp-ened point of neoliberal ideology, has grown blunter after the financial crash and warlike propensities observable in today's neoliberalism. The protests alluded to earlier may seem to have failed; but any given movement's *apparent* failure to achieve its immediate goals nevertheless often paves the way for future kindred movement gains. Contingency matters hugely: a 'coming together' of otherwise atomised members of the working classes, the precariat, new social movements and *even* social democrats offers the optimal prospect for a governmental 'crisis of legitimation', and just such a coming together can be triggered by a one-off event (like the police shooting of Mark Duggan and subsequent urban riots in London and elsewhere in August of 2011), or maybe a reaction to the suicides or premature deaths of sick and dis-abled people occasioned by the politics of austerity.

We sociologists cannot predict well. Here, nevertheless, is my scenario for change. An unanticipated trigger event might occasion a coming together of activists for change around an expediently loose coalition of overlapping interests and agendas. *The bottom line will be the widespread recruitment of those who remain dependent on wage-labour, increasingly via the brutally succinct mechanism of the zero hours contract.* It comes back to class

Box 5. Jacquet's seven criteria for effective stigmatisation (Jacquet, 2015).

1. The audience responsible for the shaming should be concerned with the transgression
2. There should be a big gap between the desired and actual behaviour
3. Formal punishment should be missing
4. The transgressor should be sensitive to the source of the shaming
5. The audience should trust the source of the shaming
6. Shaming should be directed where possible benefits are greatest
7. Scrupulous implementation

relations. Stigma and deviance alike only have bite if they are underwritten by capital and power (Link & Phelan, 2001; and see Jacquet's criteria of effectiveness in Box 5). Stigma can only be split off from deviance (making tackling it in its own right that little bit 'simpler'), *and in the process de-weaponised*, in the event of a legitimation crisis occasioned by an effective mobilisation to rein in the capitalist executive. While no such prospect seems imminent, its structural preconditions are in place. An optimal strategy for change might currently be one of *permanent reform*: that is, a series of loose alliances between movement, campaign and other groups (e.g. disability activists) challenging the local, regional and national status quo across a number of domains (Scambler & Kelleher, 2006). It would be a recipe with two key ingredients: (1) common or reconcilable interests in specific reforms, and (2) an openness to sign up to the creation of a narrative on alternative futures at micro-, meso- and macro-levels. Sociology, in my view necessarily and morally committed to lifeworld rationalisation (Scambler, 1996), should embrace yet another 'type', namely 'action sociology', or a sociology extended to counter ideological distortion in civil society and the public sphere (Scambler, 2013; Scambler, 2018).

People like those with long-term illnesses or dis-abilities have been held progressively more 'personally responsible' for their impairments, shifting in the process from 'rejects' to 'abjects'. As Foucault (1979) instructed us, felt stigma and felt deviance comprise technologies of the self that ultimately coalesce to represent a form of governmentality. But Foucault, not unlike Goffman, was stronger on *how* power is exercised than on *why*. The core thesis in this article is that phenomena like 'dis-ablism' have structural as well as cultural underpinnings, and that mechanisms like the class/command dynamic are pivotal. This is not to argue that the class/command dynamic in financial capitalism is a catch-all explanatory mechanism for stigma and deviance in all their multifarious guises, which would obviously be false. But it is to argue that an effective struggle against dis-ablism, against rejection as well as the even more pernicious forms of abjection, requires combinations of alliances across multiple fields that challenge not only policy (via a strategy of permanent reform) but expose the 'real' social structures that are critical for the maintenance and deepening of dis-ablism and a growing range of companion 'isms'. The transnational class forces unleashed within global boardrooms lead circuitously to a politics of oppression and the ratcheting up of dis-ablism.

Funding

This research received no specific grant from any funding agency in the public, commercial, or not-for-profit sectors.

References

Archer, M. (1995). *Realist social theory: The morphogenetic approach.* Cambridge, UK: Cambridge University Press.

Bhaskar, R. (1979). *The possibility of naturalism: A philosophical critique of the contemporary human sciences.* Brighton, UK: Harvester Wheatsheaf.

Bhaskar, R. (2016). *Enlightened common sense: The philosophy of critical realism.* Abingdon, UK: Routledge.

Bury, M. (1982). Chronic illness as biographical disruption. *Sociology of Health & Illness, 4,* 167–182.

Carroll, W. (2004). *Corporate power in a globalizing world.* Oxford, UK: Oxford University Press.

Clement, W., & Myles, J. (1997). *Relations of ruling: Class and gender in postindustrial societies.* Montreal, Canada: McGill-Queen's University Press.

Foucault, M. (1979). On governmentality. *Ideology and Consciousness, 6,* 5–22.

Giddens, A. (1990). *Consequences of modernity.* Cambridge, UK: Polity Press.

Goffman, E. (1961). *Asylums: Essays on the social situation of mental patients and other inmates.* Chicago, IL: Aldine.

Goffman, E. (1968). *Stigma: Notes on the management of spoiled identity.* Harmondsworth, UK: Penguin.

Goffman, E. (1971). *Relations in public: Microstudies of the social order.* New York, NY: Basic Books.

Goldthorpe, J. (2016). *Sociology as a population science.* Cambridge, UK: Cambridge University Press.

Habermas, J. (1975). *Legitimation crisis.* London, UK: Heinemann.

Harvey, D. (2007). *A brief history of neoliberalism.* Oxford, UK: Oxford University Press.

Hazan, E., & Kamo (2013). *First measures of the coming insurrection.* London, UK: Zed Books.

Jacquet, J. (2015). *Is shame necessary? New uses for an old tool.* London, UK: Allen Lane.

Jones, O. (2012). *Chavs: The demonisation of the working class.* London, UK: Verso Books.

Link, B., & Phelan, J. (2001). Conceptualising stigma. *Annual Review of Sociology, 27,* 363–385.

Oliver, M. (1990). *The politics of disablement.* London, UK: Palgrave Macmillan.

Papworth Trust. (2013). Disability in the United Kingdom 2013. Facts and figures. Retrieved from http://www.papworth.org.uk/ (accessed 6 August 2017).

Savage, M. (2015). *Social class in the 21st century.* Harmondsworth, UK: Penguin.

Sayer, A. (2015). *Why we can't afford the rich.* Bristol, UK: Policy Press.

Scambler, G. (1996). The 'project of modernity and the parameters for a critical sociology: An argument with illustrations from medical sociology. *Sociology, 30,* 567–581.

Scambler, G. (2006). Sociology, social structure and health-related stigma. *Psychology, Health & Medicine, 11,* 288–295.

Scambler, G. (2009). Health-related stigma. *Sociology of Health & Illness, 31,* 441–455.

Scambler, G. (2013). Archer and 'vulnerable fractured reflexivity: A neglected social determinant of health? *Social Theory & Health, 11,* 302–315.

Scambler, G. (2015a). Meta-reflection in sociology. Retrieved from http://grahamscambler.com/meta-reflection/ (last accessed 9 May 2018).

Scambler, G. (2015b). Shame and blame: Moving on. Retrieved from http://grahamscambler.com/shame-and-blame-moving-on/ (last accessed 9 May 2018).

Scambler, G. (2018). *Health inequalities in a fractured society: A critical realist account.* Abingdon, UK: Routledge.

Scambler, G., & Higgs, P. (1999). Stratification, class and health: Class relations and health inequalities in high modernity. *Sociology, 33,* 275–296.

Scambler, G., & Hopkins, A. (1986). Being epileptic: Coming to terms with stigma. *Sociology of Health & Illness*, *8*, 26–43.

Scambler, G., & Kelleher, D. (2006). New social and health movements: Issues of representation and change. *Critical Public Health*, *16*, 219–231.

Scambler, G., & Scambler, S. (Eds.). (2010). *New directions in the sociology of chronic and disabling conditions: Assaults on the lifeworld*. London, UK: Palgrave.

Scambler, G., & Scambler, S. (2013). Marx, critical realism and health inequalities. In W. Cockerham (Ed.), *Health sociology on the move: New directions in theory* (pp. 83–104). New York, NY: Springer Press.

Scambler, G., & Scambler, S. (2015). Theorizing health inequalities: The untapped potential of dialectical critical realism. *Social Theory & Health*, *13*, 340–354.

Standing, G. (2011). *The precariat: The new dangerous class*. London, UK: Bloomsbury.

Thomas, C. (2007). *Sociologies of illness and disability: Contested ideas in disability studies and medical sociology*. Basingstoke, UK: Palgrave Macmillan.

Thomas, C. (2012). Theorizing disability and chronic illness: Where next for perspectives in medical sociology? *Social Theory & Health*, *10*, 209–228.

Turner, B. (1987). *Medical power and social knowledge*. London, UK: Sage.

Tyler, I. (2014). *Revolting subjects: Social abjection and resistance in neoliberal Britain*. London, UK: Zed Books.

Winlow, S., Hall, S., Treadwell, J., & Briggs, D. (2015). *Riots and political protest: Notes from the post-colonial present*. Abingdon, UK: Routledge.

Wittgenstein, L. (1958). *Philosophical investigations*. Oxford, UK: Blackwell.

Wright Mills, C. (1956). *The power elite*. Oxford, UK: Oxford University Press.

Author biography

Graham Scambler is Emeritus Professor of Sociology at UCL, and Visiting Professor of Sociology at Surrey University. He has published extensively on social theory, stigma, health, and health inequalities. His latest books are *Sociology, Health and the Fractured Society* (Routledge, 2018) and, as editor, *Sociology as Applied to Health and Medicine* (Palgrave Macmillan, 2018). He is a founding editor of the international journal *Social Theory and Health* and a Fellow of the Academy of Social Sciences, UK.

Lessons from Grenfell: Poverty propaganda, stigma and class power

The Sociological Review Monographs
2018, Vol. 66(4) 65–80
© The Author(s) 2018
Reprints and permissions:
sagepub.co.uk/journalsPermissions.nav
DOI: 10.1177/0038026118777424
journals.sagepub.com/home/sor

Tracy Shildrick
Newcastle University, UK

Abstract
The Grenfell Tower fire that took place in a council owned high-rise housing block in the early hours of 14 June 2017 in the London Borough of Kensington and Chelsea represented the worst fire in Britain for many decades. This article draws, in part, on the example of Grenfell Tower to interrogate some of the most pressing issues of our time around poverty, inequality and austerity. After a period of quiet, poverty now features more regularly in popular and political conversations. This is, in part, due to the proliferation of foodbanks that in many ways have become the public face of poverty in contemporary Britain. Additionally the increased popularity of so-called 'poverty porn' exemplified by programmes such as *Benefit Street* have provoked public and political debate about the realities of poverty and its causes and consequences. Punitive policies towards out of work benefits claimants, austerity measures and the proliferation of low paid and insecure work mean poverty has been extended to more and more people, yet at the same time it is a condition that is frequently stigmatised, misrepresented and misunderstood. Whilst evidence shows increased stereotyping and stigmatisation of those experiencing poverty and other related disadvantages, there is also evidence that the British general public on the whole tend to care about fairness, equality of opportunity and that they dislike extremes of income and wealth, although importantly they also generally underestimate the realities of both. It was these extremes of inequality that Grenfell thrust so violently into the public imagination with many newspapers visually capturing the gulf between rich and 'poor' in their pictures of the burnt out shell of Grenfell set against a typical block of luxury apartments of the sort that are proliferating in London and other cities in Britain and that, particularly in London, often cost in excess of a million pounds or more. This article looks at examples of how critical work is being done by those in power to manipulate and frame the terms of the discussion around poverty, inequality and economic insecurity and its causes and its consequences.

Keywords
inequality, poverty, power, stigma

Corresponding author:
Tracy Shildrick, The School of Geography, Politics and Sociology, Newcastle University, Newcastle upon Tyne, NE1 7RU, UK.
Email: tracy.shildrick@ncl.ac.uk

Introduction

> From the top floors of the 24-storey Grenfell Tower, residents could see out across Kensington and Chelsea, one of the wealthiest local authorities in the country. Yet the tower and its residents were situated in one of the most deprived areas in England. The Borough is one of London's most unequal with extreme poverty and wealth living side by side. (Barr, 2017, *The Guardian*, 15 June)

> I would feel very resentful if those people got this for free. My husband and I work very hard to afford this. I would move out. Why should they get this for free? (Female caller to a talk show on LBC radio after the Grenfell disaster when it was revealed that a small number of those affected might be rehoused in the 'affordable' housing segment of a nearby luxury block of flats, 22 June 2017)

The fire at Grenfell Tower in the London Borough of Kensington and Chelsea on 14 June 2017 was the worst fire disasters in the UK for decades.[1] The disaster brought into critical, and at times distinctly visual, relief some of the extremes of economic inequality as well as some of the lived effects of austerity, that characterise daily life in contemporary Britain for many people. The visual images of luxury tower blocks and the haunting images of the burnt out shell of the Grenfell Tower were writ large across many of the newspapers, with the accompanying headlines of 'A tale of two cities' speaking for themselves of the gross levels of economic inequality that characterise the Greater London Borough of Kensington and Chelsea. Yet, whilst London is a city that embodies extremes of wealth and poverty – and everything in between – the disparities of life conditions and life chances that characterise the lives of those who live there are mirrored up and down the country to a greater or lesser degree (Hood & Waters, 2017). This article is primarily concerned with poverty and inequality in Britain and the UK more broadly (similar agendas have been pursued in countries such as the US, Canada and Australia as well as many Western European countries). Successive British governments have pursued a particularly aggressive neoliberal agenda of deliberately deepening inequalities since the Thatcher government of the 1980s. Since 2010 the policy of austerity that has been vigorously pursued by successive Conservative led administrations has led to deepening divisions and particularly unforgiving life conditions for those who are economically marginalised (Cooper & Whyte, 2017; Dorling, 2017; O'Connell & Hamilton, 2017; O'Hara, 2017; Pring, 2017). Whilst these trends are not particular to the UK there is little denying that the inequality agenda has been pursued with such vigour in the UK that it is now one of the most unequal countries in the Western world (Equality Trust, 2017a). Rather perversely and running parallel to these political and policy trends, those on the lowest incomes or who experience poverty and/or other multiple forms of deprivation and structural limits to their life opportunities over which they have no control have been demonised and misrepresented and are frequently portrayed in both popular and political terms as being feckless and failing to aspire or work hard enough or to be willing to work at all (Jensen, 2014; Jensen & Tyler, 2015; MacDonald, Shildrick, & Furlong, 2013; Wright, 2016). Here and elsewhere (Shildrick, 2018) I argue that these misleading, damaging and divisive depictions of those experiencing poverty and related disadvantages might best be described as poverty propaganda. In contemporary Britain poverty propaganda works to stigmatise and label those experiencing poverty and related disadvantages and thus effectively hides the real causes and consequences of poverty. Poverty propaganda has both real and ideological effects. Punitive and divisive policies towards poverty become more palatable – and even desired – by a general public who on the whole tend to accept that such responses are just, acceptable and in many cases necessary (British Social Attitudes, 2016). The narratives contained within poverty propaganda – that those experiencing poverty are workshy, lazy and culpable for their own predicaments – are so powerful, pervasive and persuasive that even people experiencing deep poverty often subscribe to their truth (Shildrick & MacDonald, 2013). Yet attitudes towards inequality, poverty and economic disadvantage are complex and multi-layered. People on the whole tend to underestimate both the extent of extreme wealth (Equality Trust, 2017a) as well as the relentless and significant everyday hardships that characterise life for those experiencing poverty (Shildrick, 2018; Shildrick, forthcoming). Even those in the top 1% of the wealthiest people in the UK tend to express views that downplay their wealth and privilege (Hecht, 2017).

Yet, episodes such as Grenfell Tower have the potential to disrupt some of this shamelessly disparaging and derogatory rhetoric around poverty, proving its deceit and aptly illustrating the vast crevice that exists between rhetoric and reality.

The article has three main parts: the first outlines the current economic and political context in the UK and looks at the role of stigma and shame and the importance of poverty propaganda in perpetuating particular views around poverty and disadvantage. The following section explores the Grenfell fire disaster in a little more detail and argues that both overtly, and in more subtle ways, the disaster not only epitomises so much that is unfair and divisive with neoliberal capitalism, but the disaster – if one looks closely enough – also reveals the shameless dishonesty of poverty propaganda. The final substantive section attempts to understand some of the issues raised in the article and offers some reflections on why poverty propaganda is so successful.

Inequality, policies that hurt and the power of poverty propaganda

In 2014 Piketty published his highly influential book *Capital in the Twenty First Century*. In it he argued that:

> For millions of people 'wealth' amounts to little more than a few weeks' wages in a checking account or low-interest savings account, a car and a few pieces of furniture. The inescapable reality is this: wealth is so concentrated that a large segment of society is virtually unaware of its existence, so that some people imagine that it belongs to surreal or mysterious entities. (2014, p. 259)

One of the major conclusions of Piketty's work was that those with economic resources were benefitting most from the way most capitalist societies were organised, resulting in gross economic inequalities. Some social scientists have expressed dismay at both the scale of inequality in Britain and its consequences for most citizens and for society more broadly (Dorling, 2014, 2015, 2017; Wilkinson & Pickett, 2010). In Britain today, the richest 1000 people own more wealth than 40% of households, or 10.2 million families. In the last year alone, the combined wealth of Britain's 1000 richest people increased by £82.5 billion to a barely believable £658 billion (Equality Trust, 2017b). In recent years increasing attention has been devoted to the top 1% who have disproportionately high incomes in comparison to those beneath them (Dorling, 2014; Hecht, 2017). The High Pay Centre points out that a chief executive can take home more in three days than one of their employees can earn in a whole year (High Pay Centre, 2015). The 'UK now [has] more billionaires per capita than any other country in the world, but London is now far and away the city with the greatest number of sterling billionaires resident globally – some 72 (compared to Moscow with 48, New York with 43, San Francisco with 42, Los Angeles with 38 and Hong Kong with 34)' (Burrows, Webber, & Atkinson, 2017, p. 189).

In contrast to this explosion of wealth at the top, poverty has been increasing at a dramatic rate as a direct result of punitive policies directed towards those experiencing poverty and disadvantage in the UK (Hood & Waters, 2017). These trends towards increasing inequality have been in train for over 40 years so it would be wrong to blame any one political party entirely, but since the election of the Coalition government led by the Conservatives in 2010 and the subsequent election of two Conservative administrations (albeit in 2017 the current one being propped up by an uneasy alliance with the Democratic Unionist Party) successive policy developments, particularly in respect of cuts made in the name of austerity, have been explicitly deployed that worsen the economic position of those on the lowest incomes (Taylor-Gooby, 2013, 2017). Poverty in the UK is widespread and has two main causes. First, paid employment that is either insecure and/or low paid is proliferating in the UK and does not take people away from poverty either far enough or for long enough to make a real difference to their lives (Shildrick, MacDonald, Webster, & Garthwaite, 2012b). It is particularly telling that in the UK the majority of households experiencing poverty now have at least one member in paid employment (Joseph Rowntree Foundation, 2016). Second, poverty is caused by inadequate financial support for out of work benefit claimants (Padley & Hirsch, 2017). Cuts to out of work benefits have been a key priority since 2010, with those forced to rely on out of work benefits faring particularly badly and being forced to engage with a punitive and hostile system that not uncommonly leaves people destitute and left for not insignificant periods of time without any income at all (Fitzpatrick et al., 2016). Disabled people have been subjected to degrading assessments through the increased use of Work Capability Assessments, which Pring describes as 'possibly the most violent and discriminatory tool ever handed to a government department' (2017, p. 51). Whilst set ups like ATOS (the company initially responsible for assessing disabled people and determining whether they were entitled to sickness benefits) profited from a £400 million government contract for its trouble, vulnerable, sick and disabled people were forced to endure intrusive and cruel and all too often completely incompetent assessments that left a great many declared 'fit to work' (many cases subsequently overturned on appeals), without essential benefits and at worse, left destitute, and in some cases to die not only without dignity but also sometimes without food in their bellies (Fitzpatrick et al., 2016; Garthwaite, 2016; Ryan, 2014). What Mills refers to as 'austerity suicides' have become all too commonplace (Mills, 2017) and financial strains add to a rising tide of mental ill health (O'Hara, 2017). In June 2016 the United Nations ruled that UK welfare reforms and austerity measures were in breach of international human rights (UN, 2016).

Yet poverty and economic disadvantage are rarely called out as being the result of policy and political decisions but are rather presented (and thus largely understood by many people) to be the result of individual behaviours. Poverty propaganda is produced via political speak, policy documents and reinforced by the media, both print and television. The production of programmes such as *Benefit Street* and *Life on the Dole* works to present a partial, highly edited and spectacular (if generally somewhat entertaining) depiction of how people on out of work benefits or experiencing multiple problems and disadvantages live their lives (Jensen & Tyler, 2015; MacDonald & Shildrick, 2014; Tyler, 2015). Furthermore, disparate groups, from rioters, so-called 'Troubled Families' and those with problematic drug and alcohol problems, can be drawn in at various moments to bolster notions of fecklessness and irresponsibility amongst those experiencing poverty and related disadvantages (Shildrick & MacDonald, 2013; Tyler, 2013). 'Welfare' in the form of out of work benefits is placed centre stage in the production of poverty propaganda, despite the fact that out of work benefits make up only a small proportion of the 'welfare' bill (Hills, 2015) and out of work benefits provide only a very limited income (Padley & Hirsch, 2017). In their attempts to garner what has been coined 'anti-welfare common sense' (Jensen, 2014), political figures and the media deploy rare, unusual and at times downright fantastical stories of supposed problematic behaviour of varying sorts that is purported to be supported by the welfare state. These examples are often carefully timed and deployed in unison to ensure the message is received and to invoke public outrage towards the welfare state and those in receipt of out of work benefits (Allen, Mendick, Harvey, & Ahmed, 2015; Jensen, 2014; Jensen & Tyler, 2015). The pervasiveness and consistency of poverty propaganda's core messages (even if the language changes with the political climate of the day), that those experiencing poverty are somehow culpable for their own poverty, mean that the realities of poverty and its causes and consequences continue to be clouded out. All of this means that episodes like the Grenfell Tower disaster can appear, and are sometimes explicitly used and positioned, to confirm rather than disrupt poverty propaganda. It is to the details of the fire and its aftermath that this article now turns.

The Grenfell Tower disaster and the dishonesty of poverty propaganda

The polar extremes of inequality that exist in contemporary Britain were most vividly and violently thrust into the public imagination by the Grenfell Tower disaster. In many respects the fire exposed many of worst aspects of contemporary neoliberal capitalism, not just in terms of inequality and social housing, but also in the ways that profits can be put before people's lives and well-being and how cuts to public services such as the police and fire services, made in the name of austerity, can have deadly consequences. The Grenfell Tower was situated in the Borough of Kensington and Chelsea, which is one of the wealthiest boroughs in London but also has significant levels of poverty. Around one-fifth (19%) of children living in Kensington and Chelsea are considered to be living in income-deprived households. In the north of the borough close to half of all children live in income-deprived households (Trust for London, 2017). On the night of the fire, a fridge cause the initial blaze that was initially contained to one flat but rapidly spread, very quickly engulfing the whole building. The Metropolitan Police have reported that the official death toll is likely to remain at 70 plus one unborn baby (BBC News, 2017). Many residents perished on the highest floors of the building where they had tried to seek refuge from the rapidly advancing flames, many adhering to the safety advice to remain in their flats in the event of a fire and the initial advice of the emergency services on the night. Those who escaped the Grenfell Tower lost family members, neighbours and friends along with all of their possessions. At the time of writing, just over nine months on from the disaster, the trauma for those directly affected inevitably continues. Very few families have been offered suitable, permanent accommodation and by the time of the one-year anniversary of the fire many families will remain in temporary accommodation. Indeed, at the time of writing in March 2018 only 62 of the 209 households have moved into new permanent accommodation (Walker, 2018). Funds that have been raised to help those affected have largely have been very slow to be released to those in need, and hundreds of people in the area have been referred to mental health services for severe anguish and distress (Rose, 2017).

Places like Grenfell Tower, predominantly social housing (just 12 of the 120 flats were owned privately) managed by the local authority, have a special place in the poverty propaganda described above (Garner, 2011; Hanley, 2012; Mckenzie, 2015). Political figures are fond of referring to 'left behind' estates' (Cameron, 2016) and perpetuating myths of despair and hopeless lives lived on estates where often three generations of the same family have never worked (Duncan Smith, 2007). As Slater (in this monograph issue) argues, the 'sink estate' has entered the political lexicon in order to condemn the very existence of social housing and at the same time to blame 'poverty on the behavioural choices of tenants'. Little wonder then that in the popular and public imaginary social housing has all too often become synonymous with the so-called 'sink estate' (Cameron, 2016), purported to be inhabited by only the hopeless, the workshy and the criminal (Hanley, 2012). Garner has described this generic stigmatisation of social housing 'Estatism', meaning 'the social dynamics associated with council estates and prejudice towards residents based on where they live' (2011, p. 1). The social housing tower block is particularly maligned. As Hanley points out, 'there is one phrase in the English language that has come to be larded with more negative meaning than "council estate" and that is the "tower block" ' (2012, p. 97). Despite these blanket negative portrayals of social housing, research with people living on council estates and in social housing shows that – despite the inevitable problems that blight areas where there are large concentrations of poverty – there is still often much that people value about their homes and their communities (Mckenzie, 2015). Indeed, it has been reported that many of the residents of Grenfell were keen to move into the flats and it was apparently the views of the London skyline that attracted two young people from Italy, who had moved to London to work as architects, to choose to live near the top of Grenfell Tower, and they regularly posted snaps of the views from their home on social media (Di Donato & Narayan, 2017).

Yet there were clearly major structural shortcomings in the quality of the accommodation and the safety of the tower block. The limited and sometimes unsafe housing conditions available to those with limited financial resources have been, at times, laid uncomfortably bare. As Watt has pointed out in respect of Grenfell Tower:

> … [it] has revealed the injustices, deprivations, expulsions and brutalities that are routine in the lives of ordinary, working class, multi-ethnic Londoners. These include: overcrowding; being 'regenerated' and watching your home and neighbourhood crumble around you: being shunted into unsatisfactory temporary accommodation; being displaced out-of-borough; being ignored and / or patronised by political elites; being invisible and not counting; and not even being properly counted. … Disposable homes, disposable lives. (2017)

Housing, particularly in London, has become a critical site of class struggle, whereby even those working in key services, such as the police or health services, struggle to access suitable housing and have virtually no chance of buying a home, and research shows that parental wealth is becoming ever more crucial for young people to access their own homes (Hood & Joyce, 2017). Housing options for those reliant on out of work benefits have been decimated, whilst expensive flats afforded only by the wealthy continue to proliferate (Watt, 2017). Many serve as second, or even third or fourth homes and others are rented out to those who are reliant on the rental market, thus further benefitting the wealthy at the direct expense of those less economically fortunate. Many people with disabilities live in social housing, such as Grenfell, despite mobility issues that render them trapped when lifts are out of order and even more vulnerable in an emergency such as the Grenfell fire. Stories emerged after the Grenfell fire of a blind man rescued from the 11th floor by the fire service and one disabled woman surviving after her son carried her down 24 flights of stairs (Springfield, 2017). As Springfield points out, 'there is no legal obligation on the part of the council workers to ensure that the disabled person can easily escape from their home in the case of fire' (2017). Ryan recently argued that around 1.8 million people are living in properties that are totally unsuitable for their needs and leaving many stranded, unable to leave their properties (Ryan, 2017).

Grenfell reveals the dishonesty of popular depictions both of poverty and of those who reside in social housing. The lists of the dead and the missing that emerged in the days and weeks after the fire make for difficult and painful reading. Grenfell was home to the young and the old, multiple generations of the same families, working-class Londoners who had lived there for decades and those newly arrived, seeking sanctuary from their own war torn homes in places like Syria. Due to reasons of space only a few examples can be noted here. Shelia (previously known as Sheila Smith) was an 84-year-old grandmother, described as a poet, artist and philosopher and an active member of the community. She died on the night of the fire and left behind two sons, six grandchildren and three great grandchildren (Rawlingson, 2017). The two young Italian architects – who so publicly and enthusiastically celebrated and shared the spectacular views they enjoyed from their home – also died. They had moved to London to take up jobs as assistant conservation architects, one of whom, Gloria Trevisan, was described by her employer as 'an extremely promising and talented graduate' (Braidwood, 2017). The first victim of the fire to be named, Mohammad Alhajali, had fled from Syria with his brother Omar, who survived the fire after being rescued, and was at the time of his death studying civil engineering at the University of West London (Forster, 2017). It is perhaps the issue of paid employment that stands out as most instructive in the Grenfell disaster. Poverty propaganda rests upon the notion that people experiencing poverty are workshy. The divisive and damaging caricature of the 'welfare' cheat, faring well on benefits, obscures the facts of everyday struggle where low paid and insecure work is now a significant cause of poverty in the UK. It is a telling fact that:

> For the first time the majority of people in poverty are actually [in] employment. The nature of poverty in Britain is changing. The idea of 'making work pay' increasingly sounds like an empty slogan to the millions of people who are hard-pressed and working hard, often in two or three jobs and struggling to make a living. (Sentamu, 2014, p. 4)

From these few short snippets of the lives of some of the individuals killed in Grenfell Tower it is clear to see that it housed many people who worked or who were retired but had previously been in paid employment. This is a simple point but it is very important. Everyday ordinary workers, many of who keep London functioning as one of the most economically vibrant and vital cities in the world, lived in Grenfell, and many like them live in social housing up and down the county. Feeders, cleaners and carers all lived in Grenfell, and continue to live in places just like it. The man who lived in the flat where the fire started was reported to work as a taxi driver (Clarke-Billings, 2017). Other victims have been emerged to be a 'retired lecturer', a 'teaching assistant', and a consultancy firm was widely reported in the media as seeking information on one of their employees who had not been seen since the fire (Rawlingson, 2017). Red Consultancy, an award winning public relations (PR) company, posted on social media that they were worried about Mo Tucca, who was missing after the fire and later confirmed to have died. They posted on Twitter on 31 July: 'today marks ten years since our friend Mo, a victim of the Grenfell fire, joined Red. Out of love and respect today we will close at 4pm' (Red Consultancy pinned tweet). A BBC report for *Newsnight* (27 September 2017) reported on the 21st floor of the tower and its residents' experiences on the night of the fire, highlighting the diversity of those who lived just on that floor. One woman was reported to be retired, having worked previously as a nanny and in a cafe. All of the other residents on that particular floor were reported to be working, in jobs as diverse as IT management consultancy, a beautician and beauty salon owner, a hospital porter and a civil engineer. One of the most widely reported deaths in the days that followed the fire was that of Khadija Saye, a promising young photographer whose work had been exhibited in Venice. An obituary from one of her tutors reads:

> Born in London, Saye lived and worked on the 20th floor in Grenfell Tower with her Gambian mother, Mary Mendy (who is also missing, and presumed dead). Saye was educated locally until age 16, when she won a full scholarship to the prestigious Rugby School; she went on to take a BA in photography at UCA Farnham, where she started to make work on identity and her Gambian heritage. She began documenting Grenfell Tower while still a student, for example; her final series, for her graduation in 2013, looked at Afro-Caribbean hairstyles and was titled *Crowned.* (Smyth, 2017)

A more fulsome study of the lives lived and lost at Grenfell would be worthy and instructive in its own right (although the truth of this is likely never to be properly known) but even on this short assessment it is very clear that Grenfell housed many ordinary – and extraordinary – people. We should not be surprised by this. Rather than some distinct 'other' (Lister, 2004), those experiencing poverty make up an increasingly significant proportion of everyday citizens in one of the richest countries in the world. Twenty-eight percent of children in the UK are growing up in poverty with the figure rising all the time (Joseph Rowntree Foundation, 2016). Furthermore, it is remarkably telling that the majority of families experiencing poverty also have at least one member in a job (Joseph Rowntree Foundation, 2016). Quite simply, those experiencing poverty tend to be workers, not shirkers, who all too often find themselves cycling in and out of low paid, insecure jobs and on and off 'welfare' (Shildrick et al., 2012b). Official unemployment rates in Kensington and Chelsea are relatively low at 5%, but research shows that 16% of people in the borough are paid below the so-called 'living wage' (Trust for London, 2017). Perhaps unsurprisingly and in contrast to the popular and political stigmatisation of places like Grenfell, the tower housed the working class. People who were all too often working and who resided in one of the richest cities in the world, and who were linked by a state that failed them in the cruellest way possible.

Discussion: Poverty propaganda and stigma as class power

This section of the article draws together some of the issues outlined above and reflects on both the impact and purpose of poverty propaganda and the ubiquitous stigma that has been explicitly and deliberately attached to poverty in the current context. Poverty propaganda is given voice, and hence power, though the mainstream media, in ways that hard evidence about poverty or the grind of day-to-day life in low paid, insecure work that fails to take people away from poverty, either far enough or for long enough, to make a real difference to their lives, very rarely is. It is most often the affluent and the powerful (and in many cases those who have the power to resolve poverty or extend the condition to more and more citizens) who hold the cards about how poverty is presented in public arenas. The voices of those with first hand experience are very rarely heard or where they are, they are moulded, shaped and represented in particular ways. For example in television programmes such as *Benefit Street* which claim to be a true-to-life representation of unemployment and poverty, depictions are partial and prone to extremes rather than the everyday and the mundane. The footage shown in such programmes is specifically orchestrated to present the participants very much as the irresponsible and feckless 'other'. Whilst even those experiencing deep poverty and related disadvantages can often subscribe to the truth of poverty propaganda, research also shows that the same people are rarely oblivious to the inequity in their life opportunities and conditions (Savage, 2015; Shildrick, 2017; Shildrick, MacDonald, Furlong, Roden, & Crow, 2012a). Evidence shows that people experiencing poverty frequently feel ignored, not listened to and powerless to challenge decisions that are made about their lives. There is not space in this piece to talk about the vote to leave the European Union that occurred in 2016 in any detail, but there is clear evidence that for some people a feeling of being denied the economic benefits of capitalism and of not being listened to or taken seriously was a factor in some people's decision to vote to leave (Goodwin & Heath, 2016). Speaking of the shock election of Donald Trump in the US in 2016 (a development that has similarly been reported to be a result of the supposedly 'left behind' white working class), Reeves argues that 'years of work lie ahead for social scientists picking over the data and trends' (Reeves, 2017, p. 2), and the same is certainly true of the vote to leave the EU in the UK. But what is becoming increasingly clear is that significant swathes of the population are not benefitting from neoliberal capitalism in the ways they have been led to believe and that perhaps most importantly, people are rarely completely oblivious to the unfairness of their real life experiences and life chances. What poverty propaganda does is to produce confusion about the root cause of inequality, blaming the supposedly feckless, the lazy and the workshy and thus deflecting attention directly away from the real causes.

The disconnect between poverty and wealth and bodies of power and powerlessness was thrown into sharp relief after the Grenfell Tower disaster as residents and those directly affected by the fire expressed their anger and frustration with the Council when it came to light that they had previously been warned that many residents had concerns about the safety of the tower block. The Grenfell Action Group had just back in November 2016 warned about 'dangerous living conditions' and concluded that 'it is a truly terrifying thought but the Grenfell Action Group firmly believe that only a catastrophic event will expose the ineptitude and incompetence of our landlord, the KCTMO' (Grenfell Action Group, 2016). Residents felt that their concerns were not listened to and evidence shows that whether these concerns were heard or not, they were never acted upon. This disconnect between power, privilege and powerlessness was further exemplified by the rather telling admission from the new leader of Kensington and Chelsea Council that she had never actually been inside any of the high-rise tower blocks in the borough before the fire (Rawlingson & Bowcott, 2017). The launch of the inquiry into the fire (and of which residents and campaigners have been highly critical both in terms of its remit and its leadership) was held in the palatial De Vere Grand Connaught Rooms in Covent Garden. The obvious and overt irony of this choice of meeting venue with its 'ornate ceilings, beautiful wood panelling and ornate chandeliers' (De Vere Connaught Rooms, 2017) was not lost on the residents who attended the meeting, as Emma Dent Coad MP said of the venue:

> We were sitting in a ballroom, dripping with chandeliers. It's the most incredibly inappropriate place. Clearly, the judge felt perfectly comfortable in a place like this – a lot of people didn't. People feel it was deliberate, to intimidate and make people feel unimportant and looked down on. (2017)

People experiencing poverty are rarely immune to its negative effects and the limits it places on their life chances and opportunities. Yet the real causes of poverty, its life limiting effects and the role governments play in perpetuating or alleviating poverty and its effects remain largely hidden by false and misleading caricatures about poverty and the people who experience it. The importance of low paid and insecure work and inadequate out of work benefits rarely features in the public and political debate. Furthermore, the ubiquitous nature of poverty propaganda means that punishing, cruel and sometimes illegal policies can be wrought on those experiencing poverty and other disadvantages with relatively little dissent, and in many cases acceptance or outright support. Thus poverty propaganda plays a crucial role in encouraging consent for and legitimising a political and economic system that further disadvantages some whilst continuing to advantage others. Link and Phelan argue that, 'When people have an interest in keeping other people down, in or away, stigma is a resource that allows them to obtain the ends they desire. We call this resource stigma power' (2014, p. 24). Tyler has also powerfully documented the ways in which stigma is increasingly utilised as a mechanism for the exercise and imposition of power by those with and in power against those without it (see Tyler, 2017, and her article in this monograph). The power of stigma, particularly as it has been developed and used to negatively label those experiencing poverty and other related disadvantages, plays a significant role in fostering a climate of distrust and a propensity to distance oneself from people at the lower end of the income scale, promoting a view of disadvantaged groups of people as 'the other' (Lister, 2004) and in one way or another culpable for their own predicaments. Such is the power of stigma and shame that are now closely associated with poverty that even those experiencing deep poverty tend to disassociate themselves from the condition. Whilst the idea that proportions of those experiencing poverty are undeserving or culpable for their experiences is nothing new (Welshman, 2013) in the current climate, such is the power and pervasiveness of poverty propaganda that virtually anyone forced to rely on out of work benefits is now perceived to be feckless and undeserving (Allen et al., 2015; Jensen & Tyler, 2015; Shildrick & MacDonald, 2013; Shildrick et al., 2012a). Despite widespread understanding of the unfairness of life conditions amongst those who are economically marginalised, poverty propaganda is so powerful and effective at manufacturing confusion about the root causes of deepening structural inequalities, that it aids the deepening of gross structural inequalities to be both perpetuated over time and tolerated as being inevitable and just and deserved. As such, poverty propaganda is a mighty political tool that orchestrates widespread consent for a political system that affords punishing life opportunities for significant numbers of its citizens whilst continuing to bolster the weight and strength of the cushions that protect the few. Neoliberal capitalism operates in this way and poverty propaganda plays an important role in its legitimation, normalising class inequality and helping to ensure its continuation. Inequalities of life chances and life conditions are presented as right, necessary and just. Even those experiencing deep poverty can be seduced by its messages, despite vehemently, and quite justifiably, rejecting such narratives as in any way reflective of their own lives and experiences (Shildrick & MacDonald, 2013).

Conclusion

Poverty propaganda works to orchestrate confusion and muddies the waters about both the causes and the consequences of poverty in Britain today. Hence it works to create misunderstanding and to hide the realities and who and what are responsible for poverty and its effects in limiting the life opportunities and life chances of many citizens. Whilst there might be growing disquiet about some of the issues discussed in this article and in particular about the ongoing commitment to austerity and its impact on public services, there is, as yet, no clear consensus. Whilst there is evidence to suggest that many people, particularly those experiencing multiple and place based disadvantages associated with decades of deindustrialisation and the degradation of working-class employment opportunities, recognise all too well that their lives are blighted by limited opportunities that are beyond their control, poverty propaganda works to distil blame and create confusion as to how and why such inequalities persist. Hence poverty propaganda is politically valuable and vital because it plays a critical role in legitimising punitive policies towards those experiencing poverty and other forms of disadvantage, whilst at the same time helping to legitimate and normalise extremes of inequality. The stigmatising narratives that make up poverty propaganda are often found to be particularly alive in deprived neighbourhoods, whereby even those in deep poverty will (quite correctly) reject scrounger narratives as bearing any relation to their own lives, problems and struggles, but vehemently believe that others in their streets or neighbourhoods exactly fit such a label (Shildrick & MacDonald, 2013; Shildrick et al., 2012b). The role of governments in fostering gross levels in inequality and inflicting sometimes dire living conditions on some of its most economically marginal citizens is permitted to go if not unseen, as at least justifiable, and due to the belief in the supposed preponderance of individual feckless and irresponsible behaviour. The role that poverty propaganda plays in stigmatising whole swathes of the population, from those living in social housing tower blocks such as Grenfell Tower, to those claiming out of work benefits, to those experiencing any number of social and economic disadvantages, allows it to work particularly effectively. Poverty propaganda is a form of stigmatisation that damages those with the least and provides a critical resource for those with power. In many respects the disaster at Grenfell Tower shone a very vivid and at times, viscerally visual light on many of the most pressing political issues of the current time. The people who died in the Grenfell Tower or have been affected by the disaster were victims of a neoliberal regime that inevitably produces casualties and losers along with its winners. Those particular victims join a long and growing list of casualties subjected to sometimes illegal and unnecessarily cruel policies that are deliberately inflicted on those with the least by those with the most. Perhaps most shamefully of all, this all takes place in one of the richest countries in the world.

Funding

This research received no specific grant from any funding agency in the public, commercial, or not-for-profit sectors.

Note

1. It is difficult to find the right terminology to describe the Grenfell Tower fire. Commentators have used various terms, including 'disaster', 'catastrophe' and some arguing that 'crime' is a more accurate description. For the purposes of this article the word disaster will be used despite its limitations

References

Allen, K., Mendick, H., Harvey, L., & Ahmed, A. (2015). Celebrity motherhood and the cultural politics of austerity. *Feminist Media Studies, 15*, 907–925.

Barr, C. (2017, June 15). Wealth and poverty sit side by side in Grenfell Tower's borough. *The Guardian.*

BBC News. (2017, November 16). Grenfell Tower final death toll stands at 71. Retrieved from http://www.bbc.co.uk/news/uk-42008279 (last accessed 2 May 2018).

BBC Newsnight. (2017). Grenfell Tower: The 21st floor. Retrieved from http://www.bbc.co.uk/programmes/p05hfh6m (last accessed 2 May 2018).

Braidwood, E. (2017, June 23). Two architectural assistants believed dead in the Grenfell tragedy. *The Architects Journal*. Retrieved from https://www.architectsjournal.co.uk/news/two-architectural-assistants-believed-dead-in-grenfell-tragedy/10020857.article (last accessed 2 May 2018).

British Social Attitudes. (2016). *British social attitudes 2016*. London, UK: Natcen.

Burrows, R., Webber, R., & Atkinson, R. (2017). Welcome to 'Pikettyville'? Mapping London's alpha territories. *The Sociological Review, 65*, 184–201.

Cameron, D. (2016, January 1). New Year's Day address.

Clarke-Billings, L. (2017, June 15). Grenfell Tower resident 'whose fridge started the deadly blaze' identified as taxi driver Dad. *Daily Mirror*. Retrieved from http://www.mirror.co.uk/news/uk-news/grenfell-tower-resident-whose-fridge-10623522 (last accessed 2 May 2018).

Cooper, V., & Whyte, D. (Eds.). (2017). *The violence of austerity*. London, UK: Pluto Press.

Dent Coad, E. (2017, September 14). Sitting in a ballroom dripping with chandeliers. *BBC News*.

De Vere Connaught Rooms Promotional web pages. (2017). Retrieved from https://www.phcompany.com/de-vere/grand-connaught-rooms/?utm_source=google&utm_medium=local&utm_campaign=localSEO (last accessed 2 May 2018).

Di Donato, V., & Narayan, C. (2017, June 17). London fire victim was on 'phone with parents when she died', says lawyer. *CNN News*.

Dorling, D. (2014). *Inequality and the 1%*. London, UK: Verso.

Dorling, D. (2015). *Injustice*. Bristol, UK: Policy Press.

Dorling, D. (2017). Austerity and mortality. In V. Cooper & D. Whyte (Eds.), *The violence of austerity* (pp. 44–50). London, UK: Pluto Press.

Duncan Smith, I. (2007). *Breakthrough Britain: Ending the costs of social breakdown*. London, UK: Centre for Social Justice.

Equality Trust (2017a). *Equality matters to human rights. We need a socio-economic duty*. London, UK: Author. Retrieved from https://www.equalitytrust.org.uk/equality-matters-human-rights-we-need-socio-economic-duty (last accessed 2 May 2018).

Equality Trust (2017b). *Scales and trends*. London, UK: Author. Retrieved from https://www.equalitytrust.org.uk/about-inequality/scale-and-trends (last accessed 2 May 2018).

Fitzpatrick, S., Bramley, G., Sosenko, F., Blenkinsopp, J., Johnsen, S., Littlewood, M., ... Watts, B. (2016). *Destitution in the UK*. York, UK: Joseph Rowntree Foundation.

Forster, K. (2017, June 16). Grenfell Tower fire victim's last phone call to brother: 'why did you leave me?' *The Independent*.

Garner, S. (2011). *White working class neighbourhoods: Common themes and policy suggestions*. York, UK: Joseph Rowntree Foundation.

Garthwaite, K. (2016). *Hunger pains: Life inside foodbank Britain*. Bristol, UK: Policy Press.

Goodwin, M., & Heath, O. (2016). *Brexit vote explained: Low skills and lack of opportunities*. York, UK: Joseph Rowntree Foundation.

Grenfell Action Group. (2016, November 20). KCTMO – Playing with fire! Retrieved from https://grenfellactiongroup.wordpress.com/2016/11/20/kctmo-playing-with-fire/ (last accessed 2 May 2018).

Hanley, L. (2012). *Estates: An intimate history*. London, UK: Granta Books.

Hecht, K. (2017). *A relational analysis of top incomes and wealth: Economic evaluation, relative (dis)advantage and the service to capital*. London, UK: LSE. Retrieved from http://www.lse.ac.uk/International-Inequalities/Assets/Documents/Working-Papers/Katharina-Hecht-A-Relational-Analysis-of-Top-Incomes-and-Wealth.pdf (last accessed 2 May 2018).

High Pay Centre. (2015). *Thinking high and low: Exploring pay disparities in society.* London, UK: Author.

Hills, J. (2015). *Good times, bad times: The 'welfare' myth of them and us.* Bristol, UK: Policy Press.

Hood, A., & Joyce, R. (2017). *Inheritances and inequalities within and across generations.* London, UK: Institute for Fiscal Studies.

Hood, A., & Waters, T. (2017). *Living standards, poverty and inequality in the UK: 2016–17 to 2021–2022.* London, UK: Institute for Fiscal Studies.

Jensen, T. (2014). Welfare, commonsense, poverty and doxosophy. *Sociological Research Online, 19,* 3.

Jensen, T., & Tyler, I. (2015). 'Benefit broods': The cultural and political crafting of anti-welfare common sense. *Critical Social Policy, 35,* 470–491.

Joseph Rowntree Foundation. (2016). *We can solve poverty in the UK.* York, UK: Author.

LBC Radio. (2017, June 22). If Grenfell residents move into my flats, I will move out. LBC radio phone-in. Retrieved from http://www.lbc.co.uk/radio/presenters/shelagh-fogarty/if-grenfell-residents-move-into-my-flats-ill-move/ (last accessed 2 May 2018).

Link, B., & Phelan, J. (2014). Stigma power. *Social Science & Medicine, 103,* 24–32.

Lister, R. (2004). *Poverty.* Cambridge, UK: Polity.

MacDonald, R., & Shildrick, T. (2014). 'Benefit Street' and the myth of workless communities. *Sociological Research Online, 19,* 1.

MacDonald, R., Shildrick, T., & Furlong, A. (2013). In search of 'intergenerational cultures of worklessness': Hunting the yeti and shooting zombies. *Critical Social Policy, 34,* 199–220.

Mckenzie, L. (2015). *Getting by: Estates, class and culture in austerity Britain.* Bristol, UK: Policy Press.

Mills, C. (2017, February 1). Suicides linked to austerity: From a psychocentric to a psychopolitical autopsy. *Discover Society.*

O'Connell, R., & Hamilton, L. (2017). Hunger and food poverty. In V. Cooper & D. Whyte (Eds.), *The violence of austerity* (pp. 94–100). London, UK: Pluto Press.

O'Hara, M. (2017). Mental health and suicide. In V. Cooper & D. Whyte (Eds.), *The violence of austerity* (pp. 35–43). London, UK: Pluto Press.

Padley, M., & Hirsch, D. (2017). *A minimum income standard for the UK in 2017.* York, UK: Joseph Rowntree Foundation.

Piketty, T. (2014). *Capital in the twenty first century.* Cambridge, MA: Harvard University Press.

Pring, J. (2017). Welfare reforms and the attack on disabled people. In V. Cooper & D. Whyte (Eds.), *The violence of austerity* (pp. 51–58). London, UK: Pluto Press.

Rawlingson, K. (2017, November 27). The victims of the Grenfell Tower fire. *The Guardian.* Retrieved from https://www.theguardian.com/uk-news/2017/jul/13/grenfell-tower-fire-victims-dead-missing-identified-named-so-far (last accessed 2 May 2018).

Rawlingson, K., & Bowcott, O. (2017, July 12). Kensington and Chelsea council leader had never been inside its high rise flats. *The Guardian.* Retrieved from https://www.theguardian.com/uk-news/2017/jul/12/kensington-and-chelsea-leader-elizabeth-campbell-never-been-inside-high-rise-flats-grenfell (last accessed 2 May 2018).

Reeves, R. V. (2017). *Dream horders: How the American upper middle class is leaving everyone else in the dust.* Danbury, CT: Westchester Publishing.

Rose, E. (2017, August 10). Hundreds from Grenfell Tower area referred to mental health services. *The Evening Standard.*

Ryan, F. (2014, September 9). David Clapson's awful death was the result of grotesque government policies. *The Guardian.* Retrieved from https://www.theguardian.com/

commentisfree/2014/sep/09/david-clapson-benefit-sanctions-death-government-policies (last accessed 2 May 2018).

Ryan, F. (2017, March 15). Trapped: The growing number of disabled people unable to leave their homes. *The Guardian*. Retrieved from https://www.theguardian.com/society/2017/mar/15/disabled-people-suffer-inaccessible-social-housing (last accessed 2 May 2018).

Savage, M. (2015). *Social class in the 21st century*. London, UK: Pelican Books.

Sentamu, J. (2014). Foreword by the Archbishop of York. In *Working for poverty: The scale and problem of low pay and working poverty in the UK*. London, UK: Living Wage Commission.

Shildrick, T. (2017, February 1). Poverty, politics and a new kind of class war? *Discover Society*. Retrieved from https://discoversociety.org/2017/02/01/poverty-politics-and-a-new-kind-of-class-war/ (last accessed 2 May 2018).

Shildrick, T. (2018). *Poverty propaganda: Exploring the myths*. Bristol, UK: Policy Press.

Shildrick, T. (forthcoming). *Poverty in Britain: Causes, consequences and myths*. Bingley, UK: Emerald.

Shildrick, T., & MacDonald, R. (2013). Poverty talk: How people experiencing poverty deny their poverty and why they blame the poor. *The Sociological Review*, *61*, 285–303.

Shildrick, T., MacDonald, R., Furlong, A., Roden, J., & Crow, R. (2012a). *Are cultures of worklessness passed down the generations?* York, UK: Joseph Rowntree Foundation.

Shildrick, T., MacDonald, R., Webster, C., & Garthwaite, K. (2012b). *Poverty and insecurity: Life in low pay, no pay Britain*. Bristol, UK: Policy Press.

Smyth, D. (2017). Obituary: Khajida Saye, fast rising artist killed tragically young in Grenfell Tower. *British Journal of Photography*. Retrieved from http://www.bjp-online.com/2017/06/obituary-khadija-saye-grenfell-tower/ (last accessed 2 May 2018).

Springfield, F. (2017). Grenfell Tower – Neglect of the most vulnerable. Retrieved from https://www.huffingtonpost.co.uk/fran-springfield/grenfell-tower-neglect_b_17239116.html (last accessed 2 May 2018).

Taylor-Gooby, P. (2013). *The double crisis of the welfare state and what we can do about it*. Basingstoke, UK: Palgrave Macmillan.

Taylor-Gooby, P. (2017). Redoubling the crises of the welfare state: The impact of Brexit on UK welfare politics. *Journal of Social Policy*, *46*, 815–836.

Trust for London. (2017). *London's poverty profile*. Retrieved from https://www.trustforlondon.org.uk/data/boroughs/kensington-and-chelsea/ (last accessed 2 May 2018).

Tyler, I. (2013). The riots of the underclass: Stigmatisation, mediation and the government of poverty and disadvantage in the UK. *Sociological Research Online*, *18*, 6.

Tyler, I. (2015). Classificatory struggles: Class, culture and inequality in neoliberal times. *The Sociological Review*, *63*, 493–511.

Tyler, I. (2017). The hieroglyphics of the border: Racial stigma in neoliberal Europe. *Ethnic and Racial Studies*. Advance online publication. doi:10.1080/01419870.2017.1361542

UN Economic and Social Council, Committee on Economic and Social Rights. (2016). Concluding observations on the sixth periodic report of the United Kingdom of Great Britain and Northern Ireland, E/C.12/GBR/CO/6. Retrieved from http://tbinternet.ohchr.org/_layouts/treatybodyexternal/Download.aspx?symbolno=E%2fC.12%2fGBR%2fCO%2f6&Lang=en (last accessed 2 May 2018).

Walker, P. (2018, March 22). Tories will break pledge to rehouse Grenfell survivors says Javid. *The Guardian*.

Watt, P. (2017). 'This place is post-something': London's housing in the wake of the Grenfell Tower fire. *City Analysis blog*. Retrieved from http://www.city-analysis.net/2017/06/23/this-place-is-post-something-londons-housing-in-the-wake-of-the-grenfell-tower-fire-paul-watt/ (last accessed 2 May 2018).

Welshman, J. (2013). *Underclass: A history of the excluded since 1880*. London, UK: Bloomsbury Press.

Wilkinson, R., & Pickett, K. (2010). *The spirit level*. London, UK: Penguin.

Wright, S. (2016). Conceptualising the active welfare subject: Welfare reform in discourse, policy and lived experience. *Policy and Politics, 44*, 235–252.

Author biography

Tracy Shildrick is Senior Lecturer at Newcastle University. She has researched and published widely in the areas of poverty, disadvantage and youth. Her co-authored book with Policy Press, *Poverty and Insecurity: Life in Low Pay, No Pay Britain*, won the British Academy Peter Townsend prize in 2013 and two new books, *Poverty Propaganda: Exploring the Myths* (Policy Press) and *Poverty in Britain: Causes, Consequences and Myths* (Emerald Publishing) will both be published in April 2018.

Stigma, housing and identity after prison

The Sociological Review Monographs
2018, Vol. 66(4) 81–97
© The Author(s) 2018
Reprints and permissions:
sagepub.co.uk/journalsPermissions.nav
DOI: 10.1177/0038026118777447
journals.sagepub.com/home/sor

Danya E. Keene
Yale School of Public Health, USA

Amy B. Smoyer
Southern Connecticut State University, USA

Kim M. Blankenship
American University, Washington, DC, USA

Abstract

Existing research suggests that individuals who are released from prison face considerable challenges in obtaining access to safe, stable, and affordable places to live and call home. This article draws on repeated qualitative interviews (conducted every 6 months over a period of 3 years) with 44 formerly incarcerated individuals, to understand how these individuals experience the search for a home after their prison release. The interviews show that the quest for a home is central to participants' reintegration projects as they seek to establish themselves as 'decent' and economically self-sufficient citizens, and shed stigmatized identities associated with incarceration, poverty, homelessness, and place. Interviews also suggest that their quest for a home is an arduous one as they encounter numerous barriers to housing arising from both structural and interpersonal forms of incarceration stigma. Somewhat paradoxically, the challenges that they face in accessing housing seem to hinder their ability to shed the stigmatized identities associated with their incarceration. Ultimately, the narratives presented here show how stigma can restrict access to a valuable material and symbolic resource (housing), resulting in ongoing stigmatization, and contributing to the enduring and discrediting mark of incarceration. In this way, the study illustrates how stigma that is enacted by both individuals and the state, that is embodied in place, and that is internalized and managed by stigmatized individuals themselves, can work to reproduce power and serve as justification for inequality.

Keywords
housing, incarceration, spatial stigma

Corresponding author:
Danya Keene, Yale School of Public Health, 60 College Street, P.O. Box 208034, New Haven, CT 06520-8034, USA.
Email: danya.keene@yale.edu

Introduction

More people are incarcerated in the United States than any other country in the world, with a vastly disproportionate impact on urban, poor, and minority populations (Wacquant, 2010a, 2010b; Western, 2006). An emerging literature has documented the numerous reintegration challenges that formerly incarcerated individuals face upon leaving prison, including barriers to employment, social services, and housing (Harding, Wyse, Dobson, & Morenoff, 2014; Solomon, Dedel Johnson, Travis, & McBride, 2004; Visher & Travis, 2011). Housing is a particular challenge for those leaving prisons (Bradley, Oliver, Richardson, & Slayter, 2001; Geller & Curtis, 2011; Harding, Morenoff, & Herbert, 2013; Herbert, Morenoff, & Harding, 2015; Lutze, Rosky, & Hamilton, 2014). Like many low-income individuals, formerly incarcerated people face a growing and severe affordable housing crisis. Fair market rents across the United States have increased at a rate that has outpaced wages such that there is currently no state in the country where full-time minimum wage work is sufficient to rent an unsubsidized fair market two-bedroom unit (Aurand, Emmanuel, Yentel, Errico, & Pang, 2017). In a context of limited housing availability, incarceration represents a significant risk factor for homelessness and housing instability (Metraux, Roman, & Cho, 2007; Roman & Travis, 2006).

For formerly incarcerated individuals, stigma associated with incarceration histories may present additional barriers to housing access that compounds issues of affordability and availability. For example, research suggests that the formerly incarcerated individuals face discrimination from landlords who can deny them a lease because of their criminal records or from potential employers who can deny them an opportunity to earn rent money (Harding et al., 2014; Pager, 2003). While these forms of exclusion are enacted by individuals, they are also the result of policies that consider incarceration or criminal justice history as legal and valid reasons to deny housing. Furthermore, the reliance on criminal background checks to screen housing applicants requires formerly incarcerated people to reveal concealable histories, turning aspects of their past into their present, and potentially activating stigma and discrimination. Indeed, formerly incarcerated people confront an array of criminal justice and social welfare policies that define a prison stay as an irredeemable mark, limit opportunities for rehabilitation and success, and restrict access to full citizenship (Kennington, 2013; Wacquant, 2010c). In this sense, incarceration represents a form of *structural stigma* that encompasses the societal conditions, cultural norms, and institutional policies that constrain opportunities, resources, and well-being of stigmatized groups (Hatzenbuehler, Phelan, & Link, 2013).

As examples of such structural stigma, punitive policies associated with the 'War on Drugs' in the United States have resulted in increased sentencing and restricted access to social resources, including housing for individuals convicted on drug-related charges (Blankenship, Smoyer, Bray, & Mattocks, 2005). In the realm of housing policy, federal and local restrictions that limit formerly incarcerated people's access to federally subsidized housing have become more stringent in the form of 'one strike' policies, mandatory bans imposed on those evicted for drug or criminal involvement, and expanded discretion granted to local public housing authorities to evict tenants and restrict access to subsidies because of a criminal record or prior incarceration (Curtis, Garlington, &

Schottenfeld, 2013). These restrictions are likely to have significant implications for formerly incarcerated people's ability to secure housing given that subsidized housing is one of the few sources of affordable housing available to low-income renters (Aurand et al., 2017; Desmond, 2016). Furthermore, they represent an added barrier to a resource that is already in short supply: only 1 in 4 eligible households receives a subsidy and waiting lists in most urban areas are measured in years (Fischer & Sard, 2017).

Link and Phelan (2001) note that one function of stigma is to limit access to resources that are needed to support well-being, and by doing so, can maintain unequal distributions of power (Parker & Aggleton, 2003). Housing is one such resource. In addition to the well-documented health benefits of housing (Benfer & Gold, 2017), it is often seen as the foundation for achieving 'reentry success' (Bradley et al., 2001; Fontaine & Biess, 2012; Metraux & Culhane, 2004). In a logistical sense, housing may provide access to spaces that allows formerly incarcerated people to parent their children, obtain jobs, desist from crime, avoid reincarceration due to parole violations, resist addiction or establish health promoting behaviors (Bradley et al., 2001; Fontaine & Biess, 2012).

However, housing is not only materially important to well-being, it also has symbolic value. Indeed, research finds that where one lives is intimately tied to one's sense of self (Cuba & Hummon, 1993; Desmond, 2016; Gieryn, 2000). Given that many formerly incarcerated people experience economic marginalization and housing challenges prior to their incarceration (Wacquant, 2010a), access to stable and decent housing may allow them to construct a new sense of economic independence and self-sufficiency, identities that provide distance from both the stigma of prison, and the stigma of economic disadvantage. Furthermore, access to decent housing may allow formerly incarcerated people to conceal potentially stigmatizing pasts.

Conversely, lack of access to decent housing may activate and reinforce stigma associated with incarceration. An emerging body of literature suggests that lack of a decent place to live may contribute to *spatial stigma*: where those who reside in or relocate from vilified and degraded locales may become marked by the perceived characteristics of their environment (Keene & Padilla, 2014; Wacquant, 2008). Residence in spaces that are associated with the criminal justice system, such as halfway houses, may represent a source of spatial stigma to potential employers, family members, and former prisoners themselves. Additionally, the challenges that formerly incarcerated individuals face in accessing decent affordable housing may restrict them to the most disadvantaged and stigmatized neighborhoods, the streets or homeless shelters. Their relegation to these discredited spaces may reinforce the stigma of prior incarceration adding to it a 'blemish of place' (Wacquant, 2008). Furthermore, the policing and monitoring of marginalized urban spaces where residents' criminal behavior is often assumed, may work to reveal concealable histories (Goffman, 2009; Wacquant, 2008).

Given the symbolic value of housing and place, lack of housing access, or relegation to marginalized spaces, may expose formerly incarcerated people to ongoing stigmatization. In turn, incarceration stigma that is enacted by individual actors and inscribed in existing policies may prevent access to decent spaces that support non-stigmatized identities. This reciprocal relationship between stigma and housing may be one way that the mark of incarceration endures beyond the prison sentence, serving as justification for an ongoing loss of rights, dignity, and citizenship. These reciprocal relationships also provide an example of what Parker and Aggleton (2003) highlight as stigma's role in reproducing relationships of power and control and subsequently, perpetuating inequality (see also Tyler, 2013). Accordingly, stigma is viewed as something that resides, not within the stigmatized individual, but in the relationships between the marginalized and the powerful, and works in the service of power to justify the existing structures of inequality (Parker & Aggleton, 2003). In particular, the activation of criminal justice stigma to deny housing access may serve to justify neoliberal cuts to social welfare spending that have rendered affordable housing an increasingly scarce resource.

This article examines the relationships between housing, stigma, and incarceration. Drawing on longitudinal qualitative data collected from 44 formerly incarcerated people, we first examine how housing contributes to stigma experienced by those who have been to prison. The article then examines how stigma associated with incarceration and criminal justice histories shapes access to housing, through both individual acts of discrimination, as well as structural forms of stigma associated with housing policies. Finally, we show how incarceration stigma may be reinforced through participants' attempts to navigate policies of discretion that require them to distance themselves from criminal justice histories in order to establish their deservingness of scarce housing resources. Ultimately, the narratives presented here show how stigma can restrict access to a valuable material and symbolic resource (housing), resulting in ongoing stigmatization and contributing to the enduring and discrediting mark of incarceration. In this way, we illustrate how stigma that is enacted by both individuals and through state-sponsored policies, that is embodied in place, and that is managed by stigmatized individuals themselves, can work to reproduce power and serve as justification for inequality.

Methods

Research setting

The interviews analyzed here were conducted in New Haven, CT, a city with approximately 130,000 residents. While small, New Haven experiences many of the challenges that larger cities face, including vast socioeconomic inequality, and high rates of poverty and incarceration (Rawlings, 2013). In 2012, there were only 47 affordable and available housing units for every 100 households earning less than 30% of the area median income in New Haven County (McDonald & Poethig, 2014). Like many urban areas, the availability of subsidized housing in New Haven does not meet the need among its low-income families. Waiting lists are long and often closed to new applicants.

Data collection

Data for this analysis come from a larger mixed method study titled Structures, Health and Risk among Re-entrants, Probationers and Partners (SHARRPP). The SHARRPP study examined movement between the criminal justice system and the community, with particular focus on sexual risk and Black/White disparities in health associated with reentry. The study involved a longitudinal survey, as well as longitudinal qualitative interviews conducted with a subset of participants. Though not its central focus, an examination of housing circumstances and experiences was one goal of the study. The study protocol was approved by IRBs at both Yale University and American University.

Eligibility for the study was restricted to individuals who were over 18 years old and released from prison or placed on probation within one year of screening (conducted from July 2010 through February 2011) for a non-violent drug-related charge. Participants were recruited through signs posted at locations throughout the New Haven area including probation and parole offices, the courthouse, offices of local social service providers, halfway houses, drug treatment programs, and community health centers. Of the 1043 individuals screened, 368 qualified as eligible for the study and 302 completed a computer-based structured survey. A subset of 45 survey participants were selected through stratified purposive sampling to complete longitudinal in-depth interviews. We limit our analysis to 44 of these participants who had prior prison or jail experiences, omitting the one participant who was recruited while on probation and had never been to prison or jail. Participants were interviewed six times at 6-month intervals. Retention was approximately 65% across waves, with the number of participants at each follow-up wave ranging from 29 to 36. All but one participant contributed more than one wave of data and 17 participants completed all six interviews. The 44 participants completed a total of 197 interviews across the six waves.

The semi-structured nature of these interviews allowed investigators to probe on main domains of interest (such as housing) but also provided an opportunity to move beyond predetermined questions by allowing participants to narrate their own stories of reentry. The primary focus of this study was on sexual risk associated with reentry, probation, and parole. In accordance with this focus, the interviews contained three primary sections on criminal justice experience, social relationships, and HIV risk behaviors. The interview also contained a section on 'current situation,' where participants were asked: 'Tell me about where you have been living since [either last criminal justice event or last interview].' Though this was the only interview question that explicitly examined housing, it often led to longer discussions encouraged by interviewer probing.

The interview sample (see Table 1) was primarily male ($n = 36$) and African American ($n = 23$) but included women ($n = 8$), Whites ($n = 13$), Latinos ($n = 5$), and people of mixed racial/ethnic identity ($n = 3$). Two women in the study self-identified as lesbian; the remainder of the participants identified as heterosexual. The average age of the sample was 40.3 years. Thirty-five participants had children. Only one participant was a college graduate, though eight participants had some college education. The majority (34) of participants had felony charges.

Thirty-seven participants had been released from prison in the year prior to their enrollment in the study. The seven others were recruited into the study while on probation, but had incarceration experiences. Twenty-one interview participants were reincarcerated during the study.

Analysis

Our analysis of the interview data involved a multi-staged inductive coding process borrowed from grounded theory (Corbin & Strauss, 2014). Prior to the start of the analysis presented in this article, each of the 197 qualitative interviews had been broadly coded

Table I. Baseline characteristics of survey and interview samples.

Characteristic	Interview sample (N = 44)	
	n	(%)[a]
Race/ethnicity		
African American	23	(52.3)
White	13	(29.5)
Latino	5	(11.4)
Other	3	(6.8)
Age (years), mean ± SD	40.3 ± 9.8	
Sex		
Male	36	(81.8)
Female	8	(18.0)
Have children		
Yes	35	(79.5)
No	9	(20.5)
Educational history		
Some high school	13	(29.5)
High school graduate	13	(29.5)
GED	10	(22.7)
Some college	7	(15.9)
College graduate	1	(2.3)
Ever employed	43 (97.8)	
Employment since last criminal justice event		
Yes	8	(18.1)
No	36	(81.8)
Number of incarcerations, mean ± SD	5.3 ± 4.3	
Years of most recent incarceration, mean ± SD	2.3 ± 3.52	
Released from prison during last year	34	(75.6)
Homeless since release	12	(26.7)
Self-reported housing challenge due to criminal record		
Unable to access subsidized housing	9	(20.5)
Unable to stay with family/friends in subsidized housing	10	(22.3)

[a]Percentages may not sum up to 100 due to rounding.

with NVivo software by the study team using a set of codes that reflected the major domains of the interview instrument. For this analysis, we began by extracting the study data that had been coded 'Housing' and 'Perceptions of Self.' The first author then read these data excerpts and utilized an open-coding process to denote important subthemes related to housing, stigma, and identity. (Stigma was not an initial focus of the interviews and therefore it had not been included in the initial rounds of coding.) Excerpts related to stigma, identity, the meaning of housing, and barriers to housing access were coded using Dedoose online software by the first author and two trained research assistants. These excerpts were then reviewed independently, often in conjunction with reading full transcripts. In presenting our results, we use pseudonyms and make small adjustments to participants' ages to protect their anonymity.

The significance of housing after prison

The quest for housing was extremely salient in participants' narratives of making a life after prison. For those on parole, housing access was literally a prerequisite for their release from prison given that parole required an eligible address. As 42-year-old Doug explained, 'You know being on parole, if you don't have an address they can basically lock you back up.' Housing was also described as a resource that could provide a foundation for other reentry goals. For example, participants described the importance of housing in providing the stability needed to maintain regular employment. Housing was understood as crucial ingredient to regaining custody of children both because participants wanted a stable environment for their children, and also in some cases, because authorities made access to housing a prerequisite for reunification. In short, housing was seen as an essential foundation upon which post-incarceration success could grow. Fifty-five-year old Jeff, who spent the first three interviews couch surfing between various friends' apartments, described the centrality of housing access in his struggle to establish himself after prison noting, 'I mean if I got housing – if they gave me a roof over my head, I could take care of the rest. That's all I want is a roof over my head. It's all I need. Yeah. That's all I hope for.'

Housing as a mark of self-sufficiency and decency

Beyond the logistics of needing a stable and affordable place to stay, where one could keep regular hours in order to get up for work in the morning, or have a spare room that children could stay in, access to housing, and certain types of housing in particular, offered participants a mark of decency to erase or mask the stigma of incarceration and poverty, and define themselves, and be defined by others, as full citizens. Participants, especially men, equated housing with economic self-sufficiency that they perceived as central to establishing a positive identity after prison. For example, according to Jeff,

> Becoming financially self-supporting. You know I want my own apartment. I want it. I got to have it. You know I want an automobile. You know. I just want to be like, you know I just want to live life, you know. And I just want my own.

Similarly, 29-year-old Darrel noted that although he enjoyed living with his girlfriend and was grateful to have a roof over his head, he wanted a place of his own, stating, 'I don't feel like it's mine. My name ain't on that lease … I really don't want that apartment. I want my own.' For 41-year-old Debra, living with someone else also interfered with her desire for independence, which she cited as the reason for moving out of her sister's apartment and into a halfway house. She explained, 'I didn't wanna live with anyone. I'm trying to do everything on my own and not go back to old things.' For Debra, moving into her own place, even if it was a temporary halfway house bed, was important to constructing a self-sufficient identity after prison.

Several participants sought 'a room of their own' where the payment of rent or a name on the lease served as markers of valorized economic self-sufficiency. For example, 45-year-old William reflected on how his stay in a subsidized transitional housing unit provided a sense of independence and also represented his broader goals of 'bettering himself' and asserting perceived masculine ideals. He stated:

> I'd never had my own place. My addiction, I was so heavily onto people, dependent on people, especially my parents and relationships, and when I got this place [the transitional housing unit], it was mine. And you know and I was going, you know I'm still going to school. I was going to school. I felt like a man. Like I was bettering myself.

Similarly, Doug, described how his acquisition of housing after a recent incarceration helped him to reestablish his identity as a provider for his family. When he was incarcerated, Doug's wife and children were unable to pay the rent and lost their family's apartment. They moved in with his sister and he joined them there upon his release. In initial interviews, Doug expressed frustration with his inability to find an apartment for his wife, stating, 'It hurts because I still wasn't in a position to put her in an apartment.' Eventually, his wife obtained a subsidized apartment on her own and they moved in together. Although he kept a separate address in a transitional housing building, because housing authority policies prohibited him from living in this subsidized unit, he considered the apartment his home and described how this home affirmed his identity as a provider for his wife and his children. He said,

> It's beautiful. I mean it makes me feel good because I'm just coming home. I'm used to being the provider. And, you know we've been waiting for – we had a place before I went to jail. A nice place, you know.

For Doug, William and others, access to decent housing seemed to provide an opportunity to distance themselves from the stigma associated with incarceration, criminal justice involvement, and economic dependency.

Housing status as a source of stigma

Just as housing access could support the construction of positive post-incarceration identities, the reverse was also true. Participants described how housing insecurity inhibited their ability to build credibility and distance themselves from stigmatized incarceration histories that were considered legitimate grounds for exclusion from resources. For example, 47-year-old Paul described the challenges of finding a job while residing in a homeless shelter.

> Unfortunately, they see [shelter address] on a job application, they go, 'Oh, that's the shelter.' That's a black-mark against you right there, most cases. Most employers want somebody who's got a steady address – a home as opposed to a bunk. And I can understand it. It's a pain in the butt to work around, but I can understand it: You're looking at a more stable individual. A lot of guys in the shelter will – 'Yeah, hire me. I'm good. I'll hang out.' A week later they're back in the bag. They forget to go to work. Or worse, they show up whacked. I've done that. I don't choose to do that anymore.

As Paul articulated, unstable housing may be associated, in the minds of employers, with personal instability or lack of reliability. This presumed assumption on the part of employers illustrates the way that a stigma of place (the homeless shelter) can be attributed to residents themselves, limiting their inability to secure key resources (in this case, employment). While Paul lamented the place-related stigma that hindered his own employment prospects, he also reproduced this stigma in his statement about homeless individuals who 'forget to go to work' or 'show up whacked.' He explained that he 'doesn't do that anymore,' differentiating his present self from other homeless individuals who may exhibit these undesirable traits.

Participants also described halfway houses as places that interfered with their ability to distance themselves from the stigma of incarceration. For example, 36-year-old Rene described how the stigma associated with halfway houses could act as a barrier to employment. She explained, 'Lot of people don't want to hire somebody who's in a halfway house … when you do get a job, they [the halfway house staff] call and call and call and call and call you. You know? A lot of people don't want to go through that.'

Rene described both the logistical challenges posed by frequent surveillance that she perceived to be an inconvenience for employers, but also suggests that the stigma of the halfway house might prevent an employer from hiring her in the first place. Rene's residence in the halfway house renders her history of criminal justice involvement visible and as a result, may serve as a barrier to moving beyond it.

In summary, housing played an important role in participants' quests to construct valorized post-prison identities, and to shed the stigmatizing mark of prison. Participants longed for independent housing, 'a room of their own,' through which they could demonstrate, to themselves and others, a self-sufficiency that distanced themselves from presumed criminality and dependency associated with incarceration. The types of housing that provided this sense of independence varied across individuals, reflecting the multiplicity of meanings that people assign to housing. In contrast, residence in stigmatized spaces such as halfway houses served to make visible histories of criminal justice involvement and economic marginalization, activating spatial stigma that then created barriers to future opportunities.

The challenge of housing access after prison

While stable housing was a salient goal for participants, it was also a challenge for many who struggled, sometimes across all six interviews, to find it. For many, these housing struggles were not new or unique to their post-prison lives. A few participants had been homeless prior to going to prison, and in fact, described their lack of housing as a key factor in their incarceration. For example, 23-year-old Jacob was first arrested when he was caught sleeping at a friend's parents' house without their permission. He was homeless and had nowhere else to go at the time. Later, while living with a girlfriend, he was arrested again for selling marijuana, which he described as an economic necessity given his girlfriend's mother's requirement that he contribute to the rent.

The barriers to affordable housing facing low-income renters like the participants in this study are pronounced and not only criminal justice related. Participants described unaffordable rents that rendered unsubsidized rental housing out of reach. As 45-year-old

Jason noted, 'My plan is to find a better job so I can get my own apartment. And I need a job with two checks – or at least one check pays my rent.' This assessment reflects the fact that in CT, like many states in the country, an individual would need to work two full-time minimum wage jobs to afford a market rate unit (Aurand et al., 2017).

Stigma as a barrier to private market housing

In addition to these affordability constraints, participants reported barriers to housing access that were uniquely associated with their incarceration histories and related stigma. For example, a few participants described the reluctance of landlords to rent to them because of their criminal record. Forty-one-year-old Natalie explained, 'I'm just going around and looking for apartments. I am just leaving people messages. Something has got to come through. *I know it's due to my background* [emphasis added]. So I'm just praying on it. Lord give somebody who has an apartment let them give me a favor, let it touch their mind and heart.' Natalie's request for 'a favor' suggests that she recognizes her 'background' as grounds for exclusion from housing and seeks an exceptional act of kindness to overcome this barrier.

Likewise, 42-year-old Phillip explained, 'So Friday, well, Monday, the apartment we were looking at the last minute decided that they didn't want us to move there because of my criminal background.' Phillip perceived his criminal background to be the reason behind the landlord's decision, perhaps representing both the landlord's views of incarcerated individuals, as well structural stigma in the form of policies that legitimize incarceration history as reason for exclusion from housing and require housing applicants to reveal concealable histories through background checks. Additionally, it is possible that the social consensus about the legitimacy of incarceration stigma may make this a more feasible reason for the denial of housing, even when other variables, such as race or family size, may be at play. Low-income renters, and in particular, low-income renters of color, face many disadvantages in their efforts to secure homes in a challenging housing market (Desmond, 2016). The stigma of incarceration thus exacerbates an already large challenge of finding housing.

Stigma as a barrier to subsidized housing access

In addition to the challenges of securing private market rental housing, participants also described the way that structural stigma, in the form of subsidized housing policies, limited their access to housing. For example, 54-year-old Gary explained that his criminal record rendered him ineligible to live in public housing, stating, 'Anybody with felonies. Misdemeanors probably can move in there but not people with felonies.' Similarly, Doug described how as a parolee, subsidized housing was off limits. He explained 'You can't parole to a project with Section 8 buildings [subsidized housing buildings]. Anything the government owns you can't parole to.' Participants also pointed to policies that prevented them from living in subsidized units that were leased by friends, partners and family members. Craig was unable to parole to his fiancée's subsidized apartment. He explained, 'I couldn't go to that place because it was housing. They don't want parolees in the housing, so I had to do something.'

Though eligibility policies vary considerably across housing authorities, and often involve considerable discretion on the part of individual case-workers who make admission decisions on a case-by-case basis, participants articulated how criminal records could serve as basis for exclusion from subsidized housing spaces (Curtis et al., 2013; Keene, Rosenberg, Schlesinger, Guo, & Blankenship, 2018). These policies, as interpreted by participants here, represent the perceived deservingness of housing for those who have criminal records. These perceived restrictions also imply that a history of criminal justice involvement can become an enduring mark that is carried beyond the prison sentence. When revealed, this history can be used to justify exclusion from scarce subsidized housing resources.

Navigating stigma in the search for affordable housing

While participants perceived restricted access to subsidized housing, they also noted the significant discretion associated with the enforcement of eligibility restrictions (Curtis et al., 2013; Keene et al., 2018). Participants described how stigma was activated in this context of discretion, and articulated their attempts to deflect this stigma by distancing themselves from their criminal records and asserting their 'deservingness' of scarce subsidized housing resources. In particular, participants emphasized evidence of 'good behavior,' such as staying clean (avoiding drugs), as a way to better position themselves in their quests for a housing subsidy. Some participants also employed the support of case managers and other officials who could advocate on their behalf and assist them in managing their self-presentation. For example, Rene, who engaged in a persistent quest for a subsidized housing unit across all six interviews, preemptively enlisted support from a case manager in appealing eligibility restrictions should a subsidized unit become available. She explained,

> If they deny because of my record, which was in 2010. It's about to be four years ago. ... I have a couple people, even a lady from City Hall that all them said they would write letters for me and you know, right, because like I said, even when I went through probation and parole and all of that, I've never given a dirty urine [failed drug test], I've never got in trouble. From then to now I've been doing good.

Here, Rene emphasized her good behavior as evidence of her deservingness of this coveted and scarce resource. Natalie described similar efforts to prove herself both eligible and deserving of a rental subsidy. She explained:

> I just signed up for [another program] and housing Section 8 [rental voucher] and I have a felony on my record, but I'm not gonna let that stop me because I'm waiting to find out that I can do appeal. I have a case manager saying that I'm doing what I have to do and they're gonna write a letter saying that I've been there such-and-such time and I haven't had a dirty urine since I came home.

In a subsequent interview, 18 months later, Natalie reiterated this effort to establish her eligibility for subsidized housing, emphasizing not only her lack of drug use but also her participation in a number of self-improvement and treatment programs, for which she has obtained certificates. She explained, 'Yeah, so my caseworker, she's advocating for me and I'm advocating for myself, bringing my certificates and everything, just letting them know that I've been clean now over five years.'

By emphasizing her participation in treatment, Natalie embraced a 'therapized identity' (Hansen, Bourgois, & Drucker, 2014) that trades the criminal stigma of incarceration for one of a diseased body that is in need of treatment and on a path to recovery. She claimed her incarceration and addiction history, while emphasizing the hard work she has put into recovery. She explained, 'Do you have a felony?' 'Yes I have a felony.' 'Why were you in prison?' 'I was in prison due to my drug addiction, using drugs. I did this. I worked on myself for these many years. I have certificates.'

Similarly, though he did not use drugs, Gary considered participation in a drug treatment program as a way to certify his commitment to rehabilitation and his deservingness of housing. He explained, 'I think you got to go to some NA meetings and be involved with that program [Interviewer: to get housing?] Yeah. I don't mind doing it, you know? An hour a day or an hour a week or something. It ain't gonna hurt me.' In emphasizing their hard work and rehabilitation, Natalie, Gary and others also suggest that these actions are needed to distance themselves from histories of incarceration and drug use given policies of discretion that require them to demonstrate their deservingness of housing. This distancing requires them to tacitly accept, and perhaps reinforce, stigma that constructs criminal justice histories as legitimate grounds for exclusion from resources.

In summary, participants viewed stigma associated with incarceration, criminal justice, and substance use histories as barriers to housing access, particularly in a context where they were competing with others for scarce affordable or subsidized units. This stigma was produced and reproduced in the actions of individual landlords and housing administrators, but also through policies that defined previous criminal justice involvement as a basis for exclusion from both private and subsidized rental housing, and required those with criminal justice histories to prove their deservingness of housing resources by distancing themselves from others who share similar experiences.

Discussion

Our analysis illustrates that the quest for housing is central to participants' experiences of making a life after prison as they seek to shed the stigmatized identity of incarceration histories and represent themselves as decent and economically self-sufficient citizens. The narratives show how lack of housing, or the right kind of housing, can serve to reinforce stigma associated with incarceration. Participants' inability to access decent homes and their relegation to marked places such as halfway houses can prevent them from concealing and moving beyond stigmatized histories. At the same time, the stigma of incarceration inhibits their ability to secure the independent housing they so desperately seek. Their quest for housing is an arduous one as they encounter both economic constraints and incarceration stigma. The latter manifests itself in the actions of individuals (potential landlords, for example) and also through policies that define incarceration histories as legitimate grounds for exclusion from housing, and that require housing seekers to reveal these histories through criminal background checks. This stigma is also strengthened and reproduced by former prisoners' own efforts to navigate policies of discretion that require them to distance themselves from the stigma they encounter

Thus, the narratives presented here illustrate the way that stigma can serve to perpetuate inequality (Parker & Aggleton, 2003; Tyler, 2013). It not only works to deny access to those resources that materially support well-being, as Link and Phelan (2006) have argued, it also restricts access to the resources that support deserving and decent identities. In this way, incarceration becomes an enduring mark that serves to justify the ongoing denial of rights and resources for those who have been to prison. This justification is particularly relevant given the shrinking of existing social safety nets that has occurred under neoliberalism. As Wacquant (2010c) and others have argued, one hallmark of neoliberal policy reforms is the use of discourses of vilification and stigmatization to justify restricted access to increasingly limited social resources (Morgen & Maskovsky, 2003; Wacquant, 2010c). In this case, discourses of vilification may work to exclude former prisoners from affordable housing, both private and subsidized, that has become an increasingly scarce commodity, rather than a guaranteed right (Pattillo, 2013).

The narratives presented here also illustrate the ways that housing serves as more than just a form of shelter, but also a symbolic good in the context of widely circulating American values of self-sufficiency and independence. These values have been reinforced through policy reforms that have made the receipt of benefits contingent on personal characteristics and labor force participation (Dohan, Schmidt, & Henderson, 2005; Pattillo, 2013; Wacquant, 2010c). Many participants found housing with family members or friends, after leaving prison, and described these housing arrangements as providing beneficial sources of mutual support. However, these same participants and others also idealized 'a room of their own,' the independent housing that was for many out of reach. The economic marginalization and lack of self-sufficiency that many participants experienced both prior to and in the wake of incarceration was not only stigmatizing, but also criminalized. The last few decades have witnessed an increase in the criminalization of poverty through, for example, the rise of debtors' prisons and anti-vagrancy laws (Aykanian & Lee, 2016; Foscarinis, 1996). The salience of participants' housing quests and their desires to present themselves as economically self-sufficient through housing acquisition may reflect a desire to distance themselves from poverty that is increasingly criminalized as well as stigmatized (Tyler, 2013).

Additionally, the narratives in this article speak to an emerging literature on spatial stigma that has documented the ways that the social construction of marginalized spaces (and in particular, spaces inhabited by low-income people of color) can work to perpetuate inequalities (Keene & Padilla, 2010; Wacquant, 2008; Wacquant & Slater, 2014). This literature shows how those who reside in a stigmatized place may become marked by a stigma of place that influences their sense of self, their daily experiences, their access to resources, and their ability to advance themselves (Keene & Padilla, 2014). As Kelaher, Warr, Feldman, and Tacticos (2010) have noted, 'neighborhood stigma may be quite literally, a way of keeping people "in their place".' Formerly incarcerated individuals may embody the spatial stigma of the penitentiary, as well as the marked spaces of halfway houses or other forms of transitional housing. In addition, they may embody, in the eyes of others, the stigma associated with the economically marginalized neighborhoods that many former prisoners hail from and return to: neighborhoods that are surveilled and policed, and where criminality of residents is often assumed (Goffman,

2009). The embodiment of these spatial stigmas, past and present, may prevent them from obtaining resources such as housing. Furthermore, their inability to obtain decent housing in decent neighborhoods may further limit their life chances.

These data also speak to participants' agency, persistence, and resilience, as they push back against incarceration stigma to construct themselves as deserving of housing by demonstrating their accomplishments and by engaging professional helpers to endorse their decency. In these efforts of self-presentation, some participants sought to neutralize the stigma of poverty by embracing medicalized identities (see Hansen et al., 2014). For example, by embracing the identity of a recovering addict, someone with an illness that can be resolved through medical interventions, Natalie was able to distance herself from the structurally produced problems of prison and poverty that have become increasingly stigmatized in a neoliberal post-welfare era (Hansen et al., 2014).

In seeking to understand the intersection of stigma and housing, this study is limited to the experience of the stigmatized. The perspectives of landlords, case managers, housing authority officials, policy makers, and other actors who might enact stigma are absent here and an important focus of future research. Furthermore, the data analyzed here were collected as part of a larger study on incarceration, well-being, and HIV risk and the interviews did not explicitly seek to examine housing quests or experiences. This may limit the depth of the analysis. However, the prevalence of themes related to housing, identity, and stigma in the data, despite the project's lack of focus on these topics, suggests that these are salient issues that require further exploration.

Prior studies have established that housing access represents an important foundation for those returning from prison, with stable housing predicting improved well-being and reduced recidivism (Bradley et al., 2001; Fontaine & Biess, 2012). This study contributes to this literature by illustrating the way that housing provides more than shelter, but is also intimately linked to the process of identity construction and stigmatization after prison.

Acknowledgements

We are grateful to the participants of the Structures, Health and Risk among Re-entrants, Probationers and Partners (SHARRPP) study for sharing their experiences with our research team. We are also thank Alana Rosenberg and Penelope Schlesinger. We would also like to thank the Connecticut Department of Correction (DOC) and Court Support Services Division (CSSD) for their cooperation with this research. The content is solely the responsibility of the authors and does not necessarily represent the official view of project funders.

Funding

The research for this article was supported by the National Institute of Drug Abuse (NIDA) (grant 1R01DA025021–01). This research was also facilitated by the services and resources provided by the District of Columbia Center for AIDS Research, a National Institutes of Health (NIH) funded program (AI117970). Additional support was received from Yale University's Center for Interdisciplinary Research on AIDS (National Institute of Mental Health grant number P30MH062294).

References

Aurand, A., Emmanuel, D., Yentel, D., Errico, E., & Pang, M. (2017). *Out of reach 2017: The high cost of housing.* Washington, DC: National Low Income Housing Coalition. Retrieved from http://nlihc.org/sites/default/files/oor/OOR_2017.pdf (last accessed 2 May 2018).

Aykanian, A., & Lee, W. (2016). Social work's role in ending the criminalization of homelessness: Opportunities for action. *Social Work (United States)*, *61*, 183–185.

Benfer, E. A., & Gold, A. E. (2017). There's no place like home: Reshaping community interventions and policies to eliminate environmental hazards and improve population health for low-income and minority communities. *Harvard Law & Policy Review Online*, S1, 11.

Blankenship, K. M., Smoyer, A. B., Bray, S. J., & Mattocks, K. (2005). Black-white disparities in HIV/AIDS: The role of drug policy and the corrections system. *Journal of Health Care for the Poor and Underserved*, *16*(4 Suppl B), 140–156.

Bradley, K. H., Oliver, R. B. M., Richardson, N. C., & Slayter, E. M. (2001, November). *No place like home: Housing and the ex-prisoner* (Policy brief). Community Resources for Justice, Inc.

Corbin, J., & Strauss, A. (2014). *Basics of qualitative research: Techniques and procedures for developing a grounded theory* (4th ed.). Thousand Oaks, CA: Sage.

Cuba, L., & Hummon, D. (1993). A place to call home: Identification with dwelling, community, and region. *Sociological Quarterly*, *34*(1), 111–131.

Curtis, M. A., Garlington, S., & Schottenfeld, L. S. (2013). Alcohol, drug, and criminal history restrictions in public housing. *Cityscape*, *15*, 37–52.

Desmond, M. (2016). *Evicted: Poverty and Profit in the American City*. New York, NY: Crown.

Dohan, D., Schmidt, L., & Henderson, S. (2005). From enabling to bootstrapping: Welfare workers' views of substance abuse and welfare reform. *Contemporary Drug Problems*, *32*, 429–455.

Fischer, W., & Sard, B. (2017). *Chartbook: Federal housing spending is poorly matched to need*. Retrieved from https://www.cbpp.org/research/housing/chart-book-federal-housing-spending-is-poorly-matched-to-need (last accessed 20 March 2018).

Fontaine, J., & Biess, J. (2012, April). *Housing as a platform for formerly incarcerated persons*. Retrieved from http://www.urban.org/sites/default/files/alfresco/publication-pdfs/412552-Housing-as-a-Platform-for-Formerly-Incarcerated-Persons.PDF (last accessed 2 May 2018).

Foscarinis, M. (1996). Downward spiral : Homelessness and its criminalization. *Yale Law & Policy Review*, *14*, 1–63.

Geller, A., & Curtis, M. (2011). A sort of homecoming: Incarceration and the housing security of urban men. *Social Science Research*, *40*, 1196–1213.

Gieryn, T. F. (2000). A space for place in sociology. *Annual Review of Sociology*, *26*, 463–496.

Goffman, A. (2009). On the run: Wanted men in a Philadelphia ghetto. *American Sociological Review*, *74*, 339–357.

Hansen, H., Bourgois, P., & Drucker, E. (2014). Pathologizing poverty: New forms of diagnosis, disability, and structural stigma under welfare reform. *Social Science & Medicine*, *103*, 76–83.

Harding, D. J., Morenoff, J. D., & Herbert, C. W. (2013). Home is hard to find: Neighborhoods, institutions, and the residential trajectories of returning prisoners. *The Annals of the American Academy of Political and Social Science*, *647*, 214–236.

Harding, D. J., Wyse, J. J. B., Dobson, C., & Morenoff, J. D. (2014). Making ends meet after prison. *Journal of Policy Analysis and Management*, *33*, 440–470.

Hatzenbuehler, M. L., Phelan, J. C., & Link, B. G. (2013). Stigma as a fundamental cause of population health inequalities. *American Journal of Public Health*, *103*, 813–821.

Herbert, C., Morenoff, J., & Harding, D. (2015). Homelessness and housing insecurity among former prisoners. *The Russell Sage Foundation Journal of the Social Sciences*, *1*, 37–54.

Keene, D., & Padilla, M. (2010). Race, class and the stigma of place: Moving to 'opportunity' in Eastern Iowa. *Health & Place*, *16*, 1216–1223.

Keene, D., & Padilla, M. (2014). Spatial stigma and health inequality. *Critical Public Health*, *24*, 392–404.

Keene, D., Rosenberg, R., Schlesinger, P., Guo, M., & Blankenship, K. (2018). Navigating limited and uncertain access to subsidized housing after prison. *Housing Policy Debate, 28*, 199–214.

Kelaher, M., Warr, D., Feldman, P., & Tacticos, T. (2010). Living in Birdsville: Exploring the impact of neighborhood stigma on health. *Health & Place, 16*, 381–388.

Kennington, M. (2013). *Ambiguous freedom: A grounded theoretical analysis of life outside prison* (Doctoral dissertation). University of Vermont. Retrieved from https://vtechworks.lib.vt.edu/handle/10919/24194 (last accessed 1 September 2017).

Link, B., & Phelan, J. (2001). Conceptualizing stigma. *Annual Review of Sociology, 27*, 363–385.

Link, B., & Phelan, J. (2006). Stigma and its public health implications. *The Lancet, 367*, 528–529.

Lutze, F. E., Rosky, J. W., & Hamilton, Z. K. (2014). Homelessness and reentry: A multisite outcome evaluation of Washington state's reentry housing program for high risk offenders. *Criminal Justice and Behavior, 41*, 471–491.

McDonald, G., & Poethig, E. (2014). *We've mapped America's rental housing crisis*. Washington, DC: Urban Institute. Retrieved from http://www.urban.org/urban-wire/weve-mapped-americas-rental-housing-crisis (accessed 1 March 2018).

Metraux, S., & Culhane, D. P. (2004). Homeless shelter use and reincarceration following prison release. *Criminology & Public Policy, 3*, 139–160.

Metraux, S., Roman, C., & Cho, R. (2007, September). *Incarceration and homelessness*. Paper presented at Toward Understanding Homelessness: The 2007 National Symposium on Homelessness, Department of Health and Human Services and US Department of Housing and Urban Development.

Morgen, S., & Maskovsky, J. (2003). The anthropology of welfare 'reform': New perspectives on US urban poverty in the post-welfare era. *Annual Review of Anthropology, 32*, 315–338.

Pager, D. (2003). The mark of a criminal record. *American Sociological Review, 103*, 937–975.

Parker, R., & Aggleton, P. (2003). HIV and AIDS-related stigma and discrimination: A conceptual framework and implications for action. *Social Science & Medicine, 57*, 13–24.

Pattillo, M. (2013). Housing: Commodity versus right. *Annual Review of Sociology, 39*, 509–531.

Rawlings, J. (2013). *Urban apartheid: A report on the status of minority affairs in the greater New Haven area*. New Haven, CT: Greater New Haven Branch of the NAACP.

Roman, C., & Travis, J. (2006). Where will I sleep tomorrow? Housing, homelessness, and the returning prisoner. *Housing Policy Debate, 17*, 389–418.

Solomon, A. L., Dedel Johnson, K., Travis, J., & McBride, E. C. (2004). *From prison to work: The employment dimensions of prisoner reentry*. Washington, DC: Urban Institute.

Tyler, I. (2013). *Revolting subjects: Social abjection and resistance in neoliberal Britain*. London, UK: Zed Books.

Visher, C., & Travis, J. (2011). Life on the outside: Returning home after incarceration. *The Prison Journal, 91*, 102–119.

Wacquant, L. (2008). *Urban outcasts*. Cambridge, UK: Polity Press.

Wacquant, L. (2010a). Class, race and hyperincarceration in revanchist American. *Daedalus, 139*, 74–90.

Wacquant, L. (2010b). Crafting the neoliberal state: Workfare, prisonfare, and social insecurity. *Sociological Forum, 25*, 197–220.

Wacquant, L. (2010c). Prisoner reentry as myth and ceremony. *Dialectical Anthropology, 34*, 605–620.

Wacquant, L., & Slater, T. (2014). Territorial stigmatization in action. *Environment and Planning A, 46*, 1270–1280.

Western, B. (2006). *Punishment and inequality in America*. New York, NY: Russell Sage.

Author biographies

Danya E. Keene is an Assistant Professor of Social Behavioral Sciences at the Yale School of Public Health. Her research focuses on the structural and policy determinants of health inequality, with a particular focus on issues related to housing and place. Her work has examined the health implications of public housing demolition, home foreclosure, and the shortage of affordable rental housing in the US. She also studies the stigmatization of place and its effects on neighborhood health inequality.

Amy B. Smoyer is an Assistant Professor of Social Work at Southern Connecticut State University. Her program of research examines the lived experience of incarceration and the impact of this experience on health outcomes. This inquiry focuses on women's health, HIV care and prevention, food justice, housing stability, and psychosocial wellness.

Kim M. Blankenship is Professor in the Department of Sociology at American University (AU) and also Founding Director of the Center on Health, Risk and Society at AU. Her research and publications focus on the social dimensions of health and structural interventions (especially community mobilization interventions) to address health, with an emphasis on HIV/AIDS among drug users, female sex workers, and populations impacted by the criminal justice system.

The
Sociological
Review
Monographs

Haunted futures: The stigma of being a mother living apart from her child(ren) as a result of state-ordered court removal

The Sociological Review Monographs
2018, Vol. 66(4) 98–113
© The Author(s) 2018
Reprints and permissions:
sagepub.co.uk/journalsPermissions.nav
DOI: 10.1177/0038026118777448
journals.sagepub.com/home/sor

Lisa Morriss
University of Birmingham, UK

Abstract

The notion of 'haunted futures' can provoke new understandings of the experiences of birth mothers living apart from their children as a result of state-ordered court removal. As 'abject figures', the mothers are silenced through the stigma and shame of being judged to be a deeply flawed mother, the justifiable fear of future children being removed, and court-ordered reporting restrictions. In this article, the author depicts how these mothers exist in a state of *haunted motherhood*: they are paralysed in anticipation of an imagined future of reunification with their children. The mothers are painfully aware that any future pregnancy will also be subject to child protection procedures; thus even their *future motherhood* continues to be stigmatised by the past. However, while the ghosts of removed children signify a traumatic loss, they also simultaneously represent hope and future possibilities of transformation through re-narrativisation. The creation of spaces for the mothers to speak about their experiences can foster a 'maternal commons'. This ending of enforced silencing can be a political act, countering the stigma caused by pathologising individual mothers and making visible how structural inequalities and governmental policies impact on the lives of the most vulnerable families in the UK.

Keywords

child protection, hauntology, motherhood, social futures, stigma

Introduction

In my last post I spent 18 months doing fieldwork as a research associate on two national projects concerned with the child protection process in the UK. My role involved reading

Corresponding author:
Lisa Morriss, Department of Social Work, University of Birmingham, 820 Muirhead Tower, Edgbaston, Birmingham, B15 2TT, UK.
Email: l.morriss@bham.ac.uk

the legal bundles and the social work electronic case files concerned with parents and children involved in care proceedings in the Family Court. These files contain numerous types of documents: social work case notes; legal orders and Judgements; psychiatric and psychological reports; care plans; police interviews; and minutes of various statutory meetings. My task as a researcher was to input this diverse material into a series of boxes in an Access data collection tool we had developed as a team: for example, was the child subject to a Child Protection Plan; who was the primary carer at each stage; and was there any mention of domestic violence? Mainly working alone, and spending long periods of time working in the archives of various government offices, I began to make sense of the material I was reading and classifying through the sociological lens of 'haunted futures'. The aim of this article is to use the lens of haunted futures to consider the impact of child protection on birth parents, usually mothers, who are subject to these practices. While this article is directly informed by this research, for ethical reasons, I am not able to quote from any of the material from the files so – with permission – it includes the work of the Mothers Living Apart from their Children project, part of the WomenCentre based in Kirklees and Calderdale, UK and that of 'Annie', a birth mother who writes and presents on her experiences of being subject to the child protection and Family Court process.

Background

Where there is reasonable cause to believe that a child is suffering – or likely to suffer – significant harm, care proceedings are issued by the Local Authority under section 31 of the Children Act 1989. Concerns that may trigger an application to the Family Court system include neglect and physical, sexual and/or emotional abuse of a child. Other prominent issues for parents include intimate partner violence, substance misuse, mental health, learning disabilities, contact with the criminal justice system, and the mother herself being subject to state care. For example, Roberts, Meakings, Forrester, Smith, and Shelton (2017) found that 27% of birth mothers and 19% of birth fathers in Wales with children placed for adoption were themselves care leavers. Thus, it is crucial to note that entering state care is not a panacea for the future well-being of a child. The majority of proceedings (over 90%) are applications for care orders, usually to place the child in state care or in adoptive placements (Harwin & Alrouh, 2017). Recently, the numbers of care cases have been increasing so rapidly that the President of the Family Court concluded that there is a 'looming crisis' (Munby, 2016). Over 43,000 birth mothers had children subject to care proceedings in the Family Court between 1 April 2007 and 31 March 2014. Broadhurst and Bedston (2017) estimate that 25.4% of women are at risk of re-appearing in care proceedings within seven years of an index episode, with the largest proportion prompted by the birth of a new baby, and mothers aged 19 or younger being the most at risk. Broadhurst et al. (2015) found that courts will remove an infant at birth far more frequently and more quickly from parents who have previously had a child removed when compared to 'first time' parents. Moreover, the Children and Families Act 2014 introduced a 26-week maximum limit for a case to be concluded in England and Wales. This means that parents (normally mothers) have a limited timeframe in which to prove they have met any conditions or made any changes required by the Local Authority, which might allow their child(ren) to remain or be returned to their care.

Remarkably, however, once care proceedings end, the mothers are effectively abandoned by the state. Children's Services do not remain involved as there is no longer a child of concern, and the Court does not monitor the provision of any of the services, be these mental health or drugs related services, recommended during the proceedings. The women involved in these cases tend not to meet the stringent criteria to access mainstream Community Mental Health services. Thus, they are left to deal with the trauma and loss of a child on their own, particularly as they may be ostracised by family and friends due to the stigma and shame of state-ordered removal. In a recent Family Court case, a young birth mother had a second child removed – a five-month baby girl – within a six-month period and placed for adoption, having experienced extreme abuse and deprivation herself but had never been offered therapeutic support. In his Judgement of what he described as a 'desperately sad case' where the mother's grief for a baby she 'loves deeply' is 'very apparent', HHJ Wildblood QC asked four critical questions:

> i) Is it right that this mother should not yet have been offered therapy, particularly bearing in mind that her first child was born three years ago and was himself the subject of lengthy proceedings?
>
> ii) If she had been offered therapy at an early stage, is there not at least a possibility that the outcome of these proceedings might have been different?
>
> iii) Even if the outcome would not have been different, would not an attempt at therapy make these proceedings more satisfactory?
>
> iv) Has the money that has been spent on issuing proceedings [£2055 is the cost of issuing a care application] and on psychological evidence [over £2000] well spent when the expenditure is incurred before attempts at therapeutic support have been made in cases of this nature. (*A Local Authority* v. *The Mother & Anor* [2017] EWFC B59)

Once their child is removed from their care, the mothers also lose any child related benefits. Furthermore, women living in social housing are at risk of losing their home once their child or children are removed due to the under-occupancy penalty (also known as the 'bedroom tax') which was introduced as part of the Welfare Reform Act 2012. In these dire circumstances, it is perhaps understandable that the women (re)turn to drugs and alcohol, remain in violent relationships, or indeed, become pregnant again as a way to ameliorate their grief. This is encapsulated in the words of one of the women in the Mothers Living Apart from their Children project:

> Instead of getting my head together and getting them back, I did the opposite and started drinking even more. I didn't care. They'd took my kids and it made me worse. I didn't care whether I lived or died. I thought my kids would be better off without me. My family wouldn't talk to me. I was disowned. I'd lost my kids. I lost my house. He was in jail. I'd lost everything. (Darby, Jones, & Beckwith, 2014, p. 29)

Thus, the loss of a child has far reaching material as well as psychological effects; what Broadhurst and Mason (2017) have described as the 'collateral consequences' of court-ordered child removal.

Being haunted

After a few weeks in the archives, reading these highly detailed and distressing accounts of mothers and children, their stories began to haunt me. The most distressing material was finding fragments of paper, handwritten letters from mothers or grandmothers, tucked within the typed bureaucratic reports, begging the Family Court Judge to let their child return home to them. The photographs within the documents were particularly haunting, as this excerpt from my fieldnotes illustrates:

> What is it about the photos that is so deeply affecting? Haunted by images. I stare at them – these photos where the children and mothers are smiling. Trying to decipher what happened, why things are going so wrong, to such an extreme. There is something about the visual that makes things more real/vivid/immediate/emotive. (Fieldnotes, 10 March 2016)

I began to 'see' the children and mothers I was reading about everywhere: on buses, trains, in shops and cafes. Outside of work, I was drawn to reading work on 'hauntology' (Derrida, 1994). Avery F. Gordon's (2008) seminal book *Ghostly Matters: Haunting and the Sociological Imagination* and an article by Debra Ferreday and Adi Kuntsman (2011) on 'haunted futures' deeply resonated with my experiences of reading the documents. To be haunted is to be in 'a heightened state of awareness; the hairs on our neck stand up: being affected by haunting, our bodies become alert, sensitive' (Ferreday & Kuntsman, 2011, p. 9). This affect had a visceral impact on me:

> The stories stay with me, haunt me, infect me, change me, impact on me (feelings of sickness, panic). (Fieldnotes, 21 February 2016)

Ghosts identify what is unsettling, difficult and painful (Gordon, 2008). In her book, Gordon (2008, pp. 23–24) explores three broad questions: first, we are part of the story – the ghost must speak to *me*; second, what does the ghost say as it speaks, barely, in the interstices of the visible and the invisible? and third, what are the alternative stories we ought to and can write about the relationship among power, knowledge and experience? This article will explore these questions in relation to the experiences of birth mothers living apart from their children following state-ordered removal. The ghost *spoke to me*: through this identification with the stories in the archives, I came to recognise that the mothers were also haunted. Being haunted is affective and magical, engendering a trans-formative recognition which brings new knowledge (Gordon, 2008). Ghosts make the political, social and economic operation of stigma visible: challenging the silencing that stigma brings, and enabling the telling of alternative stories.

Stigmatised motherhood

Mothers who have their children removed by the state are haunted by the shame of being judged to be a deeply flawed mother: 'abject figures' (Tyler, 2013) frequently stigma-tised in public forums. Here parenting is collapsed into failed mothering; an intersec-tional shaming process involving imagined moral flaws of class, gender and sexuality

(Allen & Taylor, 2012). These working class mothers are positioned as having fecund and excessive femininities (Skeggs, 2004), and become objects of disgust and repulsion. Tyler (2013) shows how disgust is political: attributed to certain bodies as part of wider social relations of power. Child protection in England is dominated by a focus on risk and risk aversion with limited attention to any economic, environmental and cultural factors (Featherstone, Gupta, Morris, & Warner, 2016). In particular, poverty is the elephant in the room in relation to child neglect (Gupta, 2017). This is in spite of the current austerity measures in the UK which are having a severe impact on the lives of low income families, particularly lone parent families, with increasing numbers struggling to provide basic essentials such as food and warmth to their children. For example, a 2017 report (Loopstra & Lalor, 2017) on surging foodbank use in the UK revealed that lone parents and their children are over-represented among people who need to use foodbanks. The report highlights the deep poverty, income insecurity, food insecurity and material deprivation of those who need to use foodbanks to feed themselves and their children.

Bywaters at al. (2016) found a strong association between children's chances of being subject to abuse or neglect and the socio-economic circumstances of their birth families. They argue that it is essential that this association 'is framed as a public issue and a matter of avoidable social inequality, not as a further source of shame and pressure on individual disadvantaged families' (Bywaters at al., 2016, p. 6). However, as Bywaters and Spark (2017) note, an inequalities perspective has only just begun to emerge in relation to child protection in the UK. It is notable that in a recent report on vulnerable children in England, the Children's Commissioner (2017) framed the 36,000 mothers in the category 'Teenage mothers aged 19 and under living with their children in 2016' as 'Children and young people whose actions put their lives at risk'. In other words, they are depicted as individually responsible, through their actions, for their own precarity and vulnerability. Thus, the structural reasons why young people may become pregnant and then struggle to be 'good enough' parents is absent in this account.

The UK government has funded a high-profile service developed specifically to work with women who have, or are at risk of, having more than one child being removed from their care. 'Pause' aims to:

> … break the cycle of repeat removal by intervening at a point when the women have no children in their care and offers them a chance to take a pause from the usual periods of chaos, anger and reaction to care proceedings … to focus on themselves with the purpose of supporting them to take control of their lives and to develop new skills and responses.[1]

It is a requirement that the women accept a Long Acting Reversible Contraceptive (LARC) in the form of a contraceptive implant for the 18 months they are part of the programme. They cannot access the well-funded resources without consenting to the LARC as this is deemed necessary to the 'success' of the project, which is predicated on working with women at a time when they do not have a child in their care or are not pregnant. Here the implication is that 'it is not deprivation and inequality which need to be "reduced", but the poor themselves' (Tyler, 2013, p. 193). Other projects working with mothers who have had a child removed, such as Mothers Living Apart from their Children and After Adoption's 'Breaking the Cycle',[2] do not require them to accept a

LARC. Notably, it is Pause that is being rolled out nationally, recently securing £6.8m of funding from the Department for Education's Innovation Fund to further extend its reach. For Pause, success is measured in the numbers of *babies not born* and these calculated numbers of unborn babies are awarded a monetary value, and are used as a primary measure of the success of the programme. For example, their Chief Executive recently specified that: 'Pause has supported 137 women – without the intervention of Pause, this group of women would have been likely to have had 27 more children taken into care per year at a cost of over £1.5 million a year to the tax payer' (Hillier, 2017). Within this calculative framework, controlling the reproductive lives of working class mothers in ways which curtail future claims upon the state is construed as a policy solution to the imagined (moral) problem of their 'failed parenting' and 'welfare dependency'. Poverty is recast as an outcome of maternal biology (Gillies, Edwards, & Horsley, 2017; White & Wastell, 2016).

Haunted motherhood

State-ordered removal disrupts the expected future for both the children and their birth mothers. For the mothers, this is a unique form of loss and trauma as their child has not died but is living elsewhere, often for the entirety of their childhood. The women are mothers and their children are alive but they are not even allowed to know where their children are living. The children are a 'ghostly presence': there and not there at the same time (Gordon, 2008, p. 6). 'Annie', the birth mother introduced above, had her newborn baby forcibly taken from her under a court order whilst she was in the maternity ward. Annie was sent home in a taxi, without her four-day-old baby, alone, bleeding, breasts leaking milk. In her blog, Surviving Safeguarding, 'Annie' (2015) writes: 'It was like a death every time I had to leave my baby after contact. … It was like I was grieving, whilst my child was still alive, all the time having to keep fighting.' Elsewhere, 'Annie' remembers 'looking outside at the sky and knowing my children were under it – but that was all I knew' (A Safeguarding Survivor, 2017a, p. 129). Furthermore, the mothers are unable to follow the customary grief rituals of bereavement as their child has not died but is alive, but somewhere unknown. Here, the past, present and future of motherhood is co-present, as a poem by one of the mothers from the Mothers Living Apart from their Children project makes clear:

> We aren't classed as mothers.
> We have no rights.
> We don't feel we have a job as a mum anymore.
> Our homes are dead…
> Being a mum never goes away in our hearts and mind.
> We have feelings.
> We have a heart. Shock anger, emotion, crying, powerless…
> Where are they now?
> We have to let them know some way we're still here for them. (Darby et al., 2014, p. 74)

The mothers exist in a state of *haunted motherhood*, living for an imagined future when their child reaches adulthood. Some have tattoos of their child's name inscribed on their skin, buy presents, and write letters to their child in preparation for reunification. Another of the mothers from the project explains that:

> I've written my daughter a letter every week to let her know she's in my thoughts and when she's older she can have them. (Darby et al., 2014, p. 77)

A third mother from the project explains how she has made her son an album:

> I put his birth certificate in his album tucked behind a photograph of me and him. No-one would know it was there. I put it there for him. (Darby et al., 2014, p. 88)

These mothers exist in the present for an anticipated future with their child; thus, their past, present and future become mutually intertwined (Urry, 2016). The mothers are living for an imagined future; one which may not even happen. This anticipated future absorbs the present. Thus, haunting is not just a matter of the past or even the present, haunting is also a matter of the future (Ferreday & Kuntsman, 2011).

A scheme called 'Letterbox Contact' allows two-way indirect contact between birth families and children who have been adopted and is set out in the final care plan as part of the court process. It usually takes the form of a letter once a year. Obviously this can be both a positive and a profoundly difficult letter for the mothers to compose and to receive. One of the women from the Mothers Living Apart from their Children project discusses a letter she had just received from her youngest daughter who had been adopted:

> She told me she looks like the princess from Disney's *Tangle*. She can write her own name, knows her colours, can ride a bike. Now when I'm out, I find myself searching for a little girl with blond hair. Social Services wouldn't let me have the photo the foster carers took of her. (Darby et al., 2014, p. 62)

Here the mother is viscerally haunted by her imagined visualisation of her daughter. In place of a photograph, and not having seen her daughter since she was adopted, she can only conceive of how she looks now based on a cartoon figure from a Disney film. Another mother from the project writes:

> I dreamed of getting my girls back. … But in my dreams it was always my four year old and two year old I got back. Last year after letter box contact with my girls, I finally got a photograph. … They were babies and now they are beaming young mothers themselves. So, that makes me a grandma and I can only hope I will be able to play a big part in their lives as I couldn't with my girls. (Darby et al., 2014, p. 88)

In her dreams, her daughters have been suspended in time as the young children she last saw before they were adopted. This apparition was only dispelled by the material evidence in the photograph. This mother is hoping for the possibility of a future where her maternality can be restored through caring for her grandchildren. These birth mothers, stigmatised as failed mothers, exist in the margins, longing for a future of successful reconciliation with their children. Thus, while ghosts usually represent a traumatic loss, ghosts also simultaneously represent future possibilities and hope (Gordon, 2008).

Stigmatised futures

During care proceedings, several imagined futures for the child(ren) will be anticipated and contested by the professionals involved in the case. For example, in any one Family Court case, consideration might be given to the child being rehabilitated back home to their mother from foster care, moving to live with their father, being placed with a relative (often a grandmother) under a Special Guardianship Order, or being adopted. Each of these possible futures will be forensically examined in turn, with the judge deciding on the plan for that child's future until they reach adulthood. Many of these children are babies removed at birth on the basis of protection from *future* significant harm. Indeed, decisions about these children are made *pre-birth*, about babies yet to be born. In other words, as with 'Annie's' baby, the child has not been subject to any actual abuse and neglect, the risk of the abuse or neglect is all deemed to be *in the future*. These alternative imagined futures are often set out in the Family Court Judgement made at the conclusion of the case. Thus, here futures are not merely imagined, they are *made*, with concrete material consequences for the lives of the mothers and children who are subject to the court orders. The objective of these imagined futures for the child is to *pre-empt* a particular happening from a range of possible futures (Amoore, 2013). However, the child may return to court as the envisaged future does not transpire as intended and a further future has to be anticipated and legislated for in a new set of proceedings.

Furthermore, the mothers are painfully aware that any future pregnancy will also be subject to child protection procedures; thus, even their *future motherhood* continues to be stigmatised by their past. In these circumstances, a mother may seek to conceal her next pregnancy in an attempt to take back control of her own future motherhood. Mothers who attempt to conceal a subsequent pregnancy in this way do so with the plan of successfully caring for their baby for a period of time in order to demonstrate that they are capable of being a 'good mother'. While the notion of 'concealed pregnancy' has been explored in the literature in terms of women hiding their pregnancy due to *not* wanting to become a mother, the consideration of concealment as an attempt *to keep* a baby is an under-examined concept. However, for child protection social workers, any attempt by a mother to conceal a pregnancy is viewed negatively and is very likely to increase the possibility of an application for removal at birth. Thus, such endeavours to exercise one's own agency 'often lead to further cycles of punishment and capture' (Tyler, 2013, p. 12).

Stigma, futures and power

Thus, the practitioners involved in care proceedings are engaged in *future-work*: imagining alternative futures for these children. Crucially, they have the *power* to 'make futures'. Urry (2016, p. 11) contends that a 'key question for social science is who or what owns the future – this capacity to own futures being central in how power works'. Here the power to determine futures lies with the state in the form of Family Court Judges, child protection social workers, barristers, Children's Guardians and court appointed experts such as psychologists and psychiatrists: 'those with institutional authority … who are in a position to give official imprint to versions of reality' (Goffman, 1983, p. 17).

For the practitioners involved in the Family Courts, planning for a child's future is simply 'business as usual'. Indeed, thinking futures and making futures can be seen as the *raison d'être* of child protection practices: these practitioners are 'specialists of the future' (Urry, 2016). While the future is elusive and cannot be accessed, known or controlled (Lyon & Carabelli, 2016), the anticipating and/or predicting of futures is specifically what the practitioners involved in child protection are doing through their decision-making practices. Moreover, although the future is an analytical object and thus 'not simply a neutral temporal space into which objective expectations can be projected' (Brown & Michael, 2003, p. 4), this is precisely the work that the court process is attempting to accomplish. The decision detailed in each Judgement clearly delineates the planned future for a child. Notably, however, for each of these futures that are taken to avoid a 'wicked future', there is a shadow of another possible future which is not taken (Tutton, 2017). However, it is crucial to note that children actually are sometimes abused and neglected in material ways by their parents; and it is the practitioners involved in the child protection system who are responsible for making decisions about these difficult and complex matters. Indeed, if a child dies, these practitioners are blamed and shamed.

Thus, there is a *politics and ethics* to futurity in relation to the making and remaking of inequality (Coleman & Tutton, 2017). Future visions are incredibly contested, saturated with conflicting social interests and have powerful consequences (Urry, 2016). This is markedly the case in relation to the mothers; having a child forcibly removed from your care can be almost too hard to bear. This is the shadow of future making: future taking (Adam & Groves, 2007). Although the state is a constellation of embodied practices (Tyler, 2013), as the Family Court hearings are closed to protect the privacy of the children, it is not possible for members of the public to observe these practices. The President of the Family Court has called for greater transparency, issuing Guidance to increase the number of Judgements available for publication in order to improve public understanding and confidence of the court process (Munby, 2014). However, Doughty, Twaite, and Magrath (2017) found that only 837 cases had been published in the two years following the Guidance, forming a tiny minority of Judgements given that between 11,000 and 12,000 children are involved in care proceedings each year. Even where Judgements are published, the anonymity of the child and members of their family must be strictly preserved and failure to do so is a contempt of court. This means that the proceedings inevitably become shrouded in an air of mystery and secrecy.

Moreover, the shame and stigma associated with having a child removed means that the mothers themselves often remain silent – or are forcibly silenced through being made subject to court-ordered reporting restrictions. 'Annie' is not allowed to use her real name or those of her children when she writes or speaks as a result of reporting restrictions made by the Family Court; thus, her very identity is directly controlled by the state and her everyday life is 'saturated with state power' (Tyler, 2013, p. 68). 'Annie' cannot even name her son who suddenly died very recently:

> I would not, could not, have started [writing] without the support of my eldest son. Because there remains, for now, a Reporting Restriction Order in place forbidding me, I cannot tell you

his name though I dearly, dearly long to. I have no choice, for now, to refer to him as 'Peter'. (A Safeguarding Survivor, 2017b)

This is a 'testimonial quieting' (Dotson, 2011, p. 242): stigma as a governmental form of classification and badging with the power to silence and constrain the (m)other (Tyler, this monograph issue). In their study of child protection, Smithson and Gibson (2017) found that the use of power by social workers – through the threat of consequences – minimised dissent, silenced parents and coerced others into signing agreements they were not actually in agreement with. Furthermore, the parents felt that they were belittled and treated as 'less than human'. These practices are part of state 'stigmacraft' – Tyler's (this issue) historical, political and economic deployments of stigma as technologies of de-humanisation.

Revolting subjects? Stigma as silencing

In her book, *Revolting Subjects*, Tyler (2013) emphasises the dual meanings of social abjection and revolt:

> ... the processes through which minoritized populations are imagined and figured as revolting and become subject to control, stigma and censure, and the practices through which individuals and groups resist, reconfigure and revolt against their abject subjectification. (Tyler, 2013, p. 4)

This section will explore the latter: how do the mothers resist, reconfigure and revolt? In their books, Tyler (2013) and Gordon (2008) both highlight mothers who revolt in the latter sense: respectively, mothers in the Yarl's Wood Immigration Removal Centre in England, and The Mothers of the Plaza de Mayo, an association of Argentine mothers whose children 'disappeared' during the state terrorism of the military dictatorship between 1976 and 1983. There are some parallels with these mothers and the birth mothers who are the focus of this article. In an interview with Tyler (2013, p. 116), one of the Yarl's Wood mothers describes how she was 'dead inside' and 'living dead'. This resonates with the experiences of the birth mothers who have had their children removed. As Joanna Latimer (this issue) argues, this can be seen as a 'body–world relation where becoming the living dead ... is an effect of how a person is stigmatized, emplaced and sequestrated by the biopolitics of late modern capitalism'. The women are positioned as less than human; their 'existence is cut to the bone' (Goffman, 1991, p. 268). However, being part of a naked protest at Yarl's Wood brought the mother 'back to life': the mothers 'stripped naked in a deliberate impersonation of their dehumanization in order to refute it' (Tyler, 2013, p. 117). In contrast, as it is a closed court, the birth mothers have to appear in the Family Court as individuals rather than as a collective. They are terrified that the outcome of the proceedings will be their child being removed so it is highly unlikely that they do anything that will jeopardise any possibility of reunification. The very real possibility of state-ordered child removal means that the mothers are silenced and any public protest is unlikely. Moreover, the very real threat of *future* children being removed compounds this silencing.

The Mothers of the Plaza de Mayo appropriated traditional norms of motherhood, protesting while wearing white shawls with the names of disappeared children and wore or carried photographs on their bodies. Gordon (2008, p. 128) argues that The Mothers recognised that haunting was central to their protest: achieving this through their ability 'to see in the face of the disappeared, or in a photo of a face, the ghost of the state's brutal authority and simultaneously the ghost of the utopian impulse the state has tried to suppress'. We have seen that the birth mothers are also haunted by photographs and imagined depictions of their children. They also carry images and the names of their children on their body in the form of tattoos. The tattoos can be seen as a literal stigma, potentially making the loss visible to others. However, the tattoos are intimate and secret, hidden on parts of the body kept invisible, or concealed in the form of symbols and images which embody the absent child. Here stigma is a form of silencing; compounded by silencing as part of the legal process through enforced anonymity and the justifiable fear of future children being removed.

However, Gordon's (2008) writing on the notion of 'disappearance' is particularly germane to making sense of the experiences of the birth mothers. Like the birth mothers, The Mothers of the Plaza de Mayo had a visceral kinship connection with their children who were missing but overwhelmingly present. Here too, temporality is merged and the distinction between the living and the dead is contravened. As with the birth mothers, this connection is affective: 'Disappearance was all around them, they smelled it, they sensed it, they felt its bewitching compulsion: it was threatening to envelop them' (Gordon, 2008, p. 113). There are further parallels: their children have disappeared through enforced absence and fearful silence. Finally, Gordon concludes that:

> Although the disappeared are only supposed to intimidate this menacing state power, the ghost cannot be so completely managed. Because making contact with the disappeared means encountering the spectre of what the state has tried to repress. (Gordon, 2008, p. 127)

Thus, in answer to Gordon's (2011) second question, the ghosts make visible how social, political and economic policies impact on mothers and their children. Moreover, haunting creates conditions that also invite action: there becomes a critical analytic moment where there is a demand for re-narrativisation and a telling of alternative stories (Gordon, 2011). It is one of the contentions of this article that making the haunting experiences of these birth mothers knowable and visible is a political project, inasmuch as it contributes to demands for better understanding of the structural causes and consequences, such as poverty and male intimate partner violence, which lead to court-ordered removals in the first place.

The ordinary magic of living with ghosts

The trauma of court-ordered child removal can, understandably, mire the mothers in a swamp of pain, shame and regret: a 'speechless bare life' (Tyler, 2013, p. 116) of enforced silencing. However, haunting, unlike trauma, is distinctive for producing a 'something-to-be-done': namely, a means of reclaiming the living present and the possibilities of potential futures through individual, social or political movement and change (Gordon, 2011). Leder's (2000) work with prison inmates, mainly serving life sentences in maximum security prisons in the US, is relevant here. Many of the inmates described living in the past or the future:

Quite a few guys try to live in the past. I like living in the future, thinking about what my life is going to be. But I think one thing most of us try to avoid is the *present*. Because the present is the most painful. (Leder, 2000, p. 86)

The inmates described this as 'time doing you'. For the mothers this involves dwelling on the past whilst dreaming of a future, with the present as a living dead. In contrast, 'doing time' is where the living present is reclaimed, as another inmate explains: 'To me, time is like a dragon I have to slay. If I can master the present, I will have used my time to *redeem* time' (Leder, 2000, p. 86). The challenge is to remain in the present and listen to what the ghosts are revealing (Ferreday & Kuntsman, 2011). For the women in the Mothers Living Apart from their Children project, this staying in the present can come from the commonality of being part of the group. As one mother explains through a poem:

in the stillness we listen
her words splintered with tears…
they hold each other laugh cry
they use ordinary magic
to keep the room safe
strong and clever women
who understand what it is
to be broken. (Darby et al., 2014, p. 87)

Thus, groups such as Mothers Living Apart from their Children, After Adoption's 'Breaking the Cycle' and the organisation Match Mothers[3] (Mothers Apart from Their Children) provide spaces where mothers can meet with others who are living with similar experiences. For example, Match Mothers recognise the isolation of being a mother apart from her children and state:

You are not alone and do not have to take the journey of being a mother apart on your own … we can offer you a confidential, safe and secure environment for you to discuss your situation with other mothers in the same situation.[4]

This collectivity of mothers living apart from their children, sharing their experiences of grief and haunting, and in doing so negotiating the stigma of been deemed 'failed mothers' by the state, can be seen as a form of 'maternal commons' (Tyler, 2013). Living with ghosts collectively in this way can allow for re-narrativisations; enabling the mothers to develop the consciousness that the situations in which they found themselves were often outside of their 'control' or 'choices' in any simple way, revealing the absence of resources and the deep structural inequalities in which they live. Anonymous blogs such as the one by 'Annie' make clear the inhumane nature of removal of a newborn baby, thus rupturing the often hidden and taken for granted practices of the current child protection process and forcing a retelling of child removal. It is important to make clear that this is not to deny or minimise the lived reality of children who are experiencing neglect and abuse. Instead, the re-narrativisation by the mothers challenges the dominant neoliberal discourse that child neglect is a result of parental pathology and individual blame which obscures the structural inequalities and poverty in which many vulnerable families live (Gupta, 2017). How many children might stay with their mothers in the context of a more equal distribution of resources and a strong welfare state with comprehensive services to support families? Featherstone, White, and Morris (2014) call for humane child protection practices where the child is seen as a relational being and there is recognition and support for families through community engagement and community development. Engaging with the sensory and affectivity imbued in haunting can probe, provoke and stimulate new imaginations of the future (Coleman, 2017). Thus, when we 'open ourselves to being haunted, we might find that the present and its possibilities are transformed, with radical consequences' (Ferreday & Kuntsman, 2011, p. 8).

Conclusion

My engagement with ghosts began when the stories of the birth mothers and children began to haunt me. The ghosts spoke to me; unsettled and disturbed me; but enabled a transformative recognition that the mothers may also be understood as being haunted. I have argued that women who have had their children removed exist in a state of haunted motherhood, suspended in the shadowlands where the living and the invisible coexist, and temporality is both disrupted and merged. Being haunted is overwhelming and affective, and almost impossible to put into words. Their children are there and yet not there; they are living and yet out of reach and invisible. Furthermore, the mothers are silenced by shame and the justifiable fear of future children also being removed through the Family Court system. Thus, stigma not only impacts on the mothers' pasts and presents, their very futures are stigmatised. The lens of haunted futures has also allowed for making visible the taken for granted child protection practices of creating futures. The ability to create futures is suffused with state power. This engagement with the future is an encounter with an intangible world but one that has very real and material consequences for the past, present and future lives of the mothers and their children.

However, ghosts appear at the interstices of the barely visible, alerting us to what has been concealed. While the ghost signifies a traumatic loss, it also simultaneously represents hope and future possibilities of transformation through a demand for re-narrativisation through the telling of alternative stories (Gordon, 2008). The creation of spaces for the mothers to speak collectively – or individually in blogs – about their experiences can foster a maternal commons, challenging the isolation, shame and stigma of being a mother living apart from her children. This ending of enforced silencing can be a political act, making visible how structural inequalities and governmental policies such as austerity impact on the lives of the most vulnerable families in the UK and countering the stigma caused by individualising and pathologising mothers. Thus, re-narrativisation makes clear the profound inhumanity of child removal in the context of poverty and the absence of any support for these families. To conclude with the words of Avery Gordon (2008, p. 208): 'ultimately haunting is about how to transform a shadow of a life into an undiminished life whose shadows touch softly in the spirit of a peaceful reconciliation'.

Acknowledgement

For Nina.

Funding

This research received no specific grant from any funding agency in the public, commercial, or not-for-profit sectors.

Notes

1. http://www.pause.org.uk/aboutpause/model
2. http://www.afteradoption.org.uk/birthparentsupport/birthties/breaking-the-cycle/
3. http://www.matchmothers.org/
4. http://www.matchmothers.org/images/rosalind3.pdf

References

A Safeguarding Survivor. (2017a). The birth parent's perspective. In A. Elvin & M. Barrow (Eds.), *Welcome to fostering: A guide to becoming and being a foster carer* (pp. 127–131). London, UK: Jessica Kingsley.

A Safeguarding Survivor. (2017b, October 9). *Primum non nocere – First, do no harm.* http://survivingsafeguarding.co.uk/2017/10/09/do-no-harm/ (last accessed 3 May 2018).

Adam, B., & Groves, C. (2007). *Future matters: Action, knowledge, ethics.* Amsterdam, The Netherlands: Brill Books.

Allen, K., & Taylor, Y. (2012). Placing parenting, locating unrest: Failed femininities, troubled mothers and riotous subjects. *Studies in the Maternal, 4*(2), Retrieved from www.mamsie.bbk.ac.uk (last accessed 3 May 2018).

Amoore, L. (2013). *The politics of possibility: Risk and security beyond probability.* Durham, NC: Duke University Press.

Broadhurst, K., Alrouh, B., Yeend, E., Harwin, J., Shaw, M., Pilling, M., & Kershaw, S. (2015). Connecting events in time to identify a hidden population. *British Journal of Social Work, 45*, 2241–2260.

Broadhurst, K., & Bedston, S. (2017). Women in recurrent care proceedings in England (2007–2016): Continuity and change in care demand over time. *Family Law*, April, 412–415.

Broadhurst, K., & Mason, C. (2017). Birth parents and the collateral consequences of court-ordered child removal: Towards a comprehensive framework. *International Journal of Law, Policy and the Family, 31*, 41–59.

Brown, N., & Michael, M. (2003). A sociology of expectations: Retrospective prospects and prospecting retrospectives. *Technology Analysis and Strategic Management, 15*, 3–18.

Bywaters, P., Bunting, L., Davidson, G., Hanratty, J., Mason, W., McCartan, S., & Steils, N. (2016). *The relationship between poverty, child abuse and neglect: an evidence review.* York, UK: Joseph Rowntree Foundation.

Bywaters, P., & Sparks, T. (2017). Child protection in England: An emerging inequalities perspective. *Journal of Children's Services, 12*, 107–112.

Children's Commissioner for England. (2017). *On measuring the number of vulnerable children in England.* London, UK: Author .

Coleman, R. (2017). A sensory sociology of the future: Affect, hope and inventive methodologies. *The Sociological Review.* Advance online publication. doi:10.1111/1467–954X.12445

Coleman, R., & Tutton, R. (2017). Introduction [Special issue: Futures in question: Theories, methods, practices]. *The Sociological Review.* Advance online publication. doi:10.1111/1467–954X.12448

Darby, D., Jones, K., & Beckwith, S. (2014). *In our hearts: Stories and wisdom of mothers who live apart from their children*. Huddersfield, UK: Women's Centre Calderdale and Kirklees.

Derrida, J. (1994). *Specters of Marx: The state of the debt, the work of mourning, and the new international* (P. Kamuf, Trans.). New York, NY: Routledge.

Dotson, K. (2011). Tracking epistemic violence, tracking practices of silencing. *Hypatia, 26*, 236–257.

Doughty, J., Twaite, A., & Magrath, P. (2017). *Transparency through publication of family court judgments: An evaluation of the responses to, and effects of, judicial guidance on publishing family court judgments involving children and young people*. Cardiff, UK: Cardiff University.

Featherstone, B., White, S., & Morris, K. (2014). *Re-imagining child protection*. Bristol, UK: Policy Press.

Featherstone, B., Gupta, A., Morris, K., & Warner, J. (2016). Let's stop feeding the risk monster: Towards a social model of 'child protection'. *Families, Relationships and Societies*. Advance online publication. doi:10.1332/204674316X14552878034622

Ferreday, D., & Kuntsman, A. (2011). Introduction: Haunted futurities. *Borderlands, 10*. Retrieved from http://www.borderlands.net.au/vol10no2_2011/ferrkun_intro.pdf (last accessed 7 May 2018).

Gillies, V., Edwards, R., & Horsley, N. (2017). *Challenging the politics of early intervention: Who's 'saving' children and why*. Bristol, UK: Policy Press.

Goffman, E. (1983). The interaction order: American Sociological Association, 1982 Presidential Address. *American Sociological Review, 48*, 1–17.

Goffman, E. (1991). *Asylums: Essays on the social situation of mental patients and other inmates*. Harmondsworth, UK: Penguin.

Gordon, A. F. (2008). *Ghostly matters: Haunting and the sociological imagination*. Minneapolis: University of Minnesota Press.

Gordon, A. F. (2011). Some thoughts on haunting and futurity. *Borderlands, 10*. Retrieved from http://www.borderlands.net.au/vol10no2_2011/gordon_thoughts.pdf (last accessed 7 May 2018).

Gupta, A. (2017). Poverty and child neglect – the elephant in the room? *Families, Relationships and Societies, 6*, 21–36.

Harwin, J., & Alrouh, B. (2017, April). New entrants and repeat children: Continuity and change in care demand over time. *Family Law*, pp. 407–411.

Hillier, J. (2017). Learning and evaluation. Retrieved from http://www.pause.org.uk/pause-in-action/learning-and-evaluation (last accessed 3 May 2018).

Leder, D. (2000). *The soul knows no bars: Inmates reflect on life, death, and hope*. Lanham, MD: Rowman & Littlefield.

Loopstra, R., & Lalor, D. (2017). *Financial insecurity, food insecurity, and disability: The profile of people receiving emergency food assistance from The Trussell Trust Foodbank Network in Britain*. Salisbury, UK: Trussell Trust Foodbank Network.

Lyon, D., & Carabelli, G. (2016). Researching young people's orientations to the future: The methodological challenges of using arts practice. *Qualitative Research, 16*, 430–445.

Munby, J. (2014). *Transparency in the family courts: Publications of Judgments. Practice guidance*. Retrieved from https://www.judiciary.gov.uk/wp-content/uploads/2014/01/transparency-in-the-family-courts-jan-2014–1.pdf (last accessed 3 May 2018).

Munby, J. (2016). *15th view from the President's Chambers: Care Cases – the looming crisis*. Retrieved from https://www.judiciary.gov.uk/wp-content/uploads/2014/08/pfd-view-15-care-cases-looming-crisis.pdf (last accessed 3 May 2018).

Roberts, L., Meakings, S., Forrester, D., Smith, A., & Shelton, K. (2017). Care-leavers and their children placed for adoption. *Children and Youth Services Review, 79*, 355–361.

Skeggs, B. (2004). *Class, self, culture*. Abingdon, UK: Routledge.

Smithson, R., & Gibson, M. (2017). Less than human: A qualitative study into the experience of parents involved in the child protection system. *Child and Family Social Work, 22*, 565–574.

Tutton, R. (2017). Wicked futures: Meaning, matter and the sociology of the future. *The Sociological Review*. Advance online publication. doi:10.1111/1467–954X.12443

Tyler, I. (2013). *Revolting subjects: Social abjection and resistance in neoliberal Britain*. London, UK: Zed Books.

Urry, J. (2016). *What is the future?* Cambridge, UK: Polity Press.

White, S. J., & Wastell, D. G. (2016). Epigenetics prematurely born(e): Social work and the malleable gene. *The British Journal of Social Work*. Advance online publication. doi.org/10.1093/bjsw/bcw157

Author biography

Lisa Morriss is a Lecturer in Social Work in the College of Social Sciences, University of Birmingham. Her research and teaching are concerned with mental health, stigma, motherhood, social futures, and qualitative methodologies.

The
Sociological
Review
Monographs

The Sociological Review Monographs
2018, Vol. 66(4) 114–138
© The Author(s) 2018
Reprints and permissions:
sagepub.co.uk/journalsPermissions.nav
DOI: 10.1177/0038026118777422
journals.sagepub.com/home/sor

Repelling neoliberal world-making? How the ageing–dementia relation is reassembling the social

Joanna Latimer
University of York, UK

Abstract

Growing old 'badly' is stigmatizing, a truism that is enrolled into contemporary agendas for the biomedicalization of ageing. Among the many discourses that emphasize ageing as the root cause of later life illnesses, dementia is currently promoted as an epidemic and such hyperbole serves to legitimate its increasing biomedicalization. The new stigma however is no longer contained to simply having dementia, it is failing to prevent it. Anti-ageing cultures of consumption, alongside a proliferation of cultural depictions of the ageing–dementia relation, seem to be refiguring dementia as a future to be worked on to eliminate it from our everyday life. The article unpacks this complexity for how the ageing–dementia relation is being reassembled in biopolitics in ways that enact it as something that can be transformed and managed. Bringing together Bauman's theories of how cultural communities cope with the otherness of the other with theories of the rationale for the making of monsters – such as the figure of the abject older person with dementia – the article suggests that those older body-persons that personify the ageing–dementia relation, depicted in film and television for example, threaten the modes of ordering underpinning contemporary lives. This is not just because they intimate loss of mind, or because they are disruptive, but because they do not perform what it is to be 'response-able' and postpone frailty through managing self and risk.

Keywords

anthropoemic, anthropophagic, biopolit, monsters, parade, response-ability

Introduction

In this article I examine the social and existential significance of an emergent biopolitics around the ageing–dementia relation and argue that this politics represents a shift from

Corresponding author:
Joanna Latimer, Department of Sociology, University of York, Wentworth College, Heslington, York, YO10 5DD, UK.
Email: joanna.latimer@york.ac.uk

emic to phagic strategies for incorporating, assimilating and transforming the Otherness that the ageing–dementia relation is made to represent. Specifically, the play upon the negative and stigmatizing effects and affects of the ageing–dementia relation runs along-side intense media, neurocultural and public health discourses that emphasize how age-ing, and specifically dementia, are plastic and malleable, and critically, if not preventable, manageable and postponable.

Public health policy worldwide represents Alzheimer's Disease, hereafter AD, as not only wrecking individual lives, but as a global 'epidemic' that threatens the social order (e.g. Alzheimer's Disease International, 2015). Most recently it has been claimed by the UK's Office for National Statistics that AD and dementia have become the major cause of death in England and Wales (Siddique, 2016). As Baroness Greengross (2014) suggests, ageing when it is associated with dementia is doubly stigmatizing:

> We know in many societies that there are strong associations with ageing and stigma and for those with dementia, it seems many are subject to a 'double jeopardy'. While this stigma to a degree is acknowledged and recognised in some communities, we still have much to understand about why dementia remains outside the realm of acceptable everyday conversation even as the profile of dementia rises. (p. 6)

The stigma of what I am calling the ageing–dementia relation has become such a truism that recent research suggests doctors charged with early detection of dementia are reluctant to give someone a dementia diagnosis because of its existential potency and potential for discrimination (Gove, Downs, Vernooij-Dassen, & Small, 2016). As Margaret Lock (2014) asserts, Alzheimer's and other Alzheimer-like dementias personify all that is most feared about growing old, a fear widely expressed in research on ageing and experiences of ageing (e.g. Bazalgette, Holden, Tew, Hubble, & Morrison, 2011). This fear is crystallized in associating the dementia–ageing rela-tion with the hollowing out of personhood (Halewood, 2016; Katz & Peters, 2008; Kontos, 2005), and with representing it as 'a living death' (Behuniak, 2011). Behuniak goes so far as to argue that it is the social construction of those with AD as zombies that:

> … generates not only negative stereotypes and stigma associated with people constructed as 'other', but also the emotional responses of disgust and utter terror. It is this politics of revulsion and fear that directly infuses the discourse about AD and shapes it. (p. 72)

Stigma is not an inherent quality of some aged and/or ill persons – it is a relation. In Goffman (1963), stigmatization, including processes of discrimination, occurs when there is a lack of fit between a body-person and the worlds of others by which they find themselves marginalized. Inasmuch as they have difficulty in passing as 'one of us', their identity is despoiled. As Twigg (2000) amongst others has asserted, the ageing body can be experienced as disgusting and repulsive because it represents deviation from what is most cherished in modernity and contemporary preoccupations with specific forms of personhood:

> Modern individualism rests on the construction of persons as self-contained, bounded entities. Incontinence and bodily disintegration threaten this. … Smell and disintegration undermine individualistic constructions of the person as stable, bounded and autonomous. (pp. 396–397)

Moreover, the parade of 'monsters' (Canguilhem, 2008) or 'revolting subjects' (Tyler, 2013) which invoke 'social disgust' (Lawler, 2005) should not be understood merely as responses to the breach in the social order that older persons with dementia invoke. Rather, proliferating media representations of older people with dementia are created spectacles of 'othering' that reaffirm the values and modes of ordering that underpin dominant forms of world-making. What is at stake in feelings of social disgust and the making of monsters is the very production and reproduction of values and moral forms. In some respects, the figure of the demented older person resembles the Sacra (Turner, 1967) – figures whose potency is exaggerated by their magnification, and which are paraded during rites of passage in order to impress those who see them with the values treasured by the culture they are to help reproduce. But in contrast, in the case of dementia, the monsters are figures that somehow contravene what is most sacred. Growing old badly, especially growing old with dementia, thus can be made to represent a deviant act – forms of otherness that are punishable by stigmatization and isolation (Schmidt, 2011) – because it contravenes what is most cherished.

Bauman (2000, 2001), drawing upon Lévi-Strauss, suggests that there are two ways of coping with the otherness of others: the strategies known as the emic (anthropoemic) and the phagic (anthropophagic). While phagic strategies involve assimilation of some kind, the emic consists of:

> … 'vomiting', spitting out the others seen as incurably strange and alien: barring physical contact, dialogue, social intercourse and all varieties of *commercium, commensality* or *connubium.* (Bauman, 2000, p. 101)

In the context of ageing, the abject demented older person represents someone who is being spat out on the basis of seeming incurably strange and alien:

> … personal losses and interpersonal ravages … replete with cliched metaphors and representations in which Alzheimer's is characteristically drawn in colourfully dramatic terms that paint vividly disturbing images of a monstrous disease. (Herskovits, 1995, p. 152)

Such monsters have to be 'sequestrated' (Giddens, 1991) – hidden away, contained. Social disgust and the creation of revolting subjects remain social processes of othering: processes in which there is a moral demand to 'efface the face' (Bauman, 1990; Latimer, 1997), and which pivot around how this 'other' is no longer fully human.

In what follows, I show how the creation of monsters, such as that bodied forth by the ageing–dementia relation, forms the background against which dominant versions of what it is to age well are being performed. I go on to suggest that there is currently a global reassembling of the dementia–ageing relation that – as at the same time as it normalizes the stigmatizing effects and affects of dementia – can also be understood as a second strategy available in the face of breaches to the social order. What Bauman calls the phagic (anthropophagic strategy) aims at the assimilation of *otherness*. So, rather than try to exile the other, this second strategy consists in:

> ... 'ingesting', 'devouring' foreign bodies and spirits so that they may be made, through metabolism, identical with, and no more distinguishable, from the 'ingesting' body. (Bauman, 2001, p. 24)

In the context of the relation between ageing and dementia, and the prediction that one in four of us will become demented by the time we are 80, emic strategies alone are no longer feasible. This is particularly so in the context of a current political climate designed to reduce rather than expand the state supported care sector. It is not just that there are not enough 'asylums' to go round, there are going to be fewer and fewer places of refuge and care for a supposedly growing population of older people figured as potential 'bedblockers' (see also Skeggs, 2017).

My original research focused on 'bedblocking' (Latimer, 1997, 1999, 2000a, 2000b) as a critical site: it illuminated the boundary work and struggles around those older people who have an acute episode of illness and are admitted to acute health services, but whose troubles can be marked as inappropriate for health care, with their needs redefined as 'personal' and/or 'social'. That study was in the 1990s. The availability of care and support in hospitals, residential homes, or in the home, is even more problematic in post-welfare societies (see for example the essays in Ceci, Purkis, & Björnsdóttir, 2011), creating even greater problems over who or what is responsible for the care and support of older people, especially older people with dementia. Under these conditions, the stigma of the dementia–ageing relation is being intensified, particularly when older people are associated with care reduced, over and over again, to its economic costs (see Figure 2, which illustrates how dementia is being figured in term of its costs – there are many, many more). Being old, demented and costly, then, potentiates the stigma of the dementia–ageing relation.

Thus, alongside the making of monsters, associations between different domains in which dementia is being reconstructed mean that dementia increasingly haunts the public imagination, including the endless invocation to age well instead of badly. Through modes of prevention, including technoscientific interventions, the goal is always to transform, even annihilate the 'foreign bodies and spirits' that dementia represents. In contrast to the literature that objects to the medicalization of ageing and of dementia, the genealogy here suggests that biomedicalization is not just helping to partially deactivate stigma (see for example Macrae, 1999; Seale, 1996) but is helping to assemble new social formations (e.g. Bond, 1992) through which to assimilate and transform dementia.[1]

I begin with analysis of a short film about Gladys Wilson and Naomi Feil that as at the same time as it appears to parade the abject older person with dementia as all that is most feared about growing old, also helps reveal a conundrum deep at the heart of the dementia–ageing relation and possibilities for the emergence of new social relations through which to reassimilate the ageing–dementia relation. I go on to show how the contemporary dominant classification of 'ageing well' rests upon complex associations. The widespread enactment of dominant notions of what counts as successful ageing (including prolonged productivity, heightened activity, self-determination, mastery of information technologies, competition of all kinds, youthful vigour and glowing health) acts as valued forms of personhood alongside actor-networks of public health, biomedicine, neuroscience and cultures of consumption that are bringing ageing and dementia into being as a bioscientific object. Together they establish that ageing is plastic, not inevitable; something to be transformed, or at least have its worst ravages postponed.

The old fools

… That is where they live:
Not here and now, but where all happened once.
                    This is why they give
An air of baffled absence, trying to be there
Yet being here. For the rooms grow farther, leaving
Incompetent cold, the constant wear and tear
Of taken breath, and them crouching below
Extinction's alp, the old fools, never perceiving
How near it is. This must be what keeps them quiet:
The peak that stays in view wherever we go
For them is rising ground. Can they never tell
What is dragging them back, and how it will end? Not at night?
Not when the strangers come? Never, throughout
The whole hideous inverted childhood? Well,
We shall find out.

(Larkin, 1973, 'The Old Fools' in *High Windows*)

Philip Larkin's poem captures something of the primordial fear of being and becoming very old and senile – of becoming a 'baffled absence', and the problem of seeming, like Gladys as we first see her, to not just be barely living but elsewhere rather than here, cowering under 'extinction's peak'.

Popular media representations of Old Fools, of old age and of dementia, proliferate (Swinnen & Schweda, 2015). These media show us monsters as at the same time as they are making the experience of the dementia–ageing relation more and more present in everyday lives (Carbonnelle, Casini, & Klein, 2009). Martin, Kontos, and Ward (2013) suggest that:

… films generate certain feelings about dementia which then become part of our popular understanding and approach to persons living with dementia. Indeed, they potentially become part of how people with dementia come to see themselves as they draw upon such films as a cultural resource for making sense of their condition. (p. 284)

But I want to press how the proliferation of books, films, television dramas and soaps which include a character with dementia is helping to body forth dementia, even give it an existence. As Cohen-Shalev and Marcus (2012) assert, these films are often from the perspective of those looking in on a person with dementia becoming other, a stranger, while others help us to get inside the experience of the person becoming-with dementia. Swinnen and Schweda (2015) suggest many depictions portray the ageing–dementia relation as an inevitable process of decline and unbecoming. Recent examples are the UK TV series *Wallander* (BBC 2016), based on the Swedish TV series, and ITV's (2016) *The Missing*, both of which depict a strong, professional man who occupies a senior position gradually losing his memory and his mind, increasingly unable to work but attempting to cover it up, and eventually becoming fragile, needy and dependent. In *The Missing*, the senior army officer, played by Roger Allam, has to be admitted to a nursing home, cared for 24 hours a day. These are tragic depictions, the decline and fall of a big man, and the gradual slide towards vulnerability, fragility and becoming a non-person. These representations of dementia parade the dementia–ageing relation unproblematically as something to be feared, as shameful and as stigmatizing. This is doubly so where, as in the case of *The Missing*, the senior army officer's 'forgetting' was tied to his hidden sense of guilt over his history of immorality and wrong doing. This is the dementia–ageing monster on parade – to be vomited up and sequestrated.

But this picture of the slide towards a living death is being disturbed by recent interventions, such as those by the well-known neurologist Oliver Saks (2007) in his and others' work on musicophilia.[2] In particular, I want to draw on one such intervention through analysis of a short film, publicly available on YouTube, by Naomi Feil, a US based validation therapist, and Michael Verde, a film-maker, about Feil's encounter with Gladys Wilson.

At first we see Gladys Wilson in a chair alone, apparently introverted and disconnected, eyes closed, very thin, but tidy and clean, sitting in a wheelchair that has been made to seem like an armchair (Figure 1). She is sitting alone in a barren, impersonal, sanitized setting. On a close-up of Gladys's face it is emaciated but peaceful. Her clothes and crooked teeth as well as the paucity of the institutional setting indicate Gladys is not a wealthy woman – not now at least.

We are told by Naomi Feil, in the voice-over, that Gladys is in her eighties and that she was diagnosed with Alzheimer's Disease (AD) nine years ago, and now has little language. For many of us, seeing Gladys like this represents our worst nightmare about growing old – abandoned, institutionalized, forced to endure a pitiful life that hardly appears to be worth living – a zombie, even perhaps repulsive and disgusting to some viewers. In many ways this figure of Gladys, co-created by us the audience together with Feil and her film team, seems to body forth all that is most feared about growing old with dementia: the hollowed-out person in a state of 'living death'.

At the same time, Gladys seems peaceful even calm – very different from the representations of the persons *becoming* demented depicted in films such as *Amour*, or TV dramas like *The Missing* or *Wallander* mentioned above. Gladys seems 'elsewhere' to the present reality of other people. She is perhaps, more or less, absent to their world-making: being *there* and not here, as Larkin's poem expresses it in the citation above. While

Figure 1. Gladys Wilson, 2009, with kind permission of Naomi Feil and Michael Verde; available at https://vfvalidation.org and https://www.youtube.com/watch?v=CrZXz10FcVM).

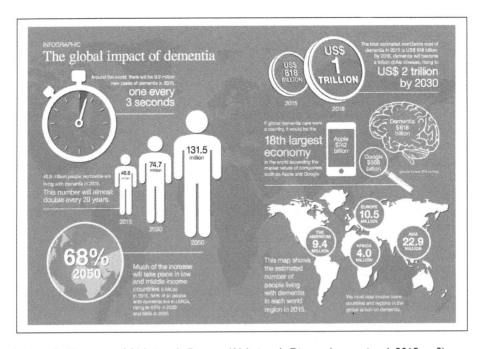

Figure 2. The costs of Alzheimer's Disease (Alzheimer's Disease International, 2015, p. 3).

this withdrawal may be due to her disease, it may also be her retreat, even a refusal, a repelling: a sign that she no longer wants to participate in the social. As in 'The Old Fools' she may be otherwise engaged, looking inward to the fading rooms and faces and moments from her past life. There may be nothing wrong with being in the world like this. Who knows?

Whichever way we want to look at the film, Naomi Feil takes a more radical position. Like Margaret Schlegel in E. M. Forster's *Howards End* (1910) she insists we should 'Only Connect!' and stresses that Gladys, like everyone else, needs and wants connection. While I am not sure about the discourse here, what I want to stress is how Naomi finds a way to become competent in Gladys's world and connect with Gladys. What we are shown is Naomi reaching Gladys: by using her body, and her voice, by taking Gladys's hands, by touching and stroking Gladys's face, by moving her face into the space of Gladys's face and touching Gladys's forehead with her own forehead, by singing a negro-spiritual hymn with her, and by holding Gladys's hands and arms and beating time together as she sings. Gradually Gladys opens: her eyes open and look into Naomi's eyes, she holds Naomi's hands, pulling her in and pushing her out as if to focus, and then she begins to sing with Naomi.

For a few moments Gladys-Naomi sings and beats time, in their jointness they become face-to-face. This is a material semiotics of bodily connection in a bodily becoming-with (Haraway, 2008). Then they separate and Gladys seems to be awakened – concentrating on Naomi, answering her questions, making a choice, having autonomy, being expressive. Naomi seems to bring Gladys into presence as participant in world-making. And as such Gladys becomes more than the living dead, regaining what most of us would recognize as the attributes of the fully human, of being, as I go on to discuss below, response-able.

In the perspective that the film unfolds Gladys is refigured: instead of her inert condition as we see it at the beginning being constituted as something inherent – the effects of ageing and AD on her brain and the rest of her body – we can begin to question whether her condition is an effect of a body–self–world relation (Latimer, 2009), and perhaps of the stigmatizing effects and affects of dementia. An extraordinary possibility is created which has the chance to completely shift how we know and understand Gladys – the supposition of her condition being that of a 'living death' may be not just an effect of her degenerating brain, but of her emplacement by a world that does not know how to reach her. Or, indeed, a world that deliberately sequestrates her as Other. From this different perspective, dementia and AD become distributed, relational and co-created.

Biopolitics and successful ageing: Managing and self-care

The figure of the abject older person becoming demented is invoked in the legitimation of a new and emergent biomedical interest in ageing. In my ethnography of biology, medicine and ageing (Cox et al., 2014; Latimer, in press; Latimer, Bagley, Davis, & Kipling, 2011; Latimer & Puig de la Bellacasa, 2013), for example, the biomedical scientists I have interviewed almost always cite dementia and AD as the worst of what ageing does to people:

So you know the ideal scenario is that you would be able to start taking some tablets when you were 55 or something like this and it would provide protection against dementia, against heart disease, against diabetes, against you know the bewildering diversity of horrible things that go wrong with you when you get older. And that would be marvellous. (Biomedical Scientist of Ageing interviewed in 2010)

Biomedicine is a dominant site of contemporary knowledge creation that is constructing and reconstructing ageing and death (Vincent, 2008, p. 331), particularly dementia (Bond, 1992). This process is reflected in worldwide programmes that are medicalizing ageing by linking between ageing, chronic illness, disability and the increasing need for care (United Nations, 2013; Vos, Ocampo, & Cortez, 2008). Problems that get high-lighted include the prevalence of multiple forms of illness associated with later life (e.g. Barnett et al., 2012; Department of Health, 2014; Kings Fund, 2012), especially, as I have already indicated, AD and dementia. At the same time, biomedicine intensifies the reorganization of health care not just around technological intervention but, increasingly, around modes of prevention and consumption (Clarke, Mamo, Fosket, Fishman, & Shim, 2010; see also Kaufman, Shim, & Russ, 2006). This is important to note as an aspect of the political economy of dementia, referred to above in relation to 'bedblocking' and the discourse of crisis in health and social care. This crisis is partly constructed around an idea that 'we cannot afford dementia', which is of course partly what is stigmatizing about it. Within this perspective the stigma associated with the dementia–ageing relation is not just the outcome of a political regime, it is helping to legitimate the biomedicaliza-tion of ageing, in general, and of dementia, in particular. In the context of so-called 'greying populations' and the associations between ageing, multi-morbidity and the pro-liferation of chronic and disabling disease in later life, ageing has rapidly become not just a policy 'problem' to be managed (Bazalgette et al., 2011), but, as Binstock, Fishman, and Johnson (2006) suggest, an exemplar scientific site for understanding 'all enhance-ment technologies'. Specifically, knowledge practices and governmental processes that position life as an object of power in contemporary capitalist societies can be understood as being played out around what constitutes ageing well or badly (Neilson, 2012), espe-cially the causes of different ageing trajectories.

The important questions, for economies, persons, families and communities, is not mortality – we are living longer than we have ever done – but *how* and *when* will we age. Globalization, individualization, labour market deregulation and restructuration of pub-lic services (Beck, 2000; Higgs & Jones, 2009; Kohli, 2007) alongside increased longev-ity have worked to produce what is sometimes labelled a de-standardized life course (Brückner & Mayer, 2005), including imaginaries of more fluid, postmodern life trajec-tories (Hockey & James, 2002; Turner, 2009) that extend 'middle age' well into later life. This fluidity is reflected in increasing emphases in health and social policy on finding ways to prolong productivity and employability (e.g. Department of Work and Pensions, 2005), especially a 'third age' (Laslett, 1989) of activity, youthfulness and health (Featherstone & Hepworth, 1993), with baby-boomer hopes and aspirations for 'time-lessness' (Katz, 2005), and an endless life of consumption and choice (Turner, 2009). How people age is thus no longer being seen as the 'natural and inevitable occurrence of growing old' (Butler, 2001–2002, p. 64), but as something that is plastic and malleable

(Moreira & Palladino, 2008) and available to enhancement (Binstock, 2003; Binstock et al., 2006).

These biomedical and public health discourses are, however, simultaneously circulating dominant versions of 'successful' ageing, which are underpinned by specific notions of value – keeping productive, independent, fit and healthy, including managing risk. Rowe and Kahn (1997), for example, state that the concept 'successful ageing' has its roots in the 1950s, was popularized in the 1980s, with 'success' classified in terms of three features: low probability of disease or disability; high cognitive and physical functional capacity; and active engagement with life. While the life course is being reimagined as more and more fluid, possibilities for successful ageing are increasingly being individualized and reconstructed as a problem of self-care and self-management of risk (Hepworth, 1995; Neilson, 2012) on the one hand, and as available to technoscientific manipulation on the other (Mykytyn, 2010). Human ageing is thus being reimagined as increasingly subject to reflexive management and manipulation, exciting a new age of consumers striving to age positively, including the incitement of a rational practice of designing one's own life course through consumption of 'anti-ageing' technology, products and activities (Schweda & Pfaller, 2014).

These discourses of successful ageing thus enact what it is to be a full person and a good consumer in late modern capitalism. Furthermore, 'ageing' as a target to be managed resembles the most sacred of 'public secrets' (Taussig, 1999). Not only must everyone age and die (eventually) but opening ageing up as a site of enhancement creates opportunities for the enactment of what is most valued and precious in neoliberal forms of modernity – to have a 'future' and be 'ready and available' for whenever the call to do this or that comes along (Latimer & Munro, 2015). The call here is to manage ageing successfully. More specifically, after Skeggs (2011), ageing bodies can be seen as bodies of value when they body forth the effects and affects of managing ageing well.

The markers and signifiers of successful ageing thus go beyond just health, fitness and engagement, and involve enactment of active engagement in *managing* ageing. Featherstone and Hepworth (1993) in their groundbreaking work on representations of ageing, written at the advent of the current form of capitalism we are experiencing today, helped to illuminate this shift in possibilities around what it is to age well. Through an examination of *Retirement Magazine* they analyse the emergence of a new discourse with images not just exemplifying a discourse of successful ageing, but as helping to construct it.

Specifically, they show how photographs of Mrs Thatcher frequently appear on the front cover, and suggest these images body forth what it is to age successfully. She appears in middle age, full of vitality, exuding not just health, but poise, grooming and wealth, each performed as *achievements*: the fruits of a steely reflexive modern relation to self through which both the world and the body can be *managed* to postpone older age. The irony of course is that Thatcher as the peon of the possibility that the third age could be stretched indefinitely was later subsumed by AD. The achievement Featherstone and Hepworth depict involves individuals investing well in their bodies as well as their other possessions as the pinnacle of individualism, and reflexive management of self (see also Callero, 2013). Here I want to stress the term 'manage' as extruding any possibility of failure:

> In contemporary Western culture, we are encouraged to think of our lives as coherent stories of success, progress and movement. Loss and failure have their place but only as a broader picture of ascendance. The steady upward curve is the favoured contour. (Stacey, 1997, p. 9 in Diedrich, 2007)

This imaginary of successful ageing – as a life course managed as a steady upward, rather than downward, curve – is represented in public health discourse and health promotional media as if it is available to everyone. Indeed, 'everyone' is represented as capable of achieving a successful and prolonged third age. Critically, the fulfilment of this utopian project is represented as an urgent issue to ensure sustainable futures for ageing societies, 'a future that takes full advantage of the powerful resource inherent in older populations' (WHO, 2011).

Just think for a moment on the images and discourses in the media that endlessly promote the relation between active and healthy lifestyles and successful ageing. We are immersed in images that characterize people in middle age as always *doing* – running, rambling, going on holiday, smiling, interacting – they are never static: as if a continuously active, mobile present is what will keep us youthful and postpone old age. This hopeful imaginary is all around and is prolific (Petersen, 2015). It continuously incites people to consume (Hurd-Clarke, 2010): to buy or to join – pension schemes, anti-ageing creams and supplements, gyms, ramblers' clubs, bicycles, five fruits and veg a day, retirement homes – the list is endless. At the same time we are bombarded with new scientific breakthroughs over what will prevent illness and disability (four hours of intense exercise each week – half an hour's walk five times a week; just walking!), as well as things to eat (low fat, low calorie; high fat, low calorie; more vitamin C, less vitamin C – superfoods abounding with new types every week) (see also MacGregor, Petersen, & Parker, 2017). Even coffee is proselytized as giving us longer life.

Public health and biomedical messages are thus coupled with a culture of consumption preoccupied with health and youthfulness (Shilling, 2002). The effect is to continuously incite consciousness of the relationship between health, ageing and identity by thrusting us into the future at all times, putting us in what Heidegger (2008) calls 'advance' of our bodies and ourselves, so that even a stroll in the countryside to a favourite spot becomes a moment for enhancement, health promotion and disease prevention as we contemplate not the extraordinary view but whether we are walking far enough and fast enough. Thus 'responsibilization' of ageing goes hand-in-hand with biomedicalization. And, as with Roger Allam's character in *The Missing* discussed above, what you do now, becomes your past, the past that shapes your ageing.

Neilson (2012) suggests this as a 'growing pressure for ageing subjects to perform practices of self-care', one that involves an existential shift because it is a 'process by which the care of self begins to eclipse the care of others' (p. 45). Healthy ageing is thus being increasingly made the responsibility of individuals and families as at the same time as it is a prime marker of positive identity. Critically then, 'response-able' (Latimer, 1999; Latimer & Munro, 2015) persons need to be seen to answer the incitements and manage their ageing well, with what counts as successful ageing prefigured as specific forms of personhood – active, productive, fit.

The biopolitics of ageing is thus being reassembled in ways that not only cut out how ageing is a relational co-produced effect, but also seem to represent a shift: from the othering of the otherness that the old represent, to a phagic strategy that impels us to manage our ageing, ingest and assimilate it, and so change its very character, to prolong being and seeming to be younger, postponing the onslaught of what the transhumanist Nick Bostrom (2005) calls the ageing dragon. Those who do not conform are not just at risk of stigmatization, they are at risk of being part of the parade of spectacles, revolting subjects, monsters.

The dementia monster and being irresponse-able

> There are around 36 million people with some form of dementia in the world and this is expected to at least double over the next 20 years, making it one of the largest neglected global health challenges of our generation. The global economic cost of dementia is estimated at over US$600 billion, and Alzheimer's Society research suggests that in the UK, one in three people over 65 will die with dementia. This is not something any of us can afford to ignore. (Piet, 2012, p. 18)

As discussed above, growing old badly is personified by the figure of the older person with dementia. Until recently dementia has not been of much interest to clinical scientists. This is partly because dementias could not be made visible as located in lesions in the body, until post-mortem, so that diagnosis was clinical, arrived at through processes of differentiation (Bender, 2003). In addition, dementias have been caught up in the inherent ageism of clinical medicine (Oliver, 2008), with dementia being constituted as intractable, inevitable and as a policy problem to be managed, rather than as a proper target for high-flying clinical research. But this is changing.

'Apocalyptic' (Robertson, 1991) demographic predictions about ageing populations plagued by dementia (see for example WHO, 2015) are typically represented in terms of their *costs* (see for example Figure 2). Cost predictions align with revolutions in technologies for detecting dementia, such as the brain scanning technology that allows for the investigation of living brains (Shine, Hodgetts, Postans, Lawrence, & Graham, 2015) and post-genomic science that enables the genetic profiling of neurodegenerative diseases (Tanzi & Bertram, 2001). Through these alignments dementia is becoming an increasingly potent site for both clinical and for technoscientific research (Milne, 2016). Critically, we are witnessing how dementia is being reconstituted across the biomedical and neurological sciences as well as mainstream psychology to grow differential dementia diagnoses (Hillman & Latimer, in press). The medicalizing of particular effects as different forms of dementia is ongoing with what Beard and Neary (2013) describe as 'nosological creep'.

More specifically, brain ageing, like ageing more generally discussed above, is beginning to be opened up as a site of prevention and enhancement (Moreira & Bond, 2008). A new frontier of scientific research is reconstituting the brain as much more plastic and malleable than originally thought (Williams, Higgs, & Katz, 2012), with hopes and expectations that have gone public:

... scientists worldwide, working in many different specialities, have found that the human brain is highly plastic, possessing the ability not only to create new neurons, but to modify networks of neurons to better cope with new circumstances. (DementiaToday, 2013)

Within this imaginary dementia is the effect of reduced brain plasticity due, for example, to biological ageing. Constructing the ageing–dementia relation in this way begins to give it a future. For example, it becomes something that is possibly preventable, with the public being incited to keep exercising their brains as a preventative strategy. Specifically, the tragic vision of the abject demented older person, such as Gladys, legitimates the enactment of specific values, namely the creation and capitalization of troubles and the triumph of endeavour, including the proliferation of science, industry and innovation through which to overcome, manage and transform dementia. It is not just that dementia in the context of ageing undoes the basis of what it is to be fully human, of personhood, in terms of memory and its loss (Katz & Peters, 2008), it is more complex than that.

Within biomedicine dementias are located as progressive or degenerative diseases of the brain in ways that increasingly somaticize mind and personhood (Lock, 2014; Moser, 2011; Pickersgill, 2013). There are disputes around whether different kinds of dementia are the natural consequence of biological decline, or whether they can be reframed as a 'terminal disease' or a mental health issue (WHO, 2015) – thereby, like cancer before it, mainstreaming how dementia can and ought to be known and 'disciplined'. This has meant that the technoscientific pursuit of knowledge about and interventions in dementia and new thinking in neuroscience about the plasticity of the brain align to form a 'neuro-culture' (Williams et al., 2012) that individuates dementia as preventable disease or, at the very least, treatable.

I want to suggest that this increasing biomedicalization of dementia – including notions that ageing, even the ageing brain, can be *managed* – reinforce a phagic strategy to transform the ageing–dementia relation through ingestion and assimilation. This strategy can be seen in the reorganization of health services and research around a programme for the 'early detection of dementia' (Swallow, 2016), and the constitution of a new category of prepatienthood, 'mild cognitive impairment' (or MCI) (Katz & Peters, 2008; Moreira, May, & Bond, 2009). It also includes, like ageing itself, a notion that dementia can be modulated, postponed or even prevented, provided individuals live the right way (Peel, 2014). So, *there* is the rub – the call for lifestyles and self-management strategies through which to nullify the potential of the ageing–dementia monster.

The shift towards reforming ageing, and even the ageing–dementia relation, as manageable depends upon individuals responding to this call to the future and to 'care for themselves' (as opposed to others). In this sense, then, the phagic strategy depends upon people responding to the call to master their futures through their 'strategic conduct' (Giddens, 1984) of the present. The figure of the aged demented subject, such as Gladys, is thus also a subject that bodies forth the figure of someone who has not responded to this call, and not managed their ageing well.

Dementia is frequently described as a neurodegenerative disease. I want to suggest that in the contemporary moment the ageing–dementia relation enacts a profound sense of *immorality*. Specifically, the dementia–ageing relation's monstrousness, its repulsiveness, comes from how it is constructed as if it threatens what is most sacred to

Euro-American notions of personhood: not just the imaginary of the sovereign subject, or even one who is merely reasonable, but of the subject who is *response-able*. To be, for example, a good 'somatic citizen' (Rose & Novas, 2004) requires someone to be response-able.

Here I am building on my earlier work (Latimer, 1999; Latimer & Munro, 2015) and the notion of personhood as situated and relational, including an effect of being 'response-able'. If we accept that personhood is not a possession, but situated, then we can also suggest that personhood is an *effect* of being 'response-able': and as I have suggested above, in terms of the relationship between ageing and persons, response-ability has very specific connotations. Being response-able involves what Goffman (1958) describes as presentation of self, which depends upon strategic conduct and reading and doing the social to get along and go along (Giddens, 1984); what Garfinkel (1967) shows as doing member, including being accountable and making actions visible and observable as rational and reasonable; what Foucault and others have shown as being positioned and being emplaced by modes of ordering as well as having the know-how of when and how to resist and transform these through negotiation, agonistics, persuasion (Foucault, 1991; Lyotard, 1984; Rabinow & Sullivan, 1979).

But as I am pressing response-ability here has an added caché: it includes being ready and available to fold into the next call to the future. From this perspective, some older people classified as having dementia can be regarded as 'socially abject' (Tyler, 2013), not because of anything essential or inherent but because of how they are not performing themselves as response-able, of how they seem to refuse and repel late modern modes of ordering by ageing unsuccessfully. To put it another way, their sensibility and experience have not been sufficiently attuned and exercised to what Adams, Murphy, and Clarke (2009) call the mode of anticipation:

> As much as speculative finance has become both a dominant mode of capital accumulation, spawning its own material and discursive effects of disaster prediction, anticipation has become a common, lived affect-state of daily life, shaping regimes of self, health and spirituality. (p. 247)

A conundrum then – through being response-able and maintaining their performativity in relation to neoliberal world-making, for example through self-care and the reflexive management of risk, people as they age can maintain their 'status honour', to use Weber's terminology. But as Minkler and Holstein (2008) suggest, this then acts to denigrate and throw into perspective those aged subjects that can be made to seem abject.

Following Skeggs, Tyler (2013) helps us to see how abject subjects are the effects of classificatory mechanisms through which specific body-persons become systematically defaced and devalued. What she goes on to show is how the rubbishing of particular kinds of body-persons is possible because of how they stand against particular neoliberal institutions of identity and personhood, not least in terms of the individuation of persons as discrete, body-selves in ways that obscure how persons are affects and effects of 'body–person–world' (Latimer, 2011) relations. Within this view people who appear as abject subjects are not just the effects of complex entanglements in the alignments between media, public health discourse and forms of governmentality working on behalf of capital. We can see how the prospect and anticipation of ageing, and the creation of monsters such as the figure of the aged person with dementia, both unconceal and intensify the precariousness of contemporary social existence characterised by a proliferation of possibilities for stigmatization.

Dwelling alongside dementia as 'a figure seen twice'

The figure of the older demented person represents something sacred that has become despoiled: what is lost is even more precious than the hollowing out of the person, the mind, the individual, their self. As Taussig (1999, p. 316) asserts, this despoiling is 'attractive in its very repulsion', because 'it creates the sacred even in the most secular of societies and circumstances'. Specifically, at moments what affronts neoliberal world-making is the abject figure of the old demented person as one who has not managed their ageing; its repulsiveness attracts because it helps recreate what is most sacred. The figure of the old demented person is also an infraction of the sacred: it helps to institute the possibility that the human can and should manage his or herself – body, mind and all – as a phagic strategy to eliminate the otherness that 'bad' ageing represents.

Bad ageing, like poverty, is performed as the *failure* of the individual because of how they fly in the face of contemporary neoliberal agendas: in Bev Skeggs's (2011) terms they are unable to (or do not want to?) embody or body forth neoliberal values. In this sense then, stigma is the effect and affects of complex alignments: political, medical, cultural. Ageing, and the extraordinary proliferation of concern and excitation of interest around ageing, is an event that brings to the surface the antithetical relation between growing old and neoliberal forms of personhood.

The inversion I want to propose requires us to '*dwell alongside*' (Latimer, 2013; Latimer, forthcoming) dementia. Dwelling alongside is a way of being with and becoming with the ageing–dementia relation and to be affected by it in ways that challenge dominant forms of what counts as successful forms of personhood. At the same time we need to hold onto the possibility that we can reassemble the social in order to find ways to bring the older person with dementia back into presence. To return for a moment to the film about Gladys Wilson, discussed earlier in the article, maybe Gladys is just as fully human at the beginning of the film, but simply different. In other words, it may be *us*, and even Naomi, that are *elsewhere* to Gladys's present reality – to her way of being in the world. Within this inversion it is we who are 'other' by virtue of the *longue durée* (Giddens, 1984) of contemporary forms of personhood. The anthropologist Clifford Geertz (1973) may help us to some extent here. In his initial encounters with the Balinese the locals seem to look at him and his wife as if it is they 'who are away'; they see through them as though they are naught but the air. Yes, at the beginning of the film Gladys seems 'away', in the sense that the Old Fools, in Larkin's poem, are away – they are *there* rather than here. But, contrastingly, drawing on Geertz's work, we have to consider that it may be 'us' that are elsewhere. Us, with our projects and our futures who are really 'away'.

The opening for care that the film conveys thus constitutes what Rudge (2009) calls a rupture of certainty. It is not just that there is no way of knowing for sure how Gladys feels about what is going on. Of course, we do not know whether she wants to be refolded into the present, 'awakened' as Saks (2007) might put it.

Rather, what I want to press is how the deep ambiguity at the heart of the ageing–dementia relation is revealed – for a moment – through Gladys and Naomi becoming differently to how they were previously shown to us. On the one hand, then, can we cherish those with dementia as 'other' than us? And on the other, can we begin to see, with Naomi, that the effects of dementia that produce the figure of Gladys as isolated and disconnected are not so much the inevitable consequences of the decline and deficit caused by ageing and dementia, but perhaps the effects of stigma and her emplacement? To use Donna Haraway's (2008) terminology – this is a moment of 'reworlding' in which the dementia–ageing relation gets figured differently. So what we need to acknowledge, even celebrate, is how this kind of radical relationality entails a possibility of 'dwelling alongside' those figures that seem most stigmatized – and so open up the figure of the ageing–dementia relation to broader perspectives.

With Michael Halewood (2016) in his recent paper on dementia, I am pressing the need to relate to people like Gladys differently and rethink 'what kind of selves we all think we are' (p. 3). This may involve getting beyond old binaries, and instead to take up Munro's (2016) challenge of 'double crossing': deliberately moving back and forth, one moment seeing ageing and dementia as relational, and as 'things' we can affect and change; and, in the next, celebrating those effects labelled 'dementia' as other forms of sociality that involve different ways of being in the world to those that dominate.

Conclusions

I started the article by suggesting that there is a proliferation of media representations that parade the abject, aged dementia subject, to bring the dementia–ageing monster into existence as a part of the everyday. The ageing–dementia relation is stigmatizing because it 'breaches', as Harold Garfinkel (1967) would say, the markers and signifiers of what makes someone up as a full person. Growing old and becoming 'demented' can seem to put someone beyond the pale.

After Bauman, I proposed that the parade of the dementia–ageing monster can be thought of not just as an emic strategy for vomiting up and sequestrating the otherness of the abject older person with dementia. Rather the alignment of the parade with a changing biopolitics of the dementia–aging relation that I have described can be understood as a phagic strategy to know, ingest and transform the dangerous and monstrous otherness that the older person with dementia is made to represent.

The phagic strategy involves the creation of a *dispositif* (Foucault, 1980), an actor-network of associations for knowing, detecting, managing and transforming dementia: public health discourses promoting healthy ageing associate with policies such as early detection and diagnosis of dementia, a proliferation of technoscientific research, media representations and an anti-ageing culture of consumption. The actor-network enacts dementia as something that can be known, transformed or even just postponed, providing individuals are response-able enough. Being a full person in late modern times, I have suggested, goes beyond memory and reason – it includes health, fitness and engagement, and the capacity to respond to the call to transform the future by participating in the active and strategic management of ageing.

The 'thinging up' (Larsen, 2013) of the dementia–ageing relation as something available to enhancement is, I am arguing, occurring against a background of the parade of monsters. Critically, I suggest, this 'double helix' is shifting dementia from simply being an object of disgust – to be shunned and excluded in processes of emesis – into a present-day reality, an imminent and present danger, which can and will be ingested and assimilated: transformed by biomedicine and the social body, as at the same time as it is transformative of the social body. On the one hand, then, the ageing–dementia *dispositif* includes incitements for people to be response-able, stand in advance of their ageing bodies and be proactive to prevent and/or postpone both ageing and dementia. On the other, it is the relation – between the older person with dementia and the world in which the older person finds themselves – that needs reordering to find ways to dwell alongside dementia.

I showed you Gladys and Naomi Feil, and how they become with each other in ways that mean that dementia is different from what it was before: that it is as much a body–world relation as it is a state of becoming other. Perhaps the ambiguity and conundrum of the ageing–dementia relation mean that it needs to be a figure seen twice (Riles, 2000): the figure of Gladys, isolated, alone and disconnected – 'elsewhere' as I have put it – can be seen as an effect of a disease, or as the effect of stigma: a body–world relation where becoming the living dead of dementia is an effect of how a person is stigmatized, emplaced and sequestrated by the biopolitics of late modern capitalism. As such, as Feil shows us, we need to find ways to reincorporate people like Gladys.

But I proposed that there is yet another way of seeing the figure of Gladys – as someone who is elsewhere, different, but still fully human, even if they are like the Old Fools, 'away'. Franco Berardi Bifo (2010), in his essay 'Exhaustion and Senile Utopia of the Coming European Insurrection', suggests that our way of being together has become apathetic, with modern culture and political imagination emphasizing 'the virtues of youth, of passion and of energy, aggressiveness and growth'. He suggests that capitalism relies on the exploitation of physical energy, with 'semiocapitalism':

> … subjugating the nervous energy of society to the point of collapse. The notion of exhaustion has always been anathema to the discourse of modernity, of romantic Sturm and Drang, of the Faustian drive to immortality, the endless thirst for economic growth and profit, the denial of organic limits.

Thus there is the possibility that in our relation to Gladys as we first see her it is us who are elsewhere. By shifting our relations to the characteristics we are being made to see as dementia, we can refigure them as ways of being in the world differently, and as such, as other ways of being human. Here I am suggesting we need to make room for those characteristics and ways of being human that we are being made to see as the signs and symptoms of dementia. Solidarity with dementia may require then a shift in perspective. What is needed here is very nuanced. Perhaps we can think then how dwelling alongside dementia is about seeing the sense in the reality and world of the person with dementia, becoming more competent in that world and letting the person who they once were 'go', at the same time as letting the person they are becoming dwell with us, dwelling alongside and cherishing their difference. Here I emphasize the importance of strategies for dwelling alongside the aged as a possible way to resist the dominant forms of person-hood mobilized in late modern capitalism, and which 'others' those no longer willing or able to be response-able and fold themselves into its demands.

In a phagic reversal of dementia's fortunes the ageing–dementia relation is becoming incorporated into the social body in ways that are helping to reassemble the social in order to transform the future. This involves the partial biomedicalization of the dementia–ageing relation alongside the circulation of hopes, even expectations, that the otherness that marks the abject dementia subject as 'bad ageing' can be postponed and even eliminated. This includes being incited today to be response-able and manage ageing in ways that keep the ageing–dementia monster at the door. The reassemblage of the dementia–ageing relation also includes opening up to dementia's otherness, with new institutions and media representations that help us trouble and even undo specific neoliberal positionings to help deconstruct the ageing–dementia relation as itself *relational*, so that there are possibilities for finding ways to dwell alongside dementia, give it room, in moments of reworlding. Here I have in mind the ways in which dementia is being partially transformed through how it is reshaping the social body, including such entities as dementia-friendly communities, dementia villages and Alzheimer's choirs. What is interesting here is the extent to which these sequestrate or assimilate dementia.

Specifically, then, I am suggesting a sensibility that does not simply reproduce old binaries between social and biomedical representations and interventions in dementia, especially those that dismiss the biomedicalization of dementia (Lyman, 1989). Rather there is a need at the very least to illuminate differences between: when it is a disease that is making someone be the ways that they are being; when it is the lack of fit between them and the world-making they are emplaced by; and when it is them becoming differently. I want to suggest then that what is required by us is to dwell alongside those other ways of being in the world – slowness, immobility, degeneration, confusion, impotency, even chaos. We know from so many carers how dementia disorders the modes of ordering that underpin our living together in the world, and that can include our own as thinkers, scientists and researchers. This means finding ways to dwell alongside what we are being made to see as a clouding of the light of the enlightenment. Attempts to eradicate the otherness of the ageing–dementia relation, and dispose of dementia or at least bring dementia to heel, are not necessarily problematic in themselves; they are problematic when they deny ways to challenge those dominant modes of ordering, and perhaps what positions the aged and the demented, that co-creates or at least intensifies dementia.

Acknowledgements

Many thanks to the editors, Tom Slater and Imogen Tyler, as well as Rob Smith and the anonymous reviewers for their insightful and affirming reading of the article.

Funding

This research received no specific grant from any funding agency in the public, commercial, or not-for-profit sectors.

Notes

1. In this article I am drawing on my ethnographic study of biology and ageing, which began in 2009 with a study funded by the RCUK New Dynamics of Ageing Program entitled 'Ageing and Biology' (see also Cox et al., 2014), a series of small grants awarded by Cardiff University and the ESRC Centre for the Social and Economic Aspects of Genetics (CESAGEN) and a Welcome Trust Project (with Alex Hillman) on Alzheimer's Disease and memory clinics as well as cultural representations of dementia (Hillman & Latimer, 2017). This research has included interviews and site visits with scientists across the UK and the US; participant observation at conferences on ageing; ongoing conversations with different scientists, clinicians and neuroscientists; participant observation at memory clinics, as well as analysis of publicly available representations of ageing, biology and dementia.
2. See https://www.youtube.com/watch?v=tqrNEmuSCis. In this video we see an older Afro-American man in a wheelchair 'away' like Gladys, someone puts headphones on him and he literally comes awake, starts singing and bopping in his chair, and afterwards he becomes perfectly capable of answering questions and interacting. We are told the music he is hearing is a composite of music he liked across his life.

References

Adams, V., Murphy, M., & Clarke, A. (2009). Anticipation: Technoscience, life, affect, temporality. *Subjectivity*, *28*, 246–265.

Alzheimer's Disease International. (2015). *The world Alzheimer report. The global impact of dementia: An analysis of prevalence, incidence, cost and trends*. Retrieved from https://dementiaroadmap.info/blog/resources/world-alzheimer-report-2015-the-global-impact-of-dementia/#.WcwRYkyZNE4 (accessed August 2016).

Barnett, K., Mercer, S. W., Norbury, M., Watt, G., Wyke, S., & Guthrie, B. (2012). Epidemiology of multimorbidity and implications for health care, research, and medical education: A cross-sectional study. *Lancet*, *380*, 37–43.

Baroness S. Greengross (2014). Foreword. In S. S. Bamford, G. Holley-Moore & J. Watson (Eds.), *A compendium of essays: New perspectives and approaches to understanding dementia and stigma* (pp. 6–7). London, UK: ILC-UK.

Bauman, Z. (1990). Effacing the face: On the social management of moral proximity. *Theory, Culture & Society*, *7*, 5–38.

Bauman, Z. (2000). *Liquid modernity*. Cambridge, UK: Polity Press.

Bauman, Z. (2001). Uses and disuses of urban space. In B. Czarniawska & R. Solli (Eds.), *Organizing metropolitan space and discourse* (pp. 15–33). Malmö, Sweden: Liber Abstrakt.

Bazalgette, L., Holden, J., Tew, P., Hubble, N., & Morrison, J. (2011). *Ageing is not a policy problem to be solved: Coming of age*. London, UK: Demos.

BBC. (2016). *Wallander, Series 4*. A Left Bank Pictures Production for BBC One. Director: Benjamin Carron; Screenplays: James Dormer, Peter Harness. Adapted from the Novels by Henning Mankell.

Beard, R. L., & Neary, T. M. (2013). Making sense of nonsense: Experiences of mild cognitive impairment. *Sociology of Health & Illness*, *35*, 130–146.

Beck, U. (2000). Living your own life in a runaway world: Individualization, globalization, and politics. In W. Hutton & A. Giddens (Eds.), *Global capitalism* (pp. 164–174). New York, NY: New Press.

Behuniak, S. M. (2011). The living dead? The construction of people with Alzheimer's disease as zombies. *Ageing & Society*, *31*, 70–93.

Bender, M. (2003). *Explorations in dementia: Theoretical and research studies into the experience of remedial and enduring cognitive loss*. London, UK: Jessica Kingsley.

Berardi Bifo F. (2010). Exhaustion and senile utopia of the coming European insurrection. *e-flux Journal, 21*, 1–8. Retrieved from http://www.e-flux.com/journal/21/67655/exhaustion-and-senile-utopia-of-the-coming-european-insurrection/ (accessed August 2016).

Binstock, H. (2003). The war on 'anti-ageing medicine'. *The Gerontologist, 43*, 4–14.

Binstock, R. H., Fishman, J. R., & Johnson, T. E. (2006). Anti-aging medicine and science: Social implications. In R. H. Binstock, L. K. George, S. J. Cutler, J. Hendricks & J. H. Schulz (Eds.), *Handbook of aging and the social sciences* (6th ed., pp. 436–455). London, UK: Academic Press.

Bond, J. (1992). The medicalization of dementia. *Journal of Aging Studies, 6*, 397–403.

Bostrom, N. (2005). The fable of the dragon. *Journal of Medical Ethics, 31*, article 5.

Brückner, H., & Mayer, K. U. (2005). De-standardization of the life course: What it might mean? And if it means anything, whether it actually took place? *Advances in Life Course Research, 9*, 27–53.

Butler, R. N. (2001–2002). Is there an 'anti-aging' medicine? *Generations, XXV*, 63–65.

Callero, P. (2013). *The myth of individualism: How social forces shape our lives*. Lanham, MD: Rowman & Littlefield .

Canguilhem, G. (2008). *Knowledge of life* (G. Geroulanos & D. Ginsburg, Trans.). New York, NY: Fordham University Press.

Carbonnelle, S., Casini, A., & Klein, O. (2009). *Les représentations sociales de la démence: De l'alarmisme vers une image plus nuancée. Une perspective socioanthropologique et psychosociale* [Les représentations sociales de la démence: De l'alarmisme vers une image plus nuancée. Une perspective socioanthropologique et psychosociale]. Bruxelles, Belgium: Fondation Roi Baudouin.

Ceci, C., Purkis, M. E., & Björnsdóttir, K. (Eds.). (2011). *Perspectives on care at home for older people*. New York, NY: Routledge.

Clarke, A. E., Mamo, L., Fosket, J. R., Fishman, J. R., & Shim, J. K. (Eds.). (2010). *Biomedicalization: Technoscience and transformations of health and illness in the U.S.* Durham, NC: Duke University Press.

Cohen-Shalev, A., & Marcus, E. L. (2012). An insider's view of Alzheimer: Cinematic portrayals of the struggle for personhood. *International Journal of Ageing and Later Life, 7*, 73–96.

Cox, L., Mason, P., Bagley, M., Steinsaltz, D., Stefanovska, A., Bernjak, A., …Davies, T. (2014). Understanding ageing: Biological and social constructions. In A. Walker (Ed.), *The new sciences of ageing* (pp. 25–76). Bristol, UK: Policy Press.

DementiaToday. (2013). *Brain plasticity & Alzheimer's disease*. Retrieved from www.dementia-today.com/brain-plasticity-and-alzheimers-disease-2/ (accessed March 2014).

Department of Health. (2014). *Better care for people with 2 or more long term conditions. Comorbidities – a framework of principles*. Retrieved from www.gov.uk/government/publications/better-care-for-people-with-2-or-more-long-term-conditions (accessed August 2016).

Department of Work and Pensions. (2005). *Opportunity age: Meeting the challenges of the 21st century*. Retrieved from http://webarchive.nationalarchives.gov.uk/20081021225600/dwp.gov.uk/opportunity_age/ (accessed January 2017).

Diedrich, L. (2007). Stories for and against the self: Breast cancer narratives from the United States and Britain. In *Treatments: Language, politics, and the culture of illness* (pp. 54–81). Minneapolis: University of Minnesota Press.

Featherstone, M., & Hepworth, M. (1993). Images in ageing. In J. Bond & P. Coleman (Eds.), *Ageing in society* (pp. 304–332). London, UK: Sage.

Foucault, M. (1980). The confession of the flesh. In C. Gordon (Ed.), *Power/knowledge: Selected interviews and other writings 1972–1977* (pp. 194–228). New York, NY: Pantheon Books.

Foucault, M. (1991). Politics and the study of discourse. In G. Burchell, C. Gordon & P. Miller (Eds.), *The Foucault effect: Studies in governmentality* (pp. 87–104). London, UK: Harvester Wheatsheaf.

Garfinkel, H. (1967). *Studies in ethnomethodology.* Englewood Cliffs, NJ: Prentice-Hall.

Geertz, C. (1973). *The interpretation of cultures: Selected essays.* New York, NY: Basic Books.

Giddens, A. (1984). *The constitution of society.* Cambridge, UK: Polity Press.

Giddens, A. (1991). *Modernity and self-identity: Self and society in the late modern age.* Stanford, CA: Stanford University Press.

Goffman, E. (1958). *The presentation of self in everyday life* (Monograph No. 2). Edinburgh, UK: University of Edinburgh, Social Sciences Research Centre.

Goffman, E. (1963). *Behavior in public places: Notes on the social organization of gatherings.* Glencoe, IL: Free Press of Glencoe.

Gove, D., Downs, M., Vernooij-Dassen, M., & Small, N. (2016). Stigma and GPs' perceptions of dementia. *Aging and Mental Health, 20*, 391–400.

Halewood, M. (2016). Do those diagnosed with Alzheimer's disease lose their souls? Whitehead and Stengers on persons, propositions and the soul. *The Sociological Review, 64*, 786–804.

Haraway, D. (2008). *When species meet.* Minneapolis: University of Minnesota Press.

Heidegger, M. (2008). The question concerning technology. In D. F. Krell (Ed.), *Basic writings: Martin Heidegger* (pp. 307–342). New York, NY: HarperCollins,.

Hepworth, M. (1995). Positive ageing: What is the message? In R. Bunton et al. (Eds.), *The sociology of health promotion: Critical analyses of consumption, lifestyle and risk* (pp. 175– 188). London, UK: Routledge.

Herskovits, E. (1995). Struggling over subjectivity: Debates about the 'Self' and Alzheimer's disease. *Medical Anthropology Quarterly, 9*, 146–164.

Higgs, P., & Jones, I. R. (2009). *Medical sociology and old age.* Abingdon, UK: Routledge.

Hillman, A., & Latimer, J. (2017). Cultural representations of dementia [Special issue: Dementia across the lifespan and around the globe]. *PLoS Medicine.* Retrieved from http://journals. plos.org/plosmedicine/article/authors?id=10.1371/journal.pmed.1002117

Hillman, A., & Latimer, J. (in press). Somaticization, the making and unmaking of *minded persons* and the fabrication of dementia. *Social Studies of Science.*

Hockey, J., & James, A. (2002). *Social identities across the life course.* Basingstoke, UK: Palgrave Macmillan.

Hurd-Clarke, L. (2010). *Facing age: Women growing older in anti-ageing culture.* Lanham, MD: Rowman-Littlefield.

ITV. (2016). *The Missing, Series 2.* Production Companies: New Pictures, Company Pictures, Two Brothers Pictures, and Playground Entertainment. Director: Ben Chanan; Created by and Screenplay by: Harry and Jack Williams.

Katz, S. (2005). *Cultural aging: Life course, lifestyle, and senior worlds.* Peterborough, ONT: Broadview Press.

Katz, S., & Peters, K. (2008). Enhancing the mind? Memory medicine, dementia and the aging brain. *Journal of Aging Studies, 22*, 348–355.

Kaufman, S., Shim, J., & Russ, A. (2006). Old age, life extension and the character of medical choice. *Journal of Gerontology: Social Sciences, 61*(B), S175–S184.

Kings Fund. (2012). *Long term conditions and multimorbidity.* Retrieved from http://www.kingsfund.org.uk/time-to-think-differently/trends/disease-and-disability/long-term-conditions-multi-morbidity#morbidity (accessed August 2016).

Kohli, M. (2007). The institutionalization of the life course: Looking back to look ahead. *Research in Human Development*, *4*, 253–271.

Kontos, P. C. (2005). Embodied selfhood in Alzheimer's disease: Rethinking person-centered care. *Dementia*, *4*, 553–570.

Larsen, T. (2013). Acts of entification: The emergence of thinghood in social life. In N. Rapport (Ed.), *Human nature as capacity: Transcending discourse and classification* (pp. 154–178). New York, NY: Berghan Books.

Laslett, P. (1989). *A fresh map of life: The emergence of the third age*. London, UK: Weidenfeld and Nicolson.

Latimer, J. (1997). Giving patients a future: The constituting of classes in an acute medical unit. *Sociology of Health & Illness*, *19*, 160–185.

Latimer, J. (1999). The dark at the bottom of the stair: Participation and performance of older people in hospital. *Medical Anthropology Quarterly*, *13*, 186–213.

Latimer, J. (2000a). Socialising disease: Medical categories and inclusion of the aged. *The Sociological Review*, *48*, 383–407.

Latimer, J. (2000b). *The conduct of care: Understanding nursing practice*. Oxford, UK: Blackwell Science.

Latimer, J. (2009). Introduction: Body, knowledge, world. In J. Latimer & M. Schillmeier (Eds.), *Un/knowing bodies* (pp. 1–22). Oxford, UK: Wiley Blackwell

Latimer, J. (2011). Home, care and frail older people: Relational extension and the art of dwelling. In C. Ceci, M. E. Purkis & K. Björnsdóttir (Eds.), *Perspectives on care at home for older people* (pp. 35–61). New York, NY: Routledge.

Latimer, J. (2013). Being alongside: Rethinking relations amongst different kinds. *Theory, Culture & Society*, *30*, 77–104.

Latimer, J. (forthcoming). *Biopolitics and the limits to life: Ageing, biology and society in the 21st century*. Abingdon, UK: Routledge.

Latimer, J., Bagley, M., Davis, T., & Kipling, D (2011). Ageing science, health care and social inclusion of older people. *Quality in Ageing & Older Adults*, *12*, 11–16.

Latimer, J., & Munro, R. (2015). Unfolding class? Culture, modernity and uprooting [Special Issue: The Great British class survey]. *The Sociological Review*, *63*, 415–432.

Latimer, J., & Puig de la Bellacasa, M. (2011). Re-thinking the ethical: Everyday shifts of care in biogerontology. In N. Priaulx (Ed.), *Ethics, law and society* (Vol. 5, pp. 153–174). Farnham, UK: Ashgate.

Lawler, S. (2005). Disgusted subjects: The making of middle-class identities. *The Sociological Review*, *53*, 429–446.

Lock, M. (2014). *The Alzheimer's conundrum: Entanglements of aging and dementia*. Princeton, NJ: Princeton University Press.

Lyman, K. A. (1989). Bringing the social back in: A critique of the biomedicalization of dementia. *The Gerontologist*, *29*, 597–605.

Lyotard, J.-F. (1984). *The postmodern condition: A report on knowledge* (G. Bennington, Trans.). Manchester, UK: Manchester University Press.

Martin, M., Kontos, P., & Ward, R. (2013). Embodiment and dementia. *Dementia*, *12*, 283–287.

Macrae, H. (1999). Managing courtesy stigma: The case of Alzheimer's disease. *Sociology of Health & Illness*, *21*, 54–70.

MacGregor, C., Petersen, A., & Parker, C. (2017, June 26). Hyping the market for 'anti-ageing' in the news: From medical failure to success in self-transformation. *BioSocieties*. https://doi.org/10.1057/s41292-017-0052-5

Milne, R. (2016). In search of lost time: Age and the promise of induced pluripotent stem cell models of the brain. *New Genetics & Society*, *35*, 383–408.

Minkler, M., & Holstein, M. B. (2008). From civil rights to … civic engagement? Concern of two critical gerontologists about a 'new social movement' and what it portends. *Journal of Aging Studies, 22*, 196–204.

Moreira, T., & Bond, J. (2008). Does the prevention of brain ageing constitute anti-ageing medicine? Outline of a new space of representation for Alzheimer's Disease. *Journal of Aging Studies, 22*, 356–365.

Moreira, T., May, C., & Bond, J. (2009). Regulatory objectivity in action: Mild cognitive impairment and the collective production of uncertainty. *Social Studies of Science, 39*, 665–690.

Moreira, T., & Palladino, P. (2008). Squaring the curve: The Anatomo-politics of ageing, life and death. *Body & Society, 14*, 21–47.

Moser, I. (2011). Dementia and the limits to life: Anthropological sensibilities, STS inferences, and possibilities of action in care. *Science, Technology & Human Values, 36*, 704–722.

Munro, R. (2016). Extension and the disposal of the world: Double-crossing systems, culture, self and language. *The Sociological Review, 64*, 424–446.

Mykytyn, C. E. (2010). A history of the future: The emergence of contemporary anti-ageing medicine. *Sociology of Health & Illness, 32*, 181–196.

Neilson, B. (2012). Ageing, experience, biopolitics: Life's unfolding. *Body & Society, 18*, 44–71.

Oliver, D. (2008). 'Acopia' and 'social admission' are not diagnoses: Why older people deserve better. *Journal of the Royal Society of Medicine, 101*, 168–174.

Peel, E. (2014). 'The living death of Alzheimer's' versus 'Take a walk to keep dementia at bay': Representations of dementia in print media and carer discourse. *Sociology of Health & Illness, 36*, 885–901.

Petersen, A. R. (2015). *Hope in health: The socio-politics of optimism*. Basingstoke, UK: Palgrave Macmillan.

Pickersgill, M. (2013). The social life of the brain: Neuroscience in society. *Current Sociology, 61*, 322–340.

Piet, P. (2012). Overcoming stigma is the first step to beating Alzheimer's disease and dementia. In N. L. Batsch & M. S. Mittelman (Eds.), *World Alzheimer report 2012. Overcoming the stigma of dementia* (pp. 17–19). Alzheimer's Disease International. Retrieved from https://www.alz.co.uk/research/WorldAlzheimerReport2012.pdf (accessed November 2016).

Rabinow, P., & Sullivan, W. M. (1979). *Interpretive social science: A reader*. Berkeley: University of California Press.

Riles, A. (2000). *The network inside out*. Ann Arbor: University of Michigan Press.

Robertson, A. (1991). The politics of Alzheimer's disease: A case study in apocalyptic demography. In M. Minkler & C. L. Estes (Eds.), *Critical perspectives on aging: The political and moral economy of growing old* (pp. 135–150). Amityville, NY: Baywood.

Rose, N., & Novas, C. (2004). *Biological citizenship*. London, UK: Blackwell Publishing.

Rowe, J. W., & Kahn, R. L. (1997). Successful aging. *The Gerontologist, 37*, 433–440.

Rudge, T. (2009). Beyond caring: Discounting the differently known body. *The Sociological Review, 6*(Special Issue 2), 233–248.

Saks, O. (2007). *Musicophilia: Tales of music and the brain*. New York, NY: Knopf.

Schmidt, W. C. (2011). Medicalization of aging: The upside and the downside. *Marquette's Elder's Advisor, 13*, article 2. Retrieved from http://scholarship.law.marquette.edu/cgi/viewcontent.cgi?article=1003&context=elders (accessed August 2016).

Schweda, M., & Pfaller, L. (2014). Colonization of later life? Laypersons' and users' agency regarding anti-aging medicine in Germany. *Social Science & Medicine, 118*, 159–165.

Seale, C. (1996). Stigma and normality. In B. Davey & C. Seal (Eds.), *Experiencing and explaining disease* (pp. 11–26). Basingstoke, UK: Palgrave Macmillan.

Shilling, C. (2002). Culture, the 'sick role' and the consumption of health. *British Journal of Sociology, 53*, 621–638.

Shine, J. P., Hodgetts, C. J., Postans, M., Lawrence, A. D., & Graham, K. S. (2015). APOE-ε4 selectively modulates posteromedial cortex activity during scene perception and short-term memory in young healthy adults. *Scientific Reports, 5*, article 16322.

Siddique, H. (2016, November 14). Dementia and Alzheimer's disease leading cause of death in England and Wales. *The Guardian*. Retrieved from https://www.theguardian.com/society/2016/nov/14/dementia-and-alzheimers-leading-cause-of-death-england-and-wales (accessed November 2016).

Skeggs, B. (2011). Imagining personhood differently: Person value and autonomist working-class value practices. *The Sociological Review, 59*, 496–513.

Skeggs, B. (2017). A crisis in humanity: What everyone with parents is likely to face in the future. *The Sociological Review Blog*. Retrieved from https://www.thesociologicalreview.com/blog/a-crisis-in-humanity-what-everyone-with-parents-is-likely-to-face-in-the-future.html (accessed September 2017).

Swallow, J. (2016). Understanding cognitive screening tools: Navigating uncertainty in everyday clinical practice. In M. Boenink, H. van Lente & E. Moors (Eds.), *Emerging technologies for diagnosing Alzheimer's disease: Innovating with care* (pp. 123–139). London, UK: Palgrave Macmillan.

Swinnen, A., & Schweda, M. (Eds.). (2015). *Popularizing dementia: Public expressions and representations of forgetfulness*. Berlin, Germany: Transcript.

Tanzi, R. E., & Bertram, L. (2001). New frontiers in Alzheimer's disease genomics. *Neuron, 32*, 181–184.

Taussig, M. (1999). *Defacement: Public secrecy and the labour of the negative*. Stanford, CA: Stanford University Press.

Turner, B. (2009). *Can we live for ever?* London, UK: Anthem Press.

Turner, V. (1967). *The forest of symbols: Aspects of Ndembu ritual*. Ithaca, NY: Cornell University Press.

Twigg, J. (2000). Carework as a form of bodywork. *Ageing & Society, 20*, 389–411.

Tyler, I. (2013). *Revolting subjects: Social abjection and resistance in neoliberal Britain*. London, UK: Zed Books.

United Nations, Department of Economic and Social Affairs, Population Division. (2013). *World population ageing*. New York, NY: United Nations.

Vincent, J. (2008). The cultural construction old age as a biological phenomenon: Science and anti- ageing technologies. *Journal of Aging Studies, 22*, 331–339.

Vos, R., Ocampo, J. A., & Cortez, A. L. (Eds.). (2008). *Ageing and development*. New York, NY: United Nations Publications.

WHO. (2011). *Global health and ageing*. Retrieved from http://www.nia.nih.gov/sites/default/files/global_health_and_aging.pdf (accessed December 2016).

WHO. (2015). *Dementia: A public health priority*. Retrieved from http://www.who.int/mental_health/neurology/dementia/dementia_thematicbrief_executivesummary.pdf?ua=1 (accessed December 2016).

Williams, S., Higgs, P., & Katz, S. (2012). Neuroculture, active aging and the 'older brain': Problems, promises and prospects. *Sociology of Health & Illness, 34*, 64–78.

Author biography

Joanna Latimer is Professor of Sociology, Science and Technology and Director of the Science and Technology Studies Unit (SATSU), University of York, UK. Having studied English Literature as an undergraduate, she then trained and worked as a nurse. She won a fellowship to do a PhD about older people in acute medicine, published as *The Conduct of Care*. Having worked at Keele as Senior Research Fellow in Nursing and then in the Centre for Social Gerontology, Joanna took up a lectureship in Sociology at Cardiff, progressing to chair in 2009. Her research focuses on the cultural, social and existential effects and affects for how science, medicine and health care are done. She works ethnographically, examining everyday processes of inclusion and exclusion. She is especially interested in the worlds people make together and the biopolitics they are entangled in and circulate. Making contributions at the leading edge of social theory, Joanna has written about the constituting of classes, motility, extension, aboutness, naturecultures, care, dwelling, the politics of imagination, body–world relations and class. Currently she is exploring the notion of the threshold. Joanna has published many articles and books, including *The Gene, The Clinic and The Family*, awarded the 2014 FSHI annual book prize. She is a longstanding member of the editorial board of *The Sociological Review*, and editor of the journal *Sociology of Health & Illness*. Currently she is writing a new book for Routledge, *Biopolitics and the Limits to Life: Ageing, Biology and Society in the 21st Century*, and co-editing two special issues, one on contemporary developments in Alzheimer's research (with Richard Milne and Shirlene Badger) and the other entitled *Intimate Entanglements* (with Daniel Lopez).

Voices in the revolution: Resisting territorial stigma and social relegation in Porto's historic centre (1974–1976)

The Sociological Review Monographs
2018, Vol. 66(4) 139–158
© The Author(s) 2018
Reprints and permissions:
sagepub.co.uk/journalsPermissions.nav
DOI: 10.1177/0038026118777423
journals.sagepub.com/home/sor

João Queirós and Virgílio Borges Pereira
University of Porto, Portugal

Abstract
This article tries to broaden the research agenda on territorial stigmatisation. It reviews some theoretical arguments on the relevance of a relational sociological reading of the processes of territorial stigmatisation, and proposes a study of these processes during a period of political revolution and social instability, through discussion of the case presented by the city of Porto, Portugal, in the mid-1970s. Based on the study of institutional archives, ethnographic work in several neighbourhoods, and semi-structured interviews with social actors involved in these processes, the article describes the urban and housing conditions of inner city Porto's working-class boroughs in the first three quarters of the 20th century and discusses the forms of political and social resistance taken up by residents from the most dilapidated neighbourhoods following the revolution of April 1974. The sociological analysis of the actions that gave origin to the *voice* of the residents in the historic centre of the city in this period reveals significant interaction with the processes of territorial stigmatisation, via organised collective resistance.

Keywords
Porto, resistance, territorial stigmatisation, voice, working classes

Introduction

It is widely acknowledged that territorial stigmatisation involves a complex system of social causality. To understand the origin and structuring of this phenomenon sociologically, one needs to address the way that institutions' mechanisms of social reproduction

Corresponding author:
João Queirós, Instituto de Sociologia, Faculdade de Letras da Universidade do Porto, Via Panorâmica, s/n,
4150-564 Porto, Portugal.
Email: jqueiros@letras.up.pt

intersect with the social reproduction strategies of individuals and their families. This article starts by reviewing some theoretical arguments on the relevance of a relational sociological reading of the processes of territorial stigmatisation. It then seeks to analyse the interactions between those social reproduction mechanisms and strategies during a period of political revolution and social instability profoundly marked by a housing crisis and by extensive processes of territorial stigmatisation and social and political relega- tion. The article presents sociological and socio-historical research that seeks to broaden the research agenda on territorial stigmatisation, through the discussion of the case pre- sented by the city of Porto, Portugal, in the mid-1970s.

The approach involves a description of the urban and housing conditions of inner city Porto's working-class boroughs in the first three quarters of the 20th century. The article then focuses on the position-taking strategies and social and political forms of resistance that were developed by the residents of the most dilapidated neighbour- hoods in Porto following the revolution of April 1974. Apart from identifying the actions taken by those residents, attention will be paid to the importance of the collec- tive work that was developed to refuse and invert the stigma attached to those areas at that time. The article also analyses how members of the city's most disadvantaged social groups were able, in a somehow paradoxical manner, to explore the contradic- tions and political opportunities of the revolutionary period, thus turning the right to housing into an achievable political goal. Their social and political accomplishments would ultimately come to be limited in scope. Nevertheless, the anatomy of these residents' actions, coming from the most socially and symbolically dilapidated neigh- bourhoods of revolutionary Porto in the 1970s, and particularly from its historic cen- tre, reveals significant interaction with the processes of territorial stigmatisation, via organised collective resistance. What is at stake here is an attempt to broaden the research on *resistance to territorial stigma*, through the identification of its corre- sponding social and symbolic properties.

Scrutinising the spatial taint in post-revolutionary Porto: Theoretical guidelines and methodological strategy

Life in physically and socially disadvantaged environments is often the object of simplis- tic readings. Therefore, it should be studied under a relational analytic framework, which can capture how residents develop symbolic and practical competences regarding their actions and probable futures. The production of these competences occurs at the intersec- tion between social agents' strategies and mechanisms of social reproduction. Here, as in other contexts, the inertia of social life and the modes of reproduction that support it are found 'in the objective probabilities inscribed in the underlying tendencies of different social fields (as tendencies to produce stable frequencies and regularities, frequently reinforced by explicit rules), and in subjective aspirations, roughly adjusted to those tendencies, which are inscribed in the inclinations of the habitus' (Bourdieu, 1994, p. 12, authors' translation).

Combining Bourdieu's theoretical and methodological relationalism with Goffman's Durkheim-inspired analysis of the 'interaction order', Wacquant reveals the importance of space, its uses and representations, 'as a distinctive anchor of social discredit' (Wacquant, 2008, Ch. 8; Wacquant, Slater, & Pereira, 2014, p. 1272). This means broadening Goffman's (1963) propositions to encompass spatial taint as another constituent of stigmatisation. Besides highlighting the relationship between processes of territorial stigmatisation and social reproduction mechanisms in advanced capitalist societies, Wacquant (2007, 2010) draws attention to the everyday strategies individuals develop to deal with territorial stigmatisation. Among social agents' strategies of material and symbolic investment (Bourdieu, 1994, p. 6), those that aim to confront territorial stigma may take on relatively plural configurations and purposes, since they are products of the 'mode of reproduction' in which they occur, and reflect the relations between the volume, composition and potential of the capitals of those putting them forward (Bourdieu, 1979/1984).

Extending Wacquant's theoretical framework, a recent study by the authors (Pereira & Queirós, 2014) drew attention to the advantages of considering the different practical and symbolic strategies developed by social agents to confront territorial stigma. The approach we proposed encompassed the notions of 'loyalty', 'voice' and 'exit' (Hirschman, 1970) as heuristic references in the sociological understanding of those strategies, and of the collective or individual actions that materialise them. The empirical evidence gathered, which built on prior research (Pereira, 2005), highlighted how significant segments of the residential population – particularly unskilled service sector workers – in one of Porto's largest social housing estates had by the end of the first decade of the 21st century found ways of deflecting the stigma attached to their place of living and thus to themselves. These included individualistic 'exit' strategies that implied – when leaving the *'bairro'* was not an option – a withdrawal to the private sphere, or distancing themselves from 'tainted' neighbours through the construction and evidencing of micro-differences. The study showed, however, that this type of strategy, and the corresponding inscription in local social space of those using it, did not account for all neighbours' everyday experiences, leaving room to examine the multidimensionality of these processes. Although individualistic 'exit' strategies were found to be highly important in this and other studies (Charlesworth, 2000; Paugam, 1991; Schwartz, 1990; Wacquant, 2008), it is equally important to consider that individual and collective strategies to find a 'voice' can also be effective as means of confronting stigmatisation in specific residential contexts. Civic action led by organised social collectives constitutes a particularly refined and socially demanding practice, given the energies of 'social physics' it requires; finding the inner city 'activists' (Krase, 1977) becomes crucial to understanding the processes enabling the production and expression of 'voice' regarding territorial stigmatisation. This effort can also cast new light on the debate on collectively experienced stigma and the politics of identity put forward by specific social groups willing to build and gain control over the image of themselves – a topic Goffman left quite underdeveloped in his works (see, for instance, Goffman, 1963, Ch. 3).

Following the general objectives of recent studies (Jensen & Christensen, 2012; Kirkness, 2014; Kirkness & Tijé-Dra, 2017; Slater & Anderson, 2012), as well as the theoretical challenges proposed by Tyler and Slater in the Introduction to this monograph issue, this article analyses the social processes through which resistance to territorial stigma is developed and enacted, by looking at the forms of social and political protest that sustained resistance to territorial stigma in the city of Porto, Portugal, during the revolutionary period after April 1974. The Portuguese case is relevant if one wishes to broaden the historical and sociological understanding of conflicts structured around urban struggles and social movements, as several sociological and socio-historical works have highlighted (Cerezales, 2003; Downs, 1989; Fishman, 2011; Hammond, 1988; Pinto, 2013; Queirós, 2015a; Topalov, 1976). In moments like the one mentioned, and in contexts like Porto, the forms of collective resistance to territorial stigma deserve analytical attention. In epistemological and methodological terms, the 'extended case method' (Burawoy, 1998, 2009) and 'short-time socio-history' (Gobille, 2008) are employed to historically reconstitute protests and daily experiences in the city's socially disadvantaged neighbourhoods, based on a wide range of data sources. These include an analysis of several institutional archives, a critical inventory of newspaper articles, ethnographic work in several neighbourhoods, and over 40 semi-structured interviews with social actors involved in these processes (neighbourhood activists, social workers, architects and decision-makers).

The next section of this article seeks to portray the configuration of the processes of social and spatial relegation that characterised Porto in the mid-1970s. Focusing on the results of the study of the collective work of neighbourhood activists in inner city Porto, the article then analyses how a course of action was designed to consolidate and evidence 'voice' and resistance to territorial stigmatisation and social and political relegation by those most affected by it. The article proposes, furthermore, a reading of the events that led to such collective action in the city.

Porto, 1974: An uneven city under social and political 'pressure'

April the 25th 1974 is one of the most decisive dates in 20th-century Portugal: at dawn that day, a group of young captains led a revolutionary military action in Lisbon that put an end to the longest dictatorship of that century in Western Europe. Forty-eight years of government by a far-right authoritarian regime ended that same day. There was minimal resistance by the overthrown regime to the military coup and the ensuing revolution spread to the rest of the country and overseas territories. It would come to be known as the 'Carnation Revolution', due to the peaceful manner in which events generally unfolded and to the impact of the image of those flowers in the barrels of soldiers' weapons. Despite the generally non-violent nature of the revolution, and the fact that the revolutionary militaries were not initially very politically minded, the following days and months were ones of intense social and political agitation, contributing to a profound reform of the organisation and structuring of politics and public policies in the country (see, for instance, Chilcote, 2010, pp. 89–116).

The effects of the revolution in Porto, the second-largest Portuguese city and the most important in the north of the country, were deep. It became the scene of strong collective mobilisations and significant urban struggles. The large demonstrations of 1 May 1974, which took over the most emblematic public spaces of Portugal's major cities, bear witness to widespread popular support for the revolution. These demonstrations initiated further political discussion and the formulation of manifestos and demands by social and political movements. In Porto, May Day demonstrations advocated primarily for the right to political freedom, a right which rapidly found expression in several priorities for action in terms of civil and social rights.

Among these, the housing question and the problem of spatial, social and symbolic inequalities gained significant importance. The residents of social housing estates made their presence clear at Porto's May Day demonstrations, bringing to the fore a set of fully defined demands: among other priorities, they demanded decent housing and, especially, the immediate revision of social housing regulations and the end of the repressive authority to which they were subject (Pereira, 2013; Queirós, 2015a).

The housing question did not emerge randomly at the core of the demands that shaped Portugal's first steps towards democracy in the mid-1970s. Indeed, and in the case of Porto, growing industrialisation in the last quarter of the 19th century defined some of the main elements of social division among the city's inhabitants; social relegation becoming increasingly intertwined with deficient housing conditions and a process of spatial relegation, which was particularly noticeable in the inner city. These transformations not only affected a large number of Porto's inhabitants, but also showed great resilience, as we will see below, and a strong capacity for reproduction over time. The start and consolidation of the process of industrialisation in Porto was shaped by very intense growth in the occupation of its historic centre. From very early on, the traditional tall, narrow houses of the medieval centre of Porto (Oliveira & Galhano, 1994) were gradually appropriated by people coming from an extensive rural exodus, originating in Portugal's inland peasant regions. Consequently, this area of the city became the first point of entry into the urban world for this migrant population. Occupation was so significant that it did not take long to exhaust the medieval area's capacity to receive more people, leaving it overcrowded for much of the 20th century. The city's expansion to the outer limits of the medieval walls meant the formation of new urban nuclei which altered – and amplified – the problem of inadequate housing that characterised the city. At the same time as this generalised urban and industrial expansion, insanitary '*ilhas*' (literally, *islands*, slum areas; see for example Figure 1) started to appear to the rear of petit bourgeois houses in the city centre and rapidly absorbed the demand for housing faced by the historic centre in previous decades. Averaging 16 square meters, these small and precarious houses, which were similar to British back-to-back houses, were relatively easy to build, since they lacked basic amenities, and thus became home to the city's working classes. These were the houses the average working-class family could afford to rent, but they were very far from representing access to decent housing conditions (Teixeira, 1996).

At the turn of the 20th century, the high population density in Porto was the cause of severe social and public health issues (Barbosa, 1906; Jorge, 1899, 1899/2011), which left a lasting mark on the city's physical and social landscape. For most of the first half of the 20th century, the medieval centre and the insanitary inner city 'islands' offered an acute representation of the spatiality of such problems. Social and health problems were the root cause of a very negative public depiction of these areas and became, early on, the focus of attention and public discussion, particularly on the part of the socialist,

Figure 1. One of Porto's *ilhas*, by the end of the 1930s.
Source: Porto City Council's General Archive (CMP-AG-DMESG-2379; exact date unknown).

republican and hygienist social and political movements that had appeared in the city from the end of the 19th century. Regardless, actual recognition of the need for state intervention was extremely slow and almost always controversial. It is estimated that about 39,000 people lived in these 'islands' at the end of the 1910s, more than a fifth of the city's population (Pereira, 1994). An important segment of the population also resided in the medieval zone, in overcrowded and dilapidated dwellings, such as those known as *'casas da malta'* (collective lodgings for workers from rural areas), as well as in other types of individual or collective improvised lodging (Queirós, 2015a). Although the Republican regime established in October 1910 passed legislation on the need for public intervention in the housing sector, new, accessible housing for the working classes, as a result of either philanthropic initiatives or state action, was scarce. Some of these new houses were of admittedly reasonable quality, with innovative architecture, but the over-all number of new houses built in the 1910s and 1920s was very low (Gonçalves, 2016; Pereira & Queirós, 2012). Later, when the march on Lisbon on 28 May 1926, and the fall of the First Republic paved the path to power for the far-right authoritarian regime (Rosas, 2012), the political priority in this domain would change. Access to housing became a significant political and ideological goal of the new regime. In the 1930s and 1940s, policies designed to promote individual housing and access to homeownership were favoured, but the fact is that state action hardly accounted for the needs of the more disadvantaged strata of the working classes living in the medieval centre and in Porto's 'islands' (Pereira, 2016; Pereira & Queirós, 2012, 2013).

For many years, local authorities voiced their concerns and conducted surveys of the insalubrious housing of these areas. But only in 1956 would a new, rent-based social housing policy be implemented, for workers poorly housed in the medieval centre and

Figure 2. Residents being transferred from the city centre to the new council housing estates in the mid-1950s.
Source: Porto City Council's Historical Archive (F-NP-CMP-04-02035; exact date unknown).

Porto's inner city 'islands'. This measure was undoubtedly influenced by struggles within the regime regarding the widely precarious living conditions experienced in Porto's 'islands'. The programme, which envisaged the building of 6000 dwellings, was fully implemented during the next 10 years and a very significant segment of the poorly housed population was moved to new council housing neighbourhoods, which were almost always located on the city's outskirts, in areas that were not at that time urbanised (Pereira, 2017). About 15–20% of the inhabitants of the central area were transferred to these new peripheral neighbourhoods. Moving to relatively small houses in the new three to four-storey buildings generally represented an improvement in the housing conditions of the relocated populations. But in many cases, it also represented a forced population transfer, which deliberately rejected the reconstitution of the original neighbourly units and created an environment of neighbourhood relationships that was subject to the repressive action of public authorities, through the implementation of a surveillance system that had a deep impact on the residents' ordinary existence and ways of life (Figure 2). The basic social problems of the relocated populations were only partially addressed by the innovative community development measures implemented in some neighbourhoods by the Catholic Church (Fernandes, 2016). Furthermore, these processes did not help the new council housing estates to become immune to processes of social and spatial segregation and symbolic denigration (Cardoso, 1983; Gros, 1982; Matos & Salgueiro, 2005; Queirós, 2015b).

Resisting territorial stigma, fighting social and political relegation in Porto: Strategies to find a *voice* in the revolution

Important segments of the working classes in Porto, and particularly in its historic centre, soon became involved in the political process which followed the military coup that put an end to the '*Estado Novo*' on 25 April 1974. The commitment with which they did so could easily seem paradoxical to those who only superficially knew that reality, and even to some residents, former residents and other past or current inhabitants of that physical and social space. The intensity of their involvement was particularly notable in the many mobilisations of the first years of the new regime, whose leitmotivs were access to decent housing and the social improvement of the city's more impoverished urban areas. The protagonists' active, committed engagement often occurred – and herein lies the apparent paradox – in spite of their relatively restricted economic and cultural resources, the extreme and persistent stigmatisation and public disregard to which they were subject, and their supposed 'unwillingness' towards, and 'distrust' of, conventional politics, state intervention and collective action (Queirós, 2015a, Ch. 2; Figure 3).

It was, in fact, in some of the most decapitalised and stigmatised socio-spatial contexts of Porto that the earliest and most fervent forms of mobilisation and popular rallying arose in this historical period. The purpose of this section is to look at this specific spatial-temporal reality as a socio-historical and sociological observatory of conditions that could allow the production of 'voice' and forms of collective action by groups marked by social relegation and territorial stigmatisation.

The example of *Bairro de S. João de Deus*, possibly the most destitute and vilified council housing estate at that time, is particularly interesting, since it was the birthplace of the first organised movement of residents in the post-revolutionary period. Their actions were in fact not merely the product of 'rage', 'desperation' or the 'audacity' of those 'who had nothing to lose', but they were rather the result of the creative and strategic claiming of the social and political opportunities opened by the April 1974 revolution. In the case of *Bairro de S. João de Deus*, collective action was built on a previous history of concerted locally based political action. In November 1973, for instance, the neighbourhood had been the focus of public attention because a group of residents had rallied together to stop a forced eviction by the local administrative and police authorities (Rodrigues, 1999, pp. 81–82). Among those who wished to express their disapproval of how council housing was managed, there were residents with no prior associative or political experience, but also several residents who had been involved for years in local cultural and sports associations, and workers who were members of professional associations, progressive Catholic groups and other associations. Among the younger 'activists',

Figure 3. A view of a street in Porto's historic centre in the 1950s.
Source: Porto City Council's Historical Archive (F-NP-CMP-07-00109; exact date unknown).

several had participated for years in community organising initiatives initiated at the local community centre by 'militant' social workers. Moreover, due to its specificity and symbolism, *Bairro S. João de Deus* – or '*Tarrafal*', as it was known,[1] the 'end of the line' estate to which public authorities sent the city's 'undesirables' – was also the focus of attention for left-wing intellectuals and political activists, who searched there for insights into the daily life of the more marginalised segments of Porto's working classes under the dictatorship, and for ways of helping to enhance their political engagement.

Without this legacy of prior experiences and the development of associative and political competences, and without the support and encouragement of social workers and the many activists in the field, it is unlikely that the numerous and organised contingent of *S.*

João de Deus's residents would have left the neighbourhood to march in the parade of May Day 1974. Indeed, in five days, between 25 April and 1 May that year, the neighbourhood's residents organised a committee, prepared a list of major demands – at the top of which was the abolition of council housing regulations and the figure of the estate 'overseer' – elaborated a critique of the dominant representation of life in council housing estates, and set forth quite skilfully their participation in the first democratic celebrations of 'Workers' Day'.

In downtown Porto, where demonstrators flocked from all over the city and surrounding areas, *S. João de Deus*'s residents stood out, with their organised presence and slogans; they would play a central role in fostering the emerging 'movement of council housing tenants' (Coelho, 1986, p. 646; Pereira, 2013, pp. 242–246). A former resident and associate leader of *S. João de Deus* recalls those intense days:

> The movement in council housing estates was born precisely on April the 30th. … At that time, I was running *Unidos ao Porto*, which was the neighbourhood's association, and R. [a political activist] showed up, with some social workers … from *Obra Diocesana* [a social institution of the Catholic Church]. … Anyway, they showed up and we grouped and right on May the 1st we marched out into the streets with a demonstration. And other associations joined us and we marched into the streets, from *São João de Deus*, and it just grew. … The first action of the council housing associations was to contest the regulations that we had by that time in council housing estates. Those regulations greatly protected the overseers. Then we started to fight for reintegration, because there were many houses. … Indeed, after April the 25th 1974, there were many empty houses in the council estates. (E1b, 62 years old, retired, lived for several decades in *Bairro de S. João de Deus*, before and after April 1974)

In Porto's historic centre, where social and housing problems were different from those in council housing estates, yet equally urgent, the first post-revolutionary urban movements were led by families living in collective dwellings and the several 'guesthouses' of the area. In an apparently 'unplanned unison' (Coelho, 1986, p. 646), dozens of families from the historic centre did exactly what many other families from dilapidated, overcrowded areas were doing, and occupied vacant council houses from the very first days of the revolutionary period. This movement was undoubtedly influenced by the sharing of relevant information and the coordination, minimal and tacit, fostered by the network of relationships that connected the movement's actors across the city. While some residents, particularly women, organised picket lines to secure the occupied houses, others were organising protests demanding the legalisation of the occupations. During May 1974, the first tenants' committees were created in the historic centre. Although 'provisional', as they were presented in those days, these committees had a decisive role in advancing the main popular demands, through the organisation of systematic protests against the City Council's representatives; they aimed to legalise the occupations, but also to promote access to other abandoned houses in council estates, to cut rents and to repress subletting practices, which were considered to be the major problem in the area (Queirós, 2015a, Ch. 3; Rocha, Teixeira, Sousa, & Meireles, 1983, pp. 106–107).

Less than a month after 25 April 1974, and confronted with the magnitude of the housing occupation movement in Portugal's major cities, the provisional government issued an order legalising the occupations that had taken place immediately after the fall of the dictatorship. Although this order prohibited further occupations, the success of the initial occupations generated enthusiasm and reinforced the capacity for mobilisation and action by neighbours' organisations. 'Revolutionary legitimacy' seemed to prevail; the advocates of a 'legality of severance' seemed to be triumphing over the advocates of a 'legality of continuity'. Consequently, the occupations continued, and the protests and demonstrations intensified (Cerezales, 2003; see also Santos, 1984). A social worker recalls:

> It was the people ... who found out that the council housing estates had several houses that were abandoned; and they came to talk to M. and I [two social workers working in the historic centre] and they said to us very clearly: '... Now, you'll come with us or you won't come with us. We're going there [to the City Hall, to talk to the provisional local government] so we can have our own house'. And so we went to the City Hall to claim the abandoned houses in the council housing estates. ... [T]hey went inside – some were dock workers, you know, strong, burly men – and they said: 'We want to talk to the Head of [Urban and Housing] Services'. There was a huge line of people waiting to be received by him ... this was in May [19]74. And he sent someone to say: 'I will see the lady but not the gentlemen'. To which they replied: 'You go there and tell him that the houses are for us or else we'll go in there right now and knock him down'. ... And then I went inside, he was very polite, but I was filled with their courage, and said: 'Mister Director, it's not even worth talking about this. You'll have to see them now, and the houses are for them, or else they'll come in here and knock you down. They asked me to tell you this.' He became very nervous, then ordered everyone out, and did not see anyone else that day, but the houses were indeed distributed to them. (ED29a, 59 years old, social worker, worked in Porto's historic centre in the 1970s)

The crisis of 'entrance rights' and the generalised disorganisation of the political and bureaucratic fields in that period gave the members of Porto's working classes unique opportunities to limit and directly influence state action. But, as in the case of *S. João de Deus* neighbourhood, in Porto's historic centre it was not only situational factors that explained the rapid and efficient way in which residents took advantage of such political opportunities: a prior history of 'everyday resistance' (Scott, 1985) and local associative participation; shared everyday experiences, practical knowledge and meanings, bolstered by proximity and neighbourliness, and transmuted into shared orientations and dispositions for common action; the presence of a 'capital of autochthony' (Retière, 2003); strong, representative local leaderships; as well as institutional support, technical and material resources, and allied social groups – all these factors were decisive in helping to create a local, alternative representation and public discourse over that specific socio-spatial configuration, and the will of collective action to bring it to fruition (see Queirós, 2015a, for analytic and empirical developments on this matter).

The interaction between residents and other social agents, such as social workers, architects, and cultural and political activists, was especially relevant, since it amplified the opportunities for the more disadvantaged social groups to explore the room for political *manoeuvre* that arose in the post-revolutionary period. The excerpt above shows the importance of these 'allies', and this is reiterated by residents from the historic centre, like this interviewee, who recalls the events of the time as follows:

From [19]74 to [19]80 it was all a bit chaotic. The residents were the ones in charge … . At the time, Architect C. was at the City Council, we had a social worker, R., who was always by our side, and we also had the president of the Parish Council here, so this was all ours. (ED12, 60 years old, former resident of Porto's historic centre transferred to a council housing estate in the mid-1970s, associative leader, retired factory worker)

Although pointing out the importance of certain 'social alliances', this sketch of urban movements in post-revolutionary Porto does not allow us to envisage them in condescending or paternalistic terms. In fact, residents were often at odds with other social groups' intentions, and frequently avoided their counselling, rejected their attempts to frame social movements institutionally or ideologically, and insisted on alternative paths of action. Particularly in the revolutionary period, the social workers, architects, cultural activists and left-wing local politicians were often 'dragged' into the wave of popular action, thus colliding with institutional hierarchies and orientations.

Table 1 gives an overview of these events and how the movement progressed in the two years after the revolution.

Under pressure from street level, provisional governments tried to deal with the flow of action and to answer popular demands. In June 1974, the Secretary of State for Housing and Urbanism discussed the basis of an urgent plan of action with members of the tenants and neighbours' associations (Cerezales, 2003, p. 94). The consequences of these meetings came shortly afterwards, in the form of significant legal and institutional innovations: by the end of July, the Ministries of Internal Affairs and of Social Equipment and the Environment approved the creation of a state 'specialised technical body' – SAAL (*Serviço de Apoio Ambulatório Local*) – whose mission was to support, through City Councils, the initiatives of poorly housed populations willing to transform their own areas. The initiative broke with the rationale and methodology that had until then been at the core of state urban and housing initiatives: apart from defining as central the active participation of neighbours, SAAL wanted to ensure the appropriation of valuable central urban locations by families from the working classes who had lived in those places for several years (see, for instance, Bandeirinha, 2007; Pereira, 2014; Portas, 1986).

Following the creation of the post of 'Government Commissioner' and a visit to Porto's historic centre from the then Secretary of State for Housing and Urbanism, the architect Nuno Portas, in July 1974, the government prepared the required legislation to take forward the urban renewal programme designed in the 1960s by architect Fernando Távora. With the creation of CRUARB, the state commission for the urban renewal of core areas of Porto's historic centre, in October 1974, urban and housing intervention in that part of the city acquired legal and institutional support. The programmed intervention claimed the will to: decongest the area, by definitively or temporarily transferring some local families to council housing estates located at the edges of the historic centre; renovate buildings and public spaces in order to enhance the local historical, cultural and social heritage, while maintaining the largest possible number of local families in their homes; ensure the return of previously expelled or relocated local families to the historic centre; combine interventions in public space with acts of social and cultural promotion; and involve tenants' and neighbours' associations in drawing up and implementing operations (see, for instance, Queirós, 2015a; Williams, 1980) (Figure 4).

Table 1. Working-class urban movements and collective action in post-revolutionary Porto: A chronology of major events (1974–1976).

The 'movement' and its action in Porto

1 May 1974: S. João de Deus tenants participate, in an organised fashion, in May Day demonstrations in the city centre. They are joined by residents' organisations from many other working-class boroughs in Porto. At this date, a 'wave' of housing occupations is already underway.

26 May 1974: In Porto, residents march towards, and protest in front of, the City Hall. They demand the elimination of the council housing regulations and the legalising of all occupations.

15 July 1974: The 'Plenary Meeting of Council Estates' Committees', gathering members from several tenants' associations, declares the abolition of former council housing regulations, and approves a set of 'Fundamental Regulatory Principles of Porto's Council Housing Estates'.

30 November 1974: In the historic centre, residents organise a rally on 'the right to adequate housing for the working classes'.

December 1974: Protests demanding the suspension of evictions intensify throughout the city; they are particularly vigorous in the historic centre, where the new neighbours' associations consolidate.

25 January 1975: Residents protest in front of the City Hall; they claim 'the right to housing' and 'the immediate dismissal of fascists from the City Council'.

17 May 1975: Demonstrations in Lisbon and Porto gather several thousands of residents and their associations; they demand new legislation on occupations and expropriations, and the public funding of new affordable housing and urban renewal.

25–27 July 1975: The first 'SAAL/North Meeting' takes place, with the participation of most of the region's tenants' committees.

August 1975: Tenants' committees call for a 'united, popular, non-affiliated' demonstration aiming to protect the 'conquests of the Revolution'; the demonstration takes place in Lisbon on 20 August and in Porto on 25 August.

September through November 1975: The 'occupation movement' goes on; families are occupying the city's abandoned houses, particularly in the housing estates that are under construction and in Porto's historic centre.

May 1976: Urban renewal in the historic centre is finally underway, but there are still reports of occupations of abandoned houses by local families.

Table 1. (Continued)

Major political events and legal-institutional innovations

19 May 1974: The 'National Salvation Committee', acting as the main political authority after the April 1974 military coup, issues a statement authorising the legalisation of occupations taking place in the previous weeks and until that date; the same statement prohibits any further occupations.

6 August 1974: A new state institution focusing on housing construction and the urban renewal of working-class areas in major Portuguese cities – 'SAAL' [*Serviço de Apoio Ambulatório Local*] – is created.

7 October 1974: A new institution focusing on housing rehabilitation and the urban renewal of Porto's historic centre – 'CRUARB' [*Comissariado para a Renovação Urbana da Área da Ribeira-Barredo*] – is created.

7 November 1974: A new decree-law establishes the 'right to free association': tenants' associations and other organisations can now be freely constituted.

January 1975: Porto's City Council provisional government abolishes previous council housing regulations, following the tenants' committees demands. Also in January 1975, a new decree-law suspends all evictions based on the unilateral termination of contracts by landlords, or resulting from illegal subletting or similar situations.

14 April 1975: A new decree-law (commonly referred to as 'the occupations' law') is published, establishing the rules necessary for the legalisation of the occupation of abandoned houses.

25 April 1975: Elections for the 'Constituent Assembly' take place.

16 May 1975: A new decree-law (commonly referred to as 'the subletting law') defines the concept of 'overcrowded housing' and takes measures against subletting practices.

September 1975: The provisional military government – which was close to the tenants' committees – is removed from Porto's City Council; the new 'Civil Administrative Commission' abolishes the 'Municipal Assembly', an organism which had been created to favour the participation of tenants' committees in the local political decision-making processes.

2 April 1976: The nation's new democratic Constitution is promulgated; article 65 defines the 'right to housing' as a constitutional right.

25 April 1976: The first general elections in democracy take place. Mário Soares ('Socialist Party', centre-left) takes office as prime minister on 23 September 1976.

26 June 1976: Ramalho Eanes wins the presidential election. He takes office on 14 July.

12 December 1976: The first democratic municipal elections take place. In Porto, Aureliano Veloso, an engineer ('Socialist Party', centre-left), becomes the first Mayor to be elected through direct, universal suffrage.

Figure 4. Vasco Gonçalves, Portuguese Prime Minister in several provisional governments after April 1974 (bottom left, in first plane), visits CRUARB's works in *Ribeira-Barredo*, Porto's historic centre.
Source: Manuel Magalhães (personal archives; June 1980).

The effect of these proposals proved to be less than initially foreseen, but the 'voices' of residents were nevertheless at least partially translated into the legislation and institutions that were then created, and the public image and discourses regarding that traditionally segregated and stigmatised area of central Porto, as well as general political discourses and concerns, started to change significantly.

Concluding remarks

In this article, we have tried to underline, following Bourdieu (1994), that the understanding of the modes of social reproduction requires analysis of the relations between strategies and systems of mechanisms of social reproduction. Managing territorial stigma involves a plural configuration of activities. These can be read within the frame of different patterns of material and symbolic investment that are typical of the strategies of social reproduction of the residents of marginalised contexts (Wacquant, 2008). Such strategies are dependent on the volume, composition and trajectory of the capitals these agents hold and on the modalities of their encounter with the fields in which agents' capitals are inscribed (Bourdieu, 1979/1984). Involving a sense of positioning in social space, as well as of the struggles that constitute it, these strategies can be transformed into civic engagement and militant activity (Mantoti & Poupeau, 2004, pp. 5–11).

In the wake of the revolution that started on 25 April 1974, and of the crisis of social reproduction that it generated during the following months and years, Porto saw the development of a significant movement of residents that originated in the most stigmatised neighbourhoods of the city. This movement, notwithstanding the inscription of their members in the most deprived regions of the city's physical and social space, sought to constitute and capitalise the political opportunities opened by the revolutionary process. Through the 'movement', residents assumed an active *voice* with the aim of improving their living conditions, under slogans that proclaimed the right to housing and tried to reverse the stigmatisation processes which affected their residential contexts. Although influenced by intellectuals, activists and members of different public bureaucracies with responsibilities in the management of the neighbourhoods, these residents quickly organised and developed a specific political agenda, deeply embedded in the neighbourhood's social relations and with a strong autochthonous inscription (Retière, 2003). The forms of contention (Tilly, 1978) employed by these residents, with housing occupations as one of its major modalities, were inscribed in disputes sustained by strategies of assumption of voice developed by neighbours who invested in proposals to emancipate the quality of the built environment, as well as of the social and cultural life of the boroughs they inhabited. In the historic centre of 1970s Porto – an area which, two decades later, would be classified as World Heritage by UNESCO, and, four decades later, would be strongly exposed to tourism and gentrification (Queirós, 2015a, 2017) – the paths towards practical and symbolic improvement of the neighbourhood were far from being evident, and their implementation was very far from being a feasible political reality. At least for a short period, the residents of the historic centre managed to make their collective *voice* heard (Figure 4).

Territorial stigmatisation remains a significant characteristic of contemporary societies. The experience of Porto's historic centre's residents during the 1970s initiated a way to give voice to a critique of territorial stigma. Scrutinising this sort of experience can contribute to improving public awareness and a sociological reading of the role of community organising and collective action in fostering resistance to the blemish of place and the reproduction of urban and social inequality.

Funding

The preparation of the final version of this article benefited from funding from the Portuguese Foundation for Science and Technology, through the Institute of Sociology of the University of Porto (Unit UID/SOC/00727/2013).

Note

1. 'Tarrafal', or 'Tarrafal Camp', was the name of a feared political prison under Salazar's regime, located on the island of Santiago in Cape Verde. The name by which the neighbourhood became known is, therefore, quite relevant. About the history of the prison, see Tavares (2006).

References

Bandeirinha, J. A. (2007). *O processo SAAL e a arquitectura no 25 de Abril de 1974* [The SAAL process and architecture on 25 April 1974]. Coimbra, Portugal: Imprensa da Universidade de Coimbra.

Barbosa, A. P. (1906). *Da tuberculose no Porto: dissertação apresentada à Escola Médico-Cirúrgica do Porto* [Tuberculosis in Porto: dissertation presented at Porto School of Medicine and Surgery). Porto, Portugal: Typographia da Empreza Artes e Letras.

Bourdieu, P. (1984). *Distinction: A social critique of the judgement of taste*. Cambridge, MA: Harvard University Press (Original work published 1979).

Bourdieu, P. (1994). Stratégies de reproduction et modes de domination [Reproduction strategies and modes of domination]. *Actes de la Recherche en Sciences Sociales, 105*, 3–12.

Burawoy, M. (1998). The extended case method. *Sociological Theory, 16*, 4–33.

Burawoy, M. (2009). *The extended case method: Four countries, four decades, four great transformations, and one theoretical tradition*. Berkeley: University of California Press.

Cardoso, A. (1983). *State intervention in housing in Portugal (1950–1980)* (PhD thesis). Reading, UK: University of Reading

Cerezales, D. P. (2003). *O poder caiu na rua: Crise de estado e acções colectivas na revolução Portuguesa 1974–1975* [The power fell in the streets: State crisis and collective action in the Portuguese revolution, 1974–1975]. Lisboa, Portugal: Imprensa de Ciências Sociais.

Charlesworth, S. (2000). *Phenomenology of working class experience*. Cambridge, UK: Cambridge University Press.

Chilcote, R. H. (2010). *The Portuguese revolution: State and class in the transition to democracy*. Lanham, MD: Rowman & Littlefield.

Coelho, M. B. (1986). Um processo organizativo de moradores (SAAL/Norte – 1974–1976) [A process of organisation of local residents (SAAL/Norte – 1975–1976)]. *Revista Crítica de Ciências Sociais, 18–19–20*, 645–671.

Downs, C. (1989). *Revolution at the grassroots: Community organizations in the Portuguese revolution*. Albany, NY: SUNY Press.

Fernandes, A. T. (2016). A igreja e a 'questão social' na cidade do Porto [The church and the social question in the city of Porto]. In V. B. Pereira (Ed.), *A habitação social na transformação da cidade: sobre a génese e estruturação do 'Plano de Melhoramentos para a Cidade do Porto' de 1956* [Social housing in the transformation of the city: on the genesis and structuring of the 1956 'Improvement Plan for the City of Porto'] (pp. 21–34). Porto, Portugal: Afrontamento.

Fishman, R. M. (2011). Democratic practice after the revolution: The case of Portugal and beyond. *Politics & Society, 39*, 233–267.

Gobille, B. (2008). L'événement Mai 68: Pour une sociohistoire du temps court [The events of May '68: A sociohistory of a brief time]. *Annales. Histoire. Sciences Sociales, 63*, 321–349.

Goffman, E. (1963). *Stigma: Notes on the management of spoiled identity*. Englewood Cliffs, NJ: Prentice-Hall.

Gonçalves, E. (2016). O alojamento operário portuense nas primeiras décadas do século XX: da casa familiar ao bloco comunitário [Working class housing in Porto in the early 1900s: from the family home to the community block]. In V. B. Pereira (Ed.), *A habitação social na transformação da cidade: sobre a génese e estruturação do 'Plano de Melhoramentos para a Cidade do Porto' de 1956* [Social housing in the transformation of the city: on the genesis and structuring of the 1956 'Improvement Plan for the City of Porto'] (pp. 9–20). Porto, Portugal: Afrontamento.

Gros, M. C. (1982). *O alojamento social sob o fascismo* [Social housing under fascism]. Porto, Portugal: Afrontamento.

Hammond, J. H. (1988). *Building popular power: Workers' and neighborhood movements in the Portuguese revolution*. New York, NY: Monthly Review Press.

Hirschman, A. O. (1970). *Exit, voice, and loyalty: Responses to decline in firms, organizations, and states*. Cambridge, MA: Harvard University Press.

Jensen, S. Q., & Christensen, A.-D. (2012). Territorial stigmatization and local belonging: A study of the Danish neighbourhood Aalborg East. *City, 16*, 74–92.

Jorge, R. (1899). *Demografia e higiene na cidade do Porto* [Demographics and hygiene in the city of Porto]. Porto, Portugal: Repartição de Saúde e Higiene da Câmara Municipal do Porto.

Jorge, R. (2011). *A peste bubónica no Porto* [The bubonic plague in Porto]. Porto, Portugal: Deriva (Original work published 1899).

Kirkness, P. (2014). The *cités* strike back: Restive responses to territorial taint in the French *banlieues. Environment and Planning A, 46*, 1281–1296.

Kirkness, P., & Tijé-Dra, A. (Eds.). (2017). *Negative neighbourhood reputation and place attachment: The production and contestation of territorial stigma*. Abingdon, UK: Routledge.

Krase, J. (1977). Reactions to the stigmata of inner city living. *Journal of Sociology and Social Welfare, 7*, 997–1011.

Mantoti, F., & Poupeau, F. (2005). Le capital militant. Essai de definition [The militant capital. A definition]. *Actes de la Recherche en Sciences Sociales, 155*, 5–11.

Matos, F., & Salgueiro, T. B (2005). Habitar nas cidades portuguesas: caracterização do parque habitacional e estratificação da habitação [Living in Portuguese cities: characterisation of the housing stock and housing stratification]. In C. A. Medeiros (Ed.), *Geografia de Portugal. Sociedade, paisagens e cidades* [The geography of Portugal. Society, landscapes and cities] (pp. 313–338). Lisboa, Portugal: Círculo de Leitores.

Oliveira, E. V., & Galhano, F. (1994). *Arquitectura Tradicional Portuguesa* [Traditional Portuguese architecture]. Lisboa, Portugal: Dom Quixote.

Paugam, S. (1991). *La disqualification sociale: essai sur la nouvelle pauvreté* [Social disqualification: an essay on the new poverty]. Paris, France: PUF.

Pereira, G. M. (1994). Housing, household, and the family: The 'Ilhas' of Porto at the end of the nineteenth century. *Journal of Family History, 19*, 213–236.

Pereira, G. M. (2014). SAAL: um programa de habitação popular no processo revolucionário [SAAL: a programme of working class housing in the revolutionary process]. *História. Revista da Faculdade de Letras do Porto, IV*, 13–31.

Pereira, V. B. (2005). *Classes e culturas de classe das famílias Portuenses. Classes sociais e modalidades de estilização da vida na cidade do Porto* [Classes and class cultures of Porto's families. Social classes and modalities of lifestyles in the city of Porto]. Porto, Portugal: Afrontamento.

Pereira, V. B. (2013). Sobre a importância de se chamar Ernesto, Avelino ou Amadeu: sobre as memórias do encontro entre o social e a política no Porto pós-revolucionário [On the importance of being Ernesto, Avelino and Amadeu: memories of the encounter between the social and the political in post-revolutionary Porto]. In B. Monteiro & V.B. Pereira (Eds.), *A política em estado vivo: uma visão crítica das práticas políticas* [Living politics: a critical perspective on political practices] (pp. 237–251). Lisboa, Portugal: Edições 70.

Pereira, V. B. (Ed.). (2016). *A habitação social na transformação da cidade: sobre a génese e estruturação do 'Plano de Melhoramentos para a Cidade do Porto' de 1956* [Social housing in the transformation of the city: on the genesis and structuring of the 1956 'Improvement Plan for the City of Porto']. Porto, Portugal: Afrontamento.

Pereira, V. B. (2017). Society, space and the effects of place: Theoretical notes and results of a sociological research on social housing in the city of Porto. In M. Mendes, T. Sá, & J. Cabral (Eds.), *Architecture and the social sciences: Inter- and multidisciplinary approaches between society and space* (pp. 99–120). Dordrecht, The Netherlands: Springer.

Pereira, V. B., & Queirós, J. (2012). *Na modesta cidadezinha: génese e estruturação de um bairro de casas económicas do Porto [Amial, 1938–2010]* [In the modest little town: genesis and structuring of an 'economic housing' estate in Porto (Amial, 1938–2010)]. Porto, Portugal: Afrontamento.

Pereira, V. B., & Queirós, J. (2013). Une maison pour le 'peuple' portugais: genèse et trajectoire d'un quartier du programme des 'maisons économiques' à Porto (1938–1974) [A house for the Portuguese people: genesis and socio-historical trajectory of a neighbourhood under the 'economic houses' programme (1938–1974)]. *Politix, 101*, 49–78.

Pereira, V. B., & Queirós, J. (2014). 'It's not a bairro, is it?'. Subsistence sociability and focused avoidance in a public housing estate. *Environment and Planning A, 46*, 1297–1316.

Pinto, P. R. (2013). *Lisbon rising: Urban social movements in the Portuguese revolution, 1974–1975*. Manchester, UK: University of Manchester Press.

Portas, N. (1986). O processo SAAL: entre o estado e o poder local [The SAAL process: between state and local power]. *Revista Crítica de Ciências Sociais, 18–19–20*, 635–644.

Queirós, J. (2015a). *No centro, à margem. Sociologia das intervenções urbanísticas e habitacionais do Estado no centro histórico do Porto* [In the centre, at the margins. Sociology of state urban and housing action in Porto's historic centre]. Porto, Portugal: Afrontamento.

Queirós, J. (2015b). Dereliction, displacement and distress in a disappearing social housing estate. In M. Allegra, E. Gualini, & J. Mourato (Eds.), *Conflict in the city: Contested urban spaces and local democracy* (pp. 180–195). Berlin, Germany: Jovis Verlag.

Queirós, J. (2017). A disappearing world: The ever-expanding 'frontier of gentrification' through the eyes of Porto's historic centre long-time residents. In A. Albet & N. Benach (Eds.), *Gentrification as a global strategy: Neil Smith and beyond* (pp. 196–209). Abingdon, UK: Routledge.

Retière, J.-N. (2003). Autour de l'autochtonie. Réflexions sur la notion de capital social populaire [Around autochthony. Reflections on the concept of popular social capital]. *Politix, 63*, 121–143.

Rocha, M. C., Teixeira, M. I., Sousa, M. V., & Meireles, M. F. (1983). *A operação de renovação urbana Ribeira-Barredo* [The urban renewal intervention in Ribeira-Barredo]. Lisboa, Portugal: Instituto Superior de Ciências do Trabalho e da Empresa.

Rodrigues, M. (1999). *Pelo direito à cidade: o movimento de moradores do Porto, 1974–1976* [The right to the city: residents' movements in Porto, 1974–1976]. Porto, Portugal: Campo das Letras.

Rosas, F. (2012). *Salazar e o poder: a arte de saber durar* [Salazar and power: the art of knowing how to survive]. Lisboa, Portugal: Tinta da China.

Santos, B. S. (1984). A crise e a reconstituição do Estado em Portugal (1974–1984) [The crisis and the reconstitution of the state in Portugal (1974–1984))]. *Revista Crítica de Ciências Sociais, 14*, 7–29.

Schwartz, O. (1990). *Le monde privé des ouvriers. Hommes et femmes du nord* [The private world of workers: Men and women of the north]. Paris, France: PUF.

Scott, J. C. (1985). *Weapons of the weak: Everyday forms of peasant resistance*. New Haven, CT: Yale University Press.

Slater, T., & Anderson, N. (2012). The reputational ghetto: Territorial stigmatisation in St. Paul's, Bristol. *Transactions of the Institute of British Geographers, 37*, 530–546.

Tavares, J. M. S. (2006). *O campo de concentração do Tarrafal (1936–1954): a origem e o quotidiano* [Tarrafal's concentration camp (1936–1954): origins and everyday life]. Lisboa, Portugal: Colibri.

Teixeira, M. (1996). *Habitação popular na cidade oitocentista* [Popular housing in the eighteenth century city]. Lisboa, Portugal: FCG/JNICT.

Tilly, C. (1978). *From mobilization to revolution*. Reading, MA: Addison Wesley.

Topalov, C. (1976). La politique du logement dans le processus révolutionnaire portugais (1974–1975) [The politics of housing in the process of the Portuguese revolution]. *Espaces et Sociétés, 17–18*, 109–135.

Wacquant, L. (2007). Territorial stigmatization in the age of advanced marginality. *Thesis Eleven, 91*, 66–77.

Wacquant, L. (2008). *Urban outcasts: A comparative sociology of advanced marginality.* Cambridge, UK: Polity Press.

Wacquant, L. (2010). Urban desolation and symbolic denigration in the hyperghetto. *Social Psychology Quarterly, 73*, 215–219.

Wacquant, L., Slater, T., & Pereira, V. B. (2014). Territorial stigmatization in action. *Environment and Planning A, 46*, 1270–1280.

Williams, A. (1980). Conservation planning in Oporto: An integrated approach in the *Ribeira-Barredo. Town Planning Review, 51*, 177–194.

Author biographies

João Queirós is an Invited Professor at the School of Education and at the School of Management and Technology of the Polytechnic Institute of Porto, Portugal. He does research at the Institute of Sociology of the University of Porto. He was a member of the Executive Board of its R&D Unit between 2010 and 2015. He also collaborates with the Centre for Research and Innovation in Education of the Polytechnic of Porto. His teaching and research interests cover: social change and urban transformations; social and housing policies; local and regional development; community studies; and adult education. He is the author of several articles, books and book chapters in this area, including *No Centro, à Margem* (Porto: Edições Afrontamento, 2015), a work on the social consequences of urban and housing policies in inner city Porto, as seen throughout the last five decades, as well as the recent 'A disappearing world: The ever-expanding "frontier of gentrification" through the eyes of Porto's historic centre long-time residents', which is part of a tribute to Neil Smith (*Gentrification as a Global Strategy: Neil Smith and Beyond*, London: Routledge, 2017).

Virgílio Borges Pereira is an Associate Professor of Sociology at the Department of Sociology of the Faculty of Arts of the University of Porto, where he has taught since 1994, and a researcher at the Institute of Sociology of the same university. He was director of its R&D Unit between 2010 and 2015. Since 2003, he has collaborated with the Faculty of Architecture of the University of Porto, where he teaches both Master's and PhD courses. His research combines sociological, historical and ethnographic approaches and focuses on the production of social and cultural inequalities in different spatial contexts in Northern Portugal, with a special interest in the study of the sociological legacy of Bourdieu's work. He has written extensively on the constitution of social spaces (*Classes e Culturas de Classe das Famílias Portuenses* [Classes and Class Cultures of Porto's Families], Porto: Edições Afrontamento, 2005), class cultures and social housing. His work has been published in different languages. Among his recent publications in English are 'The structuration of lifestyles in the city of Porto: A relational approach', in L. Hanquinet & M. Savage (Eds.), *Routledge International Handbook of Sociology of Art and Culture* (London: Routledge, 2016) and 'Society, space and the effects of place: Theoretical notes and results of sociological research on social housing in the city of Porto', in M. Mendes, T. Sá, & J. Cabral (Eds.), *Architecture and the Social Sciences: Inter- and Multidisciplinary Approaches between Society and Space* (Dordrecht: Springer, 2017).

The invention of the 'sink estate': Consequential categorisation and the UK housing crisis

The Sociological Review Monographs
2018, Vol. 66(4) 159–179
© The Author(s) 2018
Reprints and permissions:
sagepub.co.uk/journalsPermissions.nav
DOI: 10.1177/0038026118777451
journals.sagepub.com/home/sor

Tom Slater
Institute of Geography, University of Edinburgh, UK

Abstract
This article explores the history and traces the realisation of a category that was invented by journalists, amplified by free market think tanks and converted into policy *doxa* (common sense) by politicians in the United Kingdom: the 'sink estate'. This derogatory designator, signifying social housing estates that supposedly create poverty, family breakdown, worklessness, welfare dependency, antisocial behaviour and personal irresponsibility, has become the symbolic frame justifying current policies towards social housing that have resulted in considerable social suffering and intensified dislocation. The article deploys a conceptual articulation of agnotology (the intentional production of ignorance) with Bourdieu's theory of symbolic power to understand the institutional arrangements and cognitive systems structuring deeply unequal social relations. Specifically, the highly influential publications on housing by a free market think tank, Policy Exchange, are dissected in order to demonstrate how the activation of territorial stigma has become an instrument of urban politics. The 'sink estate', it is argued, is the semantic battering ram in the ideological assault on social housing, deflecting attention away from social housing not only as urgent necessity during a serious crisis of affordability, but as incubator of community, solidarity, shelter and home.

Keywords
agnotology, Bourdieu, housing, 'sink estate', symbolic power, territorial stigma, think tanks

Housing – having a roof over one's head – is absolutely central to human dignity, community, family, class solidarity and life chances (Madden & Marcuse, 2016). But intersecting with draconian welfare reforms, housing policies in the UK (particularly but not exclusively in England) are wreaking havoc upon people living at the bottom of the

Corresponding author:
Tom Slater, Institute of Geography, University of Edinburgh, Drummond Street, Edinburgh, EH8 9XP, UK.
Email: tom.slater@ed.ac.uk

class structure. A few snapshots of the situation across the UK suffice to assess the financial ruin and displacement of the poor created by four decades of housing policies tightly tethered to profit generation for owners of land and property, and correspondingly unmoored from providing shelter for people most in need. As Lansley and Mack (2015) detail in *Breadline Britain*, of the 4 million people in the private rented sector who live in poverty, a full 2 million of those are employed full-time. One-third of all private rented sector tenants in the UK are living in structurally inadequate housing, with poor insulation issues having major energy and health implications. More than 2 million households (and counting) are on the waiting list for social housing. A staggering 1.8 million households are spending over half their incomes on housing costs: the very poorest people have approximately £60 per week left for everything after housing costs are met. Local authorities have spent £3.5 billion on temporary housing in the last five years (Buchanan & Woodcock, 2016). Homelessness has become a fixture of cities and is still on the rise (there has been a substantial increase in rough sleeping since 2010) – even though there are over 750,000 empty homes across the UK. Security of tenure is a huge issue, amplified by the massive rise in 'assured shorthold tenancies' because of the explosion in 'buy-to-let' mortgages, a get-rich-quick scheme for landlords that until 2015 offered generous tax breaks, and still allows landlords to evict tenants without any reason. If food prices had risen the same rate as house prices since 1971, a fresh chicken would cost over £50 (Carylon, 2013). Under the banner of 'regeneration', social housing in English cities, particularly London, is being demolished at an unprecedented rate without replacement (Watt & Minton, 2016). Perhaps most arresting of all is that one-third of Conservative MPs have vested interests in maintaining the status quo, for they are private sector landlords.

Profit has been the guiding principle behind government housing policies for four decades. Spectacular fortunes have been made, but the cocktail of deregulation, privatisation and attacks on the welfare state has also made a spectacular mess.[1] This story is well known, having been very well documented and analysed by others (e.g. Dorling, 2014; Hodkinson, 2012; Meek, 2014). There is already an 'intimate history', rooted in personal experience, of the rise and fall of large social housing estates in the UK that tackles frontally the systematic disinvestment and profound stigma that quickly shattered the optimism over their initial construction (Hanley, 2007). Less well studied is the ongoing *ideological* assault on decommodified housing provision, particularly the institutions carrying out the ideological groundwork needed to make attractive the destructive policies deepening profound housing inequality. David M. Smith (1994) once noted that:

> Arguing for justice as equalization will inevitably face opposition from the vested interests who gain from inequality, and who have been able to marshal so much reverence for market outcomes and their association with social justice. Neoclassical economics has performed a powerful ideological role, in the hands of those whose primary purpose seems to have been to deflect criticism of distributional inequalities. (p. 123)

This article tackles one of those institutions holding the fort of vested housing interests: a free market think tank called Policy Exchange. Such think tanks have been massively influential in the formation of recent housing and welfare policies in the UK that have led to displacement and social suffering on a disturbing scale (Slater, 2016a). Given their influence, it is rather remarkable that these think tanks have not been subject to much analytic scrutiny, particularly on the housing and urban fronts. I argue that what is emerging is a *vested interest urbanism*, and free market think tanks – those who write for them, finance them and decide that their voice needs to be heard – are right at the heart of ensuring that there are certain stories that people hear and ultimately believe in respect of housing issues. These stories are truncations and distortions of social realities, and particular representations homologous to material interests. Crucially, the activation and amplification of the taint attached to certain places, which Wacquant (2007) calls 'territorial stigma', is a key tactic of think tanks deployed to control the housing narrative such that territorial stigma becomes an instrument of urban politics. In what follows, I provide an analytic dissection of the stigmatising tactics of Policy Exchange, fusing Robert Proctor's concept of agnotology with Pierre Bourdieu's concept of symbolic power to explain how the 'sink estate' has become a semantic battering ram in the ideological assault on social housing.

Agnotology and symbolic power: A conceptual articulation

> It is certain, in any case, that ignorance, allied with power, is the most ferocious enemy justice can have. (James Baldwin, 1972)

In his swashbuckling critique of the economics profession in the build up to and aftermath of the 2008 financial crisis, Mirowski (2013) argues that one of the major ambitions of politicians, economists, journalists and pundits enamoured with (or seduced by) neoliberalism is to plant doubt and ignorance among the populace:

> This is not done out of sheer cussedness; it is a political tactic, a means to a larger end. … Think of the documented existence of climate-change denial, and then simply shift it over into economics. (p. 83)

Mirowski makes a compelling argument to shift questions away from 'what people know' about the society in which they live towards questions about what people do *not* know, and why not. These questions are just as important, usually far more scandalous, and remarkably under-theorised. They require a rejection of appeals to 'epistemology' and, instead, an analytic focus on intentional ignorance production or *agnotology*. This term was coined by historian of science Robert Proctor, to designate 'the study of ignorance making, the lost and forgotten' where the 'focus is on knowledge that could have been but wasn't, or should be but isn't' (Proctor & Schiebinger, 2008, p. vii). It was while investigating the tobacco industry's efforts to manufacture doubt about the health hazards of smoking that Proctor began to see the scientific and political urgency in researching how ignorance is made, maintained and manipulated by powerful institutions to suit their own ends, where the guiding research question becomes, 'Why don't we know what we don't know?' As he discovered, the industry went to great lengths to give the impression that the cancer risks of cigarette smoking were still an open question even when the scientific evidence was overwhelming. Numerous tactics were deployed by the tobacco industry to divert attention from the causal link between smoking and cancer, such as the production of duplicitous press releases, the publication of 'nobody knows the answers' white papers, and the generous funding of decoy or red-herring research that 'would seem to be addressing tobacco and health, while really doing nothing of the sort' (Proctor & Schiebinger, 2008, p. 14). The tobacco industry actually produced research about everything except tobacco hazards to exploit public uncertainty (researchers commissioned by the tobacco industry knew from the beginning what they were supposed to find and not find), and the very fact of research being funded allowed the industry to say it was studying the problem. In sum, there are powerful institutions that want people not to know and not to think about certain conditions and their causes, and agnotology is an approach that traces how and why this happens.

Many scholars (and think tank writers) might claim that there is no such thing as the intentional production of ignorance; all that exists are people with different worldviews, interests, and opinions, and people simply argue and defend their beliefs with passion. Yet as I will demonstrate with reference to Policy Exchange, this claim would be very wide of the mark. Even when there is a vast body of evidence that is wildly at odds with what is being stated, and when the social realities of poverty and inequality expose the failures of deregulation at the top and punitive intervention at the bottom of the class structure, the 'free marketeers' become noisier and even more zealous in their relentless mission to inject doubt into the conversation and ultimately make their audiences believe that government interference in the workings of the 'free' market is damaging society. Therefore, tracking the ignorance production methods of 'the outer think-tank shells of the neoliberal Russian doll', to use Mirowski's (2013, p. 229) memorable phrasing, is a project of considerable analytic importance.

Agnotology, whilst very useful in dissecting the methods and tactics of messengers of disinformation, is less useful in explaining precisely how certain terms and categories are converted into common sense (often across the political spectrum) and become so powerful that alternative or competing terms, and the arguments they anchor, are kept off the political grid and the policy agenda. Pierre Bourdieu's concept of symbolic power is invaluable in such an analytic task. As explained by Bourdieu (1991) himself, symbolic power is:

[T]he power to constitute the given through utterances, to make people see and believe, to confirm or to transform the vision of the world and, thereby, action upon the world and thus the world itself, an almost magical power that enables one to obtain the equivalent of what is obtained through force (physical or economic) by virtue of the specific effect of mobilization. … What makes for the power of words and watchwords, the power to maintain or to subvert order, is belief in the legitimacy of the words and of those who utter them. (p. 170)

Wacquant (2017) helpfully distils these words to define symbolic power as:

…the capacity for *consequential categorization*, the ability to make the world, to preserve or change it, by fashioning and diffusing symbolic frames, collective instruments of cognitive construction of reality. (p. 57, emphasis added and reproduced with permission in the title of this essay)

Bourdieu produced an enormous body of work on symbolic power; indeed, Wacquant notes that it is 'a concept that Bourdieu elaborates over the full spectrum of his scientific life' (p. 57) and which runs from his early work on honour in Algeria to his late lecture courses at the Collège de France on the state, art and science. It is especially useful in analysing the classifying and naming powers of the state (Bourdieu, 2014; see e.g. Auyero, 2012). Even when non-state institutions such as tabloid newspapers and think tanks might be responsible for inventing and circulating particular terms and categories, symbolic power is helpful in tracing how such categories become elevated into authoritative and consequential discourses emanating from state officials and institutions:

> In the social world, words make things, because they make the meaning and consensus on the existence and meaning of things, the common sense, the doxa accepted by all as self-evident. (Bourdieu, 1996, p. 21)

In what follows I pay specific attention to a term that was invented by journalists, subsequently amplified and canonised by think tanks and then converted into doxa by politicians: the sink estate. This term has become the symbolic anchor for policies towards social housing that have resulted in considerable social suffering and intensified urban dislocation. The conceptual articulation of agnotology with symbolic power, I argue, allows us to understand the institutional arrangements and symbolic systems that fuse and feed off each other to structure the deeply unequal social relations behind such a serious housing crisis.

The sink estate: The genealogy and anatomy of a semantic battering ram

Tracing the genealogy and usage of the 'sink estate' category is instructive for any analysis of the plight of social housing estates in the UK. The etymology of *sink* dates back many centuries, and refers to a cesspit for wastewater or sewage – a receptacle that collects and stores effluent. It would therefore be somewhat simplistic to see 'sink' as a direct reference to something being poured down a kitchen sink, or just to the idea that people are sinking rather swimming in society. Wedding 'sink' to a tract of council housing – an act of symbolic violence that turns a receptacle that collects and stores effluent into a *place* that collects and stores the refuse of society – is a journalistic invention, and continues to be (though not exclusively) a journalistic trait. The first use of 'sink' by a UK newspaper to describe a geographical area was on 4 October 1972 in *The Daily Mail*, a right wing tabloid newspaper: 'The downward spiral of decline in these "sink" areas could be broken if the school led the way.' However, it was journalist Jane Morton who coined 'sink estate' in November (1976, in a short piece for *New Society* magazine, a short-lived left wing publication (absorbed by *New Statesman* magazine in 1988):

> Somewhere, in every town that has council houses at all, there's a sink estate – the roughest and shabbiest on the books, disproportionally tenanted by families with problems, and despised both by those who live there and the town at large. … As long as families on the margins of society are shunted into second best accommodation, there will be sinks. (p. 356)

Although 'sink estate' was first uttered in Parliament in 1983, the phrase did not appear in British political debate until the late 1980s, when politicians began using it to make direct links between housing tenure and deprivation; for example this statement by Labour MP Paul Boateng:

> They [the Conservative government] have set their hands to a course that is determined to create in our inner cities the development of welfare housing along American lines – sink estates to which people are condemned, with no prospect of getting out.[2]

The term cropped up occasionally after that in parliamentary debates, but 'sink estate' has circulated freely and widely since Tony Blair visited the Aylesbury Estate in south London in May 1997 to make his very first speech as Prime Minister: an event that Campkin (2013, pp. 95–104) rightfully analyses as the symbolic watershed moment in the emerging phenomenon of the 'sink estate spectacle'. Blair spoke of an 'underclass ... cut off from society's mainstream' and made a direct association between 'sink estates' and apparently self-inflicted poverty stemming from 'fatalism' and 'the dead weight of low expectations' (quoted in Crossley, 2017, p. 49).[3] Figure 1 shows the appearances of 'sink estate' in major UK newspapers over a 30-year period.[4] Campkin's assertion of the watershed moment is correct, as usage took off in 1997, and since then tabloids and broadsheets have used 'sink estate' freely. It is noteworthy that whilst a majority of major UK newspapers are right wing in political orientation, centre and left wing newspapers have used 'sink estate' just as frequently.

One thing becomes very clear from even a cursory analysis of the reporting during this timeframe – 'sink estate' is used to describe an area of council housing where the behaviour of tenants is, first, under intense moral condemnation, and second, both cause and symptom of poor housing conditions and neighbourhood malaise. The *Oxford English Dictionary* in fact lists one meaning of 'sink' as: 'A receptacle or gathering-place of vice, corruption, etc.'. In this respect there is a very important intellectual precursor to 'sink estate' that may explain why the phrase has gained such currency. The American ethologist John B. Calhoun, based on his experiments with rodents in the 1950s, developed the concept of the *behavioural sink* to warn against the dangers of overpopulation in urban environments. After putting rats in an enclosure and supplying them with an ideal 'rodent universe' (food, bedding and shelter), the animals bred rapidly, and Calhoun documented how they behaved as their enclosure became more crowded. He produced a typology of pathological crowding behaviours, and described the tendency to congregate in dense huddled knots of squalor and violence as the 'behavioural sink'.

As Ramsden and Adams (2009) explain in a paper tellingly entitled 'Escaping the Laboratory', Calhoun's concept was astonishingly influential, from its initial publication in the popular magazine *Scientific American* – where it remains one of the most cited papers ever in the field of psychology – to its influence on a generation of scholars in human ecology, social epidemiology and environmental psychology concerned with the problem of urban density; to its influence on urban planners and designers seeking physical solutions to social problems; to its popular uptake in science fiction, urban fiction (particularly the writings of Tom Wolfe), film and comic books. As Ramsden and Adams explain,

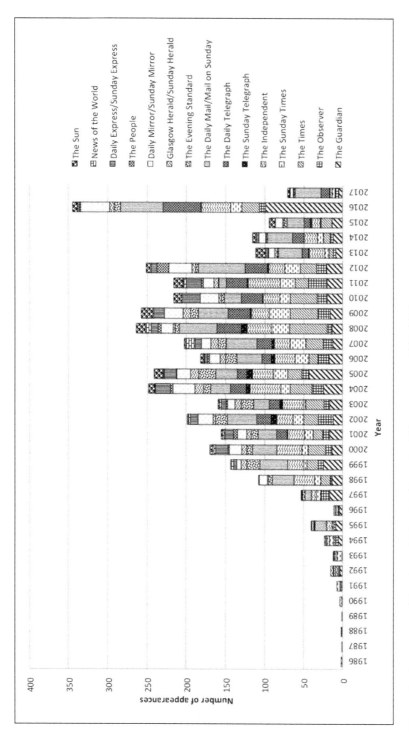

Figure 1. Appearance of the phrase 'sink estate' in major UK newspapers, 1986–2017.
Source: LexisLibrary.

Calhoun's description of the behavioral sink not only captured the sense of the city as a destructive force, but further, seemed to explain why it was that such an horrific environment seemingly acted almost as an attractor, drawing and holding together large numbers of people. The process was one of 'pathological togetherness', individuals conditioned to seek out the presence of others, even to the detriment of self and society. … Calhoun … had tapped into an extensive etymological precedent linking sinks with both cities and entropy. (2009, p. 773)

They are quick to point out that the diagnosis of problems was only one part of Calhoun's scientific life – he was convinced that within his experiments were possible solutions for the behaviours he had observed:

[H]e thought his experiments underlined the need for a revolution in the way we organise our societies and our cities. … However, in the furore surrounding the grim spectacle of the 'behavioral sink', Calhoun found that this ameliorative message was drowned out – everyone wanted to hear the diagnoses, no one wanted to hear the cure. (p. 780)

The fact that Calhoun's behavioural sink concept was 'extraordinarily appealing to popular audience' (p. 780) is not affirmation that the 'sink estate' label derives directly from it. However, when a concept circulates so widely and resonates so strongly with multiple audiences, it makes it easier for those using the related phrases that follow to gain symbolic footholds.

More elaborate media analysis of the data than can be provided here would dissect the reporting to determine the specific social and geographical contexts in which 'sink estate' was used, and continue to explain the fall in usage from 2013 to 2015. The significant spike in 2016, however, is directly because of a speech made by Prime Minister David Cameron in January of that year announcing his '100 sink estates' strategy, to be discussed shortly. As I will demonstrate in the next section, the political embrace and policy deployment of the derogatory designator 'sink estate' is a clear tactic in the ongoing condemnation of the very existence of social housing, and in blaming poverty on the behaviour/choices of tenants. However, it would be inaccurate to say that this is fuelled by newspapers, but rather by free market think tanks. It is one of these institutions in particular to which I now turn.

Policy Exchange and the marketplace of ignorance production

Policy Exchange was established in 2002, and is probably best known as former Prime Minister David Cameron's favourite think tank. It describes itself proudly as

… the UK's leading think tank. As an educational charity our mission is to develop and promote new policy ideas which deliver better public services, a stronger society and a more dynamic economy. The authority and credibility of our research is our greatest asset. Our research is independent and evidence-based and we share our ideas with policy makers from all sides of the political spectrum. Our research is strictly empirical and we do not take commissions. This allows us to be completely independent and make workable policy recommendations.[5]

The claims of independence are bold, given that it this 'educational charity' was founded by three Conservative MPs who had backed Michael Portillo's unsuccessful campaign in the 2001 Conservative Party leadership contest. Portillo was troubled by the 'nasty party' reputation of the Tories, and advocated a modernising shift towards more liberal social attitudes, whilst maintaining a commitment to Thatcherite economics. The day after Portillo withdrew from the leadership race, Archie Norman, former Conservative MP for Tunbridge Wells and the former CEO of Asda supermarkets (who masterminded its sale to WalMart in 1999 for £6.72 billion), said that he was planning to finance a new think tank: 'This is the future of the Conservative party and we would like to find a way of channeling that and harnessing it' (quoted in Sylvester, 2001). Nick Boles, currently Conservative MP for Grantham, who previously had a modest business career supplying painting and decorating tools to the DIY industry, was also involved from the start, describing Policy Exchange as his 'biggest achievement in politics so far'.[6] The third founder was Francis Maude (since 2015 Lord Maude of Horsham), a fixture on Conservative benches for over a quarter of a century. Maude felt that a new think tank should be free of the 'baggage' that he felt was affecting the Institute of Economic Affairs, Adam Smith Institute and Centre for Policy Studies, the trinity of 'policy institutes' behind the Thatcher revolution of the 1980s. He now claims that his creation 'bestrides the policy landscape like a colossus' (Maude, 2012).

Perhaps unsurprisingly, the inaugural chairman of Policy Exchange was staunch Thatcherite Michael Gove, currently Secretary of State for Environment, Food and Affairs, and one of the two central political architects of the exit of the UK from the European Union (the other being Boris Johnson). Policy Exchange's claim it does 'not take commissions' is a denegation, and an interesting choice of wording. It was registered with the Charity Commission in 2003. Registering as a charity can provide numerous advantages for a think tank, as charities do not have to pay corporation tax or capital gains tax, and donations to charities are tax free. Most significantly, think tanks can also use their charitable status to refuse requests for transparency in terms of who donates to them. *Who Funds You?* is a campaign to make the so-called think tanks more transparent, and Figure 2 shows the results of its enquiries (the methodology involved trawling through information provided on organisations' own websites, or via annual accounts where they were provided).

Many think tanks across the political spectrum are registered charities, so have the legal right not to disclose who funds them, but the more right wing and libertarian a think tank, the less likely it is to show funding transparency. In 2007, Policy Exchange was investigated by the Charity Commission after a complaint was made that it was effectively a research branch of the Conservative Party. The investigation, remarkably, found 'no evidence of party political bias'.[7]

Policy Exchange is a very busy institution. It produces an astonishing number of reports – literally hundreds of them since it was founded it 2002 – and it sponsors many events and public statements on various policy priorities like crime and justice, immigration, education, foreign affairs, and housing, planning and urban regeneration. Its influence in all these spheres has been immense in the UK over the past decade – major political speeches and catchy slogans often originate from Policy Exchange reports – but it is housing policy in particular where it is possible to see a direct imprint of think tank

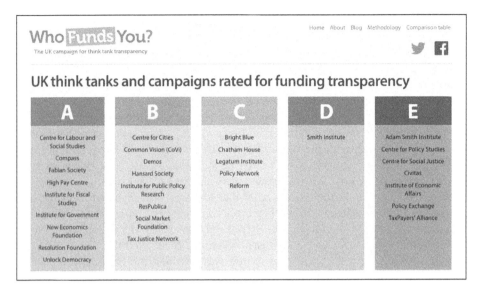

Figure 2. The funding transparency of leading UK think tanks. Those listed under 'A' name all funders who gave £5000 or more in the last reported year, and declare the exact amount given by each funder. Those listed under 'E' provide no or negligible relevant information. 'B', 'C' and 'D' lie somewhere in between in a hierarchy of transparency.
Retrieved from http://whofundsyou.org/

writing on what has been happening to people living at the bottom of the class structure in UK cities. A report entitled *Making Housing Affordable*, written by neoclassical economist Alex Morton and published in 2010, is arguably the most influential document of all. Many of the proposals in this document quickly became housing policy under the Coalition government (2010–2015) and subsequent Conservative governments, as did other work Morton authored, notably a report entitled *Ending Expensive Social Tenancies*. It was telling that, in December 2013, Alex Morton left Policy Exchange to become David Cameron's special advisor on housing policy, where he remained until Cameron resigned in June 2016.[8]

The *Making Housing Affordable* report argues that social housing of any form is a terrible disaster because it makes tenants unhappy, poor, unemployed and welfare dependent. Not only is this baseline environmental determinism, it is a reversal of causation: a very substantial literature on social housing in the UK demonstrates that the reason people gain access to social housing is *precisely because* they are poor and in need, and that it was *not social housing that created poverty and need* in the first place (e.g. Forrest & Murie, 1988; Hanley, 2007; Malpass, 2005). Nonetheless, here are just some of the things that Alex Morton says about social housing in order to denigrate it:

The real reason social housing fails is because of the incentives it creates. (p. 12)

[S]ocial housing will continually act to stop inactive tenants returning to work – essential to generate savings and reduce the welfare budget. (p. 12)

The current 'need' for social housing is not really a need for more social housing at all, but a need for new private housing. (p. 42)

Social housing has a substantial negative impact on employment per se over and above the characteristics of its tenants. (p. 51)

Social housing has always damaged equality of opportunity. … The effects of social housing are generally getting worse over time. (p. 52)

In the real world, it [prioritising those in housing need] has acted as an extremely sharp poverty trap. Welfare dependency is rewarded while independence from the state is penalized. (p. 59)

If an area is becoming gentrified the worse thing to do in terms of creating future poverty is to increase the social housing element in the area. (p. 61)

The bulk of these assertions come from cherry-picking various sound bites from a deeply problematic report on social housing written in 2007 by John Hills of the LSE (Hills, 2007) – one that embraces the highly dubious 'neighbourhood effects' thesis whilst simultaneously ignoring the question of systematic disinvestment in social housing and in people's lives – and also from numerous opinion polls commissioned by Policy Exchange, which are treated as 'robust evidence' and the definitive verdict on the topic under scrutiny. Had Morton consulted the literature on housing estates across Europe, he would have discovered that nowhere is low-income housing provided adequately by the market and also that the countries with the largest social housing sectors (Sweden, France, Holland, etc.) are those with the least problematic social outcomes (e.g. Musterd & Van Kempen, 2007; Power, 1997; Van Kempen, Dekker, Hall, & Tosics, 2005).

Having effectively argued that social housing is the scourge of British society, Alex Morton then goes on to propose what he feels are solutions to the housing crisis. Predictably, they involve helping social tenants into home ownership via the acquisition of considerable debt, and demolishing the 'worst' social housing estates and selling the land to private sector housing developers. He also posits repeatedly the hegemonic view that the housing crisis is created by too much demand and not enough supply, ignoring the inconvenient fact of over 750,000 empty homes across the UK. As Dorling (2014, 2016) has pointed out, if house prices were simply about supply and demand, then that massive surplus of homes would result in falling prices – but the opposite has happened, in that an oversupply of housing for purchase has led to unaffordability. Morton also ignores the land-banking epidemic facilitated by a system that actively rewards speculate-to-accumulate investment, and dismisses the importance of abundant mortgage credit and consistently low interest rates as factors behind the crisis (Fernandez & Aalbers, 2016). He asserts that the crisis is caused by a bloated local authority planning system aggravating NIMBYist tendencies and blocking the release of land for housing development, so he proposes that concerned local residents are given 'financial incentives' by developers to give their blessing to proposed new housing developments nearby.

Most striking of all about this report is setting the content against its title: *Making Housing Affordable*. In addition to calling for the destruction of social housing and the removal of government support for housing associations, the report proposes numerous strategies to *make housing more expensive*:

> What is needed are better quality developments that both increase housing supply and raise house prices and the quality of life for existing residents in the areas that they are built. (p. 15)

> The government should scrap all density and affordable housing targets and aspirations. (p. 23)

> It is a fallacy to assume that making new homes 'low-cost' will help increase affordability – it makes no difference to house prices whether you build cheap or expensive new homes. (p. 68)

> Social rents should rise to meet market rents. (p. 81)

It is difficult to imagine a more clear-cut case of agnotology than a report entitled *Making Housing Affordable* recommending that affordable housing targets and aspirations should be scrapped, and social housing demolished. The report won *Prospect Magazine*'s prestigious Think Tank Publication of the Year award in 2010, and, crucially, performed the ideological groundwork for the activation of the 'sink estate' designator in the reports that followed, to which I now turn.

In 2013 Policy Exchange published a report jointly authored by Alex Morton and Nicholas Boys Smith, a director at Lloyds Banking Group with an interest in architecture. Boys Smith had just founded what he calls a 'social enterprise and independent research institute', *Create Streets*, which has a mission to 'encourage and facilitate the replacement of London's multi-storey housing and the development of brownfield sites with real houses in real streets.' (Boys Smith & Morton, 2013, p. 5). The inaugural *Create Streets* report castigated all high-rise social housing estates in London, in a spectacular torrent of unsubstantiated assertions:

> Multi-storey housing is more risky and makes people sadder, badder and lonelier. (p. 29)

> The best predictor of juvenile delinquency was not population density but living in blocks of flats as opposed to houses. (p. 30)

> Multi-storey buildings create a myriad of opportunities for crime due to their hard to police semi-private corridors, walkways and multiple escape routes. (p. 32)

> [T]he evidence also suggests that tower blocks might even encourage suicide. Without wishing to be glib, tower blocks don't just make you more depressed. They make it easier to kill yourself – you can jump. (p. 30)

Under a chapter entitled 'Multi-storey Housing Creates a Spiral of Decline', 'sink estate' was used to describe the Aylesbury Estate in London – once again used to illustrate that social housing fails, regardless of the struggles to protect that estate from demolition (see Lees, 2014). The authors even claimed that multi-storey housing is bad for you regardless of income or social status, avoiding the question of how to account for the explosive growth and growing appeal of luxury condominium towers in many large cities globally. The question of how to account for any social problems in *low-rise* housing was studiously, perhaps judiciously ignored. Morton and Boys Smith concluded by saying that high-rise housing makes people 'sadder' and low-rise housing makes people 'happier'. This fitted neatly with the Conservative government's embrace of 'happiness' as their chosen catch-all indicator of well-being in austere times (Davies, 2016), and ensured that the *Create Streets* report was firmly on the political radar (as we shall see below).

The *Create Streets* report was followed two years later by another Policy Exchange report entitled *The Estate We're In: Lessons From the Front Line*, written by crime journalist Gavin Knight, author of a 'non-fiction' book entitled *Hood Rat*, 'an unflinching account of life and death in the sink estates of Britain' (Anthony, 2011), for which he spent time 'with dozens of violent criminals involved in gun and gang crime ... [and] accompanied detectives on a manhunt, firearms and drugs raids and was embedded with a CID unit over a lengthy drug surveillance operation' (Knight, 2014, p. 4). The report, which was launched with considerable fanfare,[9] opens as follows:

> The state of many of Britain's social housing estates is nothing short of a national embarrassment. Too often, crime, unemployment, gangs and violence are rife. The human cost is heart-breaking; the cost to the public purse immense. (p. 7)

A range of assertions are deployed to condemn both the design of the estates and the behaviour of people living on them, furnished with interview quotations such as, 'Sure, we have role models. Nelson Mandela. Barack Obama. They just don't live around here' (p. 13). The report concocted a relationship between social housing estates and rioting:

> Let us state the obvious: the [2011 England] riots did not start in a street of Georgian houses with spacious sash windows and manicured lawns. The riots started on a social housing estate – Broadwater Farm Estate in Tottenham, to be exact. ... The linking walkways between blocks were a gift to fleeing criminals. (pp. 13–14)

The 2011 riots did not start on the Broadwater Farm Estate. They began following a peaceful evening protest outside a police station on Tottenham High Road in London at the police killing of Mark Duggan. Not long after the protest concluded, a 16-year-old girl approached police officers to voice her anger, and was beaten back with batons (Eddo-Lodge, 2011). Two police cars, a bus and several shops were then attacked, looted and set ablaze in Tottenham, and the rioting then spread to several other districts in the capital and beyond (see Slater, 2016b). Social housing estates did not cause rioting, nor did rioting occur on them: in fact, as well as the looting and torching of stores and businesses, a large number of public buildings – such as police stations, sport centres, municipal institutions and in a few cases schools – were targeted for attack (Sutterluty, 2014). As Hancock and Mooney (2013) have argued:

> [P]articular representations of urban places as problematic on a number of different levels are mobilized. While the 2011 disorders were largely confined to inner urban areas with a significant degree of tenure mix, social housing estates (or areas where these dominate) and the populations

therein are frequently highlighted and represented as being not only vulnerable, but as particular locales where social pathologies and problems flourish. (p. 48)

Based on the unsubstantiated catalogue of nefarious properties of social housing, *The Estate We're In* report makes several predictable recommendations, best captured in this passage:

> Although Estate Recovery Plans will offer the opportunity to turn around social housing estates, we recognise that in some cases this may not be enough. In the long-term, where it is clear that an estate is beyond recovery, the government must commit to demolishing and replacing these estates. The replacement of high rise social housing must be the priority, given the strong evidence that tower blocks and multi-storey living leads to higher crime rates, weaker communities, and poorer health and education outcomes for residents. (p. 50)

The 'strong evidence' cited is a single source: the *Create Streets* report. In addition, it is not just Policy Exchange elevating 'sink estate' to semantic battering ram: the former director of the 'Centre for Social Justice', the think tank behind the current assault on the welfare state (Slater, 2014), wrote this while in post:

> 2013 is the year to tackle the tyranny of sink estates, no-go neighbourhoods and child poverty. … Look a little closer at such neighbourhoods, and we see something deeper than physical dilapidation. Behind the front doors are far too many broken and chaotic families. … Many adults could work but don't because when they do the maths, there's nothing to be gained by coming off benefits. There's usually a local school where a culture of low expectations and high truancy rates is a catalyst for underachievement and future welfare dependency. Alcohol abuse and drug addiction tend to flow through these estates like a river … (Guy, 2013, p. 10)

Tempting though it is to dismiss all the Policy Exchange documents as rhetorical ranting among like-minded free market fanatics, they are worthy of analytic scrutiny as they have had (and continue to have) major policy impacts. In April 2014 the Department for Communities and Local Government embraced many of Policy Exchange's recommendations in the three reports discussed, and created a £140m Housing Estate Regeneration Fund. It then commissioned Savills, a global real estate corporation headquartered in London with expertise in high-end, elite markets, to investigate the potential of all *Create Streets'* proposals. In January 2016 the Savills report was published (Savills, 2016) and was used as evidence to support a government strategy pledging to demolish the 'worst 100 sink estates' in England. Although the Savills report did not make a specific call for high-rise social housing demolition, it said, 'We have assumed cleared sites.' It points to current housing policy priorities that Savills was even commissioned as expert consultant on the matter of urban poverty on social housing estates, given that it stands to make vast profits from what replaces those estates.

When announcing these plans for estate demolition, David Cameron said:

> Step outside in the worst sink estates, and you're confronted by brutal high-rise towers and dark alleyways that are a gift to criminals and drug dealers. Decades of neglect have led to gangs, ghettos and anti-social behaviour. One of the most concerning aspects of these estates is just

how cut-off, self-governing and divorced from the mainstream these communities can become. And that allows social problems to fester and grow unseen.[10]

'Dark alleyways that are a gift to criminals' is too similar to Policy Exchange's 'The linking walkways between blocks were a gift to fleeing criminals' to be a rhetorical accident. In addition to the phrasing, the strategy of demolishing social housing estates is guided by the simplistic, fictitious reasoning emanating from Policy Exchange, crystallised by the sink estate label: that people who live on those estates are trapped in the culture of poverty that such estates create, and are an expensive, troublesome burden on 'taxpayers' who do not live on such estates; therefore, the only feasible solution is to bulldoze the estates and rehouse people elsewhere. But if we were to take that same logic and apply it to, say, healthcare, it is completely stranded. The argument would go: people in hospital tend to be less healthy than people who are not in hospital, so to improve health, we should demolish hospitals in fairness to the taxpayer. Since 2010 it has become *de rigueur* for UK think tanks and elected officials to frame destructive social policies as being undertaken in 'fairness to the taxpayer' (ignoring the fact that poor people are taxpayers too). But if one taxpayer considers something to be fair to them, and another taxpayer does not, then what possible arbitration procedure could there be between them? The 'fairness' approach gets us nowhere other than: if nobody paid any taxes, there would be no disagreement.

Tracking the activation of territorial stigma

Activating and amplifying the 'sink estate' – repeatedly condemning social housing estates as precipitates that collect and incubate all the social ills of the world – makes it considerably easier to justify bulldozing those estates to the ground and displacing their residents. We can also see symbolic power in the 2016 Housing and Planning Act in England and Wales, which allows social housing estates to be reclassified as 'brownfield sites' – a category normally reserved for *contaminated* ex-industrial land. The symbolic erasure of homes and entire communities thus paves the way for their literal erasure. One of the key teachings of Bourdieu's work is that symbolic systems – of which cities are major centres of production and diffusion – do not just mirror social relations, but help constitute them.

The history and use of the 'sink estate' phrase offers support for Tyler's (2013) argument that territorial stigmatisation, amplified and activated, has become a device to procure consent for punitive policies directed at those living at the bottom of the class structure; policies that cause enormous disruption. Numerous recent studies have revealed an intense and direct relationship between the defamation of place and the process of gentrification (August, 2014; Gray & Mooney, 2011; Kallin & Slater, 2014; Lees, 2014; Liu & Blomley, 2013; Slater, 2004; Slater & Anderson, 2012; Thörn & Holgersson, 2016). The taint of place can become a target and rationale for 'fixing' an area via its reincorporation into the real estate circuit of the city (Wacquant, 2008), which can have major consequences for those least able to compete for housing. Symbolic defamation provides the groundwork and ideological justification for a thorough class transformation of urban space, usually involving housing demolition, dispersal of residents, land clearance, and then the construction of housing and services aimed at a more affluent class of resident.

A substantial body of scholarship on public housing demolitions in several societies illustrates how the frequent depiction of public housing complexes as obsolete, poverty-creating failures justified the expulsion of people from their homes and the subsequent gentrification of valuable central city land tracts (e.g. Arthurson, 2004; Crump, 2002; Darcy, 2010; Goetz, 2013; Imbroscio, 2008; Kipfer and Petrunia, 2009; Minton, 2017; Steinberg, 2010). Wacquant (2007) summarises as follows:

> Once a place is publicly labelled as a 'lawless zone' or 'outlaw estate', outside the common norm, it is easy for the authorities to justify special measures, deviating from both law and custom, which can have the effect – if not the intention – of destabilizing and further marginalizing their occupants, subjecting them to the dictates of the deregulated labour market, and rendering them invisible or driving them out of a coveted space. (p. 69)

The fact that Savills was asked by the Conservative government to explore the potential of ideas to demolish tower blocks in the wake of Policy Exchange using the semantic battering ram of the sink estate illustrates how social realities are transformed through the strategic deployment of words and phrases by institutions and individuals in positions of power. Indeed, Boys Smith and Morton (2013) made their case for demolition under subheadings such as 'Building attractive streets provides the best returns for the long term landowner' and 'Plugging into the rest of the city improves economic returns'.

If social housing estates become widely renowned and reviled as epicentres of self-inflicted and self-perpetuating destitution and depravity, opposing their demolition becomes significantly more challenging. The sink estate is thus a pure exemplar of what Wacquant (2012) calls a *categoreme*, 'a term of accusation and alarm, pertaining not to social science but public polemic, that serves … to fuel the spiral of stigmatization enmeshing the impoverished districts of the urban periphery' (p. 17). Peter Marris (1986, pp. 53–54) offered a particularly succinct summary of the wider problem:

> Physical squalor is an affront to the order of society, which readily becomes associated with other signs of disorder in the public image. Crime, drunkenness, prostitution, feckless poverty, mental pathology do indeed cluster where housing is poorest – though not there only. Once this association has been taken for granted, any anomalous pattern of life embodied in shabby surroundings is easily assumed to be pathological, without much regard for the evidence. Bad housing thus becomes a symbol of complex discordances in the structure of society and so to be treated as if it were a cause of them.

Think tanks have reframed a serious crisis of housing affordability as a crisis of housing supply caused by too much state interference in the market, which, inter alia, has trapped people in failed social housing estates that can never be improved. Viewed through an analytic lens of agnotology, we can see a complete inversion going on: the structural and political causes of the housing crisis – that is, deregulation, privatisation, and attacks on welfare state – are put forward as desirable and necessary remedies for the crisis that will squash an intrusive state apparatus. Viewed through the conceptual lens of symbolic power, we can see how the already intense stigma attached to social housing estates is vamped up by think tank writers and then by political elites. A new circuit of symbolic production has thus emerged, where the framing of the 'sink estate' filters societal attention towards family breakdown, worklessness, welfare dependency, antisocial behaviour, personal irresponsibility, and away from community, solidarity, shelter and home.

In a thorough Bourdieusian analysis of the history and sociology of think tanks, Medvetz (2012) argues that their rise and influence must be set analytically 'against the backdrop of a series of processes that have contributed to the growing subordination of knowledge to political and economic demand' (p. 226). Given the realities of disinvestment in social housing and in the lives of people who are unable to afford anything else, it seems essential for scholarship to continue to analyse and expose the practices of think tanks in corroborating the need and eliciting support for regressive housing policies geared only towards profit. It is not enough to address housing precarity in the United Kingdom without a focus on both symbolic domination and the production of ignorance with respect to the transformations roiling lower-class districts of unequal cities, which, in turn, are always tightly tethered to strategies and skirmishes traversing circles of power.

Acknowledgments

An earlier version of this paper was delivered as the 13th Annual David M. Smith Lecture at Queen Mary, University of London, in November 2016. I would like to thank Alison Blunt for that invitation, and the audience on that memorable evening for their engagement. I would also like to thank Loïc Wacquant for his sharp and supportive reading of the first draft of this paper.

Funding

This research received no specific grant from any funding agency in the public, commercial, or not-for-profit sectors.

Notes

1. These issues were thrown into sharp relief by the Grenfell Tower tragedy in Kensington, London, in June 2017, when fire tore through a high-rise social housing block that had been 'regenerated' with cheap, combustible cladding solely to make it look visually more attractive to wealthy residents of the upscale district. The absolute political contempt for the rights and housing situations of Londoners on very low incomes was exposed, as indeed was the protracted disinvestment in social housing and the disregard for the repeated warnings by tenants of an impending disaster. Following the fire, it became abundantly clear that the scandalous cost of living in London had reached breaking point, as displaced tenants could not be rehoused locally due to exorbitant housing costs, nor even rehoused elsewhere in the city given the steady erosion of social housing in the capital (and this despite the existence of 1652 empty homes in Kensington and Chelsea, held for speculative purposes by absentee rentiers).
2. http://hansard.millbanksystems.com/commons/1987/jun/26/foreign-affairs#column_200
3. Lees (2014) has demonstrated that the repeated media categorisation of Aylesbury as a 'sink estate' was a crucial tactic in 'branding both the community and its residents as deviant and untrustworthy and thus justified paternalistic treatment of them' (p. 928) resulting in a massive regeneration project that has displaced many of those residents against their wishes.
4. The first appearance in a UK newspaper article was in *The Guardian* in 1982, when columnist Polly Toynbee said that the Tulse Hill Estate in Brixton, London, 'used to be a rock bottom sink estate' (Toynbee, 1982).

5. https://policyexchange.org.uk/about-us/. This description alone is enough material for an exegesis. 'Research is evidence based', if you consider what else it could possibly be, is a bit like saying, 'This water is wet' . 'Our research is strictly empirical' is the same. These two completely redundant sentences/tautologies are denegations of the deeply political nature of the knowledge produced, as indeed is 'all sides of the political spectrum' and claims of being 'completely independent'. This description is therefore symptomatic of what think tanks actually are: mongrel institutions that claim to be knowledge producers (cf. Medvetz, 2012).
6. Tellingly, it appears that Boles felt hampered by regulatory nuisances such as paying taxes. He writes on his website, 'Doing business was hard. My business career did not make me rich. But I learned a huge amount about managing people, dealing with suppliers and keeping control of the company's finances. I also saw how small interventions by government can handicap British businesses' ability to compete in a global market.' https://www.nickboles.co.uk/about-nick
7. http://powerbase.info/index.php/Policy_Exchange
8. Morton is now director of Field Consulting, a PR and communications consultancy.
9. For example, Knight wrote a short piece for right wing mouthpiece *Conservative Home* entitled 'Britain's sink estates can – and must – be turned around', saying, 'Britain's most deprived housing estates are a time-bomb of social decay. Decades of neglect and ghettoisation have led to acute, entrenched social problems that cost billions to the public purse: gang warfare, knife crime, domestic violence, illiteracy, unemployment and child neglect.' http://www.conservativehome.com/platform/2014/08/gavin-knight-britains-sink-estates-can-and-must-be-turned-around.html
10. https://www.gov.uk/government/speeches/estate-regeneration-article-by-david-cameron

References

Anthony, A. (2011, July 10). Review of *Hood Rat* by Gavin Knight. *The Guardian*.

Arthurson, K. (2004). From stigma to demolition: Australian debates about housing and social exclusion. *Journal of Housing and the Built Environment, 19*, 255–270.

August, M. (2014). Challenging the rhetoric of stigmatization: The benefits of concentrated poverty in Toronto's Regent Park. *Environment and Planning A, 46*, 1317–1333.

Auyero, J. (2012). *Patients of the state*. Durham, NC: Duke University Press.

Baldwin, J. (1972). *No name in the street*. New York, NY: Doubleday.

Bourdieu, P. (1991). *Language and symbolic power*. Cambridge, UK: Polity Press.

Bourdieu, P. (1996). On the family as a realized category. *Theory, Culture & Society, 13*, 19–26.

Bourdieu, P. (2014). *On the state: Lectures at the College de France*. Cambridge, UK: Polity Press.

Boys Smith, N., & Morton, A. (2013). *Create streets, not just multi-storey estates*. Retrieved from http://www.policyexchange.org.uk/images/publications/create%20streets.pdf (last accessed 4 May 2018).

Buchanan, M., & Woodcock, S. (2016). Councils spent £3.5bn on temporary housing in last five years. *BBC News*. Retrieved from http://www.bbc.co.uk/news/uk-38016728 (last accessed 4 May 2018).

Campkin, B. (2013). *Remaking London: Decline and regeneration in urban culture*. London, UK: I.B. Tauris.

Carlyon, T. (2013). *Food for thought: Applying house price inflation to grocery prices* (research report). Shelter. Retrieved from http://england.shelter.org.uk/professional_resources/policy_and_research/policy_library/policy_library_folder/food_for_thought (last accessed 4 May 2018).

Crossley, S. (2017). *In their place: The imagined geographies of poverty*. London, UK: Pluto Press.

Crump, J. (2002). Deconcentration by demolition: Public housing, poverty, and urban policy. *Environment and Planning D: Society and Space, 20*, 581–596.

Darcy, M. (2010). Deconcentration of disadvantage and mixed-income housing: A critical discourse approach. *Housing, Theory & Society, 27*, 1–22.

Davies, W. (2016). *The happiness industry*. London, UK: Verso.

Dorling, D. (2014). *All that is solid: The great housing disaster*. London, UK: Allen Lane.

Dorling, D. (2016, October 21). Has Brexit burst the British housing bubble? *New Statesman*. Retrieved from http://www.newstatesman.com/politics/uk/2016/10/has-brexit-burst-british-housing-bubble (last accessed 4 May 2018).

Eddo-Lodge, R. (2011, August 8). Twitter didn't fuel the Tottenham riot. *The Guardian*.

Fernandez, R., & Aalbers, M. (2016). Financialization and housing: Between globalization and varieties of capitalism. *Competition and Change, 20*, 71–88.

Forrest, R., & Murie, A. (1988). *Selling the welfare state: The privatisation of public housing*. London, UK: Routledge.

Goetz, E. (2013). The audacity of HOPE VI: Discourse and the dismantling of public housing. *Cities, 35*, 342–348.

Gray, N., & Mooney, G. (2011). Glasgow's new urban frontier: 'Civilising' the population of 'Glasgow East'. *City, 15*, 4–24.

Guy, C. (2013, February). Two nations, one mission. *Total Politics*.

Hancock, L., & Mooney, G. (2013). 'Welfare ghettos' and the 'broken society': Territorial stigmatization in the contemporary UK. *Housing, Theory & Society, 30*, 46–64.

Hanley, L. (2007). *Estates: An intimate history*. London, UK: Granta.

Hills, J. (2007). *Ends and means: The future role of social housing in England*. LSE Centre for the Analysis of Social Exclusion. Retrieved from http://eprints.lse.ac.uk/5568/1/Ends_and_Means_The_future_roles_of_social_housing_in_England_1.pdf (last accessed 4 May 2018).

Hodkinson, S. (2012). The new urban enclosures. *City, 16*, 500–518.

Imbroscio, D. (2008). Challenging the dispersal consensus in American housing policy research. *Journal of Urban Affairs, 30*, 111–130.

Kallin, H., & Slater, T. (2014). Activating territorial stigma: Gentrifying marginality in Edinburgh's periphery. *Environment and Planning A, 46*, 1351–1368.

Kipfer, S., & Petrunia, J. (2009). 'Recolonization' and public housing: A Toronto case study. *Studies in Political Economy, 83*, 111–139.

Knight, G. (2014). *The estate we're in: Lessons from the front line*. Policy Exchange. Retrieved from https://policyexchange.org.uk/wp-content/uploads/2016/09/the-estate-were-in.pdf (last accessed 4 May 2018).

Lansley, S., & Mack, J. (2015). *Breadline Britain: The rise of mass poverty*. London, UK: One World.

Lees, L. (2014). The urban injustices of New Labour's 'New Urban Renewal': The case of the Aylesbury Estate in London. *Antipode, 46*, 921–947.

Liu, S., & Blomley, N. (2013). Making news and making space: Framing Vancouver's Downtown Eastside. *The Canadian Geographer, 57*, 119–132

Madden, D., & Marcuse, P. (2016). *In defense of housing*. London, UK: Verso.

Malpass, P. (2005). *Housing and the welfare state: The development of housing policy in Britain*. Basingstoke, UK: Macmillan.

Marris, P. (1986). *Loss and change* (2nd ed.). London, UK: Routledge.

Maude, F. (2012). Ten years of modernization: Looking back and the challenges ahead. Policy Exchange. Retrieved from http://powerbase.info/images/1/14/Maude_PX_speech.pdf (last accessed 4 May 2018).

Medvetz, T. (2012). *Think tanks in America*. Chicago, IL: University of Chicago Press.

Meek, J. (2014). *Private island: Why Britain now belongs to someone else*. London, UK: Verso Books.

Minton, A. (2017). *Big capital: Who is London for?* London, UK: Penguin.

Mirowski, P. (2013). *Never let a serious crisis go to waste: How neoliberalism survived the economic meltdown*. London, UK: Verso.

Morton, A. (2010). *Making housing affordable: A new vision for housing policy*. Policy Exchange. Retrieved from https://www.policyexchange.org.uk/wp-content/uploads/2016/09/making-housing-affordable-aug-10.pdf (last accessed 4 May 2018).

Morton, J. (1976, November 18). Tough estates. *New Society*, p. 365.

Musterd, S., & Van Kempen, R. (2007). Trapped or on the springboard? Housing careers in large housing estates in European cities. *Journal of Urban Affairs, 29*, 311–329.

Power, A. (1997). *Estates on the edge: The social consequences of mass housing in Europe*. Basingstoke, UK: Macmillan.

Proctor, R., & Schiebinger, L. (Eds.). (2008). *Agnotology: The making and unmaking of ignorance*. Stanford, CA: Stanford University Press.

Ramsden, E., & Adams, J. (2009). Escaping the laboratory: The rodent experiments of John B. Calhoun and their cultural influence. *Journal of Social History, 42*, 761–792.

Savills (2016). *Completing London's streets* (Report to the Cabinet Office). Retrieved from http://pdf.euro.savills.co.uk/uk/residential—other/completing-london-s-streets-080116.pdf (last accessed 4 May 2018).

Slater, T. (2004). Municipally-managed gentrification in South Parkdale, Toronto. *The Canadian Geographer, 48*, 303–325.

Slater, T. (2014). The myth of 'Broken Britain': Welfare reform and the production of ignorance. *Antipode, 46*, 948–969.

Slater, T. (2016a). The housing crisis in neoliberal Britain: Free market think tanks and the production of ignorance. In S. Springer, K. Birch, & J. MacLeavy (Eds.), *The Routledge handbook of neoliberalism* (pp. 370–382). London, UK: Routledge.

Slater, T. (2016b). The neoliberal state and the 2011 English riots: A class analysis. In H. Thörn, M. Mayer, O. Sernhede, & C. Thörn (Eds.), *Understanding urban uprisings, protests and movements* (pp. 121–148). Basingstoke, UK: Palgrave Macmillan.

Slater, T., & Anderson, N. (2012). The reputational ghetto: Territorial stigmatization in St. Paul's, Bristol. *Transactions of the Institute of British Geographers, 37*, 530–546.

Smith, D. M. (1994). *Geography and social justice*. Oxford, UK: Blackwell.

Steinberg, S. (2010). The myth of concentrated poverty. In C. Hartman & G. Squires (Eds.), *The integration debate: Competing futures for American cities* (pp. 213–227). New York, NY: Routledge.

Sutterluty, F. (2014). The hidden morale of the 2005 French and 2011 English riots. *Thesis Eleven, 121*, 38–56.

Sylvester, R. (2001, July 21). Portillo supporters to fight on. *The Daily Telegraph*. Retrieved from http://www.telegraph.co.uk/news/uknews/1334769/Portillo-supporters-to-fight-on.html (last accessed 4 May 2018).

Thörn, C., & Holgersson, H. (2016). Revisiting the urban frontier through the case of New Kvillebäcken, Gothenburg. *City, 20*, 663–684.

Toynbee, P. (1982, February 19). Once no one wanted to live there. Now, thanks to Anne Power, the estate has been pulled back into shape. *The Guardian*.

Tyler, I. (2013). *Revolting subjects: Social abjection and resistance in neoliberal Britain*. London, UK: Zed Books.

Van Kempen, R., Dekker, K., Hall, S., & Tosics, I. (Eds.). (2005). *Restructuring large housing estates in Europe*. Bristol, UK: Policy Press.

Wacquant, L. (2007). Territorial stigmatization in the age of advanced marginality. *Thesis Eleven, 91*, 66–77.

Wacquant, L. (2008). *Urban outcasts: A comparative sociology of advanced marginality.* Cambridge, UK: Polity Press.

Wacquant, L. (2012). A Janus-faced institution of ethnoracial closure: A sociological specification of the ghetto. In R. Hutchison & B. Haynes (Eds.), *The ghetto: Contemporary global issues and controversies* (pp. 1–31). Boulder, CO: Westview Press.

Wacquant, L. (2017). Practice and symbolic power in Bourdieu: The view from Berkeley. *Journal of Classical Sociology, 17*, 55–69.

Watt, P., & Minton, A. (2016). London's housing crisis and its activisms. *City, 20*, 204–221.

Author biography

Tom Slater is Reader in Urban Geography at the University of Edinburgh. He has research interests in the institutional arrangements producing and reinforcing urban inequalities, and in the ways in which marginalised urban dwellers organise against injustices visited upon them. He has written extensively on gentrification (notably the co-authored books, *Gentrification*, 2008 and *The Gentrification Reader*, 2010), displacement from urban space, territorial stigmatisation, welfare reform, and social movements. Since 2010 he has delivered lectures in 19 different countries on these issues, and his work has been translated into 10 different languages and circulates widely to inform struggles for urban social justice.

The
Sociological
Review
Monographs

The Sociological Review Monographs
2018, Vol. 66(4) 180–200
© The Author(s) 2018
Reprints and permissions:
sagepub.co.uk/journalsPermissions.nav
DOI: 10.1177/0038026118778175
journals.sagepub.com/home/sor

Where do Black lives matter? Race, stigma, and place in Milwaukee, Wisconsin

Jenna M. Loyd
University of Wisconsin-Madison, USA

Anne Bonds
University of Wisconsin-Milwaukee, USA

Abstract

This article analyzes how the spatial metaphor of *53206*, a zip code within the city of Milwaukee, Wisconsin, connects with crises in the legitimacy of policing and politicians' claims to care about Black lives. It examines how, in the context of deepening racialized poverty, ongoing mobilizations against police violence, and increasing rates of violent crime, liberal and conservative rhetoric about *53206* largely obscures the roles that decades of deindustrialization and labor assaults, metropolitan racial and wealth segregation, and public school and welfare restructuring play in producing racial and class inequality to instead emphasize racializing tropes about 'Black-on-Black crime,' broken homes, and uncaring Black communities. Situating the examination within critical analysis of urban poverty, geographic scholarship on the racialization of space, and critical criminology, the authors consider the salience of the term *territorial stigmatization* as a means to understand how historical and contemporary processes of racialized capitalism shape Milwaukee's urban and social divides. They argue that discursive constructions of *53206* and the rhetorical posture of saving Black lives deployed by elected officials have had the effect of entrenching policing power while further rendering neighborhoods like Milwaukee's Northside as already dead and dying.

Keywords
policing, race, racial capitalism, territorial stigmatization

> Somebody has to step forward and say black lives matter when you're talking about 31 or 32 victims in four months. (Milwaukee Mayor Tom Barrett, 2015)

Corresponding author:
Jenna M. Loyd, University of Wisconsin-Madison, Madison, Wisconsin, 53706, USA.
Email: jmloyd@wisc.edu

The irony is that inner-city blacks are the ones who suffer most when the police backpedal on enforcement, because they are often the ones who have the misfortune to live where crime festers. (Opinion Author, *Milwaukee Journal Sentinel*, 2016)

Introduction

The Black Lives Matter movement marks a conjunctural moment in the United States, a marked crisis in the legitimation of policing of Black communities in cities across the United States (Gilmore & Gilmore, 2016; K.-Y. Taylor, 2016). In Milwaukee, Wisconsin, the murder of Dontre Hamilton by a Milwaukee Police Department (MPD) officer in 2014 sparked concerted mobilizations against what was then the most recent police killing of a city resident. Two years later, with political and economic conditions in the city largely unchanged, uprisings ensued in Milwaukee's Sherman Park neighborhood over three days in August 2016. These were in response to the killing of Sylville Smith by a different MPD officer. Like mobilizations in Ferguson and Baltimore, the uprising articulated a sharp critique of urban strategies of policing and prompted a larger dialogue about race, crime, policing, and inequality in the city.

The ongoing debate over meaningful police reform and community safety is shaped by prevailing racialized discourses about the relationships among violence, place, and race. Even as activists were mobilizing in the name of Dontre Hamilton and other victims of police violence, local radio and newspapers ran a series of reports on Black men in prison prompted by a study that concluded that Wisconsin has the highest rate of Black male incarceration in the nation (Pawasarat & Quinn, 2013). In popular discourse, this superlative figure about Black male incarceration circulates alongside reports that consistently rank Milwaukee as the most racially segregated city (Denvir, 2011; Florida, 2014), the second poorest city (Kennedy, 2015), the worst city in America for Black Americans (Miller, 2015; Mock, 2015), and Wisconsin as the worst place to raise Black children in the country (Annie E. Casey Foundation, 2014). A striking portion of the state's formerly incarcerated people live in just one zip code within the city – *53206* – located in the predominantly Black and heavily policed Northside of Milwaukee (Pawasarat, 2009, p. 13). Within popular discourse, *53206* has come to contain symbolically the problems of Wisconsin (and nation more broadly) – from violence to poverty to 'failing' public services. The power of this discourse has led to efforts to challenge the 'stigma attached to the ZIP code ... that it's a lost cause' (Potter, 2016).

In this article we argue that the zipcode *53206* has become a spatial shorthand for talking about race, violence, and poverty without talking about structural racism, capitalism, or the institutions of violence that sustain racial capitalism. As a spatialized narrative, *53206* offers an empirical lens through which to consider the salience of *territorial stigmatization* as a concept. We analyze how *53206*, as a discourse, serves as a spatial fix anchoring discussions of two interrelated and sustained crises over racialized poverty and policing in the city of Milwaukee, Wisconsin. *53206* fixes these problems within an apparently discrete space, where, for some, the place and people are 'lost causes.' This reification disconnects the production of poverty, segregation, and policing strategies from the broader political economy of the region, which naturalizes the effects of contemporary capitalism – including structural unemployment, austerity, and deepening concentration of wealth – and reproduces longstanding racist discourses of Black crime, economic decline, and family dysfunction (Greenbaum, 2015; Hinton, 2016; Muhammad, 2011).

Despite the political and economic rifts dividing Milwaukee from surrounding white, wealthy suburbs and much of the rest of the state, both liberal and conservative solutions to the ills of *53206* rest on racialized 'culture of poverty' narratives of capitalist urban life. The claim that the persistence of poverty could be explained by cultural attributes of impoverished groups was advanced by anthropologist Oscar Lewis in the mid-20th century and came to be most associated with Daniel Patrick Moynihan's report for the Kennedy administration, *The Negro Family*. The Moynihan report aimed to support public investment in job creation, yet it attributed Black poverty and high rates of unemployment among Black men to Black women – as both mothers and wage workers – and an ostensibly endogenous Black culture (Loyd, 2014; O'Connor, 2001).

The idea that culture or the 'breakdown' of the family are the cause of poverty – rather than racialized patterns of exploitation, economic disinvestment, and abandonment – continues to circulate through terms like *the underclass* and *concentrated poverty*. Measures for the latter routinely use categories such as 'female-headed household' and community (dis)organization, and thereby situate poverty as a property of particular people and places (Crump, 2002). Rather than conceptualizing spaces of racialized poverty as relational, as interconnected with spaces of racialized wealth, such narratives of 'bifurcation-segregation,' following geographer Katherine McKittrick, reify 'spaces of absolute otherness (slums, sites of man-made natural disaster, prisons, inner-city poverty, and death)' (2011, p. 954). This analytic simultaneously marks people inhabiting these spaces as 'actually *not* connected to us ... precisely because they are dead and dying, because they live in slums and prisons, and thus are radically outside the conceptual boundaries of emancipation, humanness, and global citizenry' (2011, p. 954, emphasis in original). As such, *53206* naturalizes the structural violence of racial capitalism and rationalizes policing as a legitimate – indeed necessary – feature of poor neighborhoods.

In the remainder of this article, we bring together literatures on the political economy of racialized poverty and critical histories of policing in order to illustrate both the shared discursive frameworks of poverty and policing and how the latter serve to naturalize racial capitalism. We situate discourses surrounding *53206* historically and theoretically in order to explore how the racialization of this space – operating through the reification of poverty and crime as products of *53206* – serves to rationalize policing as a solution to violence and to further targeted neoliberal austerity and privatization measures. Our article analyzes how the spatial metaphor of *53206* connects with crises in the legitimacy of policing and politicians' claims to care about Black lives. We conclude that the rhetorical posture of saving Black lives that is deployed by some elected officials has had the effect of entrenching policing power and further rendering the broader Northside of the city as already dead and dying (McKittrick, 2011).

Historical and conceptual background

To theorize the connections among geographies of race, poverty, and crime, we bring critical analyses of urban poverty together with critical criminology and critical theories of racism. In bringing these literatures together we emphasize the co-constitution of 'crime' and 'poverty' as racialized categories within social thought (cf. Hinton, 2016; Muhammad, 2011). As critical geographers, we draw on a tradition of scholarship that theorizes how space and social categories (such as crime or poverty) are materially and discursively produced. This work shows how interrelated processes operate across multiple scales, linking particular places, groups of people, and racial-gendered bodies (cf. Bonds, 2009; Gilmore, 2002, 2007; McKittrick, 2006, 2011, Pulido, 2000; Wilson, 2002; Woods, 1998). We draw on work in the Black radical tradition, in geography and other fields, to analyze racism as a structure and set of social relations that is constituted spatially and symbolically, and articulated with economic relations (Hall, 1980). Following Cedric Robinson (1983), we understand capitalism as always racial capitalism, an economic system that relies on and enshrines racializing differentiation and domination. As such, the uneven capitalist development of places is simultaneously a racialized process of (de)valorization and (dis)accumulation that relies upon legal and extra-legal racialized violence (Gilmore, 2007; Melamed, 2011). In the US context, white supremacy became a foundational logic through which the settler colonial dispossession of land, the attempted erasure of Indigenous peoples, and the enslavement of peoples from Africa constituted the nation, wealth, and identity (Bonds & Inwood, 2016).

Conceptualizing stigma, space, and race

Stigma has a relatively long lineage within the social sciences. As developed by Erving Goffman (1963), *stigma* has been used to analyze the systematic labeling (or 'stereotyping') and poor treatment of people with bodily and cognitive differences. *Stigma* has entered popular usage, though Goffman's concept has also been widely criticized for its individualistic and interpersonal focus. Link and Phelan write that in 'contrast to "stigma," "discrimination" focuses the attention of research on the producers of rejection and exclusion – those who do the discriminating – rather than on the people who are the recipients of these behaviors' (2001, p. 366). Link and Phelan, in turn, insist on investigating stigmatization as a power-laden process that sustains systematic discrimination and disadvantage in life chances (2001, p. 371). Imogen Tyler in this issue further develops Link and Phelan's analysis by questioning 'Goffman's decidedly apolitical account of stigma.'

The shift in scale suggested by Link and Phelan from a focus on individual interactions to broader power relations informs the development of *territorial stigmatization*, which refers to a 'consequential and injurious form of *action through collective representation fastened on place*' (Wacquant, Slater, & Pereira, 2014, p. 1278, emphasis in original). As developed by Wacquant (2007), the concept aims to bring together Goffman's work on stigmatization with Bourdieu's attention to symbolic power, and thereby focuses attention on the interrelationships among material places, representations, and the production of inequality. Part of the development of this idea came through Wacquant's engagement in scholarly debates over how to understand processes of (racial) segregation and impoverishment as US-specific and transnational phenomena (Wacquant, 2007, 2016; see also Chaddha & Wilson, 2008). The term has been used in many disciplines and with different definitions (Larsen & Delica, 2017). We focus on work developed by Wacquant and Wacquant, Slater, and Pereira, who contend that 'spatial taint is a novel and distinctive phenomenon that crystallized at [the twentieth] century's end along with the dissolution of the neighborhoods of relegation emblematic of the Fordist-Keynesian phase of industrial capitalism' (2014, p. 1270). While they acknowledge the reality of a 'traditional topography of disrepute,' they also maintain that the contemporary process of territorial stigmatization is a new phenomenon that differs from the symbolic geographies of the historical industrial city in five ways: (1) territorial stigma is partially autonomous from poverty; (2) symbols of stigmatized places circulate on national and international scale; (3) stigmatized places are represented as threats to the social fabric; (4) stigmatized places are racialized; and (5) responses to stigmatized places emphasize the penal arm of the state (2014, pp. 1273–1274).

The question we ask is whether the term territorial stigmatization is suited to the task of explaining the past and present processes of racial capitalism that shape Milwaukee's economic and social divides. Is territorial stigmatization distinctive to the contemporary 'post-industrial' moment? Does the attempt to account for change from 'traditional' symbolic geographies impose an unwitting binary chronology/typology of the (pre-)Fordist ghetto and post-Fordist stigmatized place? Does this proposed temporal break obscure continuities of both racial capitalism and racialized criminalization practices? Does a neutral sounding term like *territorial stigmatization* enable us, as white residents who live in and research racially and class-divided cities, to name how racism works?

We raise these questions in a post-Civil Rights historical context that Bonilla-Silva (2014) and Melamed (2011) describe as a 'colorblind' era of racism. This is a moment following the end of de jure segregation and discrimination in which many believe that racism is over. For Bonilla-Silva (2014), such claims to 'not see' race, or to be 'colorblind,' locate racism in the past and explain ongoing racialized inequities in terms of cultural difference and individual decisions, rather than as the result of historical and ongoing forms of structural racism, institutionalized discrimination, and systematic exploitation and dispossession. The 'colorblind' discourse of race is conjoined tightly with popular and academic accounts of deindustrialization, globalization, and persistent poverty in ways that selectively forget racially specific histories and geographies of work and public investments in housing, education, and welfare. Because this narrative that racism is over has accompanied global economic restructuring and enabled the dismantling of state spending and programs that foster greater social and economic equity, we are wary of concepts that seem to diminish the longevity and centrality of racism to US urban geographies and criminal legal system.

Conceptualizing the production of poverty, race, and space

Historian Michael Katz (2015, p. 43) identifies six prevailing frames used to explain the problem of poverty: (1) individual or family failings; (2) places; (3) the absence of resources; (4) capitalism; (5) political powerlessness; and (6) failed markets or failure to use markets. We focus on the first two frames and their interrelations. Katz argues that individual explanations of poverty often come in two versions: the 'soft' view centered on the notion that poverty results from 'laziness, immoral behavior, inadequate skills, and dysfunctional families' and the 'hard' view in which poverty is 'the result of inherited deficiencies that limit intellectual potential, trigger harmful and immoral behavior, and circumscribe economic achievement' (2015, p. 44). The first of these dominant framings has underwritten culture of poverty discourses, which as we have described, blame poverty on the values and worldviews of poor people themselves. This premise of a distinction between the 'deserving' and 'undeserving' poor continues to inform social welfare reforms.

Within the second dominant framing, poverty is spatialized and understood as a problem of place, emerging either from the conditions within a place or arising from the place itself (Katz, 2015; see also Bauder, 2002). Such place-based framings are underpinned by the notion that the spatial concentration of the poor in particular places (re)produces a range of what might be understood as stigmatized places – including crime and deviance – as well as poverty itself. Such understandings have long underpinned many reformist and liberal projects advocating tenement housing clean-ups, slum clearance, and more recent efforts to spatially 'deconcentrate' poverty (Greenbaum, 2015; Slater, 2013). These discourses make poverty a simplistic problem of concentration and local place, rather than one produced by structural and discursive processes. For example, Crump (2002) illustrates how discourses surrounding the spatial concentration of urban poverty define poverty as reproduced in inner city 'breeding grounds' (p. 583). He argues that these conceptualizations identify poverty as endemic to the inner city, and thereby suggest that poverty can be solved by dispersing poor people across space. This simplistic understanding of poverty, he argues, disconnects so-called places of poverty (i.e. the 'urban ghetto' or 'inner city') from the socioeconomic processes producing both them and places where wealth accumulates (i.e. 'the suburbs').

Reified conceptualizations of poverty – whether at the scale of the individual or place – are at odds with analyses of racial capitalism. The ideological partitioning of places that are actually interconnected naturalizes the unequal power relations that are essential to capitalism. Such reifications of poverty (and wealth) as inherent to particular people or places work to obscure government policies and capitalist processes that sustain urban inequality. Indeed, attributing the harmful outcomes of exploitative, oppressive, and extractive processes to the people and places harmed by these very processes facilitates the entrenchment of these processes. In contrast, relational conceptualizations of capitalist geographies understand that poverty and the 'inner city' are mutually produced through the same racialized sociospatial processes that work to concentrate wealth and healthy life chances elsewhere (Pulido, 2000).

In an ostensibly 'colorblind' era, apparently neutral terms like *concentrated poverty, disadvantage*, and *neighborhood effects* have circulated into popular and policy discourse in ways that displace attention to the ongoing roles that structural racism plays in producing interlinked spaces of class and racial segregation. Within this context, terms like *ghetto, inner city*, or in the case of Milwaukee, *inner core*, continue to circulate in popular and policy circuits, yet evidence for persistent segregation is discursively situated in the Jim Crow past. In other words, uneven geographies of wealth, poverty, employment, school spending, and health, etc. are viewed as the result of historical events and past racial thinking. This past is disconnected discursively from how it informs contemporary patterns of (dis)investment that continue to cement racial and economic inequality into the landscape. In turn, divisions in the contemporary metropolis ideologically can be attributed to the neutral workings of capitalist markets, public policy, and individual preference. Such explanations work to minimize racism, one of the central frames that comprise colorblind racism in Bonilla-Silva's (2014) theorization. Yet, these euphemized terms are racialized; *concentrated poverty* and *neighborhoods effects*, like earlier terms *underclass* and *culture of poverty* draw on racialized and classed conceptualizations of poverty that ostensibly can be explained by culture, behavior, and the negative and dangerous effects of concentrating poor people together (Greenbaum, 2015; Loyd, 2014). These apparently non-racial terms exemplify cultural racism, a frame that 'relies on culturally based arguments,' to buttress colorblind racism (Bonilla-Silva, 2014, p. 76).

Racialization and the co-constitution of crime and poverty

The gendered and racialized rhetoric of poverty arising from the behavior and pathology of 'stigmatized' groups and places underpins dominant framings of and solutions to crime and 'disorder.' As previously explained, culture of poverty discourses draw from racist and heteropatriarchal tropes that pathologize and blame Black women for the breakdown of the normative family structure and for young Black men's disorderliness and unemployment (Greenbaum, 2015; Hinton, 2016; Loyd, 2014). As such, the culture of poverty as an explanation imputes 'stigma' to oppressed groups, yet sidesteps the racial, gender, and class power relations constructing terms of so-called stigma (Tyler, this monograph issue). Elizabeth Hinton (2016) traces how culture of poverty discourses shaped the production of both social welfare policy *and* crime policy. 'Convinced that poverty was the root cause of crime and that community behavior was the root cause of poverty, policymakers turned to crime control to manage the symptoms of Moynihan's "tangle of pathology" while they worked to resolve the socioeconomic problems facing low-income Americans with social welfare programs' (Hinton, 2016, pp. 93–94). Her analysis reveals how liberal framings of race, crime, and poverty helped to produce solutions to urban inequality focused on crime management, rather than job creation or other structural interventions. As we discuss below, these framings remain central to understandings of how the problems of poverty and crime in Milwaukee are interconnected and their solutions.

The 'broken windows' model of policing and crime control – also known as 'order maintenance' and 'quality of life' policing – has become a paradigmatic, and controversial, model of policing in contemporary cities. Based upon a classic article by Kelling and Wilson (1982), this approach focuses on low-level crime as an indicator of community distress (Herbert, 2001; Herbert & Brown, 2006). Rather than simply react to incidents of 'crime,' the premise of broken windows policing is that managing low-level neighborhood disorder (communicated by broken windows and other signs of community decline) through increased police contact and patrols will effectively deter violent crime (Camp & Heatherton, 2016; Herbert & Brown, 2006). This deceptively simple concept became the hegemonic model for community policing (Anderson, 2016; Brown, 2015; Kelling & Wilson, 1982), an ostensibly race-neutral practice that effectively criminalized an increasing number of individuals, activities, and behaviors as part of other efforts to regulate urban space.

While some distinctions may be maintained between community policing and broken windows policing (Herbert, 2001), in popular discourse and among the officials whom we analyze, community policing and broken windows policing are treated virtually interchangeably. Like culture of poverty discourses, the logic of broken windows attributes 'disorder' to individual and community-level pathologies that are also endogenous to places that can be understood as stigmatized. As Chief Flynn, speaking about crime in *53206*, once explained '[w]here social dislocations exist we're going to have a concentration of violence' (CBS58 Staff, 2016). Indeed, Robin D. G. Kelley (2016) documents how Kelling and Wilson built on urban theorist Edward Banfield's contention that poverty and inequality in the post-Civil Rights era were the result of cultural differences rather than structural racism (pp. 25–26). The premise of intervening in small infractions to prevent larger disorder has had rhetorical appeal because it both maps onto existing racialized conceptualizations of poverty and criminality (Camp & Heatherton, 2016), and because it recasts policing as neutral in the midst of a decades-long struggle against racialized policing. Community policing distinguishes itself from previous policing practices in its use of data to map 'crime hotspots,' which ideally allows police officers to target 'bad guys' and to get police out of their cars to engage with residents (Bishop, 2009). Because 'data' commonly are understood as neutral, the use of data-driven practices lends the appearance of community policing as an objective, forward-looking, and preventative practice. The targeting of low-income communities of color is justified as a matter of rationality and necessity: policing happens where crime happens.

Analyzing *53206* as a spatial euphemism

While it is common to acknowledge that Milwaukee is segregated, this does not mean that the historical and contemporary processes fostering segregation are critically examined or condemned. For example, accounts of poverty and segregation commonly present a set of correlated statistics on crime, unemployment, female-headed households, and educational attainment. For example, a local radio broadcast explains, 'Although crime, poverty and other social factors often overlap, mapping these factors in Milwaukee shows dramatic divisions that align with the city's racial segregation' (Gordon, 2016). This description offers no account of policies, structures, or processes producing these correlations, yet citing these lamentable statistics has come to stand in for explanation. Acknowledging segregation as a 'factor' does not tell us how it works as a socioeconomic force among others contributing to racial and inequality in the region. Instead, as a term *segregation* tends to be used to discuss static *effects* of unnamed processes or places that comprise or are assumed to comprise African-American residents, not processes themselves. This reification of racial capitalist processes renders poverty, crime, and other social ills as endogenous to those spaces and disconnected from policies and processes producing wealthy neighborhoods.

During the Civil Rights movement era, Milwaukee was known to Black residents as the Selma of the North, a reference to the brutality of the South, which drew attention to this Midwestern city's own vicious struggle over racism (Jones, 2009). Although Black residents made up just 15% of the city's population in 1960, Milwaukee was already one of the most racially segregated cities in the nation at this time (Rose, 1992). Unabated racism has underpinned the city's residential patterning and urban development, confining Milwaukee's Black residents within the 'inner core' as white residents increasingly moved to the suburbs supported by urban and federal policies limiting Black mobility. The white suburbs surrounding the city encouraged and openly advertised racially restrictive housing covenants preventing non-whites from purchasing and renting housing. Recent research identifies over 100 such covenants in 16 of the 18 suburban areas in Milwaukee County, with 51 alone in the village of Wauwatosa, a wealthy suburb immediately to the west of the city (Bonds, Bettinger, & Van Eerden, 2016). These covenants, alongside the racist practices of blockbusting, real estate agreements, exclusionary zoning practices, and massive suburban investments, dramatically shaped the Milwaukee metropolitan region's racial structure. As a result, the expansion of the city's Black population was highly restricted to a narrow, northward trajectory, contained by the city's urban boundary and surrounded by the almost exclusively white suburbs in the so-called WOW counties of Waukesha, Ozaukee, and Washington.

Since the end of the Second World War, a range of public policies and private economic decisions have fueled deindustrialization, concentrated public and private economic investments in the suburbs ringing Milwaukee, and worked to dismantle public education and social welfare. As a result, the poverty rate in Milwaukee is 29%, a figure double that of the national poverty rate (14.8%) and more than double the statewide rate – a 30-year high – of 13% (Kennedy, 2015). The zip code *53206* is situated in Milwaukee's predominantly Black Northside, still referred to as part of the city's 'inner core' by longer term Milwaukee residents. It is bordered to the east by an interstate highway whose construction divided the historical Bronzeville neighborhood, and to the north, west, and south by other major urban thoroughfares (see Figure 1). The inner core was the area of focus for major urban renewal projects premised on 'slum' removal and highway building in the 1960s, resulting in the net loss of thousands of homes occupied by Black residents.

Within this polarized metropolitan landscape, *53206* has become a spatial euphemism for social and economic disadvantage in Milwaukee, regularly invoked by news media, policy makers, and residents alike as shorthand for racialized crime and poverty. As such, it serves as a form of racialized 'poverty propaganda' that powerfully shapes popular (mis)understandings of poor neighborhoods (Shildrick, this issue). *53206* has long been used as a 'bellwether for poverty changes in Milwaukee' (Quinn, 2007, p. 1). However, its use as a sociospatial reference intensified following the 2013 release of the report we noted at the outset of this article on Wisconsin's high incarceration rate among Black men (Pawasarat & Quinn, 2013). The report's findings continue to circulate widely – easily attached to other indicators identifying the city's high rate of crime and poverty and sharp racial segregation – bringing national and international attention to the city's racially unequal urban landscape (cf. Dale, 2016; Demby, 2013; Downs, 2016; 'Why does Winconsin?', 2013). Then Milwaukee Police Department Chief Edward Flynn observed, 'We have a famous ZIP code, 53206, and I always hear about it because so many prisoners come from there' (Anderson, 2015). This international spotlight contributed to urgency felt locally that resulted in a series of community forums and discussions, special programming and reporting by media, and the development of an array of new policies and calls for reform at both the level of the city and the state.

Narratives about *53206* have been produced by diverse circles: from liberal politicians and organizations calling attention to the state's racialized pattern of incarceration and the spatial concentration of poverty (e.g. Leichenger, 2014; Toobin, 2015), in academic reports and analyses of urban inequality (e.g. Levine, 2014; Pawasarat & Quinn, 2013; Quinn, 2007), a documentary entitled *53206*, and among conservative pundits and

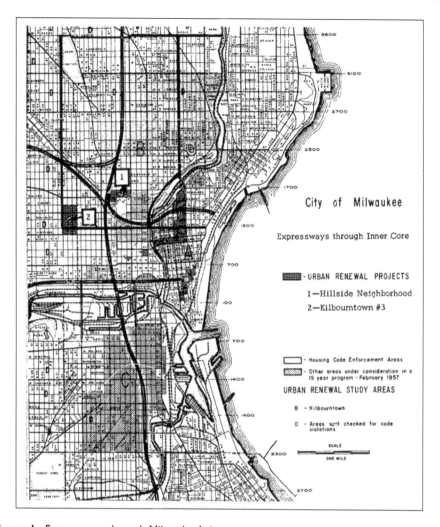

Figure 1. Expressways through Milwaukee's inner core.

elected officials decrying Milwaukee and the problems encapsulated by *53206* as the source of the state's stagnating economy and social ills. 'Yeah, a lot of bad is happening [in 53206]. But we find it funny when liberals and politicians try to come in and say they can fix things. They just drop in and use us as a backdrop and then they go' (Kaleem & Simmons, 2016). As one resident remarked when asked by a journalist about living in *53206*: 'Oh, you want to write about all us poor people' (Miner, 2017). Even as area residents and nonprofits contested how these discourses maligned their communities, and ignored ongoing grassroots efforts, their challenges often reified existing tropes about *53206* precisely by naming the factors, but not the processes. For example, a newspaper editorial seeking to disrupt these negative representations began by stating that *53206* 'has a reputation for being violent, dysfunctional and unwelcoming, a place to escape from, to abandon,' yet did little to question how this frame came about (Linnen & Gosman, 2015).

These discourses circulated in the midst of bipartisan concern about 'mass incarceration' and growing attention to policing, in part spurred by the Black Lives Matter movement. In Milwaukee as in other American cities, police violence against and mistreatment of Black residents is a decades' old issue. In the 1950s, Chicago had the highest overall number of police killings, but the disparity between Black and white residents killed by police was much higher in Milwaukee, where police killed Black people 29.5 times more frequently than white residents (Takagi, 1974/2014, p. 124). In the 1960s, MPD's tactical squad unit intimidated open housing (anti-discrimination) activists, and civil rights activists claimed that a police tear gas canister was responsible for sparking a fire that destroyed one of their organizing spaces. The death of Black Milwaukee resident Ernest Lacy at the hands of the MPD tactical squad sparked the formation of a 125-organization large coalition against police violence in 1981. NAACP president Chris Belnavis called Lacy's death 'the 23rd victim in the last ten years who has lost his life at the hands of our police' (Miner, 2013, p. 103). One officer was eventually fired, three were suspended, and the city settled a civil suit with the family. Organizing also led to legislative changes that ended the police chief's lifetime appointment, and created oversight by the mayor, common council, and Fire and Police Commission (Miner, 2013, p. 104).

The decades since have been punctuated by police abuse and neglect scandals. In the early 1990s, Jeffrey Dahmer killed 17 men and boys (many of whom were Black or Asian) in Milwaukee. Many residents contended that racism and homophobia fueled the MPD's failure to take the murders seriously (Miner, 2013, p. 104). Edward Flynn began as police chief in 2008 on the heels of a corruption scandal, specifically tasked with the role of improving community relations. Flynn initially was 'canonize[d]' as responsible for a drop in homicides and improvement in police morale (Bishop, 2009). Yet, in 2011, he refused to answer questions about a group of police officers who named themselves 'The Punishers,' calling the group a 'rumor' (Miner, 2013, p. 107). In 2012, Derek Williams died by asphyxiation in the back of a police car. That same year, eight people sued the MPD's 5th district over cavity and strip searches, forms of sexual assault, which they had endured during traffic stops. In 2016, the city settled the suit for $5 million, a settlement that one city alderman denounced as a 'whimpification' of the police (B. Taylor, 2016). The murder of Dontre Hamilton, who was resting in a downtown city park, by an MPD officer in 2014 led to a new round of organizing. His family launched Coalition for Justice, echoing efforts from the early 1980s, that used street mobilizations and other tactics to pressure for accountability and changes in MPD policy.

Amidst this sustained mobilization for police reform and increase in homicides since 2014, the repetition of language identifying *53206* as a site of high poverty, unemployment, and crime has amplified. Perhaps best capturing the convergence of liberal and conservative framings of *53206* are the responses to violent crime coming from seemingly counterposed officials: then Milwaukee Police Chief Ed Flynn and then Milwaukee County Sheriff David Clarke. Clarke, who identifies as African-American, was a law-and-order darling of Fox News, the NRA, the state Attorney General, and Republicans across the nation during his term as sheriff. As a vocal supporter of Donald Trump, he was given a platform at the 2016 Republican National Convention and was considered for a position in the Department of Homeland Security. Clarke has likened Black Lives Matter protests to terrorism, has vocally touted individual gun rights as a means of crime prevention, and claims that 'there is no police brutality in America. We ended that back in the '60s' (Mock, 2015). Police Chief Flynn was positioned in the national media as the liberal contrast to Clarke's 'get tough' style of policing (cf. Kaleem, 2016). For example, in December 2014, at the peak of street protests spurred by Dontre Hamilton's murder, Flynn participated in a Black Lives Matter rally, and he pledged, alongside Milwaukee County District Attorney John Chisholm, to address mass incarceration (Mock, 2015).

The public conflict between Clarke and Flynn expressed political schisms within the state and nation. Clarke was first elected as Milwaukee County Sheriff during a special election, running as a Democrat despite his vocal embrace of conservatism. In 2014, Clarke was re-elected for a fourth term, bolstered primarily by white suburban voters with whom his tough-on-crime rhetoric resonated (Mock, 2015). Milwaukee County had been under court order since 2001 to resolve its deadly lack of health care in its jail and corrections center when Clarke took office. Clarke outsourced medical services to a private corporation, yet staffing levels remain poor (Hovorka, 2017). Between 2008 and 2012, 10 people died while in the sheriff's custody (Barton, 2014). In 2016 alone, four people died in county custody, including an infant whose mother gave birth while held in maximum security and a man who died of dehydration after being denied water for days while in isolation in the jail (Lombardo, 2016; Willms, 2016). Amidst these and other controversies, Clarke resigned from office in 2017.

During his term as sheriff, Clarke advocated for an intensified broken windows approach to higher rates of crime, including an expanded and 'consistently visible' presence of police, increased traffic stops, and harsher penalties for low-level offenses, arguing that this approach must include 'tactics like stop-question-and-frisk' and 'continual warrant sweeps to get these bad apples off the street' (Bee & Bayatpour, 2016). He contrasted his aggressive approach to that of Chief Flynn, whom he characterized as a liberal who coddles criminals (cf. Kaleem, 2016). Yet, broken windows architect George Kelling approvingly notes that under Flynn's watch, there were 400,000 'contacts' between Milwaukee residents and police in 2015 alone (Anderson, 2016).

Flynn frequently emphasized the need to build relationships with heavily policed communities and champions broken windows policing that is data-driven and discretionary (Toobin, 2015). While Flynn promoted this approach as an alternative to racialized policing, Brian Jordan Jefferson (2018) demonstrates how predictive policing 'legitimizes the widespread criminalization of racialized districts' (p. 11). A longtime ally of former big city police commissioner and broken windows proponent William Bratton, Flynn claims that reading Kelling and Wilson's 1982 article changed the course of his career (Bishop, 2009). Flynn has been lauded widely as an epitome of community policing. Kelling, who grew up in Milwaukee and wrote a book on the history of policing in the city, recommended Flynn's candidacy for police chief. In an interview with the conservative think tank Manhattan Institute's *City Journal*, Kelling praised Flynn for his 'refocus around a geographical orientation. In the past, police departments were built around algorithms to reduce response time. Instead, community policing emphasizes building police departments around "natural neighborhoods," so that you work with the neighborhood to develop their strengths.' Kelling also approved of Flynn's implementation of another paradigm of community policing: 'preventing crime before it occurs.' Kelling concludes that Flynn was able to change the tenor of policing in Milwaukee by being 'very frank about the very nature of the problems in Milwaukee, and that was that serious crime and victimization was located in the African American community' (Anderson, 2016).

Indeed, Flynn has been vocal in this claim locally and nationally, explaining that '[t]he reality for urban police practitioners is that we respond to the overwhelming victimization of black people. … The sad fact is that most violent offenders look like their victims. So that means that everything we do is going to have a disparate impact on communities of color' (Toobin, 2015). While Clarke attributed the challenges facing poor neighborhoods of color to 'Black-on-Black violence' and failing family structures, Flynn expresses empathy for the systematic neglect of Black communities. Speaking during the uprising following the police shooting of Sylville Smith, Flynn proclaimed that 'the neighborhoods that depend on us [the police] the most are also the ones that have been the most historically ignored' (Kaleem, 2016).

One way that criticism of police violence has been countered rhetorically is through invoking the frame of 'Black-on-Black crime' as the more fundamental issue. Khalil Muhammad (2012) contends that such arguments 'play the violence card,' which 'perpetuates the reassuring notion that violence against black people is not society's concern but rather a problem for black people to fix on their own' because it stems from 'a failure of lower-class black culture … not a problem with social and institutional roots that needs to be addressed through collective effort well beyond the boundaries of black communities.' Despite their differences, Barrett, Flynn, and Clarke deploy different versions of this frame. For Clarke, the answer was law-and-order. Barrett and Flynn rework the violence card to reject the idea that violence in Black communities is solely a Black concern. For example, Mayor Barrett's quotation in the epigraph invokes Black Lives Matter as a principle for which 'somebody should step forward,' suggesting that Black people (and others) have not been working to prevent violence. In the 2016 documentary *Too Many Candles: Milwaukee Gun Violence*, Flynn similarly states that 'residents shouldn't be relegated to a life of crime because they happen to live in a particular zipcode.' Yet, this expression of a compassionate affect nonetheless rests on a racist frame in which crime flows directly from place and 'collective effort' amounts to policing.

Upon closer scrutiny, the distinctions between Clarke's law-and-order approach and Flynn and Barrett's compassionate community approaches become more difficult to discern. For all of Flynn's commitment to improving relations with low-income neighborhoods of color, in 2011, the *Milwaukee Journal Sentinel* reported that Flynn's police department stopped Black car drivers 7 to 12 times more often than they pulled over white people, a much more pronounced rate than in Clarke's countywide jurisdiction (Mock, 2015). Both Clarke and Flynn endorse the benefits of broken windows policing and advocate for an expanded police force, even as Flynn's community policing approach is represented as smoothing racial and class conflict. Illustrating the connections between liberal benevolence and institutions of social control (Murakawa, 2014; Schept, 2015), Flynn and Barrett advocate for expanded policing in low-income communities of color that is protective and preventative while disavowing the relationships among systematic policing, the city's racial inequality, and the state's racialized pattern of incarceration.

In short, the apparent dichotomy between law-and-order and community policing better represents a consensus on the legitimacy and necessity of policing.

Conclusion: Dismantling *53206?* Police reforms and other strategies to avoid ending white supremacy

The discourse of *53206* seems to offer a clear example of territorial stigmatization whereby 'noxious representations of space are produced, diffused, and harnessed in the field of power … in ways that alter social identity, strategy, and structure' (Wacquant et al., 2014, p. 1273). One of the elements of this process that Wacquant et al. identify – how particular spaces serve as 'vortexes and vectors of social *disintegration*' that threaten other spaces (2014, p. 1274, emphasis in original) – is evident in a statement that State Assembly member Janel Brandtjen made regarding Milwaukee's crime. Brandtjen, who does not represent Milwaukee, but a district in neighboring Waukesha County, warned Milwaukee Mayor Barrett: 'I will be openly advocating for funding cuts to Milwaukee unless steps are taken to dramatically cut crime in Milwaukee. I will no longer sit by while you destroy Milwaukee and its flourishing suburbs. I cannot justify financing your failed policies in Milwaukee until you take public safety seriously' (Glauber & Marley, 2016). This statement, called 'provocative' by the local news, is another example of racialized 'poverty propaganda' (Shildrick, this issue) that draws upon racialized discourses of places that threaten to harm other 'flourishing' places to advocate for punitive policy responses.

Yet, we contend that the abstraction of *territorial stigmatization* as a concept, while offering the potential for comparison across places, is a neutralizing term, which militates against the grounded histories and contemporary workings of racial capitalism. As proposed by Wacquant (2007) and advanced by Wacquant et al. (2014), territorial stigmatization is conceptualized as a process distinctive to post-industrial cities or the turn of the 21st century, and yet one that builds on earlier forms of racial and class defamation. As a concept, we are presented with distinctiveness and continuity, yet no clear reasoning for the shift, why these historical dynamics differ, and how *territorial stigmatization* better explains specific workings of racial capitalism. (To confuse matters, a recent collection on territorial stigmatization presents the concept as a 'more relevant' and 'comprehensive' term than concepts of 'segregation and the racialisation of space' [Kirkness & Tijé-Dra, 2017, p. i] even though racialization is part of the 2014 definition we have been using here.) While there has been some work using the territorial stigmatization concept that attends to how historical dynamics contribute to contemporary ones (Queirós & Pereira, this issue; Slater & Anderson, 2011), it seems in tension with the temporally distinct process theorized by Wacquant et al. (2014).

We are wary about a concept defined by a temporal break because in the US context, discourses on racism and power relations structuring segregation similarly invoke contemporary logics that are distinct from the past. During this 'colorblind' moment, history is recounted in ideological ways that serve to isolate structures of white racial rule to the past, thereby disavowing the role that accumulated white wealth and power play in the persistence of racialized poverty and racial and class conflict. For example, Republican Congressperson Jim Sensenbrenner, who represents Waukesha County, attributes his district's strong GOP support to the 1960s when 'people started fleeing into the Milwaukee suburbs due to high crime, high taxes, and bad schools' (Lewis, Silverstone, Sambamurthy, & Lapinski, 2016). Sensenbrenner invokes contemporary racialized tropes of high crime, high taxes, and bad schools that stand in for Black and Democratic Milwaukee, yet when asked about the political polarization of the state, he contends that racial segregation 'has nothing to do with it' (Lewis et al., 2016). This account of history obscures both historical white flight and white resistance to civil rights demands, and ongoing political assaults that marshal the same tropes to rationalize the dismantling of public education and services.

Similarly, Kelling's narrative of contemporary police–Black resident conflict begins in the 1960s when: 'Many of the neighborhoods were broken down. … [A]ll the agencies of social control, all the agencies of socialization really came under well-meaning, but nevertheless an assault that broke down their ability to maintain order and to keep youths, especially, under control. And so Milwaukee started, along with most other cities at the time, a movement towards increased crime, but also antagonism developed between police and the African American community' (Anderson, 2016). Kelling implicitly names the Civil Rights movement as responsible for social 'breakdown,' which then necessitates community policing to restore social order and repair community relations. Both Sensenbrenner and Kelling narrate a nostalgic and declensionist version of history in which 'crime' is always already Black and policing can restore a peaceful social order. Yet, this past can only exist by erasing the violence of Jim Crow and the longstanding role of police in maintaining this order.

Dominant framings of *53206* largely obscure the roles that decades of deindustrialization and labor assaults, metropolitan racial and wealth segregation, and public school and welfare restructuring play in the deepening of racial income and wealth gaps. Instead, bipartisan discussions rehearse racializing narratives of broken Black homes, Black-on-Black crime, and uncaring Black communities, which are largely unreconstructed from Moynihan's 1965 *The Negro Family*. The discursive linking of this space with race and violence produces its own set of solutions. Liberal and conservative solutions to the problems of *53206* advocate stronger involvement of Black men in the home, entrepreneurialism, and policing, while liberal versions add job training for Black men, prison re-entry programs, and workfare. Such moralizing terms of individual responsibility, redemption, resilience, and respectability reproduce neoliberal and colorblind myths of equal opportunity (Cope & Latcham, 2009; Lawson & Elwood, 2014).

As white scholars residing in segregated cities, we need to be able to speak about white supremacy in relation to neoliberal capitalist austerity and how state racial violence shores up sociospatial divides. Rather than treating territorial stigmatization as novel, we have traced how discourses that depict segregation as a static attribute of a bounded place, like *53206*, sustain contemporary forms of racial capitalism and policing in Milwaukee precisely by negating history and sociospatial relationships that simultaneously create wealth and poverty. The historical construction of the material places in which we live evidences continuities of racial capitalism, not departures from the past as the territorial stigmatization thesis and colorblind ideologies would have us believe. If we are to consider the power of stigmatization, in this case its power is explicitly its racialization. While racialization is an element of the territorial stigmatization concept, it is focused on the symbolic dimension of how negative meanings of places are constructed and circulated. Why not just say racialization rather than subsume it to stigmatization? Further, representations, however important, are only one part of a broader theory of racism in which concepts of oppression, domination, and exploitation continue to have salience. The symbolic or discursive racialization of space, in this case *53206*, is being used to rationalize further austerity and to entrench policing to 'protect' Black and white residents alike, thereby 'weaponizing' (Scambler, this issue) 'poverty propaganda' (Shildrick, this issue).

The Black Lives Matter movement has widened an already sustained legitimation crisis of policing and 'mass incarceration.' A bipartisan consensus has emerged around the need for reforms to the criminal legal system that aims to restore faith in the justness of the system. Residents are presented with a princess and the pea fable: that policing and incarceration can be done just right. As such, reforms such as 'community policing,' 'problem-oriented policing,' and diversion programs are held out as alternatives to uncompromising law-and-order (Brown, 2015; Camp & Heatherton, 2016; Herbert, 2001). Mutual understanding, transparency, and respect for civil rights sound appealing in comparison to militarized policing, racial profiling, and racial disparities in sentencing. Yet this good cop-bad cop routine actually erases the long history of reform driving the expansion of social control, separation, punitive, and rehabilitative practices in carceral and welfare institutions (Hinton, 2016; Murakawa, 2014; Schept, 2015). Indeed, as Ruth Wilson Gilmore and Craig Gilmore write, 'The righteous outrage against police murders and extra-heavy equipment enables a strange displacement (often unintended, yet also often cynically co-opted) of political focus from the necessarily systemic character of organized violence' (2016, p. 176). This system is one in which police agencies, whether deployed in the name of law-and-order or saving Black lives, are imagined as a neutral force, despite their actual role in underpinning the differential racial capitalist ordering of human value across urban space.

Funding

This research received no specific grant from any funding agency in the public, commercial, or not-for-profit sectors.

References

Anderson, B. C. (2016, March 23). What can we learn from the history of Milwaukee policing? *City Journal*. Retrieved from http://www.city-journal.org/html/what-can-we-learn-history-milwaukee-policing-14303.html (last accessed 10 May 2018).

Anderson, M. (2015, November 6). Documentary focuses on area of Milwaukee with highest incarceration rate. *WISN*. Retrieved from http://www.wisn.com/article/documentary-focuses-on-area-of-milwaukee-with-highest-incarceration-rate/6329328 (last accessed 10 May 2018).

Annie E. Casey Foundation. (2014). Race for results: Building a path to opportunity for all children. Retrieved from http://www.aecf.org/resources/race-for-results/ (last accessed 10 May 2018).

Barton, G. (2014, February 1). Unanswered questions surround deaths in detention in Milwaukee County. *Milwaukee Journal Sentinel*. Retrieved from http://archive.jsonline.com/watchdog/watchdogreports/unanswered-questions-surround-deaths-in-detention-in-milwaukee-county-b9979847z1–243112331.html (last accessed 10 May 2018).

Bauder, H. (2002). Neighborhood effects and cultural exclusion. *Urban Studies, 39*, 85–93.

Bee, T., & Bayatpour, A. J. (2016, June 24). Sheriff Clarke calls upon the City of Milwaukee to hire 400 new police officers. *Fox 6*. Retrieved from http://fox6now.com/2016/06/24/sheriff-david-clarke-calls-upon-city-of-milwaukee-to-hire-400-new-police-officers/ (last accessed 10 May 2018).

Bishop, D. (2009). The cop who won't stop. *Milwaukee Magazine*. Retrieved from https://www.milwaukeemag.com/TheCopWhoCantStop/ (last accessed 11 May 2018).

Bonds, A. (2009). Discipline and devolution: Constructions of poverty, race, and criminality in the politics of rural prison development. *Antipode, 41*, 416–438.

Bonds, A., Bettinger, E., & Van Eerden, J. (2016). *Mapping racial housing covenants in Milwaukee*. Unpublished manuscript.

Bonds, A., & Inwood, J. (2016). Beyond white privilege: Geographies of white supremacy and settler colonialism. *Progress in Human Geography, 40*, 715–733.

Bonilla-Silva, E. (2014). *Racism without racists: Color-blind racism and the persistence of racial inequality in America* (4th ed.). Lanham, MD: Rowman & Littlefield.

Brown, E. (2015). The social meanings of broken windows policing. *Street Sheet: A Publication of the Coalition on Homelessness*. Retrieved from http://www.streetsheet.org/?p=1788 (last accessed 11 May 2018).

Camp, J. T., & Heatherton, C. (Eds.). (2016). *Policing the planet: Why policing the crisis led to Black Lives Matter*. London, UK: Verso.

CBS58 Staff (2016, May 12). Milwaukee Police Chief Ed Flynn reveals four simple rules to not get shot in Milwaukee. *CBS 58 News*. Retrieved from http://www.cbs58.com/news/milwaukee-police-chief-ed-flynn-reveals-four-simple-rules-to-not-get-shot-in-milwaukee (last accessed 10 May 2018).

Chaddha, A., & Wilson, W. J. (2008). Reconsidering the 'ghetto.' *City & Community, 7*, 384–388.

Cope, M., & Latcham, F. (2009). Narratives of decline: Race, poverty, and youth in the context of post-industrial urban angst. *Professional Geographer, 61*, 150–163.

Crump, J. (2002). Deconcentration by demolition: Public housing, poverty, and urban policy. *Environment and Planning D: Society and Space, 20*, 581–596.

Dale, D. (2016, January 25). 'Back in time 60 years': America's most segregated city. *Toronto Star*. Retrieved from https://www.thestar.com/news/world/2016/01/25/back-in-time-60-years-americas-most-segregated-city.html (last accessed 10 May 2018).

Demby, G. (2013, April 24). Why does Wisconsin lock up more black people than any other state? *NPR Codeswitch*. Retrieved from http://www.npr.org/sections/codeswitch/2013/04/24/178817911/wisconsin-locks-up-more-of-its-black-men-than-any-other-state-study-finds (last accessed 10 May 2018).

Denvir, D. (2011, March 29). The 10 most segregated urban areas in America. *Salon*. Retrieved from http://www.salon.com/2011/03/29/most_segregated_cities/ (last accessed 10 May 2018).

Downs, K. (2016, February 8). Why is Milwaukee so bad for black people? *PBS Newshour*. Retrieved from http://www.pbs.org/newshour/rundown/why-is-milwaukee-so-bad-for-black-people/ (last accessed 10 May 2018).

Florida, R. (2014, March 24). The U.S. cities where the poor are most segregated from everyone else. *The Atlantic Citylab*. Retrieved from http://www.citylab.com/housing/2014/03/us-cities-where-poor-are-most-segregated/8655/ (last accessed 10 May 2018).

Gilmore, R. W. (2002). Fatal couplings of power and difference: Notes on racism and geography. *The Professional Geographer, 54*, 15–24.

Gilmore, R. W. (2007). *Golden gulag: Prisons, surplus, crisis, and opposition in globalizing California*. Berkeley: University of California Press.

Gilmore, R. W., & Gilmore, C. (2016). Beyond Bratton. In J. T. Camp & C. Heatherton (Eds.), *Policing the planet: Why the policing crisis led to Black Lives Matter* (pp. 173–201). London, UK: Verso.

Glauber, B., & Marley, P. (2016, June 7). Lawmaker blames Tom Barrett for crime spilling into suburbs. *Milwaukee Journal Sentinel*. Retrieved from http://archive.jsonline.com/news/statepolitics/lawmaker-blames-barrett-for-crime-spilling-into-suburbs-b99739915z1-382130961.html (last accessed 10 May 2018).

Goffman, E. (1963). *Stigma: Notes on the management of a spoiled identity*. Englewood Cliffs, NJ: Prentice Hall.

Gordon, S. (2016, May 10). How Milwaukee's economic, social disparities correspond with gun violence. *WPR*. Retrieved from https://www.wpr.org/how-milwaukees-economic-social-disparities-correspond-gun-violence (last accessed 10 May 2018).

Greenbaum, S. (2015). *Blaming the poor*. New Brunswick, NJ: Rutgers University Press.

Hall, S. (1980). Race, articulation and societies structured in dominance. In *UNESCO Sociological Theories: Race and Colonialism* (pp. 305–346). Poole, UK: UNESCO.

Herbert, S. (2001). Policing the contemporary city. *Theoretical Criminology*, *5*, 445–466.

Herbert, S., & Brown, E. (2006). Conceptions of space and crime in the punitive neoliberal city. *Antipode*, *38*, 755–777.

Hinton, E. (2016). *From the war on poverty to the war on crime*. Cambridge, MA: Harvard University Press.

Hvorka, A. (2017, June 30). Milwaukee County corrections face possible audit, fines if care for inmates does not improve. *Milwaukee Journal Sentinel*. Retrieved from http://www.jsonline.com/story/news/investigations/2017/06/30/milwaukee-county-jail-nurse-vacancies-completely-unacceptable-court-monitor-says/433800001/ (last accessed 10 May 2018).

Jefferson, B. J. (2018). Predictable policing: Predictive crime mapping and geographies of policing and race. *The Annals of the Association of American Geography*, *108*, 1–16.

Jones, P. D. (2009). *The Selma of the North: Civil rights insurgency in Milwaukee*. Cambridge, MA: Harvard University Press.

Kaleem, J. (2016, August 19). Amid Milwaukee unrest, a conservative black sheriff clashes with the city's liberal white police chief. *Los Angeles Times*. Retrieved from http://www.latimes.com/nation/la-na-milwaukee-sheriff-david-clarke-20160816-snap-story.html (last accessed 10 May 2018).

Kaleem, J., & Simmons, A. M. (2016, November 5). Trump says African Americans are living in hell. That depends on what you mean by hell. *Los Angeles Times*. Retrieved from http://www.latimes.com/nation/la-na-global-black-america-snap-20161103-story.html (last accessed 10 May 2018).

Katz, M. B. (2015). What kind of problem is poverty? The archeology of an idea. In A. Roy & E. Crane (Eds.), *Territories of poverty: Rethinking north and south* (pp. 39–78). Athens: The University of Georgia Press.

Kelley, R. D. G. (2016). Thug nation: On state violence and disposability. In J. T. Camp & C. Heatherton (Eds.), *Policing the planet: Why the policing crisis led to Black Lives Matter* (pp. 15–35). London, UK: Verso.

Kelling, G. L., & Wilson, J. O. (1982, March). Broken windows: The police and neighborhood safety. *The Atlantic*. Retrieved from http://www.theatlantic.com/magazine/archive/1982/03/broken-windows/304465/?single_page=true (last accessed 10 May 2018).

Kennedy, B. (2015, February 18). America's 11 poorest cities. *CBS Moneywatch*. Retrieved from http://www.cbsnews.com/media/americas-11-poorest-cities/11/ (last accessed 10 May 2018).

Kirkness, P., & Tijé-Dra, A. (Eds.). (2017). *Negative neighbourhood reputation and place attachment: The production and contestation of territorial stigma*. Abingdon, UK: Routledge.

Larsen, T. S., & Delica, K. N. (2017, June 21). *Conceptualizing the 'blemish of place': A review of the literature on territorial stigmatization*. Paper presented at Nordic Geographers Meeting, Stockholm, Sweden.

Lawson, V., & Elwood, S. (2014). Encountering poverty: Space, class, and poverty politics. *Antipode, 46*, 209–228.

Leichenger, A. (2014). How one zip code in Milwaukee explains America's mass incarceration problem. *Think Progress*. Retrieved from https://thinkprogress.org/how-one-milwaukee-zip-code-explains-americas-mass-incarceration-problem-66a6535d1c4/ (last accessed 11 May 2018).

Levine, M. (2014). Zipcode 53206: A statistical snapshot of inner city distress in Milwaukee: 2000–2012. *Center for Economic Development Data Brief, University of Wisconsin-Milwaukee*, Retrieved from https://www4.uwm.edu/ced/publications/53206_revised.pdf (last accessed 10 May 2018).

Lewis, P., Silverstone, T., Sambamurthy, A., & Lapinski, V. (2016, October 19). America's most segregated city: The young black voters in Milwaukee. *The Guardian*. Retrieved from https://www.theguardian.com/us-news/video/2016/oct/18/milwaukee-wisconsin-segregation-young-black-voters-election-video (last accessed 10 May 2018).

Link, B. G., & Phelan, J. C. (2001). Conceptualizing stigma. *Annual Review of Sociology, 27*, 363–385.

Linnen, J., & Gosman, M. (2015, July 8). The rest of the story behind 53206. *Milwaukee Journal Sentinel*. Retrieved from http://archive.jsonline.com/news/opinion/the-rest-of-the-story-behind-53206-b99534173z1–312674271.html (last accessed 10 May 2018).

Lombardo, C. (2016, September 15). Death in county jail ruled homicide; cause of death was dehydration. *Milwaukee Journal Sentinel*. Retrieved from http://www.jsonline.com/story/news/investigations/2016/09/15/death-county-jail-ruled-homicide-inmate-had-no-water-days/89960362/ (last accessed 10 May 2018).

Loyd, J. M. (2014). *Health rights are civil rights: Peace and justice activism in Los Angeles, 1963–1978*. Minneapolis: University of Minnesota Press.

McKittrick, K. (2006). *Demonic grounds: Black women and the cartographies of struggle*. Minneapolis: University of Minnesota Press.

McKittrick, K. (2011). On plantations, prisons, and a black sense of place. *Social & Cultural Geography, 12*, 947–963.

Melamed, J. (2011). *Represent and destroy: Rationalizing violence in the new racial capitalism*. Minneapolis: University of Minnesota Press.

Miller, J. (2015, November 3). Save Wisconsin from 'worst city for blacks' ranking. *Milwaukee Journal Sentinel*. Retrieved from http://archive.jsonline.com/blogs/purple-wisconsin/339936551.html (last accessed 10 May 2018).

Miner, B. (2013). *Lessons from the heartland: A turbulent half-century of public education in an iconic American city*. New York, NY: The New Press.

Miner, B. (2017, January 28). A closer look at Milwaukee zip code 53206. *Milwaukee Magazine*. Retrieved from https://www.milwaukeemag.com/milwaukee-zip-code-53206/ (last accessed 10 May 2018).

Mock, B. (2015, October 30). Why Milwaukee is the worst place to live for African Americans. *The Atlantic City Lab*. Retrieved from http://www.citylab.com/crime/2015/10/why-milwaukee-is-the-worst-place-to-live-for-african-americans/413218/ (last accessed 10 May 2018).

Muhammad, K. G. (2011). *The condemnation of blackness*. Cambridge, MA: Harvard University Press.

Muhammad, K. G. (2012, April 5). Playing the violence card. *New York Times*. Retrieved from http://www.nytimes.com/2012/04/06/opinion/playing-the-violence-card.html (last accessed 10 May 2018).

Murakawa, N. (2014). *The first civil right: How liberals built prison America*. Oxford, UK: Oxford University Press.

O'Connor, A. (2001). *Poverty knowledge: Social science, social policy, and the poor in twentieth-century U.S. history*. Princeton, NJ: Princeton University Press.

Pawasarat, J. (2009). Ex-offender populations in Milwaukee. Employment and Training Institute, University of Wisconsin-Milwaukee. Retrieved from http://www4.uwm.edu/eti/2009/ExOffendersMilwaukeeCounty.pdf (last accessed 10 May 2018).

Pawasarat, J., & Quinn, L. (2013). Wisconsin's mass incarceration of African American males: Workforce challenges for 2013. Employment and Training Institute, University of Wisconsin-Milwaukee. Retrieved from http://www4.uwm.edu/eti/2013/BlackImprisonment.pdf (last accessed 10 May 2018).

Potter, S. (2016). Bar code. *Milwaukee Magazine*. Retrieved from https://www.milwaukeemag.com/bar-code/ (last accessed 10 May 2018).

Pulido, L. (2000). Rethinking environmental racism: White privilege and urban development in Southern California. *Annals of the Association of American Geographers*, *90*, 12–40.

Quinn, L. (2007). New indicators of neighborhood need in 53206: Neighborhood indicators of employment, economic well being of families, barriers to employment, and untapped opportunities. Employment and Training Institute, University of Wisconsin-Milwaukee. Retrieved from https://www4.uwm.edu/eti/2007/53206N.pdf (last accessed 10 May 2018).

Robinson, C. J. (1983). *Black Marxism: The making of the Black radical tradition*. Chapel Hill: The University of North Carolina Press.

Rose, H. M. (1992). The employment status of young adult black males residing in poverty households: Recent Milwaukee County experience. Employment and Training Institute, University of Wisconsin-Milwaukee. Retrieved from http://dc.uwm.edu/eti_pubs/173/ (last accessed 10 May 2018).

Schept, J. (2015). *Progressive punishment: Job loss, jail growth, and the neoliberal logic of carceral expansion*. New York: New York University Press.

Slater, T. (2013). Your life chances affect where you live: A critique of the 'cottage industry' of neighbourhood effects research. *International Journal of Urban and Regional Research*, *37*, 367–387.

Slater, T., & Anderson, N. (2011). The reputational ghetto: Territorial stigmatization in St Paul's, Bristol. *Transactions of the Institute of British Geographers*, *37*, 530–546.

Takagi, P. (2014). A garrison state in 'democratic' society. *Social Justice*, *40*, 118–130 (original work published 1974).

Taylor, B. (2016, January 19). Milwaukee Common Council approves $5 million settlement in strip search/body cavity search case. *Fox 6*. Retrieved from http://fox6now.com/2016/01/19/milwaukee-common-council-approves-5-million-settlement-in-strip-searchbody-cavity-search-case/ (last accessed 10 May 2018).

Taylor, K.-Y. (2016). *From #BlackLivesMatter to Black liberation*. Chicago, IL: Haymarket Books.

Toobin, J. (2015, May 11). The Milwaukee experiment: What can one prosecutor do about the mass incarceration of African Americans? *The New Yorker*. Retrieved from http://www.newyorker.com/magazine/2015/05/11/the-milwaukee-experiment (last accessed 10 May 2018).

Wacquant, L. (2007). *Urban outcasts: A comparative sociology of advanced marginality*. Cambridge, UK: Polity.

Wacquant, L. (2016). Revisiting territories of relegation: Class, ethnicity and state in the making of advanced marginality. *Urban Studies*, *53*, 1077–1088.

Wacquant, L., Slater, T., & Pereira, V. B. (2014). Territorial stigmatization in action. *Environment and Planning A*, *46*, 1270–1280.

Why does Wisconsin send so many black people to jail? (2013, September 18). *BBC*. Retrieved from www.bbc.com/news/magazine-24119398 (last accessed 10 May 2018).

Willms, M. (2016, December 28). Milwaukee jailers blamed for newborn's death. *Courthouse News Service*. Retrieved from https://www.courthousenews.com/milwaukee-jailers-blamed-for-newborns-death/ (last accessed 10 May 2018).

Wilson, B. M. (2002). Critically understanding race-connected practices: A reading of WEB Du Bois and Richard Wright. *The Professional Geographer, 54*, 31–41.

Woods, C. (1998). *Development arrested: Race, power, and the blues in the Mississippi Delta*. London, UK: Verso.

Author biographies

Jenna M. Loyd is Assistant Professor of Geography at University of Wisconsin-Madison. She is the author of *Health Rights Are Civil Rights: Peace and Justice Activism in Los Angeles, 1963–1978* (University of Minnesota Press, 2014) and co-author with Alison Mountz of *Boats, Borders, and Bases: Race, the Cold War, and the Rise of Migration Detention in the United States* (University of California Press, 2018).

Anne Bonds is an Associate Professor of Geography and an affiliated faculty member of the Urban Studies Programs at the University of Wisconsin-Milwaukee. She is a feminist economic geographer with specializations in the areas of urban political economy, race and racialization, and poverty and criminalization.

Beyond legacy: Backstage stigmatisation and 'trickle-up' politics of urban regeneration

The Sociological Review Monographs
2018, Vol. 66(4) 201–216
© The Author(s) 2018
Reprints and permissions:
sagepub.co.uk/journalsPermissions.nav
DOI: 10.1177/0038026118777449
journals.sagepub.com/home/sor

Kirsteen Paton
University of Liverpool, UK

Abstract

This article explores how stigmatisation is intimately linked with neoliberal governance and capital accumulation in specific ways through processes around the Glasgow Commonwealth Games. It advances the author's previous research exploring the effects of stigma on the East End community hosting the Games, by looking at some of the processes of power and profit which motivate stigmatising processes by 'gazing up', rather than 'gazing down'. That is, looking at the role of the stigmatisers in this project and not the stigmatised. It draws loosely on Goffman's concept of 'backstage' to shed light on those who produce and profit from these stigmatisation processes, including government bodies and actors and private business interests. Looking at some of the processes through which stigmatisation is profited from reveals not only forms of power vital to this process but that it is a key form of exploitation integral to capital accumulation. Under austerity, the political economy of the Games constitutes state support of private finance and a simultaneous withdrawal of social welfare support, which transfers the burden of debt from the state to the individual and wealth from public funds to private funds.

Keywords

austerity, gentrification, neighbourhoods, territorial stigmatisation

The story goes that in the summer of 2014, a terrified athlete ran into a newsagent's shop in Dalmarnock, Glasgow. The Commonwealth Games had just begun in the city and this competitor had lost his way from the Athletes' Village and, clutching a map, was seeking directions to safety. He was in the 'red zone' – Dalmarnock – which was a designated host neighbourhood site for the Games event. The map issued to visiting athletes competing in the Games event instructed them which neighbourhoods were unsafe and to be avoided – the 'red zone' was a no-go area. The bemused newsagent looked at the map to

Corresponding author:
Kirsteen Paton, Department of Sociology, Social Policy and Criminology, School of Law and Social Justice, University of Liverpool, Eleanor Rathbone Building, Liverpool, L69 7ZA, UK.
Email: kirsteen.paton@liverpool.ac.uk

assist the lost athlete and saw that her shop – promised to experience the benefits of the Commonwealth Games 'trickle-down' of tourist consumerism – was in the 'red zone'. Yet this discovery seemed to confirm some suspicions she had. A number of local business owners were disappointed that the promised influx of visitors and 'trickle-down' capital had not materialised, which was of no wonder, then, if the neighbourhood was marked as a dangerous hinterland. There was much talk of the map as the story spread amongst East End neighbourhoods. As researchers undertaking fieldwork (Paton, McCall, & Mooney, 2017), we heard the story told countless times in various versions but largely the same message rang clear: that yet again Glasgow's East End, with a long history of being stigmatised, had been marked out, branded, excluded, deceived and designed out of the Games.

Except, they had not. The 'red zone' map did not exist. As researchers investigating the impacts of the Commonwealth Games, we drew on all the contacts we had in the field, even submitting a Freedom of Information request to find the map. Despite everyone talking about it, even claiming to have seen the map, we could not find a copy, because there was no such map. The only map that existed was a parking zone map. The idea of Dalmarnock being relegated as danger zone was a myth, a kind of local urban legend originating in the East End from its own residents and circulating around the neighbourhoods. Perhaps this myth of the red zoning of the neighbourhood is of no great surprise given the decades of negative political and media discourses heaped upon the East End: 'Glasgow's welfare capital', 'Glasgow's Guantanamo', home of the 'Shettleston Man', who dies 14 years younger than other men in the UK at 63 (Gray & Mooney, 2011; Mooney, 2009b) all epitomising 'bad' individual lifestyle decisions and choices made by 'the poor'.

I was struck by this urban myth and what it revealed about the impacts of territorial stigma and how stigma was reproduced and internalised to powerful effect (Paton et al., 2017). While in this case the 'red zone' was fictional, it echoed Stavrides's (2013) exploration of red zones as exceptional spatial formations erected as a 'state of emergency' in urban public spaces to manage transition in these spaces. These politically and spatially mediated areas are designed to be performed in ways which enact new forms of citizenship and governance (Stavrides, 2013). This resonates with how the Games were received locally. Despite the disruptions and problems caused by Games-related demolition and displacement of residents and the lofty and unsupported claims around the local 'legacy' of such mega-sporting events, many residents we spoke to had expressed support and even gratitude towards hosting the Games. There were a few strong campaign groups resisting the Games development such as Glasgow Games Monitor, Save the Accord Centre and the Jaconelli family (see below), but, broadly speaking, there was more acquiescence than opposition despite high levels of demolition, displacement and disruption. In embracing the Games, it seemed that residents were attempting to perform the 'right' identity, frontstage. It echoed Goffman's (1963) account of strategies adopted by the stigmatised in order to manage a 'spoiled identity' rather than contesting the structures that produce stigma. Given the long history of negative imagery and construction of blemish in the East End, this form of impression management is motivated by the experience and embodiment of entrenched processes of devaluation, expressed through socio-spatial abjection. However a Goffmanesque reading of stigma as a relational classification, as Tyler's article in this collection points out, can exclude, or at least make peripheral, questions of the power structures behind these social relations. The muted resistance from local residents suggested that the ongoing stigmatisation of the area acted as an effective governing force. While Goffman's (1983) later work offers recognition of the need to focus on those in a position to give an 'official imprint to reality' in order to further our understanding of the stigma project, it is through Tyler's interpretation of stigma (as) power that we can begin to see just how social *and* spatial abjection operates as a 'soft power' which is integral to governing. That is, not just those who can imprint reality but their specific interests in doing so – which are classed and centred upon exploitation and accumulation.

In this context, I conceive of stigmatisation as being central to moral and economic class projects which are realised in distinctly spatial ways. The contemporary pressures to become places and people of value under austerity and financial capitalism demonstrate the advance of this project, articulated through government policies of urban regeneration which are intimately linked to capitalist accumulation (Smith, 1996). This reading of stigma is in line with the core message of this monograph which offers a historical re-reading to situate stigma (as) power as integral to forms of governance. As Tyler in her article in this monograph rightly advocates, understanding stigma (as) power involves making the political economy of shaming practices clear. In this article, I want to extend this enquiry. Given how stigmatisation is intimately linked with neo-liberal governance and capital accumulation, I shed light on some of the processes of power and profit which motivate stigmatising processes. I do this by 'gazing up', rather than 'gazing down', that is, looking at the role of the stigmatisers in this project and not the stigmatised. In this way, I explore the notion of the 'trickle-up' of capital – a form of accumulation which is more tangible than the fabled economic principle of 'trickle-down' capital (Sowell, 2012) on which many regeneration processes are justified. I look at some of the processes through which stigmatisation is profited from, which reveals not only forms of power vital to this process but that stigmatisation is a key form of exploitation integral to capital accumulation. The political economy of the Games reveals a support for private finance and a simultaneous withdrawal of social welfare support, which transfers the burden of debt from the state to the individual and wealth from public funds to private funds. I draw loosely from another of Goffman's (1963) concepts to do this, that of 'backstage', but used here to shed light on those who produce and profit from these stigmatisation processes, which includes those in government and private business interests.

To do so I begin this article by outlining the relationship between territorial stigmatisation and gentrification. This relationship has been outlined by others (Gray & Mooney, 2011; Kallin & Slater, 2014; Slater & Anderson, 2012; Wacquant, 2007, 2008) to show how each works in tandem within urban regeneration interventions, in differing ways, to define value. Regeneration of places coincides with discourses that devalue the people living there, often via processes of territorial stigmatisation, which justifies further disinvestment. Stigmatisation helps make these sites ripe for future investment of capital, which is most often state-led gentrification (Smith, 1996). I take this argument further in this article to explore how socio-spatial abjection is amplified under austerity. Austerity performs a vital role in facilitating the shift in debt and risk from private to public assets and from the state to the individual and households (Peck, 2012). When working-class residents cannot be successfully regenerated into neoliberal consumer citizens, austerity is used to justify and advance greater welfare retraction. I argue that stigmatisation operates within these urban restructuring processes as a profoundly classed project which, first, makes places and populations manageable, valuable and, if not possible, then ultimately disposable, and second, serves class interests, including corporations and private capital, within a political economy of neoliberal capitalist accumulation.

The empirical discussion in the second part of this article takes a classic journalistic approach which 'follows the money' by presenting data on the various lands deals and profiteering which took place in relation to the Games. While Goffman's notion of backstage referred to the space where we prepare for or cast off our performed identity, 'typically out of bounds to members of the audience' (Goffman, 1959, p. 124), I use it in this context to consider the 'out of bounds' structural processes which capitalise upon stigma. Looking 'backstage' is used here to focus on how profit is generated in relation to the management, curation and orchestration of the performance of value. This notion of backstage reveals the creation of stigma for the purpose of profit and capital accumulation and in doing so brings in the power structures and class interests missing from the classic approach to studies of stigma. In presenting the political economy of stigma in relation to the Commonwealth Games Event, I advocate a sociology of stigma which connects the macro to the micro, indeed makes the very interrogation of that connection its key point of interest – and a sociology of stigma which takes seriously the role of the stigmatisers and those who profit from these processes to make clear the structural processes involved. It is a reminder that stigma serves class interests and capital accumulation processes.

Gentrification and territorial stigmatisation

Gentrification and territorial stigmatisation have been shown to have an intense symbiotic relationship (Gray & Mooney, 2011; Slater & Anderson, 2012; Wacquant, 2007, 2008). As different sides of the same coin (Kallin & Slater, 2014) they express the cycles of disinvestment in places which have been rendered surplus, whether through deindustrialisation or policy neglect. We can see this operate in how the regeneration of areas coincides with discourses that devalue the people living there. Neighbourhoods are constructed as being 'problem places', particularly areas of concentrated social housing labelled as 'sink estates' (see Slater's article in this monograph issue) and used to invoke an 'underclass' imagery of welfare dependency, crime and fecklessness. This territorial stigmatisation expresses a powerful spatial dimension to stigma whereby neighbourhoods are marked as 'places of blemish' through 'discourses of vilification' that are perpetuated in popular and political discourse (Wacquant, 2007). The devaluation of place (land) and its occupants shifts responsibility for decline to the individuals living there. Gray and Mooney (2011, p. 10) describe this political construction of place as a neoliberal alibi for accumulation strategies by and for the owners and managers of private capital:

> … the construction of place through territorial stigmatisation tends to obfuscate fundamental structural and functional differences underlying neighbourhood effects, and displaces questions of culpability and collective responsibility away from the state and business sectors.

This justifies further disinvestment as social and spatial abjection expedites the process of devaluation and this disinvestment effectively makes these sites ripe for future investment of capital/state-led gentrification. State-led gentrification is a neoliberal urban restructuring project (Smith, 1996) which operates at spatial *and* social levels. It is presented through regeneration policies as a process whereby 'capital' of social and economic varieties can be introduced into neighbourhoods via gentrification. Whether through mixed tenure developments, which invite middles-class residents to the area (Uitermark, Duyvendak, & Kleinhans, 2007), or large-scale events and developments such as mega-sporting events, this 'capital' is claimed to 'trickle-down' to benefit and valorise the wider neighbourhoods and its residents. Territorial stigmatisation and gentrification therefore help to define value: revalorising and devalorising places as a means of extracting value from land. In this context, we can see the power of stigma in action as it expedites the process of devaluation of people occupying that space: it is used strategically to devalue people and places in order to create a rent gap and forms of capital accumulation (Kallin & Slater, 2014).

The stigma-to-gentrification practice acts as part of a class project of restructuring which operates on social and spatial levels. The most obvious and grave outcome of these processes is displacement. This has proven to be the case with many large-scale regeneration initiatives, particularly mega-sporting events, as the Centre on Housing Rights and Evictions (COHRE) concluded, which entail 'massive displacements and reductions in low cost and social housing stock, all of which result in a significant decrease in housing affordability' (COHRE, 2007, p. 11). However, the processes elicit more complex effects expressed through 'soft power'. Gentrification and stigma work together to cretae a specific form of socio-spatial governance involving social and economic regulation. This also includes the manufacturing of working-class residents' aspirations towards private housing consumption to be more compatible with neoliberalism (Paton, 2014). This 'politics of aspiration' thinking underpinned much of New Labour urban and social policy (Mooney, 2009a): that poor levels of aspiration could be enhanced by social capital, including role models of middle-class residents in mixed developments (Uitermark et al., 2007). Indeed, the politics of aspiration underpinning urban regeneration is focused less on displacing residents and more on 'civilising' them (Uitermark et al., 2007), making them more productive by becoming more affluent users of private rather than collective goods, i.e. through becoming home-owners rather than social renters or benefit claimants (Paton, 2014). Stigma operates in this context as a form of 'soft power' to shame those who do not or cannot become more productive neoliberal consumer citizens. If they fail, this then compounds their pathologisation; as abjects who are holding back 'progress' and the 'legacy' that such projects are to bring (Paton et al., 2017). In this sense, gentrification and stigmatisation entrap residents – the fallacy of 'trickle-down logic' on which regeneration is premised obscures structural inequalities and instead pathologises places and their residents. This has explicit consequences in an era of fiscal discipline when it becomes more difficult for people or places to become productive in neoliberal terms, particularly in areas with high levels of poverty and underemployment and unemployment. In response, conditionality is as a government strategy to justify the retrenchment of welfare interventions (Dwyer & Wright, 2014). Welfare conditionality links welfare rights to notions of 'responsible' behaviour. That is, access to certain basic, publicly provided welfare support becomes dependent upon an individual agreeing to meet specific patterns of behaviour or obligations. Welfare conditionality also compounds stigma and enables greater extraction of value: the 'unproductive' resident in 'problem' neighbourhoods faces sanctions for failure to meet the required conditions despite the structuring forces – such as austerity and stigmatisation – which prohibit them from doing so. Thus under the conditions of austerity, the relationship between territorial stigmatisation and gentrification is intensified further involving a redistribution of wealth and debt.

Austerity: The 'trickle-up' urban policy

While the implementation of austerity following the global financial crisis in 2008 has been uneven, in the UK it became the leading policy 'wisdom' for tackling the imagined 'problem of public debt' (including the debt accrued from bailing out banks) (Clarke & Newman, 2012). It has been used to justify public spending cuts and welfare conditionality.

According to the neoliberal script, *public* austerity is a necessary response to market conditions, and the state has responded by inaugurating new rounds of fiscal retrenchment, often targeted on city governments and on the most vulnerable, both socially and spatially (Peck, 2012, p. 626).

This has resulted in what Peck (2012, p. 630) calls 'neoliberal buck-passing' – a redistribution of fiscal responsibilities. This type of buck-passing involves a further downsizing of government to local government as 'small-state' settlements (Peck, 2012) as a means of rolling out more privatisation. Fiscally constrained local governments are then forced to capitulate to market logic, rationalised by austerity wisdom. This sees local government increase their borrowing and entering into new contractual forms of public/private partnership, particularly in relation to urban policies (Aalbers, 2008; Rolnik, 2013). This buck-passing is clear in the UK government's historical set of welfare reforms in 2012, fragmenting state-level welfare provision to local delivery hubs, outsourcing the delivery of key services to private contractors and encouraging those citizens with the means to do so to take responsibility for their own welfare in the private sector.

This neoliberal austerity logic has been established as the norm, supported by political and media discourses which have fuelled moral panics about welfare recipients as 'benefits scroungers', increasing the abjection of the most vulnerable in the most deprived areas (Tyler, 2013). The hegemony of neoliberal austerity, on the one hand, increases inequalities and poverty (Cooper & Whyte, 2017; O'Hara, 2015), whilst on the other, extolling the value of self-responsibilisation, it individualises the causes of poverty (Dwyer & Wright, 2014). The withdrawal of public funding for fundamental social support and the individualisation of 'risk' also generates greater levels of debt (Ellis, 2017; O'Hara, 2015; Soederberg, 2013). Yet, the logic of austerity politics means that welfare recipients should feel gratitude for any state support that they receive or, indeed, guilt for receiving financial support in an austerity era which we are told (albeit falsely) that we are all in together. So when aspiration towards private consumption fails as it inevitably does under austerity, dispossession can be achieved with ease when the subject is indebted (Desmond, 2016; Paton & Cooper, 2016).

But where does the wealth go? Austerity has also ushered money into the Treasury 'to make the sums add up' (Chakrabortty, 2016) through large-scale privatisation sell-offs and the intentional withering of public service providers to open up new markets for private business, whether in the criminal justice and probation service (Mansfield & Cooper, 2017) or labour through workfare placements (Ellis, 2017). By stark contrast, austerity policies which affect working-class households do not touch the elites; rather austerity policies protect concentrations of elite wealth and power. There has been a consolidation of wealth amongst the top income earners: the UK's 1000 richest saw their wealth increase by £138 billion between 2009 and 2013 (Cooper & Whyte, 2017). The 2016 budget announced the threshold for the higher rate of income tax to be raised from £42,386 to £45,000. For those with valuable assets, capital gains tax will be cut from 28% to 20% (Fenton, 2016). Corporation tax has been cut from 30% to 20% since 2008 (and falling) (Cooper & Whyte, 2017). In all, there is 'a direct policy translation of trickle-down economics that cannot merely be attributed to austerity politics, but is part of the wider package of measures that are supposed to encourage economic recovery' (Cooper & Whyte, 2017, p. 17). This consolidation of wealth amongst elites also rests upon the consolidation of debt amongst low-income groups – which is exploited for capital gain by extractive markets: an additional market which profiteers from expropriation (Desmond, 2016). Debt-related poverty is particularly lucrative as demonstrated by the growth in debt and expropriation businesses which profit from debt-related poverty or, as some have called it, a 'poverty industry' (Soederberg, 2013). This poverty industry which thrives under austerity includes media and production companies which profit from televisual dramatisation of poverty which compounds stigmatisation of the most vulnerable whether as benefits claimants (Jensen, 2014; Tyler, 2015) or the tenants in debt-driven rent arrears, evicted by debt and enforcement agencies such as bailiff companies (Paton & Cooper, 2016).

In this monograph collection Tyler argues for 'reconceptualising stigma as a political economy of (de)valuation'. I suggest the practices around mega-sporting events offer an insightful political economy case study of social and spatial abjection in action, demonstrating how these government structures are embroiled with private partners and finance capital. And this approach, Tyler also suggests, requires critical methods rooted in the struggles against the structures that produce people as 'markedly inferior'. With this in mind, for the remainder of this article I will revisit the 2014 Glasgow Commonwealth Games but with a different gaze to that of my previous research study, subverting the traditional gaze upon the stigmatised to look up at those who profit from stigmatisation though Games-related development. That is, those business and government bodies and officials who profited from processes which devalued the neighbourhoods and residents in order to support and justify the Games. Many of the data are drawn from research by activist researchers and members of the Glasgow Games Monitor who carefully documented these deals and I am very grateful to them for collating and publishing this information.[1]

The Glasgow Commonwealth Games in the context of stigma production

The 2014 Glasgow Commonwealth Games had the explicit aim of being a mechanism for economy investment and regeneration in the city, specifically the East End which had

suffered from deep economic and social problems stemming from the collapse in industry there in the 1970s. Despite numerous regeneration interventions since the 1980s, the
East End still suffered from high levels of poverty. The Games was touted as being the
potential saviour of the East End of the city. The 2014 Glasgow Commonwealth Games
(CWG) policy discourse epitomised this trickle-down assumption that private sector
economic investment would filter in and down and help improve the life chances, health
and well-being of residents. This was expressed by the Scottish Government's baseline
evaluation for the CWG:

> ... there are also plans to affect social outcomes for the city, using the Glasgow 2014 Games as
> an impetus for raising aspirations, driving achievement and contributing to a positive future for
> Glasgow. Notably, there has been substantial new investment for the Games in Glasgow's east
> end, in some of the most deprived communities in Scotland. (Scottish Government Social
> Research, 2012, p. 7)

It is not possible to present a full account of how stigmatising discourses produced
helped construct the image of the East End. And in one respect, discussing the East End
in these terms contributes to the simplistic narrative of the place when it is, in reality, a
highly diverse area of complex local geographies, various histories and contrasting life
chances. However there are a few pivotal moments which compounded the reputation of
the area. In one infamous episode, then-leader of the Conservative Party and future (now
ex) Work and Pensions Secretary Iain Duncan Smith was famously reported as having
his 'Easterhouse epiphany' – his so-called conversion to 'compassionate conservatism'
after visiting the neighbourhood and being so shocked about the levels of deprivation
and poverty (Collins, 2002). This Damascene publicity performance was aimed at promoting himself and his party and certainly not to promote the East End – in fact, it condemned it (Hancock & Mooney, 2013; Toynbee, 2013). This visit informed the thinking
behind Duncan Smith's later report, *Breakthrough Glasgow* (Duncan Smith, 2008) in
which he coined the term 'Shettleston Man', an epithetical bogeyman: 'His life expectancy
is 63, he lives in social housing, and is terminally out of work. His white blood cell count
is killing him due to the stress of living in deprivation.' He seasoned this by adding that
Glasgow had the highest rate of crime in Scotland and more gangs than anywhere outside
London. These sensationalistic 'accolades' and titles associated with the East End
branded it as sick, criminal and welfare dependent. Headlines in the run up to the Games
raged that the East End was the UK's 'benefits capital', with the *Daily Mail* (Garland,
2012) reporting 'almost nine out of 10 working age adults [are] on social welfare'.
Billionaire Sir Tom Hunter, the retail entrepreneur owner of Sports Division, in response
claimed that East End residents were 'addicted to social welfare', asserting that those
relying on benefits had become 'pampered' and 'expect what others strive and graft hard
for' (*The Daily Record*, 2012). A quick 'fact check' shows that there was no basis for this
reported 'nine out of 10' claim (Fullfact, 2012). The Department for Work and Pensions
(DWP) had not at that time released any information on the topic. Instead, according to
data on the NOMIS statistics portal, figures held by the DWP at August 2011 show that
just under 45% of working age adults were claiming the DWP-administered benefits –
almost half the figure quoted (Fullfact, 2012). Such hyperbole was commonplace in

relation to the East End and the moral panic and scapegoating around welfare claimants which have been ramped up further under austerity which promotes conditionality. The point is that the derogatory epithets imprint on places and people and provided justification for wholesale landscape change and private development in this neighbourhood. The Games were promoted as an event for the 'public good' and for the 'public interest' (Gray & Porter, 2015). But the question of public good and public interest is a moot one.

Behind the scenes of the Games

It is vital then to scrutinise what goes on behind the scenes – turning the gaze onto those who profit from this production of stigma. First we know that the Games, like all mega-sporting events, are big business. Yet just how big and whose business is very revealing. The Scottish Government was one of three partners in the Games, contributing 80% to the net public cost of the Games. The other partners were Glasgow City Council, which contributed 20% to the net public cost of the Games, and Commonwealth Games Scotland. The Games have since been lauded as not only being a financial success but significantly under budget (BBC, 2015). A report by the Accounts Commission said £461.7m in public funding had been anticipated, but only £424.5m was spent. However the original Games budget was £373m which increased to £454m in 2007 prices and was since restated to £524m at cash prices (Audit Scotland, 2012). In terms of local economic benefit, the returns of mega-sporting events are entirely underwhelming (Deans, 2016). A report which emerged commissioned by the Welsh Government (2016), on the economic viability of bidding to host the next CWG, concluded that hosting the Games was not beneficial. The report revealed that short-term economic impacts from hosting the events are likely to be of a broadly similar scale as would be derived from any government investment of equivalent size such as road, rail and specific land regeneration projects. Yet these are the types of investments which could have actual material local benefits for residents – a legacy which *is* for the public good. And in the longer term, little evidence was found that the Games would have a positive impact on the wider economy (Welsh Government, 2016). There are no real surprises in these findings as they support an international body of research which challenges not only the purported legacy (Minnaert, 2012; Rojek, 2013) but which also outlines the punitive impacts and displacement that occur (COHRE, 2007; Du Plessis, 2007; Minnaert, 2012; Porter, Jaconelli, Cheyne, Eby, & Wagenaar, 2009). But who *did* profit from the Games?

The kind of 'trickle-down' of capital thought to 'save' the East End went straight into crony pockets. One of the main regeneration initiatives which had focused on the East End was Glasgow East Regeneration Agency (GERA). Founded in 2007, GERA was a charity, and one of five regeneration agencies in the city, which aimed to help fight poverty in the East End. Its aim was to help people find jobs and support that dubious 'trickle-down' of capital which would to save the East End, with the goal 'to relieve and/ or prevent poverty particularly among residents of East Glasgow'. In 2012, the five agencies were merged into a single body, Glasgow's Regeneration Agency, resulting in some staff being made redundant. The flow of capital here was straight into crony pockets as Labour MSP Ronnie Saez, the former Chief Executive Officer (CEO) of GERA, walked off with a £500,000 pay out (Glasgow Games Monitor, 2012a). The deal involved a 'severance payment' of £42,000 and a £470,000 increase to Saez's pension, including a £208,000 discretionary payment (Glasgow Games Monitor, 2012a). Following a report leaked to *The Sunday Herald* (2012), it emerged that this money had been reserved for investment in a school in Dalmarnock and thus Saez was dubbed the poverty campaigner who stole the 'poor kids' cash' (*The Sunday Herald*, 2012). While an investigation by the Office of the Scottish Charity Regulator (OSCR) ruled the incident as misconduct, no action was taken.

This so-called 'golden handshake' was signed off by three councillors, one of whom James Coleman, who had promised the users and carers of the Accord Centre a new purpose-built facility as a CWG legacy (Glasgow Games Monitor, 2012a). The Accord Resource Centre, a community centre for adults with learning disabilities, had served the East End community of Glasgow for 20 years. But it was also occupying a site earmarked for development as a car park. Despite protest from local families, city planners decided it had to be bulldozed to make way for a car park for buses for the 11-day event. Helen McCourt of the Save the Accord Campaign said, 'Over 120 people were put out. Glasgow City Council told us we'd be getting a new building but there has been nothing. They said there was £250,000 for it but now it's gone – what's happened to it?" (Ahmed & Kiernan, 2014). After promising this new replacement centre, Coleman then later claimed that money to do so was no longer available (Glasgow Games Monitor, 2012a).

Another of these councillors was George Redmond, who told Margaret Jaconelli and her family to 'take it [their eviction] on the chin' (Glasgow Games Monitor, 2012a). Home-owning resident Margaret Jaconelli was fighting a compulsory purchase order on her house as it faced demolition to make way for Games development. Her neighbours in social housing had been gradually evicted and re-housed since the initial demolition announcement in 2000 but as a homeowner, Margaret was not eligible for such resettlement. She was offered £30,000 - said to be the market value of her property, which was, in fact, independently valued at £90,000 (Gray, 2014). Yet clearly it was of much higher land value to the developers due to the rent gap on the site with the proposed development opportunity; £30,000 would not buy Margaret an equivalent property elsewhere in the city. Margaret requested a fair payment for her property with which she could purchase a similar property. Despite a lengthy campaign, Margaret and her family were forcibly evicted from their home of 35 years at 4 a.m. with around 100 police officers in attendance to 'support' the eviction.

A report by Glasgow Games Monitor (2012a) points out that across the street from where Margaret Jaconelli lived and was evicted, Labour Party donors and property developers Allan Stewart and Steve McKenna bought property in 2006 for £1.6 million. When the Athletes' Village was announced for the site, Glasgow City Council paid them £1 for the land, plus a £1.7m amount and then 'gifted' them another valuable parcel of land around the corner (Glasgow Games Monitor, 2012a). In another deal, the Games Village site was obtained by City Legacy Consortium at no cost, arriving at an undisclosed profit-sharing agreement with Glasgow City Council, the terms of which are not publicly available (Gray, 2014). Added to this, London Mayfair developer Charles Price bought up property on the earmarked Games Village site for around £8 million in 2005–2006, then sold the land to the City Council for £17 million in 2008 (Gray, 2014). Through these shady land purchases and sales the Games have involved capital and public funds, actively funnelled away from the local community into private business. Around £30 million of public subsidy from government budget was spent on remediating land, demolishing existing housing, and compensating landowners (Gray, 2014). This programme of demolition began as soon as Glasgow announced its bid to host the 2014 Commonwealth Games in 2000. The disposability and devaluation of neighbourhoods and residents were clear from the outset. There were high levels of demolition particularly in Dalmarnock where, the Games Monitor estimates, around 3000 people were removed from the area through disinvestment and demolition. Tenants of socially rented accommodation were easily dispersed to other social housing neighbourhoods across the city. Initially 1400 homes were promised on the Games Village site, but this figure was reduced to 700 homes. Only 300 of these homes have been allocated for 'social rent' (Glasgow Games Monitor, 2014).

The money generated from the Games not only lined the pockets of local elites and private funds, but leaked out of the city through corporate business sponsors. Many of the Games sponsors were corporations with ethically controversial histories and practices, such BP, drones manufacturer Selex ES and security company G4S (Glasgow Games Monitor, 2012b). One of the most notorious of the Games sponsors was ATOS. This French IT company was the outsourcing conglomeration employed by the DWP to carry out assessments on sick and disabled people. These assessments carried out by this private company on behalf of the government saw tens of thousands of sick and disabled people have their Social Security Benefit removed, reducing them to extreme poverty (Malik & Butler, 2014). It is estimated that more than 2200 people died before the assessment, known as the work capability assessment (WCS), had been completed. This policy aimed to cut the benefits bill by saving around £1bn over five years by fundamentally redefining the nature of disability (Gentleman, 2015). This process involved retesting claimants receiving the old Incapacity Benefit. Working age people who are unable to work due to illness or disability were retested to see if they were eligible for the new Employment and Support Allowance (ESA). Ironically, ATOS, a company which has direct adverse effects on people's health and well-being, was a central sponsor for a Games which local government promised would bring health and well-being to the deprived East End. What is more, they sponsored the Games in a city which has consistently had a higher percentage of the working age population claiming incapacity benefits and ESA and a higher level of reported disability among working age people in Glasgow (24%) than in Scotland as a whole (Glasgow Centre for Population Health, 2016). ATOS lost its contract after a series of controversial blunders but not before the DWP had paid ATOS and Capita £507m for conducting the tests between 2013 and 2016, despite being criticised for its carrying out of these services (Malik & Butler, 2014). Since the work assessments were introduced, more than 600,000 appeals have been lodged against ATOS judgements, which have cost the taxpayer £60m a year. In four out of 10 cases the original decisions are overturned (Malik & Butler, 2014) – all at the cost of public money. These are practices which have directly effected East End residents – a large proportion of whom have a reported disability. Residents face the double injustice of being injured by these processes but censured for failing to be 'regenerated' or become successful, productive neoliberal consumer citizens. Given the economic conditions of austerity, their failure is certain, but Glasgow's most deprived residents are blamed for this failure personally – in punitive and violent ways.

Conclusion

In this article I have presented the Glasgow Games mega-sporting event as a form of gentrification underpinned by stigmatisation. These processes of value and devaluation which facilitated the Games are central to a moral and economic class project which is realised in a distinctly spatial way. The management of working-class places and people is of material importance to neoliberal practices of elite capital accumulation, and stigmatisation helps realise this value. The increased pressure to become places and people of value under austerity demonstrates the advance of this project, articulated through government policies of urban regeneration which are intimately linked with capitalist accumulation. But, as I have outlined in this article, this requires deeper understanding of the political economy of stigma. Incorporating the gaze up, as well as down, makes the state and capital present in our understanding. Looking 'backstage' shows how profit is generated in relation to the management, curation and orchestration of the performance of value. It reveals how the creation of stigma facilitates capital accumulation in specific ways and in doing so brings in the power structures missing from the classic approach to studies of stigma. While Goffman, arguably, made some inroads, what has largely hitherto been elided is a consideration of structural and structuring relations of capital, power and class.

While the East End itself has been subject to all sorts of derogatory media epithets and metaphors, the practices of elites and corporations involved in profiteering from the Games receive far less scrutiny. The political economy of the Games reveals a support for private finance and a simultaneous withdrawal of social support, which transfers wealth from public to private and the burden of debt from the state to the individual. This political economy also involves profiteering from land and displacement while residents were expected to be grateful for this regeneration intervention and find redemption. Yet the capital trickles up rather than down. Processes of accumulation in relation to the Games point out the hypocrisy of notions of legacy, particularly those claims pertaining to well-being and health. The deep swingeing arm of austerity has caused harm to many populations (Cooper & Whyte, 2017) and welfare cuts have had a particularly damaging effect to residents in the East End, making such claims profoundly cruel. This injurious hypocrisy leaves its mark in material and physical ways, compounding, yet going far deeper than, the effects of stigmatisation and pathologisation of the neighbourhood. This shows how imperative it is to make clear the material reality around stigmatisation: how the individualisation of structural problems of poverty, itself harmful, is used to justify austerity measures which enact greater levels of harm and even violence on people. This is realised through policy processes, whether under the guise of urban regeneration or welfare reform which many powerful groups then profit from in various ways. Exposure of the political economy of stigma is not only the critical reading that has been lacking in the sociology of stigma, it brings the hidden backstage, centre stage and under the spotlight. It makes government practices, public/private partnerships and private finance interests in stigmatisation processes clear and shows their role in legitimating and profiting from the harmful and violent project of austerity.

Funding

This research received no specific grant from any funding agency in the public, commercial, or not-for-profit sectors.

Note

1. A special thanks to Margaret Jaconelli and Professor Libby Porter for their work in this area and for pointing me in the right direction in my search.

References

Aalbers, M. (2008). Financialization of home and the mortgage market crisis. *Competition & Change, 12*, 148–166.

Ahmed, C., & Kiernan, R. (2014, July 22). The real cost of the Commonwealth Games. *The Socialist Worker*. Retrieved from https://socialistworker.co.uk/art/38609/The+real+cost+of+the+Commonwealth+Games (accessed 23 July 2017).

Audit Scotland. (2012, March). Commonwealth Games 2014 Progress report 2: Planning for the delivery of the XXth Games. Retrieved from http://www.audit-scotland.gov.uk/docs/central/2012/nr_120322_commonwealth_games.pdf (accessed 23 July 2017).

BBC. (2015, March 12). Glasgow 2014 'was under budget'. *BBC News*. Retrieved from http://www.bbc.co.uk/news/uk-scotland-glasgow-west-31840344 (accessed 23 July 2017).

Centre on Housing Rights and Evictions. (2007). *Fair play for housing rights: Mega-events, Olympic Games and housing rights*. Retrieved from http://www.cohre.org/mega-events-report (accessed 1 June 2016).

Chakrabortty, A. (2016, May 24). Austerity is far more than just cuts. It's about privatising everything we own. *The Guardian*. Retrieved from https://www.theguardian.com/commentisfree/2016/may/24/austerity-cuts-privatising-george-osborne-britain-assets (accessed 23 July 2017).

Clarke, J., & Newman, J. (2012). The alchemy of austerity. *Critical Social Policy, 32*, 299–319.

Collins, V. (2002, March 23). How Iain Duncan Smith came to Easterhouse and left with a new vision for the Tory party. *The Herald*. Retrieved from http://www.heraldscotland.com/sport/spl/aberdeen/how-iain-duncan-smith-came-to-easterhouse-and-left-with-a-new-vision-for-the-tory-party-1.155218 (accessed 23 July 2017).

Cooper, V., & Whyte, D. (2017). *The violence of austerity*. London, UK: Pluto Press.

Deans, D. (2016, October 12). Commonwealth Games economic boost might have been 'zero'. *BBC News*. Retrieved from http://www.bbc.co.uk/news/uk-wales-politics-37622973 (accessed 23 July 2017).

Desmond, M. (2016). *Evicted: Poverty and profit in the American city*. New York, NY: Crown.

Du Plessis, J. (2007). Olympic scale of sport-induced displacement. *Forced Migration Review, 28*, 54–55. Retrieved from http://www.fmreview.org/sites/fmr/files/FMRdownloads/en/capacitybuilding/duplessis.pdf (accessed 23 July 2017).

Duncan Smith, I. (2008). *Breakthrough Glasgow: Ending the costs of social breakdown*. London, UK: Centre for Social Justice.

Dwyer, P., & Wright, S. (2014). Universal credit, ubiquitous conditionality and its implications for social citizenship. *Journal of Poverty and Social Justice, 22*, 27–35.

Ellis, D. (2017). The violence of the debtfare state. In V. Cooper & D. Whyte (Eds.), *The violence of austerity* (pp. 110–117). London, UK: Pluto Press.

Fenton, S. (2016, March 16). 85 per cent of Osborne's Budget benefits will go to the wealthiest half of Britain – but the austerity lie continues. *The Independent*. Retrieved from http://www.independent.co.uk/voices/85-per-cent-of-osbornes-budget-benefits-will-go-to-the-wealthiest-half-of-britain-but-the-austerity-a6934501.html (accessed 23 July 2017).

Fullfact.org. (2012, May 15). Are 9 out of 10 people claiming benefits in parts of Scotland? Retrieved from https://fullfact.org/news/are-9-out-10-people-claiming-benefits-parts-scotland/ (accessed 23 July 2017).

Garland, I. (2012, May 14). Benefits capital of Britain: The Glasgow neighbourhood where nine out of ten people are on welfare. *The Daily Mail*. Retrieved from http://www.dailymail.co.uk/news/article-2143850/Glasgow-neighbourhood-9–10-adults-welfare-crowned-benefits-capital-Britain.html (accessed 23 July 2017).

Gentleman, A. (2015, January 18). After hated Atos quits, will Maximus make work assessments less arduous? *The Guardian*. Retrieved from https://www.theguardian.com/society/2015/jan/18/after-hated-atos-quits-will-maximus-make-work-assessments-less-arduous (accessed 23 July 2017).

Glasgow Centre for Population Health. (2016). Scottish cities: economic Participation: Understanding Glasgow. *The Glasgow Indicator Project*. Retrieved from http://www.understandingglasgow.com/indicators/economic_participation/benefits/esa_and_incapacity_benefit/scottish_cities (accessed 23 July 2017).

Glasgow Games Monitor. (2012a, January 17). Dodgy land deals in Dalmarnock. Retrieved from http://gamesmonitor2014.org/dodgy-land-deals-in-dalmarnock/ (accessed 23 July 2017).

Glasgow Games Monitor. (2012b). Games of Drones: The four dodgiest companies behind the Glasgow 2014. Retrieved from http://gamesmonitor2014.org/game-of-drones-the-four-dodgiest-companies-behind-glasgow-2014/ (accessed 23 July 2017).

Glasgow Games Monitor. (2014, April 22). Public housing meeting. *Unmasking the myths of the Commonwealth Games*. Retrieved from http://gamesmonitor2014.org/public-housing-meeting-tuesday-22nd-april/ (accessed November 2016).

Goffman, E. (1959). *The presentation of self in everyday life*. Garden City, NY: Doubleday.

Goffman, E. (1963). *Stigma: Notes on the management of spoiled identity*. Englewood Cliffs, NJ: Prentice-Hall.

Goffman, E. (1983). The interaction order: American Sociological Association, 1982 Presidential Address. *American Sociological Review*, *48*, 1–17.

Gray, N. (2014). Opinion: Glasgow Commonwealth Games. *Dezeen*. Retrieved from https://www.dezeen.com/2014/07/26/opinion-glasgow-commonwealth-games-urban-regeneration-neil-gray/ (accessed 23 July 2017).

Gray, N., & Mooney, G. (2011). Glasgow's new urban frontier: 'Civilising' the population of 'Glasgow East'. *City*, *15*, 4–24.

Gray, N., & Porter, L. (2015). By any means necessary: Urban regeneration and the 'state of exception' in Glasgow's Commonwealth Games 2014. *Antipode*, *47*, 380–400.

Hancock, L., & Mooney, G. (2013). 'Welfare Ghettos' and the 'Broken Society': Territorial stigmatization in the contemporary UK. *Housing, Theory and Society*, *30*, 46–64.

Jensen, T. (2014). Welfare common-sense, poverty porn and doxosophy. *Sociological Research Online*, *1*. doi:10.5153/sro.3441

Kallin, H., & Slater, T. (2014). Activating territorial stigma: Gentrifying marginality on Edinburgh's periphery. *Environment and Planning A*, *46*, 1351–1368.

Malik, S., & Butler, P. (2014, February 17). Atos may lose fit-for-work tests contract as ministers line up rival firm. *The Guardian*. Retrieved from https://www.theguardian.com/society/2014/feb/17/atos-fit-for-work-tests-contract (accessed 23 July 2017).

Mansfield, M., & Cooper, C. (2017). The failure to protect women in the criminal justice system. In V. Cooper & D. Whyte (Eds.), *The violence of austerity* (pp. 188–195). London, UK: Pluto Press.

Minnaert, L. (2012). An Olympic legacy for all? The non-infrastructural outcomes of the Olympic Games for socially excluded groups (Atlanta 1996–Beijing 2008). *Tourism Management*, *33*, 361–370.

Mooney, G. (2009a). Reframing the poverty debate the New Labour Way. *Variant*, *29*. Retrieved from http://www.variant.org.uk/29texts/mooney29.html (accessed 23 July 2017).

Mooney G. (2009b). The 'broken society' election: Class hatred and the politics of poverty and place in Glasgow East. *Social Policy and Society, 8*, 437–450.

O'Hara, M. (2015). *Austerity bites: A journey to the sharp end of cuts in the UK.* Bristol, UK: Policy Press.

Paton, K. (2014). *Gentrification: A working-class perspective.* Farnham, UK: Ashgate.

Paton, K., & Cooper, V. (2016). It's the state, stupid: 21st gentrification and state-led evictions. *Sociological Research Online, 53.* doi:10.5153/sro.4064

Paton, K., McCall, V., & Mooney, G. (2017). Place revisited: Class, stigma and urban restructuring in the case of Glasgow's Commonwealth Games. *The Sociological Review, 65*, 578–594.

Peck, J. (2012). Austerity urbanism, *City: Analysis of Urban Trends, Culture, Theory, Policy, Action, 16*, 626–655.

Porter, L., Jaconelli, M., Cheyne, J., Eby, D., & Wagenaar, H. (2009). Planning displacement: The real legacy of major sporting events; 'Just a person in a wee flat': Being displaced by the Commonwealth Games in Glasgow's East End; Olympian masterplanning in London; Closing ceremonies: How law, policy and the Winter Olympics are displacing an inconveniently located low-income community in Vancouver; Commentary: Recovering public ethos: Critical analysis for policy and planning. *Planning Theory & Practice, 10*, 395–418.

Rojek, C. (2013). *Event power: How global events manage and manipulate.* London, UK: Sage.

Rolnik, R. (2013). Late-neoliberalism: The financialization of home ownership and housing rights. *International Journal of Urban and Regional Research, 37*, 1058–1066.

Scottish Government Social Research. (2012). *An evaluation of the Commonwealth Games 2014 legacy for Scotland report 1: Questions, methods and baseline.* Retrieved from http://www.gov.scot/Publications/2012/10/9710/2 (accessed 23 June 2017).

Slater, T., & Anderson, N. (2012). The reputational ghetto: Territorial stigmatization in St. Paul's, Bristol. *Transactions of the Institute of British Geographers, 37*, 530–546.

Smith, N. (1996). *The new urban frontier: Gentrification and the revanchist city.* London, UK: Routledge.

Soederberg, S. (2013). The US debtfare state and the credit card industry: Forging spaces of dispossession. *Antipode, 45*, 493–512.

Sowell, T. (2012). *'Trickle down' theory and 'tax cuts for the rich'.* Stanford, CA, Hoover Institution.

Stavrides, S. (2013). Contested urban rhythms: From the industrial city to the post-industrial urban archipelago *The Sociological Review, 61*(S1), 34–50.

The Daily Record. (2012, July 3). 'Pampered' Scots are addicted to benefits, claims millionaire Tom Hunter. Retrieved from https://www.dailyrecord.co.uk/news/scottish-news/pampered-scots-are-addicted-to-benefits-claims-877878 (accessed 23 June 2017).

The Sunday Herald (2012, January 15). The poverty campaigner who walked away with £500k of 'poor kids' cash'. Retrieved from http://www.heraldscotland.com/news/13044785.The_poverty_campaigner_who_walked_away_with___500k_of_poor_kids__cash/ (accessed 23 July 2017).

Toynbee, P. (2013, November 8). Iain Duncan Smith's second epiphany: from compassion to brutality. *The Guardian.* Retrieved from https://www.theguardian.com/commentisfree/2013/nov/08/duncan-smith-poverty-benefit-sanctions-easterhouse (accessed 23 July 2017).

Tyler, I. (2013). *Revolting subjects: Social abjection and resistance in neoliberal Britain.* London, UK: Zed Books.

Tyler, I. (2015, September 4). 'Being poor is not entertainment': Class struggles against poverty porn. *SARF.* Retrieved from http://www.the-sarf.org.uk/being-poor-is-not-entertainment-class-struggles-against-poverty-porn-by-imogen-tyler/ (accessed 23 July 2017).

Uitermark, J., Duyvendak, J. W., & Kleinhans, R. (2007). Gentrification as a governmental strategy: Social control and social cohesion in Hoogvliet, Rotterdam. *Environment and Planning A, 39*, 125–141.

Wacquant, L. (2007). Territorial stigmatisation in the age of advanced marginality. *Thesis, 11*, 66–77.

Wacquant, L. (2008). *Urban outcasts*. Cambridge, UK: Polity Press

Welsh Government. (2016). Wales 2026 Commonwealth Games feasibility. Retrieved from http://www.insidethegames.biz/media/file/46070/161011atisn10616doc1.pdf (accessed 23 July 2017).

Author biography

Kirsteen Paton is a lecturer at the University of Liverpool teaching and researching on the areas of class and urban sociology. She is the author of *Gentrification: A Working-Class Perspective* (Ashgate, 2014), which explores the impacts of gentrification and regeneration policies on a working-class neighbourhood. Her recent research explores regeneration and stigma in Glasgow's East End in relation to the Commonwealth Games and the rise of evictions in relation to austerity in the UK. Her forthcoming book *Class and Everyday Life* (Routledge, 2018) explores the everyday lived experiences of class in 21st-century neoliberal Britain.